Praise for *The Jesuit Guide to (Almost) Everything*

"An extraordinary blend of theological insight and flat-out sanity, both enhanced by James Martin's wonderful capacity for creativity and connection. Martin connects insights drawn from the wells of Jesuit spirituality and spirituality in general to the heartaches and headaches of everyday life. Martin is a poet, an artist, a theologian, and a Jesuit of whom we have here at his finest."

—Ronald Rolheiser, O.M.I., author of *The Holy Longing*

"This book is filled with wisdom and wit. Even Dominicans should read it!"

—Timothy Radcliffe, O.P., former superior general of the Dominican Order

"We Franciscans are often very grateful for Jesuits! Their clear heads and clean hearts both complement and complete our own romanticism. Read on for a clear head and a clean heart!"

—Richard Rohr, O.F.M., author of *Everything Belongs*

"The Spiritual Exercises of St. Ignatius Loyola is a text to be performed and not merely read. Jesuit writer James Martin shows how this is done with pages that sparkle and shine in a voice that is, by turns, deeply personal and generously inviting."

—Lawrence S. Cunningham, John A. O'Brien Professor of Theology, The University of Notre Dame

"If you find yourself at the place where deep spirituality meets everyday life, let James Martin be your guide. In this candid, insightful guide to 'almost everything,' he takes us, with both wisdom and lightness of heart, into what it means to be a Jesuit, a Christian, and a searcher after truth in today's world, and reminds us that, truly, God can be found in everything we will ever encounter."

—Margaret Silf, author of *Inner Compass*

"In this book James Martin provides a straightforward and down-to-earth program for a deeper spiritual life. Based largely on the profound wisdom of St. Ignatius Loyola, the *Jesuit Guide* shows that Ignatius's wisdom is perennial, marvelously suited to women and men of our own day. You will profit very much as you learn the lessons Ignatius teaches us through Father Martin's lens."

—John W. O'Malley, S.J., author of *The First Jesuits*

"In *The Jesuit Guide to (Almost) Everything*, Father James Martin—as usual—provides us with wonderful guidance with his characteristic light touch. It is a delight to read."

—Cardinal John Foley, Grand Master, Order of the Holy Sepulcher, Vatican City

"James Martin has struck gold again. This talented Jesuit brings his welcoming wit, honed writing skills and comprehensive knowledge of Ignatian spirituality to the reader with an amazing balance of depth and buoyancy. This is a superb resource for receiving valuable information about the essentials of spiritual growth."

—Joyce Rupp, author of *The Open Door*

"For believers of all kinds, and many nonbelievers, too, the Jesuit tradition is the strongest bridge across the growing gulf between religious faith and the modern world. That is thanks to the wisdom of the Society's founder, St. Ignatius Loyola. And now, thanks to Father James Martin, we have a wonderful 'how-to' guide to Ignatian spirituality that can renew the faith of believers and help any pilgrim on their daily struggle to cope and to find meaning. And it will make you smile! This book is a delight and a treasure."

—David Gibson, author of *The Coming Catholic Church*

"Martin's new book is a treasure! It is filled with precious gems of spiritual insight, clear applications of various aspects of St. Ignatius Loyola's Spiritual Exercises, as well as Martin's fabulous humor. Overflowing with moving stories and engaging history, this book will be a blessing for both beginners and longtime pilgrims on the spiritual journey."

—Maureen Conroy, R.S.M., author of *The Discerning Heart*

"*The Jesuit Guide to (Almost) Everything* accomplishes the seemingly impossible—a book on spirituality so interestingly written that it becomes a page-turner. Father James Martin describes Ignatian spirituality in ways that are both engaging and practical, very often humorous, filled with examples, and clearly intended to be a guide to discovering how God can be found in every dimension of a person's life. The author tackles the hard questions directly, such as 'How do I know who I'm supposed to be?,' 'How can I face suffering?,' 'How can I be happy?,' and 'How can I find God?' Martin doesn't give you pat answers but rather points out ways that Ignatian spirituality can help you, the reader, to find and to live those answers, to be alive."

—John W. Padberg, S.J., Director, Institute of
  Jesuit Sources

"Almost everyone will surely benefit from this compassionate, humane, and always entertaining 'guide to almost everything.' Drawing on the classic teachings of Jesuit spirituality, Father Martin shows how to find God in all things—including our own struggles to grow, make decisions, and find the path to our true and best selves. In this brilliant book, written with humor and love, Jim Martin comes across as the wise friend and spiritual advisor we all wish we had."

—Robert Ellsberg, author of *The Saints' Guide*
  to Happiness

"Through *The Jesuit Guide to (Almost) Everything,* Father James Martin provides an accessible resource, firmly grounded in the teaching and tradition of St. Ignatius Loyola, for charting a path through life with God. In order to fully develop our personal gifts and share them with one another, we need a means of incorporating into our lives the truth that each one of has a part to play in God's plans for the world. We need a means of including God in the myriad of decisions we make every day, particularly the ones that will have significant implications for ourselves and the people we love. Father Martin's book gives us the tools to accomplish these goals and, indeed, guides us along the way. I recommend it to you for your own use and for those whom you hold close to your heart."

—Cardinal Seán O'Malley, O.F.M., Cap., archbishop
  of Boston

"This book is a practical guide for living an authentic life, for 'being who you are' in a way that enhances your relationships with others and the world around you. Generously sharing from his own experiences, Martin introduces the major themes of Jesuit spirituality in a remarkably hospitable way, so that anyone—believer or non-believer—might come away with useful insights into the importance of shedding needless guilt, determining when religion has become a hindrance to one's spiritual growth, and the value of desire and imagination in a life of faith."

—Kathleen Norris, author of *The Cloister Walk* and
Acedia & Me

"James Martin is a brilliant thinker with a nimble mind that constantly catches you by surprise. He is a truth teller with a marvelous sense of humor, as he provides unique insights and connections between contemporary life and the great Jesuit tradition."

—Anne Lamott, author of *Traveling Mercies* and
Bird by Bird

Most Jesuits are preternaturally interesting guys, yet even in that company James Martin stands out. He is arguably the best writer on Catholic spirituality, but he's hardly just a spiritual writer, bringing wit and depth to an astonishing array of topics. Reading Martin on his own storied order is therefore my five-star, slam-dunk, can't-miss tip of the year: This book is a winner!"

—John L. Allen, Jr., author of *The Future Church*

THE JESUIT GUIDE
TO (ALMOST) EVERYTHING

St. Ignatius at prayer amid the rooftops of Rome

THE JESUIT GUIDE TO (ALMOST) EVERYTHING

A Spirituality
for Real Life

JAMES MARTIN, S.J.

HarperOne
An Imprint of HarperCollinsPublishers

Fratribus carissimis in Societate Jesu

Grateful acknowledgments are made to the following sources for granting permission to use their material: The poems of Gerard Manley Hopkins, S.J., are used with the permission of the British Province of the Society of Jesus. Selections from *A Pilgrim's Testament: The Memoirs of St. Ignatius Loyola,* translated by Parmananda Divarkar, S.J.; *The Spiritual Exercises: A Translation and Commentary,* by George E. Ganss, S.J.; and *One Jesuit's Spiritual Journey: Autobiographical Conversations with Jean-Claude Dietsch,* by Pedro Arrupe, S.J., are used with the permission of the Institute of Jesuit Sources. Selections from *The Song of the Bird,* by Anthony De Mello, S.J., and *He Leadeth Me,* by Walter Ciszek, S.J., are used with the permission of Random House, Inc. Selections from *With God in Russia,* by Walter Ciszek, S.J., are used with the permission of America Press, Inc.

Frontispiece: "St. Ignatius at prayer amid the rooftops of Rome," by the Rev. William Hart McNichols.

FIRST EDITION

Imprimi Potest: The Very Rev. Thomas J. Regan, S.J.

Library of Congress Cataloging-in-Publication Data is available upon request.

ISBN 978-0-06-143268-2

11 12 13 14   RRD(H)   20 19 18 17 16

Contents

CHAPTER ONE:
A Way of Proceeding
What Is Ignatian Spirituality?
1

CHAPTER TWO:
The Six Paths
Spiritual, Religious, Spiritual but Not
Religious, and Everything in Between
29

CHAPTER THREE:
What Do You Want?
Desire and the Spiritual Life
57

CHAPTER FOUR:
Beautiful Yesterdays
Finding God and Letting God Find You
86

CHAPTER FIVE:
Beginning to Pray
So I've Found God . . . Now What?
103

CHAPTER SIX:
Friendship with God
Father Barry's Insight
115

CHAPTER SEVEN:
God Meets You Where You Are
Ignatian Traditions of Prayer
143

CHAPTER EIGHT:
The Simple Life
The Surprising Freedom of Downward Mobility
174

CHAPTER NINE:
Like the Angels?
Chastity, Celibacy, and Love
213

CHAPTER TEN:
More by Deeds Than by Words
Friendship and Love
231

CHAPTER ELEVEN:
Surrendering to the Future
Obedience, Acceptance, and Suffering
266

CHAPTER TWELVE:
What Should I Do?
The Ignatian Way of Making Decisions
305

CHAPTER THIRTEEN:
Be Who You Is!
Work, Job, Career, Vocation . . . and Life
339

CHAPTER FOURTEEN:
The Contemplative in Action
Our Way of Proceeding
389

Acknowledgments
399

For Further Exploration
401

Index
407

CHAPTER ONE

A Way of Proceeding

What Is Ignatian Spirituality?

WHO IS ST. IGNATIUS Loyola, and why should you care?

The short answer is this: St. Ignatius Loyola was a sixteenth-century soldier-turned-mystic who founded a Catholic religious order called the Society of Jesus, also known as the Jesuits. And you should care (or, more politely, you'll be interested to know about him) because his way of life has helped millions of people discover joy, peace, and freedom and, not incidentally, experience God in their daily lives.

St. Ignatius's "way of proceeding," to use one of his favorite expressions, has led people to more fulfilling lives for over 450 years. All in all, not a bad record.

The way of Ignatius is about finding freedom: the freedom to become the person you're meant to be, to love and to accept love, to make good decisions, and to experience the beauty of creation and the mystery of God's love. It's based on an approach found in his own writings as well as in the traditions, practices, and spiritual know-how passed down by Jesuit priests and brothers from generation to generation.

While these traditions, practices, and spiritual know-how have guided members of the Jesuit Order since its founding in 1540, Ignatius wanted his methods to be available to everyone, not just Jesuits. From the first days of his Order, Ignatius encouraged

Jesuits to share these insights not only with other priests, brothers, and sisters, but also with lay men and women. "Ignatian spirituality" was intended for the widest possible audience of believers and seekers.

Maybe it's good to ask another question before we go on: what is a "spirituality"?

In brief, a spirituality is a way of living in relationship with God. Within the Christian tradition, all spiritualities, no matter what their origins, have the same focus—the desire for union with God, an emphasis on love and charity, and a belief in Jesus as the Son of God.

But each spirituality emphasizes different aspects of the tradition—one accents the contemplative life, another the active life. This one emphasizes joy, this one freedom, this one awareness, this one sacrifice, this one service to the poor. All these emphases are important in every Christian spirituality, but they are highlighted differently by each spiritual "school."

Practical Jesuits

Jesuits take their cue from Ignatius in terms of a practical spirituality. One joke has a Franciscan, a Dominican, and a Jesuit celebrating Mass together when the lights suddenly go out in the church. The Franciscan praises the chance to live more simply. The Dominican gives a learned homily on how God brings light to the world. The Jesuit goes to the basement to fix the fuses.

In his book *The Jesuits: Their Spiritual Doctrine and Practice*, first published in 1964, which I read during my first few weeks as a Jesuit, Joseph de Guibert, a French Jesuit, offers a charming analogy first made in the Middle Ages.

A spirituality is like a bridge. Every bridge does pretty much the same thing—gets you from one place to another, sometimes over perilous ground, or a river, or great heights. But they do so in different ways. They might be built of rope, wood, bricks, stone or steel; as arches, cantilevers, or suspension bridges. "Hence," writes Father de Guibert, "there will be a series of different types, with each one having its advantages and disadvantages. Each type is adaptable to given terrains and contours and not to others; yet each one in its own way achieves the common purpose—to provide a passage by means of an organic, balanced combination of materials and shapes."

Every spirituality offers you a distinctive "passage" to God.

Many of the most well-known spiritualities in the Christian tradition flow from the religious orders: Benedictines, Franciscans, Carmelites, Cistercians. Each order has developed, over the centuries, its own spiritual traditions, some directly handed down by its founder, others that come by meditating on the life and practices of the founder. Today members of those religious orders live out what Father de Guibert calls a "family tradition."

Spend time with a few Franciscans, for example, and you'll quickly notice their love of the poor and the environment, a passion shared by their founder, St. Francis of Assisi. Live for a few days in a Benedictine community, and you will soon taste their expansive, welcoming spirit, passed down from St. Benedict—not a surprise for someone who said, "All guests should be welcomed as Christ." Religious orders call this the "charism," or founding spirit, passed on by the founder. (*Charism* comes from the Latin word for "gift.")

Likewise, spend time with a Jesuit priest or brother, and you will begin to experience the distinctive spirituality of St. Ignatius Loyola and the Jesuit Order, which we'll soon describe. The sum total of the practices, methods, emphases, accents, and highlights of the Christian way of life that comes to us from Ignatius is known as "Ignatian spirituality."

That spirituality has helped the Society of Jesus do some

remarkable things in its colorful history. It's impossible for me to talk about Jesuit accomplishments without sounding too proud (something we're accused of daily), so I'll let the English historian Jonathan Wright do so instead. This thumbnail sketch is from his marvelous book *God's Soldiers: Adventure, Politics, Intrigue, and Power—A History of the Jesuits:*

> They have been urbane courtiers in Paris, Peking, and Prague, telling kings when to marry, when and how to go to war, serving as astronomers to Chinese emperors or as chaplains to Japanese armies invading Korea. As might be expected, they have dispensed sacraments and homilies, and they have provided educations to men as various as Voltaire, Castro, Hitchcock, and Joyce. But they have also been sheep farmers in Quito, hacienda owners in Mexico, wine growers in Australia, and plantation owners in the antebellum United States. The Society would flourish in the worlds of letters, the arts, music, and science, theorizing about dance, disease, and the laws of electricity and optics. Jesuits would grapple with the challenges of Copernicus, Descartes, and Newton, and thirty-five craters on the surface of the moon would be named for Jesuit scientists.

In the United States, Jesuits are probably best known as educators, currently running twenty-eight colleges and universities (including Georgetown, Fordham, Boston College, and every college named Loyola) and dozens of high schools and, more recently, middle schools in the inner city.

Since Ignatius wanted his Jesuits to be practical men who could speak to people clearly, it's not surprising that over the years Jesuits have boiled down their spirituality into a few easy-to-remember phrases. No single definition captures the richness of the tradition, but together the phrases provide an introduction to the way of Ignatius.

So here are four simple ways of understanding Ignatian spirituality. Think of them as the arches under that bridge we talked about.

Four Ways

There used to be a saying that Jesuit training was so regimented that if you asked five Jesuits from around the world the same question, you would get the same answer from all five. These days Jesuits are a more independent bunch, and you would probably get five different answers. Or six. The Italian Jesuits have a saying, "*Tre gesuiti, quattro opinioni!*" Three Jesuits, four opinions!

But there's one question that would elicit a similar answer from those five hypothetical Jesuits. If asked to define Ignatian spirituality, the first thing out of their mouths would most likely be *finding God in all things*.

That deceptively simple phrase was once considered revolutionary. It means that nothing is considered outside the purview of the spiritual life. Ignatian spirituality is not confined within the walls of a church. It's not a spirituality that considers only "religious" topics, like prayer and sacred texts, as part of a person's spiritual life.

Most of all, it's not a spirituality that says, "Well, *that*—whether it's work, money, sexuality, depression, sickness—is something to avoid when talking about the spiritual life."

Ignatian spirituality considers *everything* an important element of your life. That includes religious services, sacred Scriptures, prayer, and charitable works, to be sure, but it also includes friends, family, work, relationships, sex, suffering, and joy, as well as nature, music, and pop culture.

Here's a story to illustrate this point; it comes from a Jesuit priest named David Donovan, who will be a frequent guest in this book. David served as a parish priest in Boston before he entered the Jesuits at the age of thirty-nine. He was a proud Bostonian "by birth and by choice," as he liked to say.

After entering the Jesuits, David spent decades studying the spiritual traditions of Ignatius Loyola and, for many years, was responsible for the training of young Jesuits. A tall man who later in life sported a snow-white beard, David was also a trained spiritual director, someone who helps others with their prayer lives and relationships with God.

We first met on the day I entered the Jesuit novitiate in Boston. Over the next two years David served as my own spiritual director, guiding me along the path to God in discussions that were often filled with both laughter and tears.

Because of his extensive training, David was always in demand at retreat houses, seminaries, parishes, and convents across the world. After working in the Jesuit novitiate, he spent four years as spiritual director at the prestigious North American College, the residence where promising American diocesan priests live during their theology studies in Rome. Just a few years ago David died suddenly, from a heart attack, at age sixty-five. At the time of his death, David's sister estimated he was seeing roughly sixty people for spiritual direction. Much of what I learned about prayer I learned from him.

One afternoon I was struggling with the news of some family problems. But I was assiduously avoiding the topic since it had nothing to do with my "spiritual life." David sat in his rocking chair, sipping his ever-present mug of coffee, and listened attentively. After a few minutes, he set his mug down and said, "Is there something that you're not telling me?"

Sheepishly, I told him how worried I was about my family. But wasn't I supposed to be talking about *spiritual* things?

"Jim," he said. "It's *all* part of your spiritual life. You can't put part of your life in a box, stick it on a shelf, and pretend it's not there. You have to open that box up and trust that God will help you look at what's inside."

David's image always stuck with me. In Ignatian spirituality there is nothing that you have to put in a box and hide. Nothing has to be feared. Nothing has to be hidden away. Everything can be opened up before God.

That's why this book is called *The Jesuit Guide to (Almost) Everything*. It's not a guide to understanding everything about everything (thus the *Almost*). Rather, it's a guide to discovering how God can be found in every dimension of your life. How God can be found in everything. And everyone, too.

Here are the kinds of questions that are proper to Ignatian spirituality, which we'll discuss in the coming chapters:

How do I know what I'm supposed to do in life?

How do I know who I'm supposed to be?

How do I make good decisions?

How can I live a simple life?

How can I be a good friend?

How can I face suffering?

How can I be happy?

How can I find God?

How do I pray?

How do I love?

All these things are proper to Ignatian spirituality because all these things are proper to the human person.

After "finding God in all things," the second answer you would probably get from those five hypothetical Jesuits is that Ignatian spirituality is about being a *contemplative in action*.

That idea resonates with many people today. How would you like a more contemplative life, or simply a more peaceful one?

Wouldn't you like to disconnect from the distractions of—take your pick—cell phones, faxes, e-mail, instant messaging, iPods, iPhones, and BlackBerrys for just a little quiet? Even if you enjoy all those cool gadgets, don't you ever wish for some downtime?

Well, one insight of Ignatian spirituality is that while peace and quiet are essential to nourish our spiritual lives, most of us aren't going to quit our jobs and join a monastery to spend our days in constant prayer. And, by the way, even monks work hard. (Some of them even have e-mail now!)

So while Ignatius counseled his Jesuits always to carve out time for prayer, they were expected to lead active lives. "The road is our home," said Jerónimo Nadal, one of the early companions of Ignatius. But they were to be active people who adopted a contemplative, or meditative, stance toward the world. To be "contemplatives in action."

Most of us lead busy lives with little time for prayer and meditation. But by being aware of the world around us—in the midst of our activity—we can allow a contemplative stance to inform our actions. Instead of seeing the spiritual life as one that can exist only if it is enclosed by the walls of a monastery, Ignatius asks you to see the world as your monastery.

The third way of understanding the way of Ignatius is as an *incarnational spirituality*.

Christian theology holds that God became human, or "incarnate," in the person of Jesus of Nazareth. (The word *incarnation* comes from the Latin root *carn,* for "flesh.") More broadly, an incarnational spirituality means believing that God can be found in the everyday events of our lives. God is not just *out there*. God is right here, too. If you're looking for God, look around. To this end, one of the best definitions of prayer is from Walter Burghardt, a twentieth-century Jesuit theologian, who called it a "long, loving look at the real." Incarnational spirituality is about the real.

Ultimately, we cannot know God completely, at least in this life. St. Augustine, the fourth-century theologian, said that if you can comprehend it, then "it" cannot be God, because God is incomprehensible. But that doesn't mean we can't *begin* to know God. So while Ignatian spirituality recognizes the transcendence, or otherness, of God, it is also incarnational, recognizing the immanence, or nearness, of God in our own lives.

Finally, Ignatian spirituality is about *freedom and detachment*.

Ignatius was acutely aware of what kept him, and others, from leading a life of freedom and joy. Much of his classic text, *The Spiritual Exercises,* which was written between 1522 and 1548, was geared toward helping people find the freedom to make good decisions. Its original title was *Spiritual Exercises to Overcome Oneself, and to Order One's Life, Without Reaching a Decision Through Some Disordered Affection.* Most Jesuits just call it the Spiritual Exercises or simply the Exercises.

Buried within that clunky title are some important ideas. One comes at the end: "disordered affections" is his way of describing whatever keeps us from being free. When Ignatius says that we should be "detached," he's talking about not being tied down by unimportant things.

Here's a quick example. What happens if your overriding concern in life is making money? Well, in that case you might not be as open to spending time with people who won't advance your career. You might be less likely to take time off. You might even begin to see other people only as tools—or worse, obstacles—in your quest for upward mobility. Gradually, you might start to see everything as revolving around your job, career, and desire to make money.

Now, work is part of everyone's vocation in life. But if, over time, you find yourself sacrificing everything else to that one end, you might discover that work has become a kind of "god" for you.

When people ask me whether anyone could ever break the first commandment ("You shall have no other gods before me.") I often say that while few people today believe in multiple gods, as in the past, many more may believe in newer "gods." For some people their "god" is career. Or money. Or status.

What would St. Ignatius say about all this?

Most likely he would furrow his brow and say (in Basque, Spanish, or Latin, of course) that while you need to earn a living, you have to be careful not to let your career become a "disordered affection" that prevents you from being free to meet new people, spending time with those you love, and viewing people as ends rather than means. It's an "affection" since it's something that appeals to you. It's "disordered" because it's not ordered toward something life-giving.

Ignatius would invite you to move toward "detachment." Once you did so, you would become freer and happier.

That's why Ignatius counseled people to avoid disordered affections. They block the path to detachment, to growing more in freedom, growing as a person, and growing closer to God. If that sounds surprisingly Buddhist, it is: that particular goal has long been a part of many spiritual traditions.

So if anyone asks you to define Ignatian spirituality in a few words, you could say that it is:

1. Finding God in all things
2. Becoming a contemplative in action
3. Looking at the world in an incarnational way
4. Seeking freedom and detachment

You could say any of those things, or all of them, and you would be correct. In this book we'll talk in depth about each of these answers, and we'll also look at how each relates to, well, everything.

To understand the Ignatian vision, it helps to know about the man himself. Like all of the spiritual masters, Ignatius's experiences influenced his worldview and his spiritual practices. Plus, the story of St. Ignatius Loyola is a good reminder that everyone's life—whether sixteenth-century mystic or modern-day seeker—is primarily a journey of the spirit.

First, I'll give you a short sketch of his life. Then, throughout the book, I'll return to a few episodes to highlight various themes and insights. And you might be surprised to discover that like many people today, Ignatius wasn't always "religious" or even, to use the more popular term, "spiritual."

A (VERY SHORT) LIFE OF IGNATIUS LOYOLA

Iñigo de Loyola was born in the Basque region of northern Spain in 1491 and spent much of his young adult life preparing to be a courtier and soldier. The young Basque was something of a ladies' man and, according to some sources, a real hothead. The first sentence of his autobiography tells us that he was "given over the vanities of the world" and primarily concerned with "a great and foolish desire to win fame."

In other words, he was a vain fellow mainly interested in worldly success. "He is in the habit of going around in cuirass and coat of mail," a contemporary wrote about the twentyish Ignatius, who "wears his hair long to the shoulder, and walks around in a two-colored, slashed doublet with a bright cap."

Like many of the saints, Iñigo (he switched to the Latin-sounding Ignatius later on) was not always "saintly." John W. Padberg, a Jesuit historian, recently told me that Ignatius may be the only saint with a notarized police record: for nighttime brawling with an intent to inflict serious harm.

During a battle in Pamplona in 1521, the aspiring soldier's leg was struck and shattered by a cannonball, which led to several months of painful recuperation. The initial operation on the leg was botched, and Iñigo, who wanted his leg to look good in the fashionable tights of the day, submitted to a further series of gruesome operations. The surgery would leave him with a lifelong limp.

While he was convalescing at his family castle, in Loyola, his brother's wife gave him a book on the life of Jesus and another one on the lives of the saints. These were about the last things Iñigo wanted to read. The budding soldier preferred stirring tales of chivalry, of knights doing gallant deeds to impress noble women. "But in that house none of those he usually read could be found," he wrote in his *Autobiography*. (In his autobiography, dictated late in life to one of his Jesuit friends, Ignatius, probably out of modesty, refers to himself as "he" or "the pilgrim.")

As he idly leafed through the seemingly dull lives of the saints, something surprising happened. Iñigo began to wonder if he could emulate them. Within him stirred a strange desire—to become like the saints and serve God. He wrote, "What if I should do this which Saint Francis did and this which Saint Dominic did?" In other words, *"I could do that!"*

Here was an average man without much prior interest in religious observance assuming he could emulate two of the greatest saints in the Christian tradition.

Did Ignatius trade ambition in the military life for ambition in the spiritual life? David, my spiritual director in the Jesuit novitiate, put it differently: God used even Ignatius's overweening pride for the good. For no part of a life cannot be transformed by God's love. Even the aspects of ourselves that we consider worthless, or sinful, can be made worthwhile and holy. As the proverb has it, God writes straight with crooked lines.

This began Iñigo's transformation. Rather than wanting to chalk up heroic military exploits to impress "a certain lady," as he wrote, he felt an ardent desire to serve God, just as his new heroes, the saints, had done.

Today in Loyola, the family castle stands a few yards from a colossal church that commemorates the saint's conversion. Despite additions, the castle itself looks much as it did in the sixteenth century, with its two-meters-thick defensive stone walls on the lower floors and graceful red brickwork on the upper floors, which served as the family's living quarters.

On the fourth floor is the bedroom where Ignatius convalesced: a spacious room with whitewashed walls and a ceiling supported by massive wooden beams. A dusty brocaded canopy hangs over the location of Iñigo's sickbed. Underneath the canopy is a polychrome wooden statue of the bedridden saint holding a book in his left hand and gazing heavenward. Painted in gold on a beam overhead is a legend: *Aquí Se Entrego à Dios Iñigo de Loyola.* Here Ignatius of Loyola surrendered to God.

After recuperating, Iñigo considered the insights he had received and, despite his family's protests, decided to relinquish the soldier's life and devote himself entirely to God. So in 1522, at the age of thirty-one, he made a pilgrimage to the Benedictine abbey in Montserrat, Spain, where, with a dramatic gesture right out of his beloved books on chivalry, he stripped off "all his garments and gave them to a beggar." Then he laid his armor and sword before a statue of the Virgin Mary.

Afterward he spent almost a year living in a small town nearby, called Manresa, and embarked on a series of austere practices: fasting, praying for hours on end, and allowing his hair and fingernails to grow, as a way of surrendering his previous desire for a pleasing appearance. It was a dark period in his life, during which he experienced a great spiritual dryness, worried obsessively about his sins, and was even tempted to commit suicide.

The difficulty of what he was about to do—trying to live like a saint—tempted him to despair. How could he ever change his life so dramatically? "How will you be able to endure this [new] life for the seventy years you have to live?" a voice within him seemed to say. But he rejected those thoughts as not coming from God. With God's help, he decided, he *could* change. So he moved away from despair.

Gradually he moderated his extreme practices and regained a sense of interior equilibrium. Later in Manresa he underwent a series of mystical experiences in prayer that convinced him he was being called to a deeper relationship with God.

For Iñigo this was a time of learning about the spiritual life. In a touching analogy, he wrote, "God treated him at the time as a schoolmaster treats a child whom he is teaching."

One day, walking on the banks of the nearby Cardoner River, deep in prayer, Iñigo experienced a mystical sense of union with God. The passage in his autobiography describing this pivotal experience deserves to be quoted in full.

> As he went along, occupied with his devotions, he sat down for a little while with his face toward the river which was running deep. While he was seated there, the eyes of his understanding began to be opened; though he did not see any vision, he understood and knew many things, both spiritual things and matters of faith and of learning, and this was with so great an enlightenment that everything seemed new to him.
>
> The details that he understood then, though there were many, he cannot set forth, except that he experienced a great clarity in his understanding. This was such that in the whole course of his life, through sixty-two years, even if he gathered up all the many helps he had had from God and all the many things he knew and added them together, he does not think they would amount to as much as he received at that one time.

The time in Manresa formed him anew. It also helped to form the ideas that would one day be collected in *The Spiritual Exercises*. He began to "note some things in his book; this he carried along carefully, and he was greatly consoled by it."

After several false starts, including a pilgrimage to the Holy Land (where he found it impossible to receive official permission to work), Iñigo decided that he could best serve the church with an education and by being an ordained priest. So the proud swashbuckler recommenced his education at two Spanish universities, after dutifully enrolling in lower-level classes with young boys, studying remedial Latin. Eventually, he made his way to the University of Paris, where he begged alms to support himself.

While in Paris he gathered around him several new friends who would become the original "companions," or first Jesuits. These included men like Francisco Javier, later known as the great missionary St. Francis Xavier. In 1534 Iñigo and six friends bound themselves together with a communal vow of poverty and chastity.

In time, Ignatius (as he now called himself, mistakenly thinking that Iñigo was a variant of this Latin name) decided that his little group could do more good if they received approval from the pope. Already they were showing their "detachment." They would do whatever the pope felt was best, since he presumably had a better idea of where they could do the most good.

Ultimately, Ignatius and his companions asked the pope for formal approval to start a new religious order, the *Compañia de Jesús,* or the Society of Jesus. They had a tough time winning approval. As early as 1526, when Ignatius was studying in the Spanish town of Alcalá, his new ideas on prayer attracted suspicion, and he was thrown in jail by the Inquisition. "He was in prison for seventeen days without being examined or knowing the reason for it," he wrote.

The notion of being "contemplatives in action" also struck many in the Vatican as nearly heretical. Some prominent clerics believed that members of religious orders should be cloistered behind monastery walls, like the Cistercians or Carmelites, or at least lead a life removed from the "follies of the world," like the Franciscans. That a member of a religious order would be "in the world," without gathering for prayer every few hours, was shocking. But Ignatius stood firm: his men were to be contemplatives *in action,* leading others to find God in all things.

Some found even their name arrogant. Who were these unknown men to claim that *they* were the Society of Jesus? The name

"Jesuit" was initially applied derisively soon after the founding of the Order, but it was eventually taken up as a badge of honor. Today we use it proudly. (Some say too proudly!)

In 1537, Ignatius and several other companions were ordained. The newly humble man postponed celebrating his first Mass for over a year, to prepare himself spiritually for this signal event and perhaps, he hoped, to celebrate it in Bethlehem. When that proved impossible, he settled on a Mass at St. Mary Major Church in Rome, which was believed to contain the "true crib" of Jesus.

In time, Ignatius won over his critics by carefully explaining the aims of his group and also by leading a few of his detractors through the Spiritual Exercises. In 1540, the Society of Jesus was officially approved by Pope Paul III. The goal of the Jesuits was both simple and ambitious: not, as is usually thought, to "counter" the Protestant Reformation, but, rather, to "help souls." This is the phrase that appears most often in the early documents of the Society of Jesus.

Ignatius spent the rest of his life in Rome as the superior of the Jesuits, writing the Jesuit *Constitutions,* sending men to all corners of the globe, corresponding with the Jesuit communities, continuing his spiritual counseling, starting Rome's first orphanage, opening the Collegio Romano (a school for boys that soon developed into a university), and even founding a house for reformed prostitutes called the Casa Santa Marta. Ignatius continued his work on the *Constitutions* and his management of the increasingly large religious order until his death.

By the end, years of asceticism had taken a toll. In the last year of his life, he suffered from liver problems, high fevers, and physical exhaustion, in addition to the stomach problems that had plagued him all his life. Eventually he was confined to his room. In his final days, the Jesuit infirmarian, the one in charge of those who were ill, reported hearing "Father Ignatius" sighing during his prayer and calling out softly, *"Ay, Dios!"* He died on July 31, 1556.

Ignatius Among the Stars

At night [Ignatius] would go up on the roof of the house, with the sky there up above him. He would sit quietly, absolutely quietly. He would take his hat off and look up for a long time at the sky. Then he would fall to his knees, bowing profoundly to God. . . . And the tears would begin to flow down his cheeks like a stream, but so quietly and gently that you heard not a sob or a sigh nor the least possible movement of his body.

—Diego Laínez, S.J., one of the early Jesuits

Today St. Ignatius Loyola may not elicit the kind of warm affection that many other saints do—like, say, Francis of Assisi or Thérèse of Lisieux, the "Little Flower." Perhaps this is a result of the austere tone of his autobiography. Perhaps it is because his letters are often concerned with practical matters, including begging money for the new Jesuit schools. Perhaps it is because some portraiture shows him not as a lighthearted young man but as a grim-faced administrator seated at his desk—though Peter Paul Rubens's painting, now in the Norton Simon Museum in California, depicts him gazing heavenward, wearing richly brocaded red vestments, his face streaming with tears of joy. Rubens had better insight into Ignatius than most artists: he belonged to a group of lay Catholics organized by the Jesuits.

Contemporary accounts portray Ignatius as an affectionate man, given to laughter and frequently moved to tears during Mass or while in prayer. Still, some modern-day Jesuits persist in envisioning him as a stern father. An elderly Jesuit once said to me about the prospect of heaven, "I have no problem with Jesus judging me. It's *Ignatius* who worries me!"

But his ability to gather devoted followers shows that there must have been tremendous warmth to the man. His deep compassion also enabled him to bear with some difficult personalities in the Society of Jesus. One of his contemporaries wrote, "He is mild, friendly, and amiable so that he speaks with the learned and unlearned, with important and with little people, all in the same way: a man worthy of all praise and reverence."

In all things, actions and conversations he [Ignatius] contemplated the presence of God and experienced the reality of spiritual things, so that he was a contemplative likewise in action (a thing which he used to express by saying: God must be found in everything).

—Jerónimo Nadal, S.J., one of the early Jesuits

The founder of the Society of Jesus was ambitious, hardworking, and practical. "Saint Ignatius was a mystic," wrote William James, the American philosopher, "but his mysticism made him one of the most powerfully practical human engines that ever lived." At every juncture, he fought for the Society of Jesus. But he was also flexible. Thanks to his spiritual practices, Ignatius enjoyed remarkable interior freedom: he considered himself "detached" about even the Jesuit Order. He once said that if the pope ever ordered the Jesuits to disband, he would need only fifteen minutes in prayer to compose himself and be on his way.

Still, it was probably a good thing that he wasn't around in 1773, when the Holy See *did* disband the Jesuits. A welter of European political powers forced the pope to suppress the Society, mainly because they thought its universality and devotion to the papacy impinged upon their own sovereignty. Pope Clement XIV formally issued a document of "suppression," abolishing the Society of Jesus. (The empress Catherine the Great, no fan of Clement, refused to promulgate the decree in Russia, thus legally keeping the Jesuits alive.)

After four decades, the political winds changed, and the Jesuits, many of whom had kept in close touch with one another in the intervening years, were officially "restored" in 1814. Not everyone was happy about the restoration of the Society of Jesus. Two years later, John Adams wrote breathlessly to Thomas Jefferson. "I do not like the late resurrection of the Jesuits," he wrote, "shall we not have swarms of them here, in as many shapes and disguises as ever a king of gypsies . . . himself assumed?"

THE SPIRITUAL EXERCISES AND THE CONSTITUTIONS

While he was busy writing the *Constitutions,* Ignatius was also putting the finishing touches on his classic text, *The Spiritual Exercises,* his manual for a four-week period of meditation on the life of Jesus, first published in 1548. And to understand what follows in this book, you have to know something about the Spiritual Exercises, the primary gift of Ignatius to the world. (Hereafter, references to the text of *The Spiritual Exercises* will be italicized; references to overall experience of the Spiritual Exercises will be left in plain text.)

The Spiritual Exercises

The Exercises are organized into four separate sections, which Ignatius calls "weeks." One version calls for a person to withdraw from daily life for four weeks of meditation, with four or five prayer periods daily. Today this version is usually done in a retreat house, where the retreatant is guided by a spiritual director. So the Spiritual Exercises are usually made over the course of a full month. (Often you'll hear Jesuits refer to the Thirty-Day Retreat or the Long Retreat.)

But Ignatius wanted as many people as possible to enjoy the Exercises, so he included several notes, or annotations, in his text for the sake of flexibility. Some people might not be ready for the whole Exercises, he wrote, so they could complete them only in part. Others might profit from having the *insights* of the Exercises taught to them.

In his nineteenth annotation, he suggests that those involved in "public affairs or pressing occupations" could do the Exercises over a longer period while continuing with their daily responsibilities. Rather than praying for one month straight, you might pray for one hour a day and stretch the retreat over several months. Today this is called the 19th Annotation Retreat or the Spiritual Exercises in Daily Life.

As John W. O'Malley, the eminent Jesuit historian, wrote in his study of the early years of the Society, *The First Jesuits,* "Ignatius's most fundamental teaching was that individuals had to find the way that suited them best."

The Exercises follows a careful plan, which is based on the path of spiritual progress that Ignatius noted in himself and, later, in others. *The First Week* looks at gratitude for God's gifts in your life and, then, at your own sinfulness. Sometimes a deep sin is revealed, like selfishness. In the end, you are usually led to realize that you are a sinner (or a flawed human being) who is still loved by God.

The Second Week is a series of meditations taken directly from the New Testament, focusing on the birth, young adult life, and eventual ministry of Jesus of Nazareth. Here you follow Jesus in his preaching, healings, and nature miracles, which bring you in contact, in an imaginative way, with Jesus in his earthly ministry.

The Third Week focuses on the Passion: Jesus' final entry into Jerusalem, the Last Supper, his trial, crucifixion, suffering on the cross, and death.

The Fourth Week is based on the Gospel accounts of the Resurrection and, once again, God's love for you.

Along the way, like mileposts, Ignatius includes specific meditations on ideas like humility, decision making, and choosing between good and evil.

Some classic works of spirituality are meant to be read contemplatively. The Spiritual Exercises are different. They are meant to be experienced, not read. Frankly, they read more like a tedious instruction manual than a moving treatise on prayer. For example: "After the preparatory prayer and the three preludes, it is profitable to use the imagination and to apply the five senses to the first and second contemplations, in the following manner." Snooze.

In a sense, the Exercises are like a dance. If you want to learn how to dance, you can't simply read a book on dancing; you have to dance! Or at least have someone help you to dance. What I'll try to do in this book is offer some insights from the Exercises, that is, tell you a little about what happens in that dance. And encourage you to start dancing yourself.

When Jesuits think about the Exercises, they often think of a particular style of prayer that Ignatius often recommends: using your imagination as an aid to prayer, as a way of picturing yourself within specific stories from Scripture. So the Exercises are not only a program of prayer; they also embody a *way* of prayer. And a certain worldview. (More about all that later.)

Overall, the Spiritual Exercises are one of the main repositories for understanding the way of Ignatius: what leads to God, what elicits greater freedom, and what helps you live a purposeful life.

The Constitutions

During his years in Rome, Ignatius spent much of his time writing the Jesuit *Constitutions,* the series of guidelines that governs Jesuit life—in the communities, in the various works we do, in the way that we relate to one another—almost every aspect of our lives. Ignatius worked on the *Constitutions* until his death and, as with the Spiritual Exercises, was always tinkering with it. It is another resource for understanding his distinctive spirituality.

Every religious order has something similar to the *Constitutions.* Usually it's called a "rule," as in the *Rule of St. Benedict,* which governs life in the Benedictine order. Each rule is a window into the underlying spirituality, or "charism," of the religious order. You can learn a great deal about the Benedictines by reading their *Rule.* And you can learn a lot about Ignatian spirituality by reading the *Constitutions*. (Technically our "rule" also includes the original papal documents, issued by Pope Paul III and Pope Julius III, establishing the Jesuits.)

For the Jesuit, if the Exercises are about how to live your own life, the *Constitutions* are about how to live your life with others. The Exercises are about you and God; the *Constitutions,* at least for Jesuits, are about you, God, and your brother Jesuits.

Into the *Constitutions* Ignatius poured his ideas for the way that Jesuits should be trained, how they should live with one another, how they should work best together, what works they should undertake, how superiors should behave, how the sick should be cared for, and which men should be admitted to the order—in short, every facet of Jesuit life he could think of. Seeking guidance, he would pray fervently about anything before setting it down on paper.

In the process, he consulted with some of his original companions about the best course of action. So the *Constitutions* are a result of his own experience and prayer as well as the advice of trusted friends. Thus, they reflect an eminently sensible spirituality. André de Jaer, a Belgian Jesuit, says they embody "a spiritual realism, ever mindful of the concrete and practical."

Here's an example of that practicality: while the *Constitutions* lay out precise rules for life in Jesuit communities, Ignatius recognized the need for flexibility. After a lengthy description of what was required for community life, he would add a proviso, knowing that unforeseen circumstances always call for flexibility: "If something else is expedient for an individual," he writes about Jesuits studying a particular academic course, "the superior will consider the matter with prudence and may grant an exemption." Flexibility is a hallmark of this document.

Much in the *Constitutions* is concerned with the daily running of the order. But you'll also find suggestions about living a simple lifestyle, making decisions, working toward a common goal with others, and relying on friends. So it is a great resource not only for Jesuits but for everyone interested in the Ignatian way.

LETTERS, ACTIVITIES, SAINTS, LIVING RULES, AND EXPERTS

The *Autobiography,* the Spiritual Exercises, and the *Constitutions* are three of the main sources for Jesuit spirituality. But not the only three. Several other resources can help us understand the way of Ignatius.

The first is his vast series of *letters.* During his lifetime he wrote an astonishing 6,813 letters to a wide array of men and women. He was one of the most prolific letter writers of his age, writing more than Martin Luther and John Calvin combined, and more than Erasmus, one of the great letter writers of the time. Between managing a new religious order, opening schools at a breathtaking clip, receiving Vatican officials and European ambassadors, requesting permissions from church and state authorities, praying and celebrating Mass, as well as corresponding with men and women—Jesuit priests, sisters, lay men and women, members of royal families—around the world, Ignatius must have been one of the original multitaskers.

These were not e-mails written on the fly. Some of his letters are minor masterpieces of the genre, combining encouragement, advice, a little news, and heartfelt promises of support and love. Like many public figures of the sixteenth century, Ignatius saw letter writing as an art. And like many religious figures, he saw it as a ministry. He advised Jesuits in official positions, particularly missionaries, to write two letters in tandem: the first would offer information for public consumption, "edifying" stories for fellow Jesuits and the public. The second would contain more personal news; these he referred to by the Spanish word *hijuela,* or "little daughter." In those letters, "one might write hurriedly out of abundance of the heart."

In this way Ignatius kept in touch with people from all walks of life from across Europe (and, later, with missionaries overseas), considering their questions and problems and answering them with care. His letters were a way to love and serve others. From them we can glean some of his spiritual insights too.

Another resource for understanding the Ignatian way is Jesuit *activities.* In *The First Jesuits,* John W. O'Malley, S.J., points out that to understand Ignatian spirituality, it is important to look not simply at what Jesuits wrote, but also at what they *did.* "That source is not a document," writes O'Malley. "It's the social history of the order especially in its early years."

What Does *S.J.* Mean?

After every Jesuit's name come the letters *S.J.* Abbreviations like this are traditional ways of identifying members of a religious order. Benedictines use O.S.B. for the Order of St. Benedict. Franciscans, O.F.M. for the Order of Friars Minor. Jesuits use S.J. for the Society of Jesus. One alternative designation came from a woman who wrote an angry letter to *America* magazine, complaining about something I had written. "In your case," she wrote, "S.J. obviously stands for Stupid Jerk!"

Knowing, for example, that the early Jesuits set up such varied ventures as schools for boys and a house for reformed prostitutes, while serving as advisors to popes and an ecumenical council, gives a sense of their openness to new ministries in a way that reading the *Constitutions* does not. And reading about their early work in education underlines the emphasis that Ignatius placed on reason, learning, and scholarship.

The history of the Jesuit *saints* who followed Ignatius is another resource for understanding his way. These men applied their own insights to the Ignatian way in both everyday ways and in extreme environments. Whether they were working among the Huron and Iroquois peoples in seventeenth-century "New France," like St. Isaac Jogues and St. Jean de Brébeuf, or secretly ministering to sixteenth-century English Catholics while enduring persecution under the crown, like St. Edmund Campion. Or surviving in a Soviet labor camp in the 1940s, '50s, and '60s, like Walter Ciszek. Or working alongside the poor, like the Salvadoran Jesuits who would be martyred in the 1980s. Each of the lives of these saints and holy men highlights a specific facet of Ignatian spirituality.

But holiness is not confined to the past. Over the last two decades I have met many holy Jesuits who have given me the gift of their examples.

In many religious orders, the members whose lives embody the ideals of their order are called "living rules." Were the community somehow to lose its rule or constitution, it would need only to look at these men or women to understand it again. These *living rules,* whose stories I will share, are another source of insight on Ignatian spirituality.

Finally, there is the resource of *experts* who have made the study of Ignatian spirituality their lives' work. Happily, this extends far beyond Jesuit priests and brothers. In a development that would have delighted Ignatius—who welcomed anyone onto his spiritual path—Catholic sisters, priests and brothers from other religious orders, clergy and laypersons from other Christian denominations, and men and women from other religious traditions have all embraced the way of Ignatius. Some have become among the most astute commentators on his spirituality.

THE WAY OF IGNATIUS

The way of Ignatius has been traveled by hundreds of thousands of Jesuits over the past 450 years, in all parts of the world and in almost every conceivable situation, many of them perilous.

Ignatius's insights inspired the Italian Jesuit Matteo Ricci to live and dress as a Mandarin in order to be granted entry into the imperial Chinese court in the 1600s. They encouraged Pierre Teilhard de Chardin, a French paleontologist and theologian, to set out for (literally) groundbreaking archeological digs in China in the 1920s. They galvanized John Corridan, an American social scientist, to work for labor reform in 1940s New York. (His story partly inspired the film *On the Waterfront*.) They consoled Alfred Delp, a German Jesuit, when he was jailed and awaiting execution for aiding the Resistance movement allied against the Nazis. They comforted Dominic Tang, a Jesuit who, beginning in the late 1950s, spent twenty-two years in a Chinese jail for his loyalty to the Catholic Church. They motivated Daniel Berrigan, the American peace activist, in his protests in the 1960s against the Vietnam War.

And thousands of Jesuits somewhat lesser known to the world have found Ignatian spirituality a guide for their daily lives. The high-school teacher struggling to connect with inner-city children. The physician working in a remote refugee camp. The hospital chaplain counseling a dying patient. The pastor comforting a grieving parishioner. The army chaplain accompanying soldiers trying to find meaning in the midst of violence. This particular list is closer to home, since I've known each of these men.

Add to this roster the millions of lay men and women who have come into contact with Ignatian spirituality through schools, parishes, or retreat houses—husbands, wives, fathers, mothers, single men and women, from all walks of life, from around the world—who have found a way to peace and joy, and you begin to glimpse the remarkable vibrancy of this ancient but living tradition.

In short, Ignatian spirituality has worked for people from an astonishing variety of times, places, and backgrounds. And it's worked for me. It helped to move me from feeling trapped in life to feeling free.

This book is an introduction to the way of St. Ignatius Loyola, at least as I've learned it in my twenty-one years as a Jesuit. It's not meant to be overly scholarly or academic. Instead, it's a friendly introduction for the general reader. It's not meant to be exhaustive either. You can't summarize almost five centuries of spirituality in a few pages, and each of these chapters could easily spawn four or five books. So I won't be touching on every single aspect, for example, of the Spiritual Exercises or the *Constitutions*—only those areas that I think would be of greatest interest, and use, to the average reader.

But Ignatian spirituality is so capacious that even an introduction will touch upon a broad spectrum of topics: making good choices, finding meaningful work, being a good friend, living simply, wondering about suffering, deepening your prayer, striving to be a better person, and learning to love.

The way of Ignatius means there is nothing in our lives that is not part of our spiritual lives. To use David's homey image, all those "boxes" that you might be tempted to keep closed—marital difficulties, problems at work, a serious illness, a ruptured relationship, financial worries—can be brought out of the dark box and opened up to the light of God.

We'll look at how to find God in everything and everything in God. And we'll try to do so with a sense of humor, an essential element in the spiritual life. There's no need to be deadly serious about religion or spirituality, because joy, humor, and laughter are gifts from God. So don't be surprised by occasional humor, especially at my expense. (Don't be surprised by the occasional Jesuit joke, too.)

And we'll also look at some clear and simple ways to incorporate Ignatian spirituality into your own daily life. Spirituality should not be complex, and so I'll offer simple practices and real-life examples.

Another final but important aside: you don't have to be Catholic, Christian, religious, or even spiritual to benefit from some of the insights of St. Ignatius Loyola. When I've described for nonbelievers the Ignatian techniques for making a good decision, for instance, they are invariably delighted by the results. And when I've told atheists why we try to live simply, they appreciate the wisdom of Ignatius.

But it would be crazy to deny that for Ignatius "being spiritual" and "being religious" wasn't the most important thing in the world. It would be equally crazy to separate God or Jesus from Ignatian spirituality. It would render Ignatius's writings absurd. God was at the center of Ignatius's life. The Jesuit founder would have some pointed things to say—most likely in a very long letter—about someone who tried to separate his practices from his love of God.

But Ignatius knew that God meets people where they are. We're all at different points on our paths to God. And on different paths, too. Ignatius himself traversed a circuitous route, and he recognized that God's activity cannot be limited to people who consider themselves "religious." So Ignatian spirituality naturally embraces everyone from the devout believer to the tentative seeker. To use one of Ignatius's favorite expressions, his path is "a way of proceeding" along the way to God.

So I'll do my best to make Ignatian spirituality understandable, useful, and usable for everybody, no matter where you are in life, but I'll also be clear about the centrality of God in the Ignatian worldview, and in my own, too.

Overall, don't worry if you don't feel close to God at the moment. Or if you've never felt close to God. Or if you have doubts about God's existence. Or even if you're reasonably sure that God doesn't exist at all. Just keep reading.

God will take care of the rest.

CHAPTER TWO

The Six Paths

*Spiritual, Religious, Spiritual but Not Religious,
and Everything in Between*

SINCE YOU'RE ALREADY READING this book, I figure that besides being interested in making good choices, finding meaning in your work, enjoying healthy relationships, and being happy in life, you're at least *mildly* interested in religious questions. So let's begin with a tough question.

Since the Ignatian way is founded on the belief that there is a God and that God desires to be in relationship with us, it's important to think about God first. At the very least, it will make everything that comes afterward seem easy by comparison.

This doesn't mean that you need to believe in God in order to find Ignatius's insights useful. But to do so, you have to understand where God fits into his worldview.

So: how do I find God?

That question marks the starting point for all seekers. But, surprisingly, many spirituality books downplay or ignore it. Some books assume you already believe in God, that you have already found God, or that God is already part of your life. But it is ridiculous not to address that question in a book like this. It would be like writing a book about swimming without first talking about how to float.

To begin to answer that question—How do I find God?—let's start with something more familiar. Let's look at the various ways people seek God.

Even though there are as many individual ways to God as there are people on the earth, for the sake of clarity I'll break down the myriad ways into six broad paths.

Each has its benefits and pitfalls. You may find yourself on several different paths during your lifetime. You may even feel like you're on more than one path at the same time.

SIX PATHS TO GOD
The Path of Belief

For people on this first path, belief in God has always been part of their lives. They were born into religious families or were introduced to religion at an early age. They move through life more or less confident of their belief in God. Faith has always been an essential element of their lives. They pray regularly, attend religious services frequently, and feel comfortable talking about God. Their lives, like every life, are not free from suffering, but faith enables them to put their sufferings into a framework of meaning.

The early life of Walter Ciszek, an American Jesuit priest who spent twenty years in Soviet prisons and Siberian labor camps beginning in the 1940s, reflects this kind of upbringing. In his autobiography, *With God in Russia,* published after his return to the United States, Ciszek describes growing up in a devout Catholic family in the coal belt of Pennsylvania. Family life centered on the local parish: Sunday Masses, special feast days, weekly confessions. So it is not a surprise when Ciszek says this in his book's first chapter: "It must have been through my mother's prayers and example that I made up my mind in the eighth grade, out of a clear blue sky, that I would be a priest."

What for many people would be a difficult decision was for young Walter Ciszek the most natural thing in the world.

The benefits of walking along the path of belief are clear: faith gives meaning to both the joys and struggles of life. Faith in God means that you know that you are never alone. You know and are known. Life within a worshipping community provides companionship. During times of hardship, faith is an anchor. And the Christian faith also holds out the promise of life beyond this earthly one.

This kind of faith sustained Walter Ciszek during his years in the Soviet labor camps and enabled him, as he finally left Russia in 1963, to bless the country whose government had caused him untold physical and mental suffering. At times he struggled with his belief—who wouldn't in such conditions?—but ultimately his faith remained firm. *With God in Russia* ends with these haunting words, describing what Ciszek does as his plane takes off: "Slowly, carefully, I made the sign of the cross over the land I was leaving."

Others sometimes envy people who walk along the path of belief. "If only I had faith like you!" one friend often tells me. While I understand her sentiment, that perspective makes faith seem like something you *have* rather than have to work at keeping. It's as if you're born with unquestioning faith, like being born with red hair or brown eyes. Or as if faith were like pulling into a gas station and filling your tank.

Neither metaphor is apt. Ultimately, faith is a gift from God. But faith isn't something that you just have. Perhaps a better metaphor is that faith is like a garden: while you may already have the basics—soil, seeds, water—you have to cultivate and nourish it. Like a garden, faith takes patience, persistence, and even work.

If you envy those on the path of belief, don't worry—many people go through a period of doubt and confusion before they come to know God. Sometimes for a long time. Ignatius finally accepted God's presence at an age when many of his peers were well on their way to raising a family and achieving financial success.

None of these six paths is free from dangers. One pitfall for those on the path of belief is an inability to understand people on other paths and a temptation to judge them for their doubt or disbelief. Certainty prevents some believers from being compassionate, sympathetic, or even tolerant of others who are not as certain in their faith. Their arrogance turns them into the "frozen chosen," consciously or unconsciously excluding others from their cozy, believing world. This is the crabbed, joyless, and ungenerous religiosity that Jesus spoke against: spiritual blindness.

There is a more subtle danger for this group: a complacency that makes one's relationship with God stagnate. Some people cling to ways of understanding their faith learned in childhood that might not work for an adult. For example, you might cling to a childhood notion of a God who will never let anything bad happen. When tragedy strikes, since your youthful image of God is not reflected in reality, you may abandon the God of your youth. Or you may abandon God completely.

An adult life requires an adult faith. Think of it this way: you wouldn't consider yourself equipped to face life with a third-grader's understanding of math. Yet people often expect the religious instruction they had in grammar school to sustain them in the adult world.

In his book *A Friendship Like No Other,* the Jesuit spiritual writer William A. Barry invites adults to relate to God in an adult way. Just as an adult child needs to relate to his or her parent in a new way, he suggests, so adult believers need to relate to God in new ways as they mature. Otherwise, one remains stuck in a childlike view of God that prevents fully embracing a mature faith.

Like all of the six paths, the path of belief is not without its stumbling blocks.

The Path of Independence

Those on the path of independence have made a conscious decision to separate themselves from organized religion, but they still believe in God. Maybe they find church services meaningless, offensive, dull, or all three. Maybe they've been hurt by a church. Maybe they've been insulted (or abused) by a priest, pastor, rabbi, minister, or imam. Or they feel offended by certain dogmas of organized religion. Or they find religious leaders hypocritical.

Or maybe they're just bored. Believe me, I've heard plenty of homilies that have put me to sleep, sometimes literally. As the Catholic priest and sociologist Andrew Greeley once wrote, sometimes the question is not why so many Catholics leave the church—it's why they stay.

Catholics may be turned off by the church's teachings on a particular moral question, or its stance on a political question, or by the scandal of clergy sex abuse. Consequently, while they still believe in God, they no longer consider themselves part of the church. They are sometimes called "lapsed," "fallen away," or "recovering" Catholics. But, as one friend said after the sex abuse crisis, "I didn't fall away from the church. It fell away from *me*."

Though they keep their distance from churches, synagogues, or mosques, many people in this group are still firm believers. Often they find solace in the religious practices they learned as children. Just as often they long for a more formal way to worship God in their lives.

One strength of this group is a healthy independence that enables them to see things in a fresh way—something that their own religious community often desperately needs. Those on the "outside," who are not bound by the usual restrictions on what is "appropriate" and "not appropriate" to say within the community, can often speak more honestly.

The main danger for this group, however, is a perfectionism that sets up any organized religion for failure.

Not long ago, a friend stopped attending his family's church. My friend is an intelligent and compassionate man who believes in God and whose parents had deep roots in Episcopalianism. But he believed his local church was too aligned with the affluent. So he decided to search for a community that recognized the place of the poor in the world.

After he left his church, he toyed with the idea of joining the local Catholic church, which he noticed many of the poor attended on Sundays. But my friend disagreed with their prohibition on ordaining women. So he rejected Catholicism.

Next he experimented with Buddhism, but he found it impossible to reconcile his belief in a personal God, and his devotion to Jesus Christ, with the Buddhist worldview.

Finally, he ended up at the local Unitarian church, which initially seemed to suit him. He appreciated their broad-minded Christian-based spirituality and commitment to social justice, as well as their welcome of people who feel unwelcome in other churches. But he eventually ran into a problem: the Unitarians didn't espouse a clear enough belief system for my friend. In the end, he decided to belong to no church. Now he stays at home on Sundays.

My friend's experience reminded me that the search for a perfect religious community is a futile one. As the Trappist monk Thomas Merton wrote in *The Seven Storey Mountain,* "The first and most elementary test of one's call to the religious life—whether as a Jesuit, Franciscan, Cistercian or Carthusian—is the willingness to accept life in a community in which everybody is more or less imperfect." That holds for *any* religious organization.

This is not to excuse all the problems, imperfections, and even sinfulness of religious organizations. Rather, it is a realistic admission that as long as we're human, we will be imperfect. It's also a reminder that for those on the path of independence—believers who have left organized religion—the search for a perfect religious community may be one without end.

The Path of Disbelief

Those traveling along the path of disbelief not only find that organized religion holds no appeal (even if they sometimes find its services and rituals comforting), but have also arrived at an intellectual conclusion that God may not, does not, or cannot exist. Often they seek proof for God's existence, and finding none, or encountering intense suffering, they reject the theistic worldview completely.

The cardinal benefit of this group is that they take none of the bland reassurances of religion for granted. Sometimes they have thought more deeply about God and religion than some believers have. Likewise, sometimes the most selfless people in our world are atheists or agnostics. Some of the hardest working aid workers I met in my time working with refugees in East Africa were nonbelievers. The "secular saint" is real.

They also have a knack for detecting hypocrisy, cant, or lazy answers: a religious-baloney detector. Tell a person in this group that suffering is part of God's mysterious plan and needs to be accepted unquestioningly, and he will rightly challenge you to explain yourself. One of my college friends practices his atheism religiously; his questions have kept me on my toes for the last thirty years. Try telling him about "God's will," and you will find yourself on the receiving end of a pointed lecture on personal responsibility.

The main danger for this group is that they sometimes expect God's presence to be proven solely in an intellectual way. When something profound happens in their emotional lives, something that touches them deeply, they reject the possibility that it could be a sign of God's activity. Their intellect may become a wall that closes off their hearts to experiences of God's presence. They may also be unwilling to attribute to God anything that the believer might see as an obvious example of God's presence.

It's like the story of the atheist caught in a flood. The fellow figures that the flood threatening his house is the chance to prove conclusively whether God exists. So he says to himself, *If there is a God, I will ask him for help, and he will save me.* When he hears a warning on the radio advising listeners to move to higher ground, he ignores it. *If there is a God, he will save me,* he thinks. Next, a firefighter knocks on his door to warn him to evacuate. "If there is a God, he will save me," he says to the firefighter. When the floodwaters rise, the man climbs to the second floor. The coast guard boat motors by his window and offers him rescue. "If there is a God, he will save me," he says and refuses help from the coast guard.

Finally, he ends up on the roof, with the waters rising around him. A police helicopter hovers over the house and drops a rope to climb. "If there is a God, he will save me!" he shouts over the roar of the helicopter's blades.

Suddenly a giant wave sweeps over him, and the man drowns and finds himself in heaven. When God comes to welcome him, the atheist is first surprised. And then furious. "Why didn't you save me?" he asks.

"What do you mean?" says God. "I sent the firefighter, the coast guard, and the police officer, and you still wouldn't listen!"

The Path of Return

This path gets more crowded every year. People in this group typically begin life in a religious family but drift away from their faith. After a childhood in which they were encouraged (or forced) to attend religious services, they find them either tiresome or irrelevant or both. Religion remains distant, though oddly appealing.

Then something reignites their curiosity about God. Maybe they've achieved some financial or professional success and ask, "Is that all there is?" Or after the death of a parent, they start to wonder about their own mortality. Or their children ask about God, awakening questions that have lain dormant within themselves for years. "Who is God, Mommy?"

Thus begins a tentative journey back to their faith—though it may not be the same faith they knew as children. Perhaps a new tradition speaks more clearly to them. Perhaps they return to their original religion but in a different, and more committed, way than when they were young.

That's not surprising. As I mentioned, you would hardly consider yourself an educated adult if you ended your academic training as a child. Yet many believers cease their religious education as children, and expect it to carry them through adulthood. People in this group often find that they need to reeducate themselves to understand their faith in a mature way.

When I was a boy, for instance, I used to think of God as the Great Problem Solver who would fix all my problems if I just prayed hard enough. Let me get an A on my social studies test. Let me do well in math. Better yet, let tomorrow be a snow day.

If God was all good, I reasoned, then he would answer my prayers. What possible reason could God have for *not* answering them?

As I grew older, the model of God as the Great Problem Solver collapsed—primarily because God didn't seem interested in solving all of my problems. I prayed and prayed and prayed, and all my problems still weren't solved. *Why not?* I wondered. Didn't God care about me? My adolescent narcissism led to some serious doubts, which led me to consider the possibility that God didn't exist.

This lukewarm agnosticism came to a boil during my college days at the University of Pennsylvania. During freshman and sophomore years at Penn, my friends and I spent many late nights arguing loudly about religion (usually after too many beers or too much pot). Those late-night sessions raised doubts about the God to whom I had prayed when I was young. But at the time they were just random doubts and unconnected questions.

They coalesced when my freshman-year roommate was killed in an automobile accident during our senior year. Brad was one of my closest friends, and his death was almost too much to bear.

At Brad's funeral, on a humid spring day in a wealthy suburb outside of Washington, DC, I sat in a tasteful Episcopal church, surrounded by Brad's shattered family and my grieving friends, and thought about the absurdity of believing in a God who would allow this. By the end of the service I had decided not to believe in a God who would act so cruelly. The Great Problem Solver wasn't solving problems but creating them.

My newfound atheism was invigorating. Not only did I feel like a person with a first-rate intellect, I was proud to have rejected something that obviously had not worked. Why believe in a God who either couldn't or wouldn't prevent suffering? Atheism was not only intellectually respectable but also had some practical benefits: I now had my Sunday mornings free.

So I firmly stepped onto the path of disbelief.

This journey continued for a few months until a conversation with a mutual friend of Brad. Jacque (she pronounced it "Jackie") came from a small town outside of Chicago and was what my friends derisively called a "fundamentalist," though we had scant idea of what that meant. (It meant that her faith informed her life.) Jacque had lived in the same dorm with Brad and me during freshman year. Though wildly different from Brad in outlook and interests, the two became close.

After an accounting class one day, standing in a snowfall outside of our old freshman dorm, I told Jacque how angry I was at God, and how I had decided I would no longer go to church. My comments were flung at her like a challenge. *You're the believer,* I thought, *explain this.*

"Well," she said softly, "I've been thanking God for Brad's life." I can still remember standing in the cold and having my breath taken away by her answer. Rather than arguing about suffering, she was telling me that there were other ways to relate to God, ways other than as the Great Problem Solver.

Jacque's response nudged me onto the path of return. She hadn't answered my question about suffering. Rather, her words reminded me that the question of suffering (or the "mystery of evil" as theologians say) is not the only question to ask about God. Her reply said that you can live with the question of suffering and still believe in God—much as a child can trust a parent even when he doesn't fully understand all of the parent's ways. It also reminded me that there are other questions that are equally important—such as "Who is God?" Not being able to answer one question does not mean that others are not equally valid. Her answer opened a window onto another vista of faith.

Yet I was still stuck with a big question: if God wasn't the Great Problem Solver, the God of my youth, who was He? Or She? Or It?

Not until I entered the Jesuits and began hearing about a different kind of God—a God who was *with* you in your suffering, a God who took a personal interest in your life, even if you didn't feel that all your problems were solved—did life started to make more sense. That's not to say I ever found an entirely satisfying answer for the mystery of suffering—or for why my friend's life was ended at twenty-one. But it helped me understand the importance of being in relationship with God, even during difficult times.

When I was a novice, one of my spiritual directors quoted the Scottish philosopher John Macmurray, who contrasted "real religion" and "illusory religion." The maxim of "illusory religion" is as follows: "Fear not; trust in God and He will see that none of the things you fear will happen to you." "Real religion," said Macmurray, has a different maxim: "Fear not; the things you are afraid of are quite likely to happen to you, but they are nothing to be afraid of."

The Path of Exploration

A few years ago, I worked with an Off-Broadway acting company that was producing a new play about the relationship between Jesus and Judas called *The Last Days of Judas Iscariot*. After some meetings with the actor who would play Judas, as well as the playwright and the director, I was invited to help the cast better understand the subject material. In time they asked me to serve as "theological consultant" for the play. This isn't as strange as it may seem: the Jesuits have historically been active in theater, having used it extensively in their schools from the earliest days. (More about "Jesuit theater" later on.)

Over the course of six months, I found myself talking with the actors not simply about Jesus and Judas but also about their spiritual lives, answering questions prompted by our freewheeling discussions about the Gospels, about sin and forgiveness, and about faith.

Several of the actors had toggled between one religious tradition and another, seeking something that would "fit." One actor, named Yetta, who played Mary Magdalene, told me that her mother was Catholic and her father was Jewish. They decided to let her choose her own religion when she was grown. "But," she said, "I haven't chosen yet." (By the way, when I quote people in this book, or tell their stories, it is with their permission.)

My time with the actors was one of not only discovering the theater but also meeting people who were traveling along a path I hadn't encountered before. They were on the path of exploration.

Given their profession, this was not surprising. A good actor often researches a new role by spending time with a person from a particular background. An actor prepping for a role in a police drama, for instance, will hang out with real-life police officers. So the idea of "exploration" comes naturally to them. Stepping into another person's shoes for a time is not that different from entering into another religious tradition for a time.

Others—not just actors—more settled in their religious beliefs often find that their own spiritual practices are enhanced through interactions with other religious traditions. Several years ago I was astonished by the richness of my prayer one Sunday morning in a Quaker meeting house near my parents' home outside Philadelphia. While I had ample experience praying contemplatively on my own, and worshipping together during Catholic Masses, the Quakers' "gathered silence" (praying silently *together*) was a type of contemplation I'd never before imagined. Their tradition enriched my own.

I have wandered freely in mystical traditions that are not religious and have been profoundly influenced by them. It is to my Church, however, that I keep returning, for she is my spiritual home.

—Anthony de Mello, S.J. (1931–1987)

Exploration comes naturally to Americans in particular and is a theme celebrated not only in U.S. history but in our great works of literature: Huckleberry Finn is an explorer. So are the heroes and heroines of the novels of Jack London and Willa Cather, to name but two favorite authors. Our homegrown religious writers—especially the transcendentalists Ralph Waldo Emerson and Henry David Thoreau—were inner explorers. "Afoot and lighthearted, I take to the open road," wrote Walt Whitman, "Healthy, free, the world before me, / The long brown path before me leading wherever I choose."

Exploration comes naturally in American faith as well. Turned off by their childhood faith, or by the failings of organized religion, and lacking extensive religious training, many Americans searching for a religion that "fits" embark on a quest—itself a spiritual metaphor.

The benefit of walking along the path of exploration is plain. After a serious search, you may discover a tradition ideally suited to your understanding of God, your desires for community, and even to your own personality. Likewise, returning to your original community may give you a renewed appreciation for your "spiritual home." Explorers may also be more grateful for what they have found and are not as likely to take their communities for granted. The most grateful pilgrim is the one who has finished the longest journey.

The pitfall for this path is similar to the one for the path of independence: the danger of not settling for any tradition because none is perfect. An even greater danger for explorers is not settling on any one religious tradition because it doesn't suit *them:* God may become someone who is supposed to satisfy their needs. God becomes what one writer called a "pocket-size God," small enough to put in your pocket when God doesn't suit you (for example, when the Scriptures say things that you would rather not hear) and take out of your pocket only when convenient.

Another danger is a lack of commitment. Your entire life may become one of exploration—constant sampling, spiritual grazing.

And when the path becomes the goal, rather than God, people may ultimately find themselves unfulfilled, confused, lost, and maybe even a little sad.

The Path of Confusion

This final path crosses all the other ones at various points. People on the path of confusion run hot and cold with their childhood faith—finding it relatively easy to believe in God at times, almost impossible at others. They haven't "fallen away," but they've not stayed connected either. They cry out to God in prayer and then wonder why there doesn't seem to be an answer. They intuit God's presence during important moments, and perhaps even during religious services, but find themselves bothered by the problems of belonging to a church, synagogue, or mosque. They may pray from time to time, particularly when in dire need, and they may go to services on key holidays.

But for this group, finding God is a mystery, a worry, or a problem.

The main benefit of this path is that it often helps people to fine-tune their approach to their childhood faith. Unlike those who consider themselves clearly religious or clearly nonreligious, these people have not yet made up their minds, and so they are constantly refining their ideas about a religious commitment.

But confusion can lapse into laziness. Avoiding worship services because of a particular criticism can lead to leaving organized religion entirely because it's too much work, or because it takes too much energy to belong to a group that demands, say, charity and forgiveness.

Much of my adult life, before entering the Jesuits, was spent on this path. As a boy, I was raised in a loving family with a lukewarm Catholic background. My family went to church regularly, but we didn't engage in those practices that mark very religious Catholics—saying grace at meals, speaking regularly about God, praying before going to bed, and attending Catholic schools. And in college I grew increasingly confused about God.

After Jacque's mysterious answer moved me to give God another chance, I returned to church, but in a desultory way. I wasn't sure exactly what, or who, I believed in. So for several years God the Problem Solver was replaced by a more amorphous spiritual concept: God the Life Force, God the Other, God the Far-Away One. While these are valid images of God, I had no idea that God could be anything *but* those abstract ideas. And I figured that things would stay that way until I died.

Then, at age twenty-six, I came home one night after work and turned on the television set. After graduation, I had taken a job with General Electric but was beginning to grow dissatisfied with the work. After six years of working late at night and on the weekends, I had also started to develop stress-related stomach problems and was wondering how much more I could take.

On television that night was a documentary about Thomas Merton, a man who had turned his back on a dissolute life to enter a Trappist monastery in the early 1940s. Something about the expression on his face spoke to me: his countenance radiated a peace that to me seemed unknown, or at least forgotten. The show was so interesting that the next day I purchased and began reading Merton's autobiography, *The Seven Storey Mountain*.

Gradually, I discovered within myself a desire to do something similar to what Thomas Merton had done; maybe not join a monastery (since I'm too talkative) but somehow lead a more contemplative, more religious, life. That experience helped me to step off the path of confusion and onto the path of belief, which led to the Jesuits.

THOSE ARE THE SIX paths on which many seem to travel. What does St. Ignatius have to say to people on each of those paths about finding God? The answer is: plenty.

The way of Ignatius is an invitation to those who have always believed in God, who believe in God but not in religion, who have rejected God, who are coming back to God, who are exploring, and who are confused. Ignatius's approach meets you on your path and leads you closer to God.

SPIRITUAL BUT NOT RELIGIOUS

Before we tackle the question of how to find God, a digression on two important ideas: religion and spirituality. Everybody seems to be spiritual these days—from your college roommate to the person in the office cubicle next to yours to the subject of every other celebrity interview. But if "spiritual" is fashionable, "religious" is unfashionable. This is usually expressed as follows: "I'm spiritual but not religious." It's even referred to by the acronym SBNR.

There are so many people who describe themselves as SBNR that sometimes I wonder if the Jesuits might attract more people if they promoted the *Spiritual but Not Religious Exercises*.

The thinking goes like this: being religious means abiding by the arcane rules and hidebound dogmas, and being the tool of an oppressive institution that doesn't allow you to think for yourself (which would have surprised many thinking believers, like St. Thomas Aquinas, Moses Maimonides, Dorothy Day, and Reinhold Niebuhr). Religion is narrow-minded and prejudicial—so goes the thinking—stifling the growth of the human spirit (which would have surprised St. Francis of Assisi, Rabbi Abraham Joshua Heschel, St. Teresa of Ávila, Rumi, and the Rev. Dr. Martin Luther King Jr.).

Or worse, as several contemporary authors contend, religion is the most despicable of social evils, responsible for all the wars and conflicts around the world.

Sadly, religion is responsible for many ills in the modern world and evils throughout history: among them, the persecution of Jews, endless wars of religion, the Inquisition, not to mention the religious intolerance and zealotry that leads to terrorism.

You can add to this list smaller things: your judgmental neighbor who loudly tells you how often he helps out at church, your holier-than-thou relative who trumpets how often she reads the Bible, or that annoying guy at work who keeps telling you that belief in Jesus is sure to bring you amazing financial success.

There is a human and sinful side to religion since religions are human organization, and therefore prone to sin. And, frankly, people within religious organizations know this better than those outside of them.

Some say that on balance religion is found wanting. Still, I would stack up against the negatives the positive aspects: traditions of love, forgiveness, and charity as well as the more tangible out-growths of thousands of faith-based organizations that care for the poor, like Catholic Charities or the vast network of Catholic hospitals and schools that care for poor and immigrant populations. Think too of generous men and women like St. Francis of Assisi, St. Teresa of Ávila, St. Catherine of Siena, Mother Teresa, and the Rev. Dr. Martin Luther King Jr. Speaking of Dr. King, you might add abolition, women's suffrage, and the civil rights movements, all of which were founded on explicitly religious principles. Add to that list the billions of believers who have found in their own religious traditions not only comfort but also a moral voice urging them to live selfless lives and to challenge the status quo.

And Jesus of Nazareth. Remember him? Though he often challenged the religious conventions of his day, he was a deeply religious man. (This is something of an understatement.)

By the way, atheism doesn't have a perfect record either. In his book *No One Sees God: The Dark Night of Atheists and Believers,* the writer Michael Novak points out that while many atheist thinkers urge us to question everything, especially the record of organized religion, atheists often fail to question their own record. Think of the cruelty and bloodshed perpetrated, just in the twentieth century, by totalitarian regimes that have professed "scientific atheism." Stalinist Russia comes to mind.

On balance, I think religion comes out on top. And when I think about the maleficent effects of religion, I remember the English novelist Evelyn Waugh, a dazzling writer who was by many accounts a nasty person. (He once wrote to his wife, "I know you lead a dull life now. . . . But that is no reason to make your letters as dull as your life. . . . Please grasp that.") One of Waugh's friends, Nancy Mitford, once expressed astonishment that he could be so mean-spirited and a Christian. "You can't imagine," said Waugh, "how much worse I should be if I were not religious."

Still, it's not surprising that, given all the problems with organized religion, many people would say, "I'm not religious," adding, "I'm serious about living a moral life, maybe even one that centers on God, but I'm my own person."

Spiritual, on the other hand, is taken to mean that, freed from unnecessary dogma, you can be yourself before God. The term may also imply that you have sampled a variety of religious beliefs that you have integrated into your life. You meditate at a Buddhist temple (which is great); participate in Seders with Jewish friends at Passover (great too); sing in a gospel choir at a local Baptist church (great again); and go to Midnight Mass on Christmas Eve at a Catholic church (also great).

You find what works for you, but you don't subscribe to any one church: that would be too confining. Besides, there's no one creed that represents exactly what you believe.

But there's a problem. While "spiritual" is obviously healthy, "not religious" may be another way of saying that faith is something between you and God. And while faith is a question of you and God, it's not *just* a question of you and God. Because this would mean that you, alone, are relating to God. And that means there's no one to suggest when you might be off track.

We all tend to think we're correct about most things, and spiritual matters are no exception. Not belonging to a religious community means less of a chance of being challenged by a tradition of belief and experience. It also means less chance to see that you are misguided, seeing only part of the picture or even that you are wrong.

Let's consider a person who wants to follow Jesus Christ on her own. Perhaps she has heard that if she follows Christ, she will enjoy financial success—a popular idea today. Were she part of a mainstream Christian community, though, she would be reminded that suffering is part of the life of even the most devout Christian. Without the wisdom of a community, she may gravitate toward a skewed view of Christianity. Once she falls on hard times financially, she may drop Christ, who has ceased to meet her personal needs.

Despite our best efforts to be spiritual, we make mistakes. And when we do, it's helpful to have the wisdom of a religious tradition.

This reminds me of a passage from a book called *Habits of the Heart,* written by Robert Bellah, a sociologist of religion, and other colleagues, in which they interviewed a woman named Sheila about her religious beliefs. "I believe in God," she said. "I'm not a religious fanatic. I can't remember the last time I went to church. My faith has carried me a long way. It's Sheilaism. Just my own little voice."

More problematic than Sheilaism are spiritualities entirely focused on the self, with no place for humility, self-critique, or a sense of responsibility for the community. Certain New Age movements find their goal not in God, or even the greater good, but in self-improvement—a valuable goal—but one that may degenerate into selfishness.

Religion can provide a check to my tendency to think that I am the center of the universe, that I have all the answers, that I know better than anyone about God, and that God speaks most clearly through me.

By the same token, religious institutions need themselves to be called to account. And here the prophets among us, who are able to see the failures, weaknesses, and plain old sinfulness of institutional religion, play a critical role. Like individuals who are never challenged, religious communities can often get things tragically wrong, convinced that they are doing "God's will." (Think of the Salem witch trials, among other examples.) They might even encourage us to become complacent in our judgments. Unreflective religion can sometimes incite people to make even *worse* mistakes than they would on their own. Thus, those prophetic voices calling their communities to continual self-critique are always difficult for the institution to hear, but nonetheless necessary. Ignatius, for example, exercised a prophetic role by asking Jesuits not to seek high clerical office in the church—like that of bishop, archbishop, or cardinal. In fact, Jesuits make a promise not to "ambition" for high office even within their own order. In this way, Ignatius not only tried to prevent careerism among the Jesuits, but also spoke a word of prophecy to the clerical culture rampant in the Catholic Church of his time.

It's a healthy tension: the wisdom of our religious traditions provides us with a corrective for our propensity to think that we have all the answers; and prophetic individuals moderate the natural propensity of institutions to resist change and growth. As with many aspects of the spiritual life, you need to find life in the tension.

Isaac Hecker was a nineteenth-century convert to Catholicism who became a priest and founded the American religious order known as the Paulists. He may have summed it up best. Religion, said Hecker, helps you to "connect and correct." You are invited into a community to connect with one another and with a tradition. At the same time, you are corrected when you need to be. And you may be called to correct your own community—though a special kind of discernment and humility is required in those cases.

Religion can lead people to do terrible things. At its best, though, religion modifies our natural tendency to believe that we have all the answers. So despite what many detractors say, and despite the arrogance that sometimes infects religious groups, religion at its best introduces humility into your life.

Religion also reflects the social dimension of human nature. Human beings naturally desire to be with one another, and that desire extends to worship. It's natural to want to worship together, to gather with other people who share your desire for God, and to work with others to fulfill the dreams of your community.

Experiencing God also comes through personal interactions within the community. Sure, God communicates through private, intimate moments—as in prayer or reading of sacred texts—but God also enters into relationships with us through others in a faith community. Finding God often happens in the midst of a community—with a "we" as often as an "I." For many people this community is a church, a synagogue, or a mosque. Or more broadly, religion.

Finally, religion means that your understanding of God and the spiritual life can more easily transcend your individual understanding and imagination. Do you imagine God as a judge? That's fine—if it helps you become a more moral and loving person. But a religious tradition can enrich your spiritual imagination in ways that you might not be able to discover by yourself.

Here's an example: one of my favorite images of God is the God of Surprises, which I first encountered in the novitiate. My own idea of God at the time was limited to God the Far-Away One, so it was liberating to hear about a God who surprises, who waits for us with wonderful things. It's a playful, even fun, image of God. But I would have never come up with it on my own. It came to me from David Donovan, my spiritual director, who had read it in a book of that same title, by an English Jesuit named Gerard W. Hughes, who borrowed it from an essay by the German Jesuit Karl Rahner.

That image was amplified when I read the conclusion of one of the great modern spiritual novels, *Mariette in Ecstasy*. Ron Hansen, an award-winning writer who is also an ordained Catholic deacon, penned the story of the religious experiences of a young nun in the early 1900s, loosely based on the life of St. Thérèse of Lisieux, the French Carmelite. At the end of the story, Mariette, who had left the monastery many years before, writes to her former novice director and assures her that God still communicates with her.

> We try to be formed and held and kept by him, but instead
> he offers us freedom. And now when I try to know his will,
> his kindness floods me, his great love overwhelms me, and I
> hear him whisper, Surprise me.

The image of the God who surprises and the God who waits for surprises came to me from three Jesuit priests and the religious imagination of a Catholic writer.

In other words, that idea was given to me by religion.

Overall, being spiritual and being religious are *both* part of being in relationship with God. Neither can be fully realized without the other. Religion without spirituality can become a dry list of dogmatic statements divorced from the life of the spirit. This is what Jesus warned against. Spirituality without religion can become a self-centered complacency divorced from the wisdom of a community. That's what I'm warning against.

For St. Ignatius Loyola the two went hand in hand. (If anything, Ignatius was criticized for being too spiritual, as his way struck some people as not centered enough on the church.) His way understands the importance of being both spiritual *and* religious.

FINDING GOD IN ALL THINGS

After Ignatius's conversion, his life was focused on God. The introduction to the *Spiritual Exercises* reads, "Human beings are created to praise, reverence, and serve God our Lord, and by means of doing this to save their souls." God, says Ignatius, is at the center of everything and provides meaning for our lives.

Another way of understanding that worldview is with a quotation from Pedro Arrupe, S.J. Father Arrupe was the head of the Jesuit Order from 1965 to 1981, a period of volcanic change in the Catholic Church. He is perhaps best known for reminding the Jesuits that part of their original work was with the poor and marginalized. In the 1970s a journalist asked Father Arrupe this question: who is Jesus Christ for you?

One can imagine the journalist anticipating a boilerplate answer like "Jesus Christ is my Savior" or "Jesus Christ is the Son of God." Instead, Arrupe said, "For me Jesus Christ is everything!" That is a good shorthand for how Ignatius looked at God.

But not everyone reading this book has that kind of relationship with God. Maybe few people do. For people on the path of independence, the path of disbelief, the path of exploration, or the path of confusion, the question is less about devoting oneself to God entirely and more about something else, the question that began our discussion: how do I find God?

Here is where we can turn to an important insight of Ignatius: God can speak directly with people in astonishingly personal ways. This can lead even the doubtful and confused and lost to God. The key, the leap of faith required, is believing that these intimate experiences are ways God *communicates* with you.

In his *Spiritual Exercises,* Ignatius wrote that the Creator deals "immediately with the creature and the creature with its Creator." God communicates with us. Seekers, then, need to be aware of the variety of ways that God has of communicating with us, of making God's presence known.

In other words, the beginning of the path to finding God is awareness. Not simply awareness of the ways that you can find God, but an awareness that God desires to find you.

That brings us to the first important moment in the life of Ignatius: his initial conversion. By focusing more carefully on this one particular incident, you can see how God can use everything to find you. So let's return to that event and look at it in greater detail.

LITTLE BY LITTLE

Iñigo of Loyola, as I mentioned earlier, was thirty years old when his leg was shattered by a cannonball during the siege of a castle by the French military in Pamplona in 1521. This pivotal incident, which might have been merely a tragic setback to another person, marked the beginning of Ignatius's new life.

After Ignatius stayed in Pamplona for several days, his French captors, who treated him "with courtesy and kindness," brought him back to his family's castle, where the doctors reset the bone. To do so, they had to break the leg. "This butchery was done again," he writes in his *Autobiography*. His condition worsened, and those around him, worried that he was about to die, arranged for him to have the last rites.

Finally he recovered. Yet Ignatius noticed something troubling: the bone below one knee had been poorly set, shortening his leg. "The bone protruded so much that it was an ugly business." Now his vanity took over. "He was unable to abide it," he wrote, "because he was determined to follow the world." He couldn't abide the idea of being thought unattractive.

Despite the pain involved, he asked the surgeons to cut away the bone. Looking back, the older Ignatius recognized his foolishness. "He was determined to make himself a martyr to his own pleasure," he wrote.

During his subsequent convalescence, Ignatius was unable to find books on what he most enjoyed reading: adventure stories and tales of chivalry. The only things available were a life of Jesus and the lives of the saints. To his surprise, he found that he enjoyed the tales of the saints. Thinking about what the saints had done filled him with a sense that they would be "easy to accomplish."

Still, he was attracted to the ideals of knightly service, and when he wasn't reading about the life of Christ or the lives of the saints, he mused about doing great deeds for "a certain lady." Even though her station was higher than a countess or a duchess, Ignatius was obsessed on winning her over with daring exploits. In this way he wasn't very different from some men in our time, or any time for that matter.

So he went back and forth, thinking about doing heroic things for the noble lady and doing heroic things for God.

Then a strange thing happened, something that would influence not only Ignatius but the life of every Jesuit and anyone who has followed the way of Ignatius.

Ignatius slowly realized that the *aftereffects* of these thoughts were different. After he thought about impressing his "certain lady" with exploits on the battlefield, he felt one way. After thinking about doing great things and undergoing hardships for God, he felt another.

I'll let him describe it in one of the most famous passages in his autobiography:

> Yet there was a difference. When he was thinking about the things of the world, he took much delight in them, and afterwards, when he was tired and put them aside, he found that he was dry and discontented. But when he thought of going to Jerusalem, barefoot and eating nothing but herbs and undergoing all the things that the saints endured, not only was he consoled when he had these thoughts, but even after putting them aside, he remained content and happy.
>
> He did not notice this, however; nor did he stop to ponder the difference until one day his eyes were opened a little, and he began to marvel at the difference, realizing from experience that some thoughts left him sad and others happy. Little by little he came to recognize the difference between the spirits that agitated him, one from the enemy and one from God.

Ignatius began to understand that these feelings and desires might be ways that God was communicating with him. This is not to say that Ignatius found God and women in opposition. Rather, he began to see that his desires of winning fame by impressing others drew him away from God. His desires to surrender to a more generous and selfless way of life drew him toward God. What religious writers call a "grace" was not simply that he *had* these insights, but that he *understood them as coming from God*.

As a result of his experience, Ignatius began to understand that God wants to communicate with us. Directly.

This idea would get Ignatius in trouble with the Inquisition and land him in jail. (Ignatius had his own problems with "religion" at times.) Some critics suspected that Ignatius was trying to bypass the institutional church. If God could deal with humanity directly, they wondered, what need was there for the church?

As I've mentioned, religion enables people to encounter God in profound ways in their lives. But Ignatius recognized that God could not be confined within the walls of the church. God was larger than the church.

Today the Ignatian notion of the Creator's dealing directly with human beings is less controversial. It's assumed by those on the "spiritual but not religious" journey. The far more controversial idea these days is that God would speak to us through religion.

But Ignatius's insight is as liberating today as it was in his time. And it is here that Ignatian spirituality can help even the doubtful find God.

Some agnostics or atheists await a rational argument or a philosophical proof to demonstrate the existence of God. Some will not believe until someone can show them how suffering can coexist with the belief in God. A few may even hope for an incontrovertible physical "sign" to convince them of God's presence.

But God often speaks in ways that are beyond our intellect or reason, beyond philosophical proofs. While many are brought to God through the mind, just as many are brought to God through the heart. Here God often speaks more gently, more quietly, as he did during Ignatius's convalescence. In these quiet moments God often speaks the loudest.

Let's look at some examples of these quiet, heartfelt moments in our own lives.

You are holding an infant, maybe your own, who looks at you with wide-open eyes, and you are filled with a surprising sense of gratitude or awe. You wonder: *Where do these powerful feelings come from? I've never felt like this before.*

You are walking along the beach, and as you cast your eyes to the horizon, you are filled with a sense of peace that is all out of proportion to what you expect. You wonder: *Why am I getting so emotional about the beach?*

You are in the midst of a sexual encounter with your husband or wife, or an intimate moment with your girlfriend or boyfriend, and you marvel at your capacity for joy. You wonder: *How can I be so happy?*

You are out to dinner or with a friend and feel a sudden sense of contentment, and you recognize how lucky you are to be blessed with her friendship. You wonder: *This is an ordinary night. Where did this deep feeling come from?*

You have finally been able to come to terms with a tragedy in your life, a sickness or death, or you find yourself consoled by a friend, and you are overcome with calm. You wonder: *How is it that I am finally at peace in the midst of such sadness?*

Gratitude, peace, and joy are ways that God communicates with us. During these times, we are feeling a real connection with God, though we might not initially identify it as such. The key insight is accepting that these are ways that God is communicating with us. That is, the first step involves a bit of trust.

Conversely, during times of stress and doubt and sorrow and anger, we can also experience God's communication.

You accompany a good friend or relative struggling with a horrible illness, or maybe you are ill. You think: *How could this happen?* And you feel a desperate need, an urgent longing, for some comfort or connection.

You are in the midst of a stressful time and wonder how you can ever get through the day. Then someone says something that goes straight to your heart, consoling you out of all proportion to the words, and you feel supported and loved. You think: *How could just those few words help me?*

You are at a funeral and wonder over the meaning of human life. Or you are tired and stressed from your life and wonder how much more you can take. You think: *Is there anyone out there aware of me, who is looking out for me?*

In each of these times—happy and sad, consoling and confusing, intimate and overwhelming—something special is happening, something more than just emotional "projection." The excess of feeling seems disproportionate to the cause, or perhaps it's hard to see *any* obvious cause. As well, there is a certain expansion of the soul, a loss of inhibition, and perhaps even an increase in one's feelings of love and generosity. (Abraham Maslow, the social psychologist, spoke of these as "peak experiences.") There may even be a change in one's outlook on life, and a great sense of peace or joy.

During these times, I believe, you are feeling a manifestation of your innate attraction to God. You are feeling what St. Augustine described in the fourth century. "Lord, our hearts are restless," he wrote, "until they rest in you." The pull that draws you to God comes from God.

Now we need to talk about that attraction from a different angle, and using another word. We're going to talk about something that Ignatius considered to be at the heart of the spiritual life. And it might surprise you.

We're going to talk about desire.

CHAPTER THREE

What Do You Want?

Desire and the Spiritual Life

TWO OF THE GOSPELS include the deceptively simple story of Jesus of Nazareth meeting a blind beggar along the road. In the Gospel of Mark, he is given a name: Bartimaeus, which in Hebrew means "son of Timaeus" (see Mark 10:46–52).

Bartimaeus is seated by the side of the road, begging for alms, when Jesus and his disciples pass by. The Gospels say that a "large crowd" was following Jesus, so there must have been a great commotion. You can easily picture the blind man wondering what is going on.

When Bartimaeus hears who is passing by, he shouts, "Son of David, have mercy on me!" Here is some irony: as Mark tells it, most in the crowd have no idea who Jesus is. Jesus' true identity as the Messiah is kept hidden from most people. (Theologians call this the "Messianic secret.") The blind man, however, sees.

The crowd shushes Bartimaeus. But he is insistent and shouts out again. The blind man, who has probably been ignored for most of his life, wants Jesus to notice him. The unseen man wants to be seen.

Finally, Jesus hears him and invites him over. In a bit of storytelling that has the ring of truth, the man's friends, who had previously been shushing him, now say, "Get up, he is calling you." With a gesture of freedom, he throws off his cloak and approaches Jesus.

Jesus says to Bartimaeus, "What do you want me to do for you?"

"My teacher," he says, "let me see again."

"Receive your sight," says Jesus in the Gospel of Luke. "Your faith has saved you." Bartimaeus is healed and follows Jesus along the way.

When I first heard this story as a Jesuit novice, it baffled me. Why would Jesus ask Bartimaeus what he wanted? Jesus could see that the guy was blind. And Jesus already had several healings to his credit, so he knew not only that the sick wanted to be healed but that he *could* heal them.

So why does he ask that question? Gradually, an answer dawned on me: Jesus asks Bartimaeus what he wants, not so much for himself as for the blind man. Jesus was helping the man identify his *desire,* and to be clear about it.

Desire has a disreputable reputation in religious circles. When most people hear the term, they think of two things: sexual desire or material wants, both of which are often condemned by some religious leaders. The first is one of the greatest gifts from God to humanity; without it the human race would cease to exist. The second is part of our natural desire for a healthy life—for food, shelter, and clothing.

Desire may be difficult for some people to accept in their spiritual lives. One of the best books on the way of Ignatius is *The Spiritual Exercises Reclaimed,* written by Katherine Dyckman, Mary Garvin and Elizabeth Liebert, three Catholic sisters. In their book, they suggest that some dynamics of Ignatian spirituality may present obstacles for women and may need to be reimagined. Desire is one of them. "Women may often feel that paying attention to their desires is somehow selfish and that they should not honor their desires if they are being truly generous with God." The authors encourage women to "notice" and "name" their desires.

Why this emphasis on desire? Because desire is a key way that God speaks to us.

Holy desires are different from surface wants, like "I want a new car" or "I want a new computer." Instead, I'm talking about our deepest desires, the ones that shape our lives: desires that help us know who we are to become and what we are to do. Our deep desires help us know God's desires for us and how much God desires to be with us. And God, I believe, encourages us to notice and name these desires, in the same way that Jesus encouraged Bartimaeus to articulate his desire. Recognizing our desires means recognizing God's desires for us.

Here's a dramatic story to illustrate this. At least it was dramatic for me.

FATHER? FATHER? FATHER?

A few months before I was to be ordained a deacon (the final step before the priesthood), I started to get migraine headaches—almost every week. At the time I was in the middle of theology studies in Cambridge, Massachusetts. Life was only moderately stressful, and I had suffered from migraines before, but never with such intensity. I decided to see a doctor.

After some tests, the doctor informed me that he had seen a "spot" on my test results. He suspected that it was a small tumor under my jaw that would have to be removed.

At the time, I was something of a hypochondriac, so even though my father had had the same operation thirty years before and had recovered, I was terrified. What if it were cancer? What if I were disfigured? What if? What if?

Fortunately, my friend Myles is a Jesuit physician. (That doesn't mean that he is a physician who takes care of Jesuits only; he's a physician who's also a Jesuit.) Myles offered to arrange the surgery at the Catholic hospital in Chicago where he worked, with a doctor he knew well. By way of convincing me, he invited me to stay in his Jesuit community during the subsequent recuperation. What a relief! I was grateful for his friendship, his professional help, and his compassion.

Until this time I had never had major surgery. Fear welled up within me, and with it self-pity. Yet when I saw all the others in the hospital waiting room a few weeks before the surgery, I realized the truth of what Myles had said: When you get your diagnosis you ask, "Why me?" When you meet others who suffer, you ask, "Why not me?"

On the morning of the surgery, lying on a cold hospital table, with tubes snaking out of my arms, I was consumed with fear. Myles entered the room in his surgeon's gown and introduced me as a Jesuit to the physicians and nurses in the operation room. After saying a few words of encouragement and promising he would pray for me, he left.

A nurse stuck a needle in my arm, placed a mask over my face, and asked me to count backward from one hundred. I had seen this dozens of times in the movies and on television.

Suddenly an incredible desire surged up from deep within me. It was like a jet of water rushing up from the depths of the ocean to its surface. I thought, *I hope I don't die, because I want to be a priest!*

The Energy of Life Itself

We tend to think that if we desire something, it is probably something we ought not to want or to have. But think about it: without desire we would never get up in the morning. We would never have ventured beyond the front door. We would never have read a book or learned something new. No desire means no life, no growth, no change. Desire is what makes two people create a third person. Desire is what makes crocuses push up through the late-winter soil. Desire is energy, the energy of creativity, the energy of life itself. So let's not be too hard on desire.

—Margaret Silf, *Wise Choices*

I had never felt it so strongly before. Of course I had thought about the priesthood from the day I entered the novitiate and felt drawn to the life of a priest throughout my Jesuit training. But never was there a time when I felt that desire so ardently. Perhaps it was something of what Bartimaeus felt when Jesus was passing by.

When I awoke hours later, it was as if I had been asleep for only a few moments. In my foggy state I dimly heard someone calling my name. Since Myles had told the physicians and nurses that I was a Jesuit, they assumed I was already ordained (which I wasn't). So the first thing I heard, seemingly immediately after having this intense desire to become a priest, was a nurse saying softly, "Father? Father? Father?"

For me it was a surprising confirmation of my desire from the God of Surprises. During my recuperation I realized another reason why Jesus may have asked Bartimaeus what he wanted. Naming our desires tells us something about who we are. In the hospital I learned something about myself, which helped free me of doubts about what I wanted to do. And who I wanted to be. It's freeing to say, "*This* is what I desire in life." Naming our desires may also make us more grateful when we finally receive the fulfillment of our hopes.

Expressing these desires brings us into a closer relationship with God. Otherwise, it would be like never telling a friend your innermost thoughts. Your friend would remain distant. When we tell God our desires, our relationship with God deepens.

Desire is a primary way that God leads people to discover who they are and what they are meant to do. On the most obvious level, a man and a woman feel physical, emotional, and spiritual desire for each other, and in this way they discover their vocations to be married. A person feels an attraction to being a doctor or a lawyer or a teacher, and so discovers his or her vocation. Desires help us find our way. But we first have to know them.

The deep longings of our hearts are our holy desires. Not only desires for physical healing, as Bartimaeus asked for (and as many ask for today), but also the desires for change, for growth, for a fuller life. And our deepest desires, which lead us to become who we are, are God's desires for us. They are one manner in which God speaks to you directly, one way that, as Ignatius says, the Creator deals with the creature. They are also the way that God fulfills God's own dreams for the world, by calling people to certain tasks.

A few weeks after the operation, I shared all this with Myles, who always combines prayerfulness with playfulness. He agreed that it was a grace to have this recognition, but then he laughed and said, "Wouldn't it have been nice if you didn't have to have major surgery to realize this?" (As it turned out, the tumor was benign and had nothing to do with the migraines.)

Laughing, I replied that if I hadn't had the operation, I probably wouldn't have realized any of this. Not that God wanted me to be sick, or caused me to be sick, so that I could recognize his presence in this way. No more than Jesus caused Bartimaeus to be blind. Rather, when my defenses were down, I was able to see things more clearly.

These are a few reasons why Ignatius asks us repeatedly in the Spiritual Exercises to pray for our desires. At the beginning of each prayer, Ignatius asks you to ask God "for what I want and desire." For instance, if you are meditating on the life of Jesus, you ask for a deeper knowledge of Jesus. The practice reminds you of the importance of asking for things in the spiritual life and of realizing that whatever you receive is a gift from God.

Desire plays an enormous role in the life of a Jesuit. A young Jesuit who dreams of working overseas, or studying Scripture, or working as a retreat director, will be encouraged to pay attention to his desires. Likewise, Jesuit superiors reverence these desires when making decisions about where to assign a particular Jesuit. This is part of the decision-making process known as "discernment" in the Jesuits. (More about making decisions later.)

Sometimes a Jesuit might find himself lacking the desire for something that he *wants to desire*. Let's say you are living in a comfortable Jesuit community and have scant contact with the poor. You may say, "I know I'm *supposed* to want to live simply and work with the poor, but I have no desire to do this." Or perhaps you know that you *should* want to be more forgiving of someone in the community, but you don't desire it. How can you pray for that with honesty?

In reply, Ignatius would ask, "Do you have the *desire for this desire?*" Even if you don't want it, do you want to want it? Do you wish that you were the kind of person that wanted this? Even this can be seen as an invitation from God. It is a way of glimpsing God's invitation even in the faintest traces of desire.

Some people find that their deep desires are difficult to identify. What then? Margaret Silf, an English spiritual writer, retreat director, and popular lecturer, provides one answer in her book *Inner Compass: An Invitation to Ignatian Spirituality*.

She suggests two ways that you may come to know your hidden desires. One is "Outside In"; the other "Inside Out." The Outside-In approach considers those desires already present, which may point to deeper ones. Desires like "I want a new job" or "I want to move" may signify a longing for greater overall freedom.

The Inside-Out approach uses archetypal stories as signposts to your desires. What fairy tales, myths, stories, films, or novels appealed to you when you were young? The same could be asked about stories from your sacred Scriptures. Are you drawn toward the story of Moses' freeing the Hebrew slaves? Or Jesus' healing the blind man? Why? Might these real-life stories hold clues about your holy desires?

Desire is a key part of Ignatian spirituality because desire is a key way that God's voice is heard in our lives. And ultimately our deepest desire, planted within us, is our desire for God.

EXPERIENCES OF THE DESIRE FOR GOD

Maybe you're surprised by the notion that everyone has an innate desire for God. If you're an agnostic, you might believe that intellectually but haven't experienced it yourself. If you're an atheist, you might flat-out disbelieve it.

So for the disbelieving, the doubtful, and the curious (and everyone else, for that matter), let's turn to *how* these holy desires manifest themselves in everyday life. What do they look like? What do they feel like? How can you become aware of your desires for God?

Here are some of the most common ways that our holy desires reveal themselves. As you read, you might take a moment and consider which have been at work in your own life.

Incompletion

Many of us have had the feeling that, even though we have had some success and happiness, there is something missing in life. Way back in the 1960s Peggy Lee sang "Is That All There Is?" In the 1980s, U2 sang "I Still Haven't Found What I'm Looking For." We all feel that restlessness, the nagging feeling that there must be something more to life than our day-to-day existence.

Feelings of incompletion may reflect dissatisfaction with our daily lives and point us to something that needs to be rectified. If we are trapped in a miserable job, a dead-end relationship, or an unhealthy family situation, it might be time to think about serious change. Dissatisfaction doesn't have to be stoically endured; it can lead to a decision, change, and a more fulfilled life.

Yet no matter how happy our lives are, part of this restlessness never goes away; in fact, it provides a glimpse of our longing for God. "Our hearts are restless until they rest in you," as Augustine wrote, 1,500 years before Peggy Lee and Bono. This longing is a sign of the longing of the human heart for God. It is one of the most profound ways that God has of calling us. In the echoes of our restlessness we hear God's voice.

Sometimes those feelings are stronger than simple incompletion and feel more like an awful emptiness. One writer called this emptiness within our hearts the "God-shaped hole," the space that only God can fill.

Some people try to fill that hole with money, status, or power. They think: *If only I had more I would be happy.* A better job. A nicer house. Yet even after acquiring these things, people may still feel incomplete, as if they're chasing something they can never catch. They race ahead, straining to reach the goal of fulfillment, yet it always seems tantalizingly out of reach. The prize of wholeness is elusive. Emptiness remains.

That was my experience early in my business career. After graduating with a business degree, I thought that once I landed a good job, pumped up my bank account, and filled my closet with elegant suits, I would be happy. But even with a job, money, and the best suits I could afford, I wasn't satisfied. Something was missing. It would take me several years to figure out what it was.

One of the best reflections on this topic comes from the twentieth-century spiritual writer Henri Nouwen. Nouwen, a Dutch Catholic priest and psychologist, wrote a perceptive book called *The Selfless Way of Christ* in which he examined this relentless quest to fill the empty hole in our lives. He observes that those rushing to fill that hole already sense that it is a useless quest.

> Somewhere deep in our hearts we already know that success, fame, influence, power, and money do not give us the inner joy and peace we crave. Somewhere we can even sense a certain envy of those who have shed all false ambitions and found a deeper fulfillment in their relationship with God. Yes, somewhere we can even get a taste of that mysterious joy in the smile of those who have nothing to lose.

In their drive to fill this hole, some are pulled toward addictive behaviors, anything to fill them up: drugs, alcohol, gambling, shopping, sexual activity, compulsive eating. But those addictions lead only to a greater sense of disintegration, a more cavernous emptiness and, eventually, to loneliness and despair.

This hole in our hearts is the space from which we call to God. It is the space where God wants most to meet us. Our longing to fill that space comes from God. And it is the space that only God can begin to fill.

Common Longings and Connections

Sometimes you experience a desire for God in very common situations: standing silently in the snowy woods on a winter's day, finding yourself moved to tears during a movie, recognizing a strange sense of connection during a church service—and feeling an inexpressible longing to savor this feeling and understand what it is.

In the first few years after my sister gave birth to my first nephew, I often felt overwhelmed with love when I was with him. Here was a beautiful new child, a person who had never existed before, given freely to the world. One day I came home from a visit to their house and was so filled with love that I wept—out of gratitude, out of joy, and out of wonder. At the same time, I longed to connect more with this mysterious source of joy.

Common longings and heartfelt connections are ways of becoming conscious of the desire for God. We yearn for an understanding of feelings that seem to come from outside of us. We experience what the sixteenth-century Spanish mystic St. John of the Cross calls the desire for "I know not what."

Many of us have had experiences like this. We feel that we are standing on the brink of something important, on the edge of experiencing something just beyond us. We experience wonder. So why don't you hear more about these times?

Because many times we ignore them, reject them, or deny them. We chalk them up to being overwhelmed, overwrought, overly emotional. "Oh, I was just being silly!" you might say to yourself. Or we are not encouraged or invited to talk about them as spiritual experiences. So you disregard that longing you feel when the first breath of a spring breeze caresses your face after a long dark winter, because you tell yourself (or others tell you) that you were simply being emotional. This happens even to those practiced in the spiritual life: often, after an intense experience in prayer during a retreat, people are tempted to dismiss it as simply something that "just happened."

Or we simply don't recognize these moments as possibly having their origins in God.

"I don't believe in God, but I miss Him." That's Julian Barnes, beginning his memoir *Nothing to Be Frightened Of*. Barnes is the acclaimed author of many books, including *Flaubert's Parrot*. (More about that unusual bird later.) He takes as his subject his overpowering fear of death. Barnes writes, "I miss the God that inspired Italian painting and French stained glass, German music and English chapter houses, and those tumbledown heaps of stone on Celtic headlands which were once symbolic beacons in the darkness and the storm."

Barnes misses God. Who is to say that this "missing" does not arise from the very desire for God, which comes from God?

One friend, a self-described workaholic who hadn't been to church for many years, once went to a baptism of a friend's child. Suddenly she was overtaken by powerful feelings—mainly the desire to live a more peaceful and centered existence. She began to cry, though she didn't know why. She told me that she felt an intense feeling of peace as she stood in church and watched the priest pour water over the baby's head.

To me, it seemed clear what was happening: she was experiencing in that moment, when her defenses were down, God's desires for her. And it makes sense that a religious experience would happen in the context of a religious ceremony. But she laughed and dismissed it. "Oh," she said, "I guess I was just being emotional." And that was that.

It's a natural reaction: much in Western culture tries to tamp down or even deny these naturally spiritual experiences and explain them away in purely rational terms. It's chalked up to something *other than* God.

Likewise we may dismiss these events as being too common, too simple to come from God. Mike, a Jesuit high school teacher, once preached a short homily in our house chapel. The reading for the day was a story from the Old Testament, 2 Kings 5:1–19, about Naaman the Syrian. Naaman, commander of the Syrian king's army, is suffering from leprosy and is sent by the king to ask the prophet Elisha for healing. In response Elisha tells him to do something simple: bathe in the Jordan River seven times.

Naaman is furious. He thought that he would be asked to wash in some *other* river, some more *important* river. His servants say, "If the prophet had commanded you to do something difficult, would you not have done it?" (v. 13). In other words, why are you looking for some spectacular task? Do the simple thing. Naaman does it and is healed.

Mike said that our search for God is often like Naaman's. We're searching for something spectacular to convince us of God's presence. Yet it is in the simple things, common events and common longings, where God may be found.

You may also *fear* accepting these moments as signs of the divine call. If you accept them as originating with God, you might have to accept that God wants to be in relationship with you or is communicating with you directly, which is a frightening idea.

Fear is a common experience in the spiritual life. Confronted with an indication that God is close to you can be alarming. Thinking about God wanting to communicate with us is something that many of us would rather avoid.

That is why so many stories in the Bible about men and women encountering the divine begin with the words, "Do not be afraid." The angel announcing the birth of Jesus to Mary says, "Do not be afraid" (Luke 1:30). Nine months later, on the eve of the birth of Jesus, the angel in the fields greets the shepherds with "Do not be afraid" (Luke 2:10). And when Jesus performs one of his first miracles in front of St. Peter, the fisherman falls to his knees out of awe and fear. "Go away from me!" says Peter. And Jesus says, again, "Do not be afraid" (Luke 5:10).

Fear is a natural reaction to the divine, to the *mysterium tremendum et fascinans,* as the theologian Rudolf Otto says, the mystery that both fascinates and leaves us trembling.

Religious experiences are often dismissed—not out of doubt that they aren't real, but out of fear that they *are* real after all.

Uncommon Longings

Also in the broad category of longing are more intense experiences. Sometimes we feel an almost mystical sense of longing for God, or having a connection to God, which can be triggered by unexpected circumstances.

Mysticism is often dismissed as a privileged experience for only the superholy. But mysticism is not confined to the lives of the saints. Nor does each mystical experience have to replicate exactly what the saints describe in their writings.

In her book *Guidelines for Mystical Prayer,* Ruth Burrows, a Carmelite nun, says bluntly that mysticism is not simply the province of the saints. "For what is the mystical life but God coming to do what we cannot do; God touching the depths of our being where man is reduced to his basic element?" Karl Rahner, the German Jesuit theologian, spoke of "everyday mysticism."

What does it mean to have a mystical experience?

One definition is that a mystical experience is one where you feel filled with God's presence in an intense and unmistakable way. Or you feel lifted up from the normal way of seeing things. Or you are overwhelmed with the sense of God in a way that seems to transcend your own understanding.

Needless to say, these experiences are hard to put into words. It's the same as trying to describe the first time you fell in love, or held your newborn child in your arms, or saw the ocean for the first time.

During his time meditating in Manresa, Ignatius described experiencing the Trinity (the Father, Son, and Holy Spirit of Christian faith) as three keys that play one musical chord, distinct but unified. Sometimes people describe finding themselves close to tears, unable to contain the love or gratitude they feel. Recently, one young man described to me an experience of feeling almost as if he were a crystal vase with God's love like water about to overflow the top of the vase. It was an experience of being "filled up," he said.

While they may not be daily occurrences, mystical experiences are not as rare as some would believe. Ruth Burrows writes that they are "not the privileged way of the few."

Such moments pop up with surprising frequency not only in the lives of everyday believers but also in modern literature. In his book *Surprised by Joy,* the British writer C. S. Lewis describes an experience he had when he was a boy.

As I stood beside a flowering currant bush on a summer day there suddenly arose in me without warning, and as if from a depth not of years but of centuries, the memory of that earlier morning at the Old House when my brother had brought his toy garden into the nursery. It is difficult to find words strong enough for the sensation which came over me; Milton's "enormous bliss" of Eden (giving the full, ancient meaning to "enormous") comes somewhere near it. It was a sensation, of course, of desire; but desire for what? . . . Before I knew what I desired, the desire itself was gone, the whole glimpse withdrawn, the world turned commonplace again, or only stirred by a longing for the longing that had just ceased.

That's a good description of the desire for more. I don't know what a currant bush looks like but I know what that desire feels like. It may be difficult to identify exactly what you want, but at heart, you long for the fulfillment of all your desires, which is God.

This is closely aligned with the feeling of awe, which Rabbi Abraham Joshua Heschel identified as a key way to meet God. "Awe . . . is more than an emotion; it is a way of understanding. Awe is itself an act of insight into a meaning greater than ourselves. . . . Awe enables us to perceive in the world intimations of the divine, to sense in small things the beginning of infinite significance, to sense the ultimate in the common and the simple."

In my own life I have encountered these feelings a few times. Let me tell you about one.

When I was young, I used to ride my bike to school in the mornings and back home every afternoon. Sometimes I would ride to school with a boisterous group of friends from the neighborhood. We would start off early in the morning, carefully lining up all our bikes in front of a neighbor's house, each jockeying for the lead position.

But some mornings I would ride to school by myself. There were few things I enjoyed more than sailing downhill through our neighborhood, down the clean sidewalks, past the newish early-1960s houses, beneath the leafy trees, under the orange morning sun, the wind whistling past my ears.

Closer to our school was a small concrete path that ran between two houses in our neighborhood; the school lay at the far end of the path, behind what seemed a vast tract of land. At the end of the path was a set of six steps, which meant that I had to dismount and push my big blue Schwinn up the stairs.

At the top of the stairs lay one of my favorite places in the world, the memory of which, though I am writing this over forty years later, uplifts me. It was a broad meadow, bordered on the left by tall oak trees and on the right by baseball fields. And in each season of the year it was beautiful.

On cold autumn mornings, clad in my corduroy jacket, I would pedal my bike over the bumpy dirt path through a meadow of crunchy brown leaves, desiccated grasses, and dried milkweed powdered in frost. In the winter, when I would not ride but walk to school, the field was often an open landscape of silent snow that rose wetly over my galoshes as my breath formed in cottony clouds before me.

But in the springtime the little meadow exploded with life. On those days, I felt as if I were biking through one of the science experiments we did in school. Fat grasshoppers jumped among the daisies and black-eyed Susans. Crickets hid in the grasses and among old leaves. Bees hummed above the Queen Anne's lace and the tall purple and pink snapdragons. Cardinals and robins darted from branch to branch. The air was fresh, and the field was alive with creation.

One spring morning, when I was ten or eleven, I stopped to catch my breath in the middle of the field. The bike's metal basket, packed with my schoolbooks, swung violently to one side, and I almost lost my homework to the grasshoppers. Standing astride my bike, I could see so much going on around me—so much color, so much activity, so much *life*.

Looking toward the school on the brow of the hill, I felt an overwhelming happiness. I felt so happy to be alive. And I felt a fantastic longing: to both possess and be a part of what was around me. I can still see myself standing in this meadow, surrounded by creation, more clearly than almost any other memory from childhood.

In such uncommon longings, hidden in plain sight in our lives, does God call us.

Exaltation

Similar to these longings are times that might be best described not as ineffable desires or strong connections, but times when one is lifted up or feels a sense of exaltation or happiness. Different from longing to know what it's all about, here you are feeling that you are very close to, or about to meet, the object of your desire.

Here you feel the warm satisfaction of being near God. You are in the middle of a prayer, or are in the middle of a worship service, or are listening to a piece of music, and suddenly you feel overwhelmed by feelings of beauty or clarity. You are lifted up and desire more.

Pied Beauty

Gerard Manley Hopkins (1844–1889) was an English Jesuit priest and poet renowned in the literary world for his creative use of language. In the religious world he is also renowned for his desire to find God in all things. In his poem *Pied Beauty,* Hopkins evinces a love of God, nature, and wordplay. It is a prayer of exaltation.

Glory be to God for dappled things—
For skies of couple-colour as a brinded cow;
For rose-moles in all stipple upon trout that swim;
Fresh-firecoal chestnut-falls; finches' wings;
Landscape plotted and pieced—fold, fallow, and plough;
And áll trádes, their gear and tackle and trim.
All things counter, original, spare, strange;
Whatever is fickle, freckled (who knows how?)
With swift, slow; sweet, sour; adazzle, dim;
He fathers-forth whose beauty is past change:
Praise him.

One evening, the English poet W. H. Auden gathered together with his fellow teachers at the Downs School, when something unexpected happened to him. He describes it in the introduction to a book edited by Anne Fremantle called *The Protestant Mystics:*

> One fine summer night in June 1933 I was sitting on a lawn after dinner with three colleagues, two women and one man. We liked each other well enough but we were certainly not intimate friends, nor had we any one of us a sexual interest in another. Incidentally, we had not drunk any alcohol. We were talking casually about everyday matters when, quite suddenly and unexpectedly, something happened. I felt myself invaded by a power which, though I consented to it, was irresistible and certainly not mine. For the first time in my life I knew exactly—because thanks to the power, I was doing it—what it means to love one's neighbor as oneself. . . . My personal feelings toward them were unchanged—they were still colleagues, not intimate friends—but I felt their existence as themselves to be of infinite value and rejoiced in it.

Auden seems almost to have met the desire of his heart, almost to have found exactly what he was looking for, but when he arrived at the place, he was just as quickly taken away from it. Such powerful experiences increase our appetite for a relationship with God in the future, even if we never again experience God's presence in quite so clear a way.

Beauty as a passage to God is a similar experience, and it crops up in fiction almost as often as it does in real life. In Evelyn Waugh's novel *Brideshead Revisited,* about a Catholic family in England in the 1920s and 1930s, one of the characters, Sebastian Flyte, a young aristocrat, confesses that he is drawn to the beautiful stories in the Gospels. His friend Charles Ryder, an agnostic, protests. One can't, Charles says, believe in something simply because it's lovely.

"But I *do,*" Sebastian says. "That's how I believe."

Clarity

There is a *New Yorker* cartoon that features a wizened, monkish-looking man hunched over a large book. He looks up and says to himself, "By God, for a minute there it suddenly all made sense!"

Sometimes we feel that we are tantalizingly close to understanding exactly what this world is about. On the day of my ordination, at a church in Chestnut Hill, Massachusetts, I entered the back of the church a few hours before the Mass was to begin. The choir was rehearsing, and as I stood in the empty church, which would soon be filled with friends and family, I thought, *This is right where I should be.*

Feelings of clarity may be similar to feelings of exaltation. Indeed, many of the feelings we're looking at may overlap. In some of the cases described in this chapter, we might also experience what Ignatius calls in the *Spiritual Exercises* "consolation without prior cause," a sense of God's communicating with us directly and giving us encouragement. "When the consolation is without a preceding cause there is no deception in it," he writes, "since it is coming only from God our Lord."

Isak Dinesen spoke of such clarity in her book *Out of Africa*. She writes about the "transporting pleasure" of being taken up in an airplane by her friend Denys Finch-Hatton. "You may at other times fly low enough to see the animals on the plains and to feel toward them as God did when he had just created them, and before he commissioned Adam to give them names." Moviegoers will remember this scene from the 1985 film of the same name, in which Meryl Streep speaks lines from the following passage. Dinesen writes:

> Every time that I have gone up in an aeroplane and looking down have realised that I was free of the ground, I have had the consciousness of a great new discovery. "I see:" I have thought, "This was the idea. And now I understand everything."

Desires to Follow

Desires to follow God are more explicit. It is not a desire for "I know not what" but for "I know exactly what." And you may be able to identify it as the desire for God.

In the First Week of the Spiritual Exercises, spiritual directors often invite you to meditate on the gifts that God has given you, and then, as Ignatius suggests, on your own sinfulness. This is not as formulaic as it sounds. After spending time thinking about blessings in their lives, people often feel, in a sense, unworthy of what they have received. Not that they're bad people. Rather, they ask, *What have I done to deserve all this?*

At this point in the Exercises your faults may come to the fore. As Bill Creed, a Jesuit spiritual director, once told me, "In the bright sunshine of God's love, your shadows begin to emerge."

This can lead to the realization that you are, as Jesuits say, a "loved sinner," imperfect but loved by God. Typically this prompts gratitude, which leads to a desire to respond. You may feel so overwhelmed by God's love for you, even in your "imperfect" state, that you want to say "Thank you! What can I do in return?"

For Christians this often takes the form of a desire to follow Christ. The response to the urge comes in the Second Week in the Exercises: a series of meditations on the life of Christ. In the Second Week, the desire is more explicit than one for "I know not what." It is for a particular way of life, that is, following Christ.

You don't have to be in the middle of the Spiritual Exercises for this kind of desire to manifest itself. You may be reading something about religion or spirituality and think, *This is what I've always wanted, to follow this path.* You may be sitting in a church service, hear about Jesus, and think, *Why don't I follow him?* You may remember the way you felt about God as a child and think, *What would happen if I returned to that path?* Your desires are more formed in this case. You are able to identify clearly your desire to follow a specific path, or to follow God. This is another way that God calls us.

Desires for Holiness

An attraction to examples of holiness is another sign of the desire for God. This can be triggered in at least two ways: first, learning about holy people in the past; and second, meeting holy people today.

In the first case, one famous example of this experience is that of Ignatius. There he was lying on his sick bed, reading about the lives of the saints, when he started to think, in essence, *Hey, I could do something like that.* His vanity was attracted to their great deeds, but a more authentic part of himself was attracted to their holiness.

This is one way that God can call you to holiness—through a heartfelt attraction to holy men and women and a real desire to emulate their lives.

But holiness resides not only in canonized saints like Ignatius but also in the holy ones who walk among us—that includes the holy father who takes care of his young children, the holy daughter who attends to her aging parents, and the holy mother who works hard for her family. Nor does holiness mean perfection: the saints were always flawed, limited, human. Holiness always makes its home in humanity.

So we can be attracted to models of holiness both past and present. Learning about past examples of holiness and meeting holy people today often makes us want to *be* like them. Holiness in other people is naturally attractive, since it is one way that God attracts us to himself. Experiencing the attractiveness of sanctity today also enables us to understand why Jesus of Nazareth attracted great crowds of people everywhere he went. Holiness in others calls out to the holy parts of ourselves. "Deep calls to deep," as Psalm 42:7 says.

This is something of what Marilynne Robinson, author of the novel *Gilead,* had in mind when she wrote in an article, "What I might call personal holiness is in fact openness to the perception of the holy, in existence itself and above all in one another."

Vulnerability

Here's an often misunderstood and misinterpreted statement: many people feel drawn to God in times of suffering.

During a serious illness, a family crisis, the loss of a job, or the death of a loved one, many people will say they turn to God in new ways. More skeptical minds may chalk this up to desperation. The person, they say, has nowhere else to turn and so turns to God. God is seen in this light as a crutch for the foolish, a refuge for the superstitious.

But in general, we do not turn to God in suffering because we suddenly become irrational. Rather, God is able to reach *us* because our defenses are lowered. The barriers that we erected to keep out God—whether from pride or fear or lack of interest—are set aside, whether intentionally or unintentionally. We are not less rational. We are more open.

Remember my story of being on that operating table and realizing—with blinding clarity—my desire to be a priest? That is one reflection of this same phenomenon. The desire was always there, as was God's call within that desire. But with my defenses lowered, it was much easier to see it.

When he was in his late fifties, my father lost a good job. After a long while, he found a new position but one that he found unsatisfying. As many people know, it is difficult to find work and start a new career later in life, at an age when many people are looking forward to retirement. It was hard for him and for my mother.

His job required an hour-long commute from our home in suburban Philadelphia. One dark night, in the parking lot of his office, far from home, my father had a dizzy spell, lost his balance, and fell. He ended up in the hospital. Tests showed what everyone feared: cancer. Cancer of the lungs had spread to his brain, which had caused the fall. (My father had been a heavy smoker for much of his life.)

During the next nine months, my father's physical condition went steadily downhill, despite chemotherapy. Soon he was bedridden and began to rely on my mother to care for all of his physical needs at home. The last month of his life, when my mother could no longer help him out of bed, he said, "I think I should go to the hospital." So we moved my father to a subacute care facility.

But while his physical condition declined, his spiritual condition seemed to improve.

Near the end of his life, my father started to talk more frequently about God. This was a complete surprise. While he had been raised Catholic and graduated from Catholic grammar school and high school, and while he attended Mass during important feast days, he had, as long as I had known him, never been overtly religious.

But as he neared death, he asked my Jesuit friends to pray for him, he treasured holy cards that people sent him, he mused about which family members he longed to see in heaven, he asked what I thought God would be like, and he made some suggestions about his funeral Mass. My dad also became more gentle, more forgiving, and more emotional.

I found these changes both consoling and confusing.

One of the last people to visit him was my friend Janice, a Catholic sister, who had been one of my professors during my theology studies. After his death, I remarked that my dad seemed to have become more open to God. In response, she said something that I had never heard but seemed to have already known.

"Yes," she said. "Dying is about becoming more human."

Her insight was true in at least two ways. First, becoming more human for my father meant recognizing his inborn connection to God. All of us are connected to God, though we may ignore it, or deny it, or reject it during our lives. But with my father's defenses completely lowered, God was able to meet him in new ways. Whatever barriers that had kept God at a distance no longer existed.

This, not desperation, is why there are so many profound spiritual experiences near death. The person is better able to allow God to break through.

But there is a second way that Sister Janice's insight made sense. My father was becoming more human because he was becoming more loving. Drawing closer to God transforms us, since the more time we spend with someone we love, the more we become like the object of our love. Paradoxically, the more human we become, the more divine we become.

This is not to say that God desires for us to suffer. Rather, when our defenses fall, our ultimate connection is revealed. Thus, vulnerability is another way in which we can experience our desire for God.

THESE EXPERIENCES, WHICH MANY of us have had—feelings of incompletion, common longings and connections, uncommon longings, exaltation, clarity, desires to follow, desires for holiness, and vulnerability—are all ways of becoming aware of our innate desire for God.

Anyone, at any time, in any of these ways, can become aware of his or her desire for God. Moreover, finding God and being found by God are the same, since those expressions of desire have God both as their source and goal.

Thus, the beginning of the path to God is trusting not only that these desires are placed within us by God, but that God seeks us in the same way we seek God.

That's another wonderful image of God: the Seeker. In the New Testament, Jesus often used this image (see Luke 15:3–10). He compared God to the shepherd who loses one sheep out of one hundred, and leaves the other ninety-nine behind to find the one lost. Or the woman who loses a coin and sweeps her entire house in order to find it. This is the seeking God.

But my favorite image is one from the Islamic tradition, which depicts God as seeking us more than we seek God. It is a *hadith qudsi,* which Muslim scholars translate as a divine saying revealed by God to the Prophet Muhammad. "And if [my servant] draws nearer to me by a handsbreadth, I draw nearer to him by an armslength; and if he draws nearer to me by an armslength, I draw nearer to him by a fathom; and if he comes to me walking, I come to him running."

God wants to be with you. God desires to be with you. What's more, God desires a relationship with you.

GOD MEETS YOU WHERE YOU ARE

When I entered the Jesuit novitiate, I was baffled about what it meant to have a "relationship" with God. We novices heard about that quite frequently. But what was I supposed to *do* to relate to God? What did that mean?

My biggest misconception was that I would have to change before approaching God. Like many beginners in the spiritual life, I felt I wasn't worthy to approach God. So I felt foolish trying to pray. I confessed this to David Donovan. "What do I need to do before I can relate to God?" I asked.

"Nothing," he said. "God meets you where you are."

That was a liberating insight. Even though God is always calling us to constant conversion and growth, and even though we are imperfect and sometimes sinful people, God loves us as we are *now*. As the Indian Jesuit Anthony de Mello said, "You don't have to change for God to love you." This is one of the main insights of the First Week of the Spiritual Exercises of St. Ignatius: you are loved even in your imperfections. God *already* loves you.

The Christian can see this clearly in the New Testament. Jesus often calls people to conversion, to cease sinning, to change their lives, but he doesn't wait until they have done so before meeting them. He enters in relationship with them as he finds them. He meets them where they are and as they are.

But there is another way of understanding this. Not only does God desire to be in relationship with you now, but God's way of relating with you often depends on where you are in your life.

So if you find happiness primarily through relationships, this may be how God wants to meet you. Look for God through friendship. If you are a parent, God may meet you through your son or daughter (or grandson or granddaughter). Just the other day a man told me that he was having a hard time being grateful. When I asked where he most found God, his face immediately brightened and he said, "My children!" It was easy for him to find God once he knew where to look.

Do you find joy through nature? Look for God in the sea, the sky, the woods, and the fields and streams. Do you engage the world through action? Look for God in your work. Do you enjoy the arts? Go to a museum, or to a concert, or to the movies, and seek God there.

God can meet us anywhere. One of my closest Jesuit friends is a prison chaplain named George, who has recently started giving the Spiritual Exercises to inmates in a Boston jail. Not long ago, one inmate told George that he was about to punch a guy in the face, when he suddenly felt God was giving him "some time" to reconsider. He decided against violence. Here was God meeting an inmate in his prison cell.

> Seek grace in the smallest things, and you will also find grace to accomplish, to believe in, and to hope for the greatest things.
>
> —Blessed Peter Favre, S.J., one of the first Jesuits

God also meets you in ways that you can *understand,* in ways that are meaningful to you. Sometimes God meets you in ways like those

I've just described, and sometimes in a manner that is so personal, so tailored to the unique circumstances of your life, that it is nearly impossible to explain to others.

One of my favorite instances of this in fiction comes from Gustave Flaubert's luminous short story, "A Simple Heart," written in 1877, which tells the tale of a poor servant named Félicité.

For many years Félicité, a goodhearted young woman, patiently bears up under her grim employer, the imperious Madame Aubain. At one point in the story, Madame Aubain gives her hardworking maid a brightly colored parrot named Loulou, really the only extraordinary thing that Félicité has ever owned. (This is the eponymous bird in *Flaubert's Parrot,* by Julian Barnes, the English author who "misses God.")

Then disaster strikes: her beloved Loulou dies. In desperation, Félicité sends the bird to a taxidermist, who stuffs him. When it is returned, Félicité sets it atop a large wardrobe with other holy relics that she keeps. "Every morning," writes Flaubert, "as she awoke she saw him by the first light of day, and then would recall the days gone by and the smallest details of unimportant events, without sorrow, quite serenely."

After her mistress dies, Félicité grows old and retreats into a simple life of piety.

"Many years passed," writes Flaubert.

Finally, at the moment of her own death, Félicité is given a strange and beautiful vision: "When she breathed her last breath she thought she saw, as the heavens opened, a gigantic parrot, hovering over her head."

God comes to us in ways we can understand.

Let me give you an example of this from my own life: At one point during my Jesuit training I spent two years in Nairobi, Kenya, working with the Jesuit Refugee Service. There I helped East African refugees who had settled in the city start small businesses to support themselves. At the beginning of my stay, cut off from friends and family in the States, I felt a crushing loneliness. After a few months of hard work, I also came down with mononucleosis, which meant two whole months of recuperation. It was a trying time.

Happily, I worked with some generous people, including Uta, a German laywoman with extensive experience in refugee work in Southeast Asia. After I had recovered from my illness, our work flourished: over time Uta and I would help refugees set up some twenty businesses, including tailoring shops, several small restaurants, a bakery, and even a little chicken farm. Together we also founded a small shop that sold the refugee handicrafts, located in a sprawling slum in Nairobi.

It was a remarkable turnaround—from lying on my bed, exhausted, wondering why I had come there, anguished that I would have to return home, puzzled over what I could accomplish, to busily working with refugees from all over East Africa, managing a shop buzzing with activity, and realizing that this was the happiest and freest I had ever felt. Many days were difficult. But many days I thought, *I can't believe how much I love this work!*

One day I was walking home from our little shop. The long brown path started at a nearby church, on the edge of the slum, which was perched on a hill that overlooked a broad valley. From there the bumpy path descended through a thicket of floppy-leaved banana trees, thick ficus trees, orange day lilies, tall cow grass, and corn fields. On the way into the valley I passed people silently working on their plots of land, who looked up and called out to me as I passed. Brilliantly colored iridescent sunbirds sang from the tips of tall grasses. At the bottom of the valley was a little river, and I crossed a flimsy bridge to get to the other side.

When I climbed the opposite side of the hill, I turned to look back. Though it was around five in the afternoon, the equatorial sun blazed down on the green valley, illuminating the long brown path, the tiny river, the people, the banana trees, the flowers, the grass.

Quite suddenly I was overwhelmed with happiness. *I'm happy to be here,* I thought. After the loneliness, the sickness, and the struggles, I felt that I was exactly where I was supposed to be.

It was a surprising experience. Here was God speaking to me where I was—physically, emotionally, and intellectually—and offering what I needed on that day.

Was it clarity? Uncommon longing? Common longing? Exaltation? Hard to say. Maybe all of those things. But it was especially meaningful to where I was at the time.

God speaks to us in ways we can understand. God began to communicate with Ignatius during his recuperation, when he was vulnerable and more open to listening. With me, on that day in Nairobi, God spoke to me through the view of that little valley.

God can also meet you at any *time,* no matter how crazy things may seem. You don't have to have a perfectly organized daily life to experience God. Your spiritual house does not need to be tidy for God to enter.

In the Gospels, Jesus often meets people in the midst of their busy lives: Peter mending his nets by the seashore, Matthew sitting at his tax collector's booth. Just as often he encounters people when they're at their absolute worst: an adulterous woman about to be stoned, a woman who has been sick for many years, a possessed man not even in his right mind. In each of these situations God said to these people, busy, stressed out, worried, frightened, *"I'm ready to meet you, if you're ready to meet me."*

If God meets you where you are, then where you are is a place to meet God. You don't have to wait until your life settles down, or the kids move out of the house, or you've found that perfect apartment, or you recover from that long illness. You don't have to wait until you've overcome your sinful patterns, or you're more "religious" or you can pray "better."

You don't have to wait for any of that.

Because God is ready now.

CHAPTER FOUR

Beautiful Yesterdays

Finding God
and Letting God Find You

FOR IGNATIUS AND HIS friends, finding God often meant noticing where God was already active in their lives. And we can notice God not only in peak moments, like the ones we just discussed, but also in daily events where God's presence is often overlooked. God is always inviting us to encounter the transcendent in the everyday. The key is noticing.

This insight—that finding God is about noticing—helps the seeker in two ways. First, it makes the quest straightforward. As I mentioned, Walter Burghardt, S.J., defined prayer as "a long, loving look at the real." Contemplating the real, rather than trying to grasp an abstract concept like the transcendence of God, or trying to puzzle out a complicated philosophical proof, is an easier place for most people to start.

This is not to deny the appeal of the intellectual path. In his book *A Testimonial to Grace,* first published in 1946, Avery Cardinal Dulles, a distinguished theologian and the first American Jesuit named a cardinal, wrote that his own religious awakening was encouraged by Greek philosophy, which helped him to see the world as an ordered whole. "The Platonic ideal of virtue," he wrote, "had enormous consequences in my personal philosophy."

Still, this most rational of men was finally moved to recognize God when he linked the philosophical idea of God with the natural world. His epiphany came as an undergraduate at Harvard, while he was walking along the Charles River in Cambridge and spied something more commonplace than a philosophical proof—a "young tree."

> On its frail, supple branches were young buds attending eagerly the spring which was at hand. While my eye rested on them the thought came to me suddenly, with all the strength and novelty of a revelation, that these little buds in their innocence and meekness followed a rule, a law of which I as yet knew nothing.

"That law came from God," wrote Dulles, "a Person of Whom I had no previous intuition."

That brings us to the second reason for the importance of noticing, like Avery Dulles's awareness of that tree. Noticing helps you realize that your life is already suffused with the presence of God. Once you begin to look around and allow yourself to take a chance to believe in God, you will easily see God at work in your life.

At this point you might be saying, "That's fine. But how do I *do* this?" Here's where the way of Ignatius can help.

THE EXAMEN

In the Spiritual Exercises, Ignatius includes a prayer designed to enable believers to find God in their lives. (Actually, it's more accurate to say that he popularized the prayer, since versions of it had been around for some time.) He called it the "examination of conscience." And he used to say that it was so important that even if Jesuits neglected all other forms of prayer in their day, they should never neglect this one.

The prayer goes by many names today. The Jesuit George Aschenbrenner, a spiritual director and writer, popularized the term "examination of consciousness" or "consciousness examination," since he feels that the English word "conscience" has "narrow moralistic overtones" that push people to focus primarily on their sinfulness. (In other languages, like Spanish and Italian, that single word expresses both meanings: conscience and consciousness.) Many Jesuits refer to the prayer by its original Spanish name—the *examen.* English-speaking Jesuits pronounce it "examine." Which is not such a bad way of thinking about it. Because what you're doing is examining your day for signs of God's presence.

The examen is a simple prayer with five easy steps.

It can be done once a day (usually before going to bed) or twice (usually during midday and evening). Here's how it goes:

As with every prayer, you prepare by asking for God's *grace.* It's a way of consciously inviting God to be with you and reminding yourself that you are in God's presence.

The traditional first step is *gratitude.* You recall the good things that happened to you during the day, and you give thanks for any "benefits," as Ignatius wrote. This is an essential step. As David Fleming, S.J., an expert on spirituality, recently wrote me in a letter, "Ignatius saw the examen as prayer, not just focused on the person, but as directed to God. That's why the examen begins with thanks to God, establishing the focus. It's not simply self-examination or dreamy introspection, it is a way of prayer, a way of being with God."

Ignatius meant "benefits" in the broadest possible sense. Obvious things would include any good news, a tender moment with a spouse, finishing an important project at work. But also less-obvious things: the surprising sight of sunlight on the pavement in the middle of a bleak midwinter's day, the taste of a ham-and-cheese sandwich you had for lunch, satisfaction at the end of a tiring day spent caring for your children.

For Ignatius many things—no matter how seemingly inconsequential—are occasions for gratitude. You recall them and you "relish" or "savor" them, as he would say.

Savoring is an antidote to our increasingly rushed lives. We live in a busy world, with an emphasis on speed, efficiency, and productivity, and we often find ourselves hurriedly moving on to the next task at hand. Life becomes an endless series of tasks, and our day becomes a compendium of to-do lists. We become "human doings" instead of "human beings."

Savoring slows us down. In the examen we don't recall an important experience simply to add it to a list of things that we've seen or done; rather, we savor it as if it were a satisfying meal. We pause to enjoy what has happened. It's a deepening of our gratitude to God, revealing the hidden joys of our days. As Anthony de Mello said, "You sanctify whatever you are grateful for."

The second step in the examen is asking for the *grace to "know my sins,"* to see where you have turned away from the deepest part of yourself, the part that calls you to God. Where did you act contrary to your better judgment or to God's voice inside you, to the divine spark within? Perhaps during a mean-spirited conversation about a coworker you contributed your own snotty remark. Perhaps you treated someone in your family or at work without the respect everyone deserves. Perhaps you ignored someone who was truly in need.

Reflecting on your sinfulness sounds like an unhealthy outgrowth of the stereotypical Catholic emphasis on guilt. But today guilt may be undervalued. The voice of our conscience, which tells us we did something wrong and moves us to make amends, is a voice that can lead us to become more loving and, ultimately, happier. In his diaries, Peter Favre, one of the early Jesuits, when speaking about his sins, calls it a "certain good spirit" that moves him to remorse.

When thinking about your sins, you might consider a helpful idea from my moral theology professor, James F. Keenan, S.J.

Father Keenan observed that, in the New Testament, when Jesus condemns people for sinful behavior, he typically does not condemn weak people who are trying to do better, that is, public sinners struggling to make amends. Time and again Jesus reaches out to people who are ready to change and invites them to conversion.

More often, Jesus condemns the "strong" who could help if they wanted, but don't bother to do so. In the famous parable of the Good

Samaritan, those who pass by the poor man along the road are fully able to help him, but simply don't bother. Sin, in Father Keenan's words, is often a "failure to bother."

St. Francis Xavier on the Examen

Twice a day, or at least once, make your particular examens. Be careful never to omit them. So live as to make more account of your own good conscience than you do of those of others; for he who is not good in regard to himself, how can he be good in regard to others?

This insight can help you see where you failed to respond to God's invitation in your day. Where did you fail to bother? Where could you have been more loving? Perhaps you neglected to help a friend who needed just a few minutes of your time, or a sick relative hoping for a friendly phone call. You could have, but you didn't—you failed to bother. This is a new way of meditating on what theologians call "sins of omission."

Does reviewing your sins still seem a manifestation of the worst stereotypes of Christianity? Well, an admission of our own sinfulness, or our inability to do what is right, helps not only to move us closer to God, but also to become more loving people. We are also able to see more clearly our *need* for God, who invites us to grow in love, no matter how many times we take a step backward. This second step of the examen reminds us of our humility. We become more aware of the way that we hurt others and can move away from those parts of ourselves that prevent others from loving us back.

That is, as long as you don't get mired in guilt. An awareness of your sins can be an invitation to growth but also a trap. Sometimes guilt mistakenly leads a person to believe either that he cannot be forgiven by God or that sinfulness makes him worthless. This leads to despair, a sure sign of moving away from God. All of us struggle with sin, all of us must seek forgiveness from God and others, yet all of us are still loved by God—more than we can ever imagine. Jesus' parable of the Prodigal Son (Luke 15:11–32), where the father not only forgives the wayward son but lavishes him with love, captures some of this insight, expressed in Ignatian spirituality as the "loved sinner." Guilt is a means to an end, not the end of the story.

Awareness of one's sinfulness is important for spiritual growth. This is why Anthony de Mello wrote, "Be grateful for your sins. They are carriers of grace."

The traditional third part of the examen is the heart of the prayer, a *review of your day*. Basically you ask, "What happened today?" Think of it as a movie playing in your head. Push the Play button and run through your day, from start to finish, from your rising in the morning to preparing to go to bed at night. Notice what made you happy, what made you stressed, what confused you, what helped you be more loving. Recall everything: sights, sounds, feelings, tastes, textures, conversations. Thoughts, words, and deeds, as Ignatius says. Each moment offers a window into where God has been in your day.

Now you may say, "I already *know* what happened today!" But without the discipline of the examen you could miss it. That's something I learned, in a very surprising way, during my philosophy studies in Chicago.

When my Jesuit brothers and I were in the midst of our philosophy studies, after our time as novices, we were also expected to do ministry. Though our superiors instructed us that our primary work was studying philosophy, we were not to lose touch with the outside world or to forget that our studies had a practical end, the end to which Ignatius geared his studies: to help souls.

During my first year of philosophy at Loyola University in Chicago I worked in an outreach program for members of street gangs in the inner city. During my second year, I was assigned to a community center in a lower-middle-class neighborhood near our Jesuit residence. Using my business experience, I helped unemployed men and

From the Spiritual Exercises

Here's the examen in the words of St. Ignatius Loyola, straight from *The Spiritual Exercises:*

The First Point is to give thanks to God our Lord for the benefits I have received.

The Second is to ask grace to know my sins and rid myself of them.

The Third is to ask an account of my soul from the hour of rising to the present examen, hour by hour or period by period; first as to thoughts, then words, then deeds, in the same order as was given for the particular examination.

The Fourth is to ask pardon of God our Lord for my faults.

The Fifth is to resolve, with his grace, to amend them. Close with an Our Father.

women with the ins and outs of finding a job: writing résumés, learning how to track down job openings, and preparing for interviews.

After the challenges of working with the street gangs, working at the community center seemed comparatively easy. And more physically comfortable: working with gang members meant standing outside of public housing projects and speaking with them during Chicago winters, when the bitterly cold Lake Michigan wind cut through however many layers of clothing I wore. At least the Howard Area Community Center had heat.

But where the gang ministry was exciting, this work seemed more prosaic. And it didn't feel particularly Christian. Where was God? I enjoyed the friendly staff at the community center, and I enjoyed meeting the unemployed men and women, who seemed interested in what I was teaching them. But the work itself seemed dull. On top of that, the clients were having a hard time finding jobs. I felt bored and unsuccessful at the same time.

One woman, whom I'll call Wanda, embodied this. Wanda was overweight and unkempt (neither surprising, given her limited finances) and had faced an unbroken string of bad breaks. Her education consisted mainly of high school and a desultory few months at a local community college.

Out of work for several months, Wanda was desperate for a job; this drew her to the community center. We met several times, and together we crafted a résumé that highlighted her skills, pored through the newspaper want ads, and ran through some practice interviews.

But no matter how hard we worked, Wanda never found a job, and I began to feel frustrated working with her.

One day, I confessed this to my Jesuit spiritual director, named Dick, a cheerful middle-aged priest with a great deal of experience in Ignatian spirituality. As with many spiritual directors, you felt that you could tell Dick anything. And he knew when you *weren't* telling him everything.

"Is your ministry coming up in your examen much?" he asked.

It wasn't. Since my primary work was studying, I said, I was more focused on that. In my examen, I would carefully review what experiences I had in my classes, during my study time, and over lunch and dinner with my Jesuit friends in community. The work with Wanda and the other clients was an afterthought. Or not even a thought at all.

"Maybe one reason that the work seems dull is because you're not bringing it up before God in prayer," said Dick.

"No," I said, "it's dull because it's dull."

Dick reminded me that when we feel resistance to something in prayer, it's often because we're resisting God's invitation to growth. So the next day after I spent some time at the center with Wanda, I promised myself that I would remember her during the review part of the examen.

That night I settled down in the chapel of our Jesuit community and began my examen. After a long day, I recalled the events related to my studies and community life. Then, when I reached the part of the day spent at the community center, I reminded myself to pause. It was strange to feel resistance, but I forced myself to remember the faces of the people that I had seen that day: the unshaven homeless man who had struggled with being out of work for many years; the wheelchair-bound, middle-aged man who had been searching for a job for months; and, finally, Wanda.

Wanda and I had spent an hour that day preparing for an interview that might not come for months, or might never come. Suddenly in my prayer I saw her face and was filled with an intense sadness that nearly overwhelmed me. Things seemed so hopeless for her. It was as if I had tapped into an endlessly deep well of pity. Before I knew it, I was crying for someone I barely knew.

The next week I told Dick how surprised I had been. "Perhaps you were feeling God's compassion for her," he said. "How else would God communicate his hopes for Wanda other than to work through you?" It was not surprising, Dick suggested, that I had earlier felt resistance to thinking about those with whom I worked—perhaps out of fear of the strong emotions that lay just beneath the surface.

The next time I met Wanda, it was like meeting someone holy, someone God loved in a special way. Of course God loved all the people at the community center, but prayer reminded me that Wanda was the one for whom God had asked *me* to care, even if in a small way. That one step of the examen—the review—changed the way I related to my ministry, changed the way I related to the people with whom I worked, and, more important, changed the way I related to Wanda (whom I would never see again after my time in Chicago ended). It had helped me to see God not simply in retrospect, but in the moment.

As Margaret Silf writes in *Inner Compass,* "You will quickly find that you start to look out for God's presence and his action in places you would not have thought to look before."

> The present moment holds infinite riches beyond your wildest dreams but you will only enjoy them to the extent of your faith and love. The more a soul loves, the more it longs, the more it hopes, the more it finds.
>
> —Jean-Pierre de Caussade, S.J. (1675–1751),
> *The Sacrament of the Present Moment*

The fourth step of the examen is asking for *forgiveness* from God for anything sinful that you've done during the day. Catholics may feel the need to follow this up with the sacrament of confession if there has been a grave sin. You may also recognize the desire to seek forgiveness from the person you offended.

Asking for forgiveness for our sins can be freeing, reminding us of God's desire to welcome us back—like the father in Jesus' parable of the Prodigal Son—no matter what we've done, if we are truly sorry. In theology studies, one of our professors, Peter Fink, S.J., told our class that the emphasis in confession needs to be not on how bad I am, but on how good God is.

Finally, in the last step of the examen you ask for the *grace* of God's help during the next day, and you can close with any prayer you like. Ignatius suggests the Our Father. Those who aren't Christian might want to close with a prayer from their own tradition.

EXAMEN(S)

Even though Ignatius told the Jesuits never to omit it from their day, the examen doesn't need to be followed slavishly. For Ignatius the examen went like this: gratitude, awareness of sins, review, forgiveness, grace.

But Jesuits pray it in a variety of ways. For me, it's hard to identify sinfulness without first reviewing the day. It's also easier to ask for forgiveness after thinking about my sins. So my examen goes like this: gratitude, review, awareness of sins, forgiveness, grace.

Others find that the steps overlap. Some run through the review and, in the process, recall something sinful and immediately ask for forgiveness.

The examen was meant for everyone, not just Jesuits. Dorothy Day, the American-born founder of the Catholic Worker Movement, talks about the examen in her journals, published as *The Duty of Delight*. "St Ignatius says never omit 2 examens, 15 minutes each," she writes on April 11, 1950. Then she gives her own way of doing it.

1. Thank God for favors.
2. Beg for light [that is, the grace to see clearly]
3. Survey
4. Repent
5. Resolve

Day found the examen not only reminded her of the simple joys of life, but goaded her to self-improvement. "We all do too much talking," she wrote in 1973, at the age of seventy-five. She had been complaining and gossiping too much, she felt. "I must stop." The examen led her to action.

"There is no 'right' way to pray," as David told me. So pray it in whatever way draws you closer to God.

There is, however, one common pitfall: doing the examen as if it were simply a list to be completed. Many Jesuits (including me) fall prey to this temptation. For busy people it's tempting to plop down at the end of the day and race through the day on their own: I did this, then I did that, then I did this, and so on.

To guard against this, you might remind yourself that you're doing the examen *with God*. Recalling this makes it not only more prayerful but more like a dialogue and less like a task that needs to be completed. Sometimes just recalling that you're in God's presence is enough.

The Examen in Five Steps

Here is how I like to do the examen. It's only slightly modified from what St. Ignatius suggests in the Exercises.

Before you begin, as in all prayer, remind yourself that you're in God's presence, and ask God to help you with your prayer.

1. Gratitude: Recall anything from the day for which you are especially grateful, and give thanks.
2. Review: Recall the events of the day, from start to finish, noticing where you felt God's presence, and where you accepted or turned away from any invitations to grow in love.
3. Sorrow: Recall any actions for which you are sorry.
4. Forgiveness: Ask for God's forgiveness. Decide whether you want to reconcile with anyone you have hurt.
5. Grace: Ask God for the grace you need for the next day and an ability to see God's presence more clearly.

You Shall See Me Pass

The examen builds on the insight that it's easier to see God in retrospect rather than in the moment. To highlight that insight, let me tell you a story.

A few years ago, I edited a book called *How Can I Find God?* in which I asked the famous and not-so-famous to address that question. Somewhat boldly, I wrote to the superior general of the Society of Jesus, Peter-Hans Kolvenbach, and was delighted when he mailed back a concise essay. His approach accented the practice of "looking back" to find God.

Father Kolvenbach recounted the story of an abbot in the Middle Ages who would speak to his monks every day "on finding God, on searching for God, on encountering God." One day a monk asked the abbot if he ever encountered God. Had he ever had a vision or seen God face-to-face?

After a long silence the abbot answered frankly: no, he hadn't. But, said the abbot, there wasn't anything surprising in this because even to Moses in the Book of Exodus (33:19–20) God said, "You cannot see my face; for no one shall see me and live." God says that Moses will see his back as he passed by him.

"Thus," Father Kolvenbach wrote, "looking back over the length and breadth of his life the abbot could see for himself the passage of God."

The examen helps you see God in retrospect. And what Father Kolvenbach said about the search for God could be applied to this daily prayer. "In this sense, it is less a matter of searching for God than of allowing oneself to be found by Him in all of life's situations, where He does not cease to pass and where He allows Himself to be recognized once He has really passed."

Likewise, while we frequently ask God for help in specific areas of life, we just as frequently fail to recognize God's help when it comes. Sometimes the examen can help answer the question, "Why doesn't God answer my prayer?"

Suppose you start a new job, enter a new school, or move to a new town and are feeling lonely. You ask God for help: Help me feel less lonely. Help me find friends.

Typically we expect a dramatic change: an instant new friend the next day. Normally, that doesn't happen; real friendships don't progress that quickly.

Instead you might start to grow friendly with a few people, very slowly. Perhaps the day after your prayer someone offers a friendly remark or asks if you need help. If you're looking only for that "instant friend," perhaps something as small as a kind remark will go unnoticed. The examen helps you notice that God often works gradually—which reminds me of one of my favorite images of God.

God, an elderly Jesuit once suggested to me, is something like an old carpenter in a small village in Vermont. If you ask the townspeople where to turn for carpentry work or repairs, they will say, "There's only one person to call. He does excellent work. He's careful, he's precise, he's conscientious, he's creative, he makes sure that everything fits, and he tailors his work exactly to fit your needs. There's just one problem: he takes *forever!*"

With the examen you're less likely to overlook that slow work of God.

Over time, you'll also begin to notice *patterns* of God's activity in your life. Maybe you recall every night that you're happiest when helping others with their physical needs—say, helping an elderly neighbor clean her house. You may think, *That's interesting. I've never noticed that before. Maybe I should do that on a more regular basis.* Or you notice that every night you thank God for the same person in your workplace. *That's interesting,* you think. *Maybe I should tell him how grateful I am for his friendship.*

Finding God in your examen makes you more likely to look for him during the day. You become more aware of where God *was* and where God *is.* Gradually you realize that God is active every moment of the day. Finding God by looking behind you makes it easier to see God right in front of you.

The examen can also be used to contemplate the presence of God over the long term. In her book *Inner Compass,* Margaret Silf tells of a leisurely driving trip she took in the Scottish countryside with her relatives, when they came upon a sign that said, "This is the source of the River Tweed." In just a short time they watched the stream,

In All People

Finding God in all things also means finding God in all people. St. Alphonsus Rodríguez (1532–1617) was a Jesuit brother who for forty-six years served at the Jesuit college in Majorca, Spain, in the humble job of a porter, or doorkeeper. Joseph Tylenda, S.J., writes in his book *Jesuit Saints and Martyrs*: "His duty was to receive the visitors who came to the college, search out the fathers or students who were wanted in the parlors, deliver messages, run errands, console the sick at heart who, having no one to turn to, came to him, give advice to the troubled, and distribute alms to the needy." St. Alphonsus was devoted to finding God in the present moment. "Lord, let me know you. And let me know myself," he would pray. Each time the bell rang, he looked to the door and envisioned that it was God himself who was standing outside seeking entrance. On his way, he would say, "I'm coming, Lord!"

which began as an insignificant spring, spread and grow, finally becoming a "stately presence in the valley town," a great river spanned by a bridge, fished in by fishermen, a source of beauty in the countryside. By car they traversed the path of the river in a few minutes.

Silf asks us if we consider our lives in this way. Can we use the examen to look backward, to find the hidden sources of the "landscape of your circumstances"? What parts of our landscapes resisted the flow of water, and what encouraged them? (Remember Félicité, the heroine of "A Simple Heart"? Flaubert describes her as every morning recalling "the days gone by and the smallest details of unimportant events, without sorrow, quite serenely.")

Put another way, can we use the examen to look back over our entire life? You might call this the "life examen."

BEAUTIFUL YESTERDAYS

The daily examen is of special help to seekers, agnostics, and atheists. For them it can be altered into a "prayer of awareness." The first step is to be consciously aware of yourself and your surroundings. The second step is to remember what you're grateful for. The third is the review of the day. The fourth step, asking for forgiveness, could be a decision to reconcile with someone you have hurt. And the fifth is to prepare yourself to be aware for the next day. Gradually they may begin to connect the events of their lives with God's love, presence, and care for them.

A few years ago, I started to lead large groups in this prayer. Most were familiar with Christian spirituality. But even people who had never prayed before were enthusiastic about the examen. And around the same time, as I mentioned, I was invited to work with a group of actors putting together an Off-Broadway play. The summer after the play closed I was invited to their summer workshop, where they staged brand-new plays and offered courses on various facets of theater arts. Most "guests" were asked to offer the company a workshop on something like Shakespearean drama, or voice, or movement.

What could I offer? I had had zero acting experience. Then it dawned on me: the examen. One afternoon, in an airy dance studio, I led about fifteen actors, writers, directors, and playwrights through the five steps. Some had meditated before, others hadn't, some believed in God, others didn't, some weren't sure, others didn't say. At the end of the session we discussed what we had felt.

My favorite response came from a young New York actor who said he always had a hard time meditating and wasn't even sure if he believed in God. But when the examen was finished, he said, "I never knew that my yesterday was so beautiful."

That's the theme of Thornton Wilder's play *Our Town,* first performed in 1938 and beloved by high school performing-arts groups. One character, Emily Webb, who has died in childbirth, asks to return to the world of the living. As she sees the simple things that make up our days—ironing, hot baths, meals, sleeping, and waking up—she says, "Do any human beings ever realize life while they live it?"

The examen helps you to "realize" the presence of God. For me, it transcends any proofs for the existence of God by asking you to notice where God *already exists* in your life, where your yesterdays were beautiful. With that awareness you will begin to notice God's presence more and more in your day.

Let me end our discussion of the examen with a story from the Indian Jesuit Anthony de Mello. His book *The Song of the Bird* includes several marvelous parables about the awareness of God. This one is called "The Little Fish."

> "Excuse me," said an ocean fish. "You are older than I, so can you tell me where to find this thing they call the ocean?"
>
> "The ocean," said the older fish, "is the thing you are in now."
>
> "Oh, this? But this is water. What I'm seeking is the ocean," said the disappointed fish as he swam away to search elsewhere.

"Stop searching, little fish," says de Mello. "There isn't anything to look *for*. All you have to do is *look*."

CHAPTER FIVE

Beginning to Pray

So I've Found God . . . Now What?

THE EXAMEN IS AN easy way to discover God in your daily life. But as useful as the examen is, there is lots more to prayer than looking back over your day.

The best way for me to talk about prayer is to tell you something about my own first steps in the life of prayer, which might give you the confidence to start, or continue along, your own journey. Since I knew very little about prayer until later in life, it's easy for me to sympathize with newcomers.

But, in fact, all of us are newcomers to prayer, because our relationship with God changes over time and is constantly being renewed.

CAN I ASK GOD FOR HELP?

When I was a boy, I used to pray a lot.

In the first grade, I used to envision God not as the Creator or the Almighty or the Supreme Judge but, as I mentioned, the Great Problem Solver, the one to whom you turned to fix things, to change things, or to help you out of a scrape. And since there were lots of things I wanted fixed (my baseball prowess, my trumpet skills, my math ability), I turned to God frequently.

It's as natural to turn to God in need as it is for a child to ask a parent for help, or for an adult to ask a favor from a friend. Being human means being in relationship. Being human also means being in need. So being human means sometimes asking for help.

As a boy, my preferred method of asking for help from God was to repeat rote prayers, like the Our Father and Hail Mary, over and over, with the number of repetitions in direct proportion to the desired outcome. Nerves about a spelling quiz would prompt a Hail Mary as I walked to school. If I was worried about a Little League tryout or a big solo in band practice, I would pray *many* Hail Marys. The more I wanted something, the more prayers I said.

This type of prayer—asking for help—is called petitionary prayer and is probably the type of prayer with which most of us are familiar. Asking God for something you want is both common and natural.

Still, every form of prayer has its pitfalls. One danger of petitionary prayer is that it can remove from our spiritual lives an awareness of God's freedom and may move into the realm of superstition or even magic. You might feel that if you pray a certain prayer, or in a certain way, or use a fixed number of repetitions, you just *might* be able to cajole God into doing something, to force God to respond. But prayers are not spells or incantations designed to "make" something happen. (Which was exactly what I was hoping for as a boy!)

Perhaps because of this fear of superstition, many people have told me they feel guilty when they use petitionary prayer. Or selfish. They say, "There are so many people in the world who need so much more than I do. How could I possibly ask God for something?"

Never Mind

One joke about petitionary prayer has a man desperately searching for a space in a church parking lot on a wedding day. As best man in the wedding, he can't be late. "God," he prays in desperation, "I'll go to church every Sunday for the rest of my life, if you just find me a space!"

Suddenly a spot opens up. "Oh, never mind God," he says. "I just found one."

There are certainly many people who need things more than you (and I) do. But while it's important to keep your own needs in perspective, it is impossible *not* to pray this way: I don't know anyone who does not feel the need to call to God for help.

God, I believe, also wants us to be open about what we need. This is part of having an honest relationship with God. Let's say that you've just lost your job or just received a frightening diagnosis from your doctor. How could you not cry out to God for help?

Petitionary prayers likely began as soon as human beings became aware of the limitations of their own existence. Their forms may have originated in some practices of prehistory—requesting favors from the various gods, deities, and spirits through prayer, ritual, and sacrifice.

But this does not mean that the modern believer should shun them: prehistoric petitionary prayers may simply reflect the inchoate human desire for relationship with God. And petitionary prayers have a long lineage in Jewish and Christian history. They are at least as old as the psalms. "Hear my voice, O God, in my complaint," says the writer of Psalm 64. Nearly all the major figures of the Old Testament, as well as the prophets, at one time or another, called on God for help.

This way of relating to God continues unabated through the New Testament. Think of Bartimaeus, the blind beggar, who cried out even when his friends told him to be silent. "What do you want me to do for you?" asked Jesus. Jesus himself instructs his disciples to pray, "Give us this day our daily bread." This is simple petitionary prayer.

Petitionary prayer is natural, human, and common. It expresses our very real need for God's help. It was the primary way that I prayed as a boy.

But it never dawned on me that prayer could be anything else.

Making Lists, Getting a Tan, and Finding God

That changed at age twenty-six, when I began thinking about entering a religious order. At point I was still praying the way I had when I was nine years old. Still praying all those Hail Marys and Our Fathers whenever I needed something badly.

The first person with whom I discussed entering the Jesuits was Father Jim Kane, the vocations director, in charge of recruiting and screening applicants. Father Kane, a friendly, fortyish man with a sunny disposition, said that in addition to completing an application, writing a brief spiritual autobiography, being interviewed by several Jesuits, gathering a series of recommendations, and undergoing a battery of psychological tests, he wanted me to complete a directed retreat.

A what?

From reading about Thomas Merton's life in the monastery, I knew that a retreat meant spending time secluded somewhere in prayer. But what was a *directed* retreat? Maybe, I thought, they directed you to different parts of the Bible.

But I wanted to enter the Jesuits, so I agreed. "How many days should I reserve for the retreat?" I asked.

"Well," said Father Kane, "it's an eight-day silent retreat."

"Eight days!" I said. How could anyone pray for eight days?

I imagined sitting immobile in a dark room with my eyes closed for the length of the retreat. Or maybe sitting on an uncomfortable pew in some dusty chapel. It also seemed an insane amount of time to take off—over half of my annual vacation days. And silent? Praying for eight days was hard enough. Staying silent for that long seemed impossible.

The next day I asked Father Kane to fax the agenda to me, so I could prepare for my trip. He laughed. "There's no agenda," he said. "It's a retreat."

One of my most vivid memories of that time is sitting at my desk, hearing Father Kane's response and thinking, as any businessperson might, *No agenda? For eight days? Who* are *these people?*

But my desire to join the Jesuits (and escape my old life) was so powerful that I asked my manager for time off and made plans to drive to the Campion Renewal Center in Weston, Massachusetts, where I would spend eight silent, agendaless days.

A few weeks later, in the middle of June, I arrived in Weston, a leafy suburb outside of Boston, and found my way to Campion Renewal Center. Formerly a school of philosophy and theology for Jesuit seminarians, the immense brick complex, built in 1926, now served as a combination retreat house and infirmary for the elderly Jesuits in New England. It took its name from St. Edmund Campion, one of the Jesuits martyred in the sixteenth century during the reign of Elizabeth I for ministering to Catholics in Protestant England.

My spartan room on the fourth floor was furnished like every other retreat-house room I've seen since: a bed (single of course), a desk and chair, a sink, a rocking chair, and a crucifix on the wall. It was also enormously hot, owing to the sticky Boston summer that year. An ancient fan did its best to move the sultry air around my room. Most mornings I woke up sweating, feeling like a turkey being roasted in an oven.

Shortly after I arrived, I met with Ron, a young Jesuit who explained that he would be directing me, helping to guide me through my prayer. I pretended to know what he was talking about. Then he said I should spend the first day enjoying nature. I was relieved—I could do that.

The next day was more pleasant than anticipated. For one thing, silence wasn't all that difficult. For another, the novelty of possibly entering religious life was still fresh, so I could imagine myself as a silent, holy, humble Jesuit as I paced the marble floors of Campion Center and strolled the spacious grounds, carrying a Bible. After six years in a stressful corporate environment, the opportunity to lie out on the grass, read books, and work on my tan was welcome.

The next day I told Ron how relaxing the day had been. At the end of our conversation, Ron said, "Why don't you spend some time over the next day thinking about who God is."

Aha! A trick! The Jesuits were fiendishly clever, or so I had heard. Evidently, they were testing my religious education, to ascertain if I knew enough to be a good priest.

That afternoon I lay down on the broad lawn beside the retreat house and tried to figure out how I should describe God.

Let's see, I thought, *God is:*

1. Creator
2. Love
3. Almighty

Though *almighty* was more of an adjective, I figured this was an impressive list. The next afternoon I presented to Ron my answers, which I hoped would cement his appreciation for my awesome intellect. "Okay," Ron said, leaning back slightly in his rocking chair. He chatted about my list but, sadly, seemed unimpressed with my theological acumen. Then he said, "Maybe today you could spend your time thinking about who Jesus is."

Another trick—more devious than the first one! "Well, Jesus *is* God," I said. "Right?"

I expected Ron to congratulate me on slipping through his Jesuitical trap. Instead he said, "Well, that's true. But why don't you think about who Jesus is for *you*. In your own life."

After lunch I stretched out on the soft grass under the sun, and came up with a new list. Jesus was:

1. Savior
2. Messiah
3. Prince of Peace

I finished in ten minutes and settled back to work on my tan.

Suddenly a word popped into my mind: *friend.* Jesus was a friend. That was something I had never thought of before. Nor did I remember anyone's suggesting it to me. Or, if they did, I hadn't paid much attention.

For a few minutes I lay on my back, peered into the cloudless blue sky, and imagined what it would be like to have Jesus as a friend.

If Jesus were my friend, he would be happy to listen to me. He would celebrate with me over my successes and be sad with me over my disappointments. He would want the best for me. And he would want to spend time with me and hear about my life.

Then I wondered what Jesus of Nazareth was really like. Of course I had heard the Gospel readings during Mass, understood something about his life, and knew about his miracles and his resurrection, but now I wondered what he was like as a person. What was it like for the apostles to hang around with Jesus? It must have been wonderful to be around him, to have him give you support, to answer your questions. It felt good, comforting, even exciting, to think about Jesus like this. I started to think about wanting him as a friend.

Then, with a start, I realized I was being distracted from the real reason I was supposed to be thinking about this. Dutifully I forced myself to return to my list. What else should I add?

Jesus was also:

4. Good Shepherd
5. Judge
6. Lamb of God (whatever that was)

The next morning I ticked off my list for Ron. He listened patiently and then chatted with me about those images.

As a guilty afterthought, I added, "You know, the funniest thing popped into my mind. For a moment I thought about Jesus as a friend. For some reason, I thought about the apostles and imagined them spending time with Jesus. It felt good to think about Jesus as a friend. It made me happy."

As soon as the words were out of my mouth, I was horrified. Surely Ron would accuse me of wasting time. I waited for the inevitable reproach. And I wondered if he would tell me that I was unfit to be a Jesuit.

Instead, Ron leaned back in his rocking chair and asked me to talk more about what I felt about having Jesus as a friend. After I did, he smiled and said, "I think you're beginning to pray."

It was a liberating moment, one in which I realized the possibility of a different kind of relationship with God. Ron wasn't saying that this was the right way, or the wrong way, or the only way, to pray. Rather, he was saying that thinking about Jesus as a friend was a kind of prayer. That it was okay to have *feelings* about God in addition to thinking about God. And that using your imagination in prayer was also okay.

Ron's words implied something else, too. Through these highly personal thoughts, feelings, and desires—being attracted to the idea of Jesus as a friend, thinking about what it was like for the apostles, wondering if Jesus could be my friend, hoping that I might someday experience this friendship—God was *communicating* with me. That was revelatory.

Strange as it sounded, God apparently wanted to be in a relationship with me.

For the beginner, that's a key insight about prayer. God desires to communicate with us and can use all sorts of means to do so.

In Chapter Two we talked about how we become aware of the desire for God. During this retreat my desire manifested itself in the simple attraction to the idea of Jesus as friend. For others their first memorable experience of prayer may arrive as they contemplate a weird-looking insect making its way across a leaf or as they listen to a Mozart concerto. But this insight—that God *wants* to communicate with us—is central to the way of Ignatius.

What Is Prayer, Anyway?

A few weeks after my retreat at Campion Center in the summer of 1988, I entered the Jesuit novitiate. At the time, the novitiate for the New England region was housed in a grand old brick house next to an even grander brick church in the Jamaica Plain section of Boston, then a neighborhood comprised primarily of poor Latino and African American families. In past decades the house had served as a convent for the sisters who taught at the elementary school next door. As a result, the common rooms were huge, the bedrooms tiny: a twin bed and a desk barely fit. "You have to go into the hall to change your mind," one novice said, only half-jokingly.

The first month in the novitiate was glorious: I was overjoyed to be a Jesuit. And I relaxed instantly into the daily schedule, which included studying Jesuit history and spirituality and working outside the house (which for me, that fall, was in a hospital for the seriously ill).

It also meant lots of prayer.

The day began with morning prayer in common, at 7:00 a.m., every day except Saturdays (when we cleaned the house in the morning) and Sundays (when we were expected to attend Mass in a local parish).

Traditionally, one of the novices led the morning prayer, which took a variety of forms. One day it might be the standard prayer for Catholic priests and brothers (called the Daily Office and contained in a book called a breviary). It consists mainly of psalms and readings from the Old and New Testaments.

Another day, morning prayer might be a simpler version of the Daily Office, with a novice choosing a single psalm, leaving more time for silent meditation. The psalms were prayed antiphonally, with one side of the room speaking one stanza, and then the other side, and back and forth, much as they do in monasteries.

As much as I disliked getting up early, I loved that part of the day: praying with the rest of the community while the early-morning sunlight poured through the clear windows of our plain, airy chapel. (Or often *didn't* pour in, since this was Boston, not Florida.) Morning prayer centered me for the remainder of the day.

At 5:15 p.m. we attended Mass, the central prayer of the church, which was celebrated by one of the priests in the novitiate. This was absolutely my favorite time of the day. Before entering the Jesuits, I had never been to a daily Mass and so didn't know what to expect. What did people do during a weekday Mass, anyway? Was it the same as Sunday Mass? Did they sing? Was there a homily? Were the prayers the same?

As it turned out, daily Mass was nearly the same as Sunday Mass, but more austere: the same prayers, always a homily, not as much singing. Instead of sitting in pews, we sat on simple wooden chairs, and during the Liturgy of the Eucharist (the time when the priest consecrates the bread and the wine) we stood silently around the plain wooden altar.

My favorite part of Mass was the readings from the Old and New Testaments. Since I had had little formal religious education, I was familiar with only a few of these stories. While most of the other novices knew by heart the story of, say, Joseph in Egypt, I had no idea what was going to happen. For me, it was like following an exciting novel or a movie.

And during the feast days of the Jesuit saints, I was introduced to the lives of the men whom we were encouraged to emulate. How wonderful to hear these stories during the Mass, during a time of prayer with my new brothers.

Catholics mark the feast day of a saint—the day of his or her death, or entry into heaven—with special readings and prayers. For the well-known saints, like Peter or Paul, the entire church marks the day. A few Jesuits, like Ignatius and Francis Xavier, are included in this elite group.

But often the feast days of Jesuit saints are celebrated only in Jesuit communities. On these days the homilist would tell stories of priests and brothers who had slogged through Amazon jungles to work with indigenous peoples, or risked martyrdom in England for ministering to Catholics, or paddled with Native Americans through the rivers of New France to spread the Gospel. Listening to those stories was itself like prayer.

Besides morning prayer and the Mass, we were to give one hour each day to contemplative prayer. "At *least* one hour," said Gerry, our novice director. We were asked to develop a personal relationship with God. But we were free to pray any way we liked. Without fail, though, at the end of the day we were to pray the examen.

Even with all this time for contemplative prayer, for Mass and for the examen, and even with all the encouragement from the novitiate staff, I began to feel frustrated about my spiritual "progress." Perhaps because of the focus on prayer, I was anxious about any possible "failures" in my spiritual life.

And despite my positive experiences during the eight-day retreat at Campion Center, I began to worry in the novitiate: How would I know if I was praying well? Or praying at all? How would I know if it wasn't all in my head? How did I know if God was communicating to me in prayer? What was the best way to pray? How did one go about praying?

All these confusing questions seemed to coalesce into one question about prayer: What is it?

There are many definitions of prayer. A traditional one, from St. John Damascene in the seventh century, is that prayer is a "raising of one's mind and heart to God." He also says prayer is the "requesting of good things from God." (That's petitionary prayer.) St. John's "raising of the mind and heart" reminds us that prayer is not simply an intellectual exercise, but an emotional one, too.

But that seemed too one-sided. It described what I was trying to do, but it left out God. What was God doing? Waiting for me to lift my mind and heart to him? It seemed too passive an image of God. This is what Mark Thibodeaux, S.J., characterizes in his book *Armchair Mystic,* as the first stage of prayer: "Talking *at* God." (His others are talking *to* God, listening to God, and being with God.)

Karl Rahner, the twentieth-century Jesuit theologian, wrote that prayer is "God's self-communication, given in grace and accepted in freedom." While I liked that idea, it still felt one-sided, but on the other side—as if all we did was sit around and wait for God. It left out *our* part of the relationship.

David's favorite definition, which I've already alluded to, was Walter Burghardt's: prayer is "a long, loving look at the real."

Prayer is "long," said Burghardt, because it is done in a quiet, unhurried way. "Loving" because it happens in a context of love. Prayer is a "look" because it has to do with being aware. "I do not analyze or argue it, define or describe it," wrote Burghardt. "I am one with it." Finally, prayer is "real" because our spiritual life is primarily about what happened in our daily life. His superb definition emphasized the groundedness of prayer.

But that still seemed to leave out God's role. What was God doing while we were looking lovingly at the real? It seemed too static, as if we were just looking and not much more.

St. Teresa of Ávila said that prayer is conversation with God. That definition seemed to fill in some of the gaps, since it emphasized the relational aspect of things: prayer was a two-way street.

But St. Teresa's definition raised almost as many questions as it answered. If it was a conversation, was I supposed to hear voices? How was I supposed to listen to God? How was I supposed to converse with God? That might work for a mystic like Teresa, but what about an average believer like me?

In essence, my question about prayer was the same as it is for many newcomers: what happens when you close your eyes? Thanks to some wise Jesuits, I would soon find out.

CHAPTER SIX

Friendship with God

Father Barry's Insight

WHEN MY CONFUSION PEAKED, David gave me a short book called *God and You: Prayer as a Personal Relationship* by William Barry, the popular spiritual writer and former provincial superior of the Jesuits in New England. The key insight of this marvelous book is that prayer is like a personal relationship with God, which can be fruitfully compared to a relationship with another person.

Obviously that's an imperfect analogy. After all, none of our friends created the universe *ex nihilo*. And prayer is not simply the relationship itself, but also the way that the relationship is expressed. Perhaps you could say that prayer is the conversation that happens in a personal relationship with God.

But Father Barry's general point was revelatory: the way you think about friendships can help you think about, and deepen, your relationship with God.

At first blush Barry's insight sounds strange. But if we look at what makes a healthy friendship, we'll see that some of the same traits help make for a good relationship with God. So I'll use Barry's work as a jumping-off point to talk about prayer. What makes for a good friendship makes for a good relationship with God, and that makes for good prayer. So what are we invited to do in our relationship with God?

Spending Time

A friendship flourishes when you spend time with your friend. So also with your relationship with God. You wouldn't say that you are someone's friend if you never spend any time with her. Yet some people do that with God. Some believers say, "God is the most important thing in my life!" But when you ask how much time they spend with God in an intentional way, they will admit that it's not much.

What kind of relationship do you have if you never carve out time for the other person? One that is superficial and unsatisfying for both parties. That's why prayer, or intentional time with God, is important if you want a relationship, a friendship, with God.

That's not to say that the only way to spend time with God is through private prayer. As you know by now, one hallmark of Jesuit spirituality is "finding God in all things." You can find God through worship services, reading, work, family—everything, really.

But, as with any friendship, sometimes you need to spend time *one on one* with God. Just as sometimes you need to block out time to spend with a good friend, you need to do the same with God, and to let God do this with you—assuming you want to sustain and deepen your relationship. As the Book of Amos says, "Do two walk together unless they have made an appointment?" (3:3).

Seeing friends on the fly or at work or in groups is fine, but from time to time you need to give a friend undivided attention. Prayer is like that: being attentive to God. How much time are you willing to spend, one on one, with God?

Learning

One of the most enjoyable parts of a new friendship is finding out about a friend's background—discovering his hobbies and interests, hearing funny stories about his childhood and getting to know his joys and hopes. When two people fall in love, there is an even more intense desire to know the other person, which is another way of being intimate.

The same holds true in your relationship with God. Particularly in the early stages, you may feel a powerful desire to learn as much about God as possible. You find yourself thinking about God and wondering: *What is God like? And how can I learn about God?*

One of the easiest ways to discover answers to these questions is to listen to *other people* talk about their own experiences of God.

A few years ago, when I edited the book *How Can I Find God?* I received a beautiful essay from Sister Helen Prejean, the author of *Dead Man Walking.* She wrote, "The most direct road that I have found to God is in the faces of poor and struggling people." Sister Helen talked about how working with the poor, specifically men and women on death row, had led her to places "*beyond* the part of us that wants to be safe and secure and with the comfortable and the familiar."

Later in her essay Sister Helen offered the analogy of a boat on a river. When you begin to seek God, your sails fill up with wind, and your boat is taken to places that you may not expect. But prayer is an essential part of that journey. Your boat, she says, needs not only sails but a rudder, too. Sister Helen's answer reminded me how much there is to learn about God through other people's experiences of God.

Each essay taught me something new about God—for instance, I had never thought of God as a rudder. Letting others tell us about their experiences of God is like having a friend introduce us to one of her friends. Or like discovering something new about an old friend.

Another way of learning about God is through *Scripture*. One of my favorite essays in that same book is by Daniel J. Harrington, S.J., who teaches New Testament at Boston College and was one of my favorite professors during theology studies. In his essay he told a moving story about coming to know God.

When Harrington was a little boy, he stuttered. At age ten, he read in a newspaper that Moses stuttered, too. He looked it up in the Book of Exodus, and, sure enough, Moses says to God, "I am slow of speech and slow of tongue." The boy read the rest of the story in Exodus (chap. 4), which tells how God promised to be with Moses and ultimately liberated the people of Israel.

"I read that story over and over," wrote Harrington, "and it gradually worked upon me so that it has shaped my religious consciousness to this day. As a boy of ten or eleven years of age I found God in the Bible, and I have continued to do so ever since."

But there was more to the story than that. As a Scripture scholar, Harrington now spends a great deal of time studying and teaching the Bible. As a priest, he preaches on the Bible. And sometimes, "in the midst of these wonderful activities . . . I occasionally stutter."

Then he makes this connection:

And this brings me back to where my spiritual journey with the Bible began. Though I am slow of speech and tongue like Moses, I still hear the words of Exodus 4:11–12: "Who gives speech to mortals? Who makes them mute or deaf, seeing or blind? Is it not I, the LORD? Now go, and I will be with your mouth and teach you what you are to speak."

Scripture is an ancient path to knowledge of God. First, reading Scripture helps to inspire us, in the literal sense of that word—placing God's spirit into us. Second, Scripture tells us about the history of God's relationship with humanity, and therefore it tells us something about God. Third, it tells of the ways that people throughout that history—from the Old Testament prophets to the apostles to St. Paul—related to God. In Scripture you see God relating to you, to humanity and to individuals. In all these ways Scripture helps you to come to know God better.

> Knowing God is more important than knowing about God.
>
> —Karl Rahner, S.J. (1904–1984)

For Christians, knowing God also means knowing a person: if you want to know more about God, learn more about *Jesus*. One reason that God became human was to show us more clearly what God was like. Jesus literally embodied God, and so anything you can say about Jesus you can say about God.

Here's another way of looking at that, through the lens of the parable, a story from everyday life that opens up your mind to new ways of thinking about God.

The parable form is one of the primary ways in which Jesus of Nazareth communicates his understanding of elusive but important concepts. In Luke's Gospel, for example, Jesus tells the crowd that one should treat one's neighbor as oneself. But when he is asked, "Who is my neighbor?" Jesus offers not a precise definition but instead spins out the story of the Good Samaritan, where the Samaritan man helps a neighbor in distress (Luke 10:29–37). When asked to explain what he means by the "Kingdom of God," the central message of his preaching, Jesus offers short stories about mustard plants, wheat and weeds, and seeds falling on rocky ground (Mark 4).

Where a strictly worded definition closes down thought and can be shallow, a story opens the hearer's mind and is endlessly deep. Stories carry meaning without having to be converted into a rigid statement. Parables also went against the normal expectations of the audience, as when the Samaritan, hailing from a hated ethnic group (at least for Jesus' crowd), was ultimately revealed as the good guy who cares for the stranger.

In a sense, Jesus of Nazareth was a story told by God. As Jesus communicated spiritual truths through parables, you might posit the same about God the Father. In order to communicate an essential truth, God offered us a parable: Jesus.

Jesus is the parable of God. So for the Christian, if you want to learn about God, get to know Jesus.

You can also learn about God through the *lives of holy men and women,* and witness how God leads them to fulfill God's dreams for the world.

For me, few things are more enjoyable than reading the lives of the saints, especially the Jesuit saints. When I read stories of how much they loved God, and how they experienced God's love in their own lives, I learn more about the source of that love.

For example, Pierre Teilhard de Chardin, the French Jesuit and paleontologist who lived from 1881 to 1955, found God not simply in the celebration of the Mass and in the other more obvious duties of a priest, but in his work as a scientist and naturalist, work that took him around the globe. During his lifetime Teilhard wrote extensively about the interplay between science and religion. (For a time, his works were considered too controversial by the Vatican, which was suspicious of some of his new ways of speaking about God.)

Teilhard encountered God through many avenues, including the contemplation of nature. "There is a communion with God," he wrote, "and a communion with earth, and a communion with God through earth." When I first read that, it helped me better understand that experience I had on my bike on the way to elementary school. Teilhard understood that you can learn about God through the natural world, by seeing how God reveals beauty and order in the universe and is forever creating and renewing the physical world.

We can learn about God through the experiences of such holy men and women, as well as through the men and women *themselves.* Through them we can glimpse the transcendent. Not that they are divine. Rather, they are like a clean window through which the light of God can shine.

Closer to home than Teilhard de Chardin is a Jesuit named Joe. When I first met Joe, he was in his late sixties and was living with us in the novitiate as a "spiritual father," a resource and example for the younger men.

Joe was one of the freest people I've ever known. Once, on a trip to visit some Jesuits in Kingston, Jamaica, his plane was delayed for five hours in Boston. Ultimately, the flight was canceled and Joe returned home. That night I ran into Joe in the living room of the novitiate, calmly reading a book. "You're back!" I said. "What happened?"

"The funniest thing!" he said. "We were supposed to take off, and then we were delayed for an hour, and then waited another hour until they delayed us again." Joe chuckled as he recounted the delays that led to his trip's eventual cancellation. Afterward, he tracked down his luggage and took a long ride on the subway (the T in Boston) to get home. "So here I am!" he laughed.

Had that happened to me, I would have been boiling over in frustration. "Weren't you angry?" I said, amazed.

"Angry? Why?" he said. "There was nothing I could do about it. Why get upset over something you can't change?"

Equanimity in the face of stress does not make you holy. Much less does it make you a saint. But it's a start. Detachment, freedom, and a sense of humor are signposts on the road to holiness. Joe, a man well acquainted with the way of Ignatius, knew that a healthy spirituality requires freedom, detachment, and openness. Often when you would ask this elderly priest if he wanted to do something new—say, see a controversial new movie, go to a newly opened restaurant, check out a Mass at a faraway parish—he would answer, "Why *not?*"

Why not indeed? People like Joe show the fruits of friendship with God: spontaneity, openness, generosity, freedom, love. Time with Joe taught me not simply about this particular Jesuit priest but about the way God acts in the lives of men and women. Holy people teach you something about how God works, and in this way you learn about God.

Overall, learning about God—through other people's experiences of God, through Scripture, through holy men and women—is part of nourishing your spiritual life, because learning about God is part of being in relationship with God.

BEING HONEST

"O Lord, you have searched me and known me," says Psalm 139. Letting God come to know *you* is also essential—as it is in any relationship. Letting yourself be known by God means more or less the same thing it means in a friendship: speaking about your life, sharing your feelings, and revealing yourself openly.

Honesty is an important part of this process. Father Barry suggests thinking about what happens when you're not honest in a relationship. Usually, the relationship begins to grow cold, distant, or formal. If you're avoiding something unpleasant, the relationship devolves into one defined by nothing more than social niceties. Eventually the relationship stagnates or dies.

It's the same with prayer. If you are saying only what you think you *should* say to God, rather than what you want to say, then your relationship will grow cold, distant, and formal. Honesty in prayer, as in life, is important.

Not long ago I became friendly with a Jesuit whom I greatly admired. He seemed to lead a charmed life: he was happy, optimistic, hardworking, friendly, and prayerful. For a long time I tried to figure out what his secret was. What enabled him to lead this almost perfect life?

A few years later, this same friend went through a wrenching personal crisis and turned to me, among others, for help. In a series of conversations he poured out his pain and showed a part of himself that I had previously not seen.

Happily, the crisis passed. But after he had opened up to me, I felt closer to him, and he told me that he felt closer to me. Both of us were grateful for our friendship. Though I knew he didn't lead the perfect life, I liked him even more. His honesty changed the relationship.

How can you be honest with God in prayer? One easy way is to imagine God right in front of you. You might imagine God, or Jesus, sitting across from you in a chair, or sitting beside you on a couch—use whatever image feels most comfortable. Then speak in a familiar way, in silence or out loud, about your life.

Of course God already knows what's going on in your life. Still, this kind of openness is an important part of the spiritual life. Once again, comparing it to a friendship is instructive. Let's say a loved one has died. A good friend already knows how sad you are, and probably doesn't need to be told. But you tell her anyway, right?

Not too long ago I had lunch with a friend who lost his brother at a young age to cancer. My friend is a warm and generous person, and I knew that he was devastated by his brother's loss. But it was still a privilege for me to hear him talk about what had happened, to see his tears, and to listen to him recount funny stories about his brother.

Telling your friend *anyway* helps to make the loss more concrete for you, it gives you the opportunity to accept your friend's consolation, and it reminds you that you are known by another in an intimate way.

Being honest with God means sharing everything with God, not just the things that you think are appropriate for prayer, and not simply your gratitude and praise. Honesty means sharing things you might consider inappropriate for conversation with God.

Anger is a perfect example. It's natural to be angry with God over suffering in our lives. Disappointment springs from all of us. Anger is a sign that we're alive.

God can handle your anger no matter how hot it burns. God has been handling anger as long as humans have been praying. Just read the Book of Job in the Old Testament, where Job rails against God for causing his seemingly endless pain. Usually Job is seen as a patient man, and in the beginning of that book he is. But eventually Job loses his patience and begins to curse the day he was born. "I loathe my life," he says. "I will give free utterances to my complaint; I will speak in the bitterness of my soul" (Job 10:1).

Anger, sadness, frustration, disappointment, and bitterness in prayer have a long history. Why shouldn't you allow yourself to express those same honest feelings too?

A few years ago, I told my spiritual director I was so frustrated that God didn't seem to be doing anything to help me and that I used an obscenity in my prayer. One night I was so angry that I clenched my fists and shouted aloud, "How about some @#$% help, God!"

Some readers might be shocked that a priest would use language like that, especially in prayer. And I thought my spiritual director, a wise and gentle Jesuit priest named Damian, would reproach me. Instead Damian said, "That's a good prayer."

I thought he was kidding.

"That's a good prayer because it's honest," he said. "God wants your honesty, Jim." Being honest also made me feel that God now knew exactly how I felt. Have you ever had the experience of confiding something to a friend and feeling relief? It felt like God could now better accompany me, as a good friend might. Or, more accurately, I would be able to allow God to accompany me.

Saying it aloud also brought me face-to-face with my lamentable lack of gratitude. Sure, there was a big problem in my life, but there were some wonderful things going on at the same time. It was like an adolescent saying to his parent, "I hate you!" because he was asked to go to bed early or turn off his video games or take out the trash. Hearing myself talk like that—out loud—revealed how part of my re-

Thou Art Indeed Just, Lord

This poem by the English Jesuit Gerard Manley Hopkins (1844–1889), based on a lament from the Book of Jeremiah, expresses the poet's frustration with God. Like most of

Hopkins's complex poems, you have to read it carefully to puzzle out what he's saying, but once you get it, it packs a real punch.

Thou art indeed just, Lord, if I contend
With thee; but, sir, so what I plead is just.
Why do sinners' ways prosper? and why must
Disappointment all I endeavour end?
 Wert thou my enemy, O thou my friend,
How wouldst thou worse, I wonder, than thou dost
Defeat, thwart me? Oh, the sots and thralls of lust
Do in spare hours more thrive than I that spend,
Sir, life upon thy cause. See, banks and brakes
Now, leavèd how thick! lacèd they are again
With fretty chervil, look, and fresh wind shakes
Them; birds build—but not I build; no, but strain,
Time's eunuch, and not breed one work that wakes.
Mine, O thou Lord of life, send my roots rain.

lationship with God was childish and how much I wanted to change my approach to prayer.

So Damian was right: it *was* a good prayer!

Sadness is something else that some people feel reluctant to share with God. Someone once told me of the experience of going to a movie with a close friend. Because the subject material intersected with his life, he began to sob at the end of the movie and was embarrassed. Later on, as the two sat together in a car in the parking lot, his friend sat silently and simply let him cry.

His friend wasn't the only one showing love. The person weeping allowed another to enter into his life, giving the gift of intimacy. Can you share with God the intimate gift of your true self, your true emotions, even when you are grieving?

But when it comes to prayer, the most inappropriate emotion, at least in many minds, is sexual desire.

One of the best books on prayer is *God, I Have Issues,* by Mark Thibodeaux, one of the most lighthearted Jesuits I know. Each chapter addresses prayer during different moods. The moods are organized alphabetically so that you can thumb through the book when you are: Addicted, Afraid, Angry, Angry at You, and so on.

One chapter is titled "Sexually Aroused." Mark begins his essay bluntly: "Good Christian people often worry about their sexual feelings. They are embarrassed and ashamed of them."

Mark reminds us that sexuality and sexual activity are wondrous gifts from God to be celebrated. On a natural level they draw people together for the sake of companionship and creating new life. On a spiritual level those feelings remind us of the love that God has for us. Many spiritual writers use erotic love as a metaphor for God's love for humanity. (Check out the Bible's Song of Songs if you have any doubts.)

But like any gift, sexuality must be used wisely. If motivated by selfishness, it can turn into a desire for possessiveness. On a much more benign level, sexual thoughts during prayer can also be a distraction. So what do we do with those feelings in prayer?

Again, the solution is being honest. "Instead of hiding these experiences, we should share them with God," says Mark, "and use them to remind us how great it is to be alive, how great it is to be a creature of God and how wondrously we are created." If that doesn't work, or if those feelings are troublesome because they are directed to a person with whom you cannot have a relationship, just be honest with God about your struggles.

Be honest with God about everything.

LISTENING

Friendship requires listening. You would scarcely consider yourself a good friend if all you did was talk and talk and talk. But that's what happens in some relationships with God. People sometimes find their prayer is just a recitation of things they need (too much petitionary prayer) or an endless stream of letting God know how they are (too much talking). As in any friendship, we need to listen.

But what does it mean to "listen" to God? This baffled me in the novitiate. Does it mean hearing voices?

Few people say they have heard God's voice in a physical way. (That is, few sane people.) But it does happen. Mysterious notations in Ignatius's personal diaries, speaking about his prayer, refer to *loquela,* loosely translated as speech, discourse, or talking.

The most recent example may be Mother Teresa, who wrote that in 1946 she "heard" God ask her to work with the poorest of the poor in the slums of Calcutta. Earlier, Mother Teresa had made a promise to God to never refuse anything that God asked of her. Then, years later, as she told her spiritual director, when she heard God's voice asking her to leave behind her work in a girls' school, she, not surprisingly, was reluctant to leave behind her work for something new and, it seemed, dangerous.

She reported that God, as if recalling her earlier promise, said to her, "Wilt thou refuse?" Mother Teresa accepted God's invitation to work among the poor. (By the way, she could have said no. Our relationship with God does not obliterate free will.)

But the kinds of experiences reported by Mother Teresa are exceedingly, exceedingly rare. So it's probably best for the rest of us to set aside our pious hopes—or unwarranted fears—that we're going to hear voices in a literal way.

In twenty-one years as a Jesuit I've only met two people who have told me they have heard God speak to them. One is Maddy, a joyful and prayerful woman who is a member of the Sisters of St. Joseph of Springfield, Massachusetts. Maddy and I first got to know each other when we were both working in East Africa in the 1990s. Today she works at the Jesuit retreat house in Gloucester, Massachusetts, where we have often directed retreats together.

Since we are longtime friends, I figured I knew her well. But this no-nonsense woman surprised me during one of these retreats when, during an afternoon talk to the retreatants, she said that when she was young and considering entering a religious order, she heard God's voice saying, "I have chosen you to be with me. You will find your way."

Before entering the Jesuits, I would have thought Maddy was insane. But now I believe that those moments—while very rare indeed—can be privileged experiences of God's presence. Still, we have to weigh them carefully, ruling out any psychological illness, comparing them to what we know about God, and submitting them to experienced spiritual guides.

Most of us will never have that kind of experience. (I never have.) So if you're worried about hearing voices, don't be. Or if you're frustrated that you're *not* hearing God speak to you in that way, don't be.

On the other hand, many people say that during prayer, even though they don't audibly hear God's voice, they feel *as if* God were speaking with them. This can happen in ways both subtle and not so subtle. It can even happen outside of formal prayer. For example, a friend may say something so insightful that it is almost as if a window into your soul had just been opened: you may feel as if your friend's words are a way that God is communicating with you.

Another example: my mother once told me that she was looking out the window and said to God, "Do you love me?" And the words "More than you know!" instantly came to mind. "It wasn't a voice; it just popped into my head." My mother wasn't seeking that answer; it came spontaneously. And of course God *does* love her more than she can know. But for many people these experiences are rare, too.

So, are there other ways to listen to God? Absolutely.

Sometimes, for example, when you try imagining yourself speaking with God, you might also try imagining what God would say in return. That's a popular way of prayer for many Christians, and it is something that Ignatius suggests as one technique in the Spiritual Exercises.

Praying in that particular way is difficult for me. But for some people it's not difficult at all. When they picture themselves speaking with God, they can easily imagine God speaking to them, naturally and easily. Sometimes it helps to imagine listening to Jesus in a familiar place from Scripture—like by the Sea of Galilee or even in his house at Nazareth. However, what you imagine him saying must always be tested against what you know about God, what you know about yourself, and what your faith community believes about God. Does it lead you to be more loving and compassionate? Does it sound authentic? "God's words," as Vinita Hampton Wright says in *Days of Deepening Friendship,* "have the ring of truth."

If that kind of prayer is too difficult, you might try something that I stumbled upon recently: imagine what you think God *would* say based on what you know about God.

Here's where the friendship analogy is again helpful. Let's say you have an elderly friend who is known for giving excellent advice. She's experienced, wise, and compassionate. Over the years, you have come to appreciate, and know, her outlook on life. When you tell her a problem, sometimes you don't even have to wait for her to respond: you *know* what she's going to say.

Since it's hard for me to imagine God literally speaking to me, I sometimes ask myself, "Given what I know about God through Scripture, through experience, and through tradition, what would God *probably* say about this?" Usually it's not hard to imagine at all. And, as the authors of *The Spiritual Exercises Reclaimed* note, "Often communication is 'felt' or intuited, rather than heard as ordinary conversation."

But for most people the idea of listening to God is even more subtle than the ways I've just been describing. So let's look at how God *most often* communicates in prayer with people. The following are more common ways to listen to God's voice in prayer.

Listening Carefully

Emotions are a key way that God speaks in prayer. You might be praying about a favorite Bible passage, and suddenly you feel happiness over being closer to God, or anger over how Jesus or the prophets were mistreated, or sorrow over the plight of the poor. God may be speaking to you through those emotions. Remember the story of Wanda, the unemployed woman in the community center? During my prayer, I felt sorrow for her, which seemed to have been one way that God was leading me to care for her.

These invitations to listen can be easily overlooked because they are often fleeting. If we're not careful, we'll miss them.

Insights are another way that God speaks in prayer. Perhaps you're praying for clarity, and you receive an insight that allows you to see things in a new light. You may see a novel way of approaching an old problem.

Or you may, in a flash, perceive something surprising about God. Let's say you're reading a Gospel story that speaks of Jesus going off to pray by himself. You might have heard this story many times, but this time an insight arrives: *If even* Jesus *could take time off from his busy schedule to pray, perhaps I could do the same.* Here the experience is not so much emotional as intellectual.

While a few spiritual directors may privilege emotional moments in prayer, it's important not to neglect the way that an intellectual insight can be as meaningful.

Memories also float to the surface in prayer. Here God may invite you to remember something that consoles or delights you. What is God saying to you through those consoling memories?

A few years ago, for example, during a retreat in Gloucester, Massachusetts, I became consumed with doubts about chastity and concerned about loneliness as a celibate man. Not that I was thinking of breaking my vow. It was more of an abstract worrying. And I asked God to take away the loneliness.

Suddenly, as if a valve had been opened, warm memories flooded into my mind. Memories of the friends I had made since entering the Jesuits—this Jesuit from my novitiate; this sister in East Africa; this young woman I knew during my theology studies; even someone who worked at the retreat house where I was staying—arose into my consciousness. These memories reminded me of the love that I've been given in my Jesuit life.

> The fundamental attitude of the believer is of one who listens. It is to the Lord's utterances that he gives ear. In as many different ways and on as many varied levels as the listener can discern the word and will of the Lord manifested to him, he must respond.
> —David Asselin, S.J. (1922–1972)

Many might dismiss that as a coincidence: happening to remember these people just when I was praying about loneliness. But God often gives us such consoling memories as a way of saying, *Remember what I have done.*

In the Gospel of Luke (1:26–38), the angel Gabriel visits Mary to foretell the birth of Jesus. She questions Gabriel, saying, "How can this be, since I am a virgin?" Gabriel tells her that the Holy Spirit will "overshadow" her. He also reminds her that her elderly cousin, Elizabeth, is pregnant. "This is the sixth month for her who was said to be barren." In other words, see, and remember what God has already done.

Memories may reveal bitter things, too. One of the best examples comes from William Maxwell's novel *So Long, See You Tomorrow,* the tale of a friendship between two young boys. Written in retrospect, the narrator tells the story of how his friend Cletus was ostracized by his schoolmates after his father murdered another man. One day in school, the narrator willfully ignores his former friend. Years later the narrator writes, in sorrow,

Five or ten years have gone by without my thinking of Cletus at all, and then something reminds me of him. . . . And suddenly there he is, coming toward me in the corridor of that enormous high school, and I wince at the memory of how I didn't speak to him. . . . But it isn't only my failure that I think about. I also wonder about him, about what happened to him.

Memories can both console us and move us to sorrow for our sins.

Feelings are also important. Besides recognizable emotions—like joy and sorrow—more indistinct feelings, like a sense of peace or communion with God, can be signs of God's voice. You may feel strongly connected with God in a way that may be incommunicable to others but deeply meaningful to you. You experience a strange desire for, coupled with a strange fear of, "I know not what." Trust those moments, even though they are difficult to explain or, sometimes, understand.

Ignatius himself sometimes found what happened in prayer difficult to communicate. The fragments of his diary for 1544 include phrases like "with flashes of understanding too great to be written down," "an experiencing . . . that cannot be explained," and "a wonderful depth of reverence that I find impossible to explain." Just because you can't explain it or put it into words, doesn't mean it's not real.

Pay attention to *physical feelings* as well. Recently, I chatted with Matt, a young Jesuit in training, who had just directed a retreat for a group of young adults and spoke with them about how to listen to God. In addition to feelings of peace and comfort, and even inexplicable and incommunicable feelings, Matt added bodily feelings, another indication of God's presence.

Let's say you're reading Psalm 23, which talks about God's leading you through "green pastures" and "still waters," and you feel your body relaxing physically. Pay attention. Or you come upon a passage in Scripture that you feel is inviting you to do something that you would rather avoid (like forgive someone) and you start feeling fidgety. What's going on? Is God speaking to you through your physical reaction? Listen to your body, where God dwells.

Finally—as if we have to mention them again!—come *desires*. They arise in prayer frequently. There is the desire for God, which makes itself known in the ways we've discussed: the desire for holiness, the desire for change and growth in life, and all the desires we described in the past few chapters. Prayer is a key time for holy desires to arise.

In each of these cases it's helpful to remember the story of Elijah, in the First Book of Kings, who patiently waits in a cave for the manifestation of God. First he hears a great wind, but God is not there. Then an earthquake, but God is not there. Then he sees a fire. But God is not there. Finally there is, as one translator has it, a "still small voice," and Elijah covers his face, because he understands this as one way God communicates (1 Kings 19:12).

In such "still small" ways as emotions, insights, memories, feelings, and desires, God speaks to us in prayer.

But don't forget to pay attention to what is going on in your *daily life*. That's why the examen is so critical: it helps you listen to your day. Everyday events are perhaps the easiest part of your life to overlook; especially if you've been praying for some time you may inadvertently start privileging the contemplative over the active.

Reflecting on our daily lives is also an important way to discover how prayers are answered. Frequently we pray for something that we need and don't receive what we had asked for. (That should be clear from anyone's life.) But often we have to listen carefully for God's response, to that "still small" voice.

We may also ask for something and fail to recognize that God is answering our prayer in a hidden or unexpected way. On that retreat, for example, I asked for an end to loneliness. In God's response, I received the gift of memories, which helped me see that while there will always be some loneliness in my life, there is also an abundance of love.

It was a different answer to my prayers, but an answer nonetheless. Had I not been listening, I would not have heard the answer.

As in any good friendship, you not only have to listen, you have to listen carefully.

CHANGING

Another aspect of healthy relationships is *change*. Friendships that began in childhood and adolescence can be among the richest of all. Yet if we don't allow the other person to change, the friendship will not deepen and mature. Still, as with a friendship, change can be threatening in a person's relationship with God.

Many believers assume that their relationship to God will remain the same—or should remain the same—as it was when they were children. Some adults feel, for instance, that they cannot be angry or disappointed with God, since they did not harbor those sentiments when they were young. Or, more likely, they were told that those feelings were wrong.

Recently an elderly Catholic woman sent me a copy of some questions from the *Baltimore Catechism*, the religious-instruction book used by many Catholic children from the end of the nineteenth century to the late 1960s. At the end of the chapter on sin, there were questions to help children better understand their faith. But some of them sound more like questions from a law-school exam. She marked the following with the ironic notation "a personal favorite."

> Giles is murdered by a Communist just as he leaves the church after his confession. Giles had been away from the church for 28 years. He just about satisfied the requirements for a good confession, having only imperfect contrition, aroused during this week's mission. The Communist de-

manded to know if Giles was a Catholic, threatening to kill him if he was. Fearlessly, Giles said: "Yes, thank God!" Did Giles go immediately to heaven, or did he go to purgatory for a while? Give a reason for your answer.

Pity poor Giles! And pity the poor third grader who had to puzzle out the answers. Of course religious rules and regulations have been around since (at least) the Ten Commandments. Jesus of Nazareth, during his short ministry, offered his own set of rules to his disciples. And nearly every organized religion has its own share of rules. (Check out the Catholic Church's *Code of Canon Law* if you want a good example.) So do religious orders: my version of the Jesuit *Constitutions* runs to 502 pages.

Rules are an essential part of any community, since they enable us to live healthy lives in relationship with others. Rules bring order to the group. They also help order our personal lives. Ironically, some critics of religious rules designed to lead to spiritual health follow an even stricter set of rules designed to lead to physical health. Diet plans and exercise programs are often as draconian as any canon law.

But an overreliance on a rules-based religion can lead to an image of God as a stern traffic cop concerned only with enforcing the law or, as one friend said, a parole officer. How many children who memorized the *Baltimore Catechism* concluded that spiritual life was not an invitation to a relationship from a loving God but a series of complicated rules from a tyrant God?

This style of instruction may be necessary to educate young children, but if that teaching is never deepened it can hinder their ability to relate, as adults, to God. It would be as if in your twenties you related to your parents the same way you did in elementary school. The most obvious example of being stuck in a childhood idea of God, which I've heard from almost every person I've directed, is the tendency to see God not only as a judge but, worse—to use the image of the French philosopher René Descartes—as an "evil genius."

When a person starts to be intentional about the spiritual life, prayer is usually delightful. Like any relationship, the initial period is one of infatuation. Reading Scripture and spiritual books is fun, talking with fellow believers about your spirituality is enjoyable, church services are rich. Everything is natural, easy, and joyful, just as in the start of a love affair. *Hooray,* you think, *I love being spiritual!*

But soon you are invited—through prayer, conversation, or the voice of conscience—to amend your ways, to turn away from sinful behaviors, to surrender to a new way of life. In a word, to change. You may see that selfishness is inconsistent with your newfound beliefs. You may feel called to forgive someone against whom you've held a bitter grudge. You might feel drawn to living a simple life based on the Scriptures.

That's when the fear comes.

It's natural. Change is frightening. But this fear is different: it's a fear of where God is leading you. It's the fear that God is inviting you to something bad or dangerous. You think, *Even though I feel called to forgive this person, I'm sure it will be a disaster for me. God is going to trick me!* One young man, thinking about joining the Jesuits, feared that by following God's invitation, he would end up miserable.

That's when people may need to revisit their image of God. In these situations it's helpful to dig deeper and ask, *Who is God for me?* Often one's image is stuck in the third grade. Or the image is not life-giving: the stern judge, the distant father, or the unforgiving parent. "The particular image we have of God will depend very much on the nature of our upbringing and how we have reacted to it," writes Gerard W. Hughes, S.J., in *God of Surprises,* "because our ideas and our felt knowledge derive from our experience."

> On the day you cease to change you cease to live.
> —Anthony de Mello, S.J. (1931–1987)

Religion itself may be a hindrance to developing a healthy image of God. In his book *God's Mechanics,* the Jesuit scientist Guy Consolmagno, who works at the Vatican Observatory and has an advanced degree from MIT, speaks of a scientist's faith in God. He notes, "One obvious way we can let a religion limit our view of the universe is by insisting that its doctrines are a complete and final description of nature and God." God is bigger than religion.

Your childhood image of God may need to grow. When you're a child, you may see God as I did: the Great Problem Solver. Later on, you might relate to God as parent. As you mature, you might relate to God in still different ways: Creator, Spirit, Love. Christians might find themselves looking at Jesus in a different way, too: not only as Savior and Messiah, but perhaps as brother and friend.

The way you relate to God often mirrors relationships in other parts of your life, particularly with parents or authority figures. But remember that while the image of parent is helpful (for some people), God is not your mother or father. This is especially important for anyone who has suffered physical, emotional, or mental abuse from a parent. Richard Leonard, a Jesuit priest, once said we're relating to the best possible father or mother when we relate to God as parent.

Even if you feel drawn to the image of God as parent, remember that adult children relate to their parents in ways that differ from those of a child. In *A Friendship Like No Other,* Father Barry points out that when preachers speak of God as parent, they often use the image of the parent with a child. Barry believes that the "relationship between an *adult child* and his or her parent is a better image of the relationship God wants with us as adults."

You also may be surprised to discover fresh images of God buried within ancient traditions. In her book *She Who Is,* Elizabeth Johnson, C.S.J., a Catholic sister and theologian, writes about feminine imagery of God from the Jewish and Christian Scriptures. To offer just two examples from her groundbreaking work, the Hebrew word for "spirit," *ruah,* is feminine. Likewise, the Greek word *Sophia,* or Wisdom, is a traditionally female image of God. The Wisdom of Solomon says, "She reaches mightily from one end of the earth to the other, and she orders all things well." In Islam, the Prophet Muhammad speaks of the ninety-nine names of God, each highlighting an attribute of the divine, including the Gentle One, the Restorer to Life, and the Guide. Each is an invitation to imagine God in new ways.

One of my favorite images can be found in the Book of Jeremiah, which is especially useful for those who fear God may be the evil trickster inviting them to change, only to trap them into a miserable life. Jeremiah's God says otherwise: "'Surely I know the plans I have for you,' says the LORD, 'plans for your welfare and not for harm, to give you a future with hope'" (Jer. 29:11). God wants only the best for you, says Jeremiah.

You may also find some newer, more modern, images like the God of Surprises, who astonishes you with new and unexpected invitations to grow. Or perhaps you'll come up with images of your own. One Jesuit friend was once on a long cross-country trip and ended up stranded in an unfamiliar airport, with all his flights canceled. A cheery travel agent patiently helped him sort everything out so he could book a new flight. It was a striking image of God, he said: someone who helps you find your way home.

Change may also be part of your growing relationship with organized religion. Some of us were born into strongly religious families. Some remain rooted in their original religious traditions and develop a mature faith that nourishes them. (You'll remember those as traveling on the "path of belief," which we discussed in the first chapter.) Others discard old religious beliefs, since they no longer work for them as adults, and begin the search for new religious traditions (the "path of exploration"). Also common are those who separate themselves from religion for a time and then find their way back to the same tradition, on their own terms, reappropriating a more adult faith that works for them (the "path of return").

In each case the relationship with God will change as well. As the Spanish Jesuit Carlos Vallés wrote in his book *Sketches of God,* "If you always imagine God in the same way, no matter how true and how beautiful it may be, you will not be able to receive the gift of the new ways he has ready for you."

BEING SILENT

Are you open to *silence* in your spiritual life? Sometimes God seems distant, and sometimes nothing at all seems to be happening in your daily life or in your prayer.

The revelations in Mother Teresa's letters and journals, collected by Brian Kolodiejchuk, M.C., in *Mother Teresa: Come Be My Light,* talked about her painful "dark night"—a long period of prayer when it felt as if God were absent—and reminded people that silence is common, even in the lives of the saints. Many believers were astonished, even scandalized, that she spoke frequently of not feeling God's presence in her prayer. Some secular critics even pointed to her descriptions of silence as proof that her faith was weak. Or that God does not exist.

But silence is part of any relationship. Think about times when spouses or lovers are separated from each other by physical distance. Or, more positively, think about taking a long car trip with a friend. Does your friend have to talk every minute? Think about two lovers walking side by side down the beach, without saying a word. Sometimes silence can be painful and confusing between friends, but sometimes a companionable silence is consoling.

Sister Maddy, my friend at the retreat house in Gloucester, noted another similarity between silence in prayer and silence in friendship. "Sometimes I don't hear from friends for a time," she said. "But whether I hear from them or not, I know they're still my friends. It's the same in prayer. Whether or not I feel God's presence, I know God's there."

When I was a novice, silence in my prayer drove me crazy. One day I told David Donovan, "This is ridiculous! Nothing's happening in my prayer. It's a waste of time."

David said, "What do you mean?"

"Well," I said. "I sit down to pray, and not a thing happens. I just sit with God for an hour. It's a waste of time."

David laughed. "Being with God is a waste of time?"

Despite myself, I had to laugh. It's never a waste of time to be in the presence of God—even if it doesn't feel like much is happening.

You can delight in someone's company wordlessly. As Margaret Silf recently wrote in a letter to me, you can be silent together, trusting that silence does not mean that God has left you. Or you may simply enjoy being in God's presence.

Another way of looking at this comes from Aristotle, who believed that we become like the object of our contemplation. Have you ever met an elderly couple who seem to have taken on each other's attributes? They share the same interests, they finish each other's sentences, they sometimes even look alike. Likewise with God: the more time you spend with God, even in complete silence, when it feels that nothing is happening, the more you will grow, because being in the divine presence is always transformative. Think of Moses coming off Mount Sinai with his face shining. "Wasting time with God," one of David's favorite descriptions of prayer, even during silent moments, turns out not to be a waste of time at all.

But there is another reason we may have trouble with silence in prayer: we no longer value silence *at all*.

Electronic gadgets—iPods, BlackBerrys, cell phones, laptops—have created a world of constant stimulation. Most of this is good, efficient, and even fun. Why not have all your favorite tunes ready for when you're stuck in a traffic jam? Why not have the television, radio, and Internet to keep up to date on the world around us? Those are the fruits of the digital age.

Yet are we growing addicted to these gadgets? The amount of media we consume each day continues to grow, and our ability to be detached from digital devices diminishes.

Just the other day, a film executive called me from her cell phone in the car to ask about a particular music selection she was hoping to use in a new movie about the Catholic Church. What would be the most appropriate Catholic hymn to use? she asked. When I started making a few suggestions, she said, "Wait, I have to text this to someone as we're talking." Amazed, I said, "You're driving the car, talking to me on the phone, and texting someone all at once?"

We are gradually losing the art of silence. Of walking down the street lost in our own thoughts. Of closing the door to our rooms and being quiet. Of sitting on a park bench and just thinking. We may fear silence because we fear what we might hear from the deepest parts of ourselves. We may be afraid to hear that "still small" voice. What might it say?

Might it ask us to change?

You may have to disconnect in order to connect—disconnect with the world of noise to connect with silence, where God speaks to you in a different way. You cannot change our noisy world, but you can disconnect from time to time, to give yourself the gift of silence.

Being silent is one of the best ways to listen to God, not because God is not speaking to you during your noisy day, but because silence makes it easier to listen to your heart. To use the friendship analogy, sometimes you need to be silent and listen very carefully when your friend is trying to make a point. As my sister sometimes tells her children, "You have two ears and one mouth for a reason: listening is more important than talking."

If your environment (inside and outside) is too noisy, it might be hard to hear what God, your friend, is trying to say.

THE NEW WAYS GOD HAS READY

While friendship is a terrific analogy for a relationship with God, it is not perfect. As I mentioned, none of our friends created the universe. And God, unlike any other friend, always remains constant. As Richard Leonard writes in his book *Preaching to the Converted,* "If you feel distant from God, guess who's moved away from whom!"

Nonetheless, using Father Barry's rich insight—thinking about prayer in terms of a personal relationship—can help to clarify your relationship with God. If you're dissatisfied with your relationship with God, think about it in terms of a friendship, and consider ways that you might be neglecting that friendship and how you can nourish it.

That model can also make the spiritual life less daunting. It helps to make a relationship with God more understandable, something that you can incorporate into your life, rather than something designed only for saints and mystics.

Even the *progress* of the spiritual life mirrors that of a relationship. At the beginning of many relationships, as I mentioned, there's often a period of infatuation. All you want is to spend time with the other. But the relationship has to move beyond that superficial level and into something deeper and more complex. It will also move into places that you couldn't have imagined when you first fell in love. It will have its ups and downs, its times of silence, its times of frustration. Just like any friendship will.

Your relationship with God will change over your lifetime: sometimes it will happen naturally, almost easily, and feel rich and consoling; at other times it will seem difficult, almost a chore, yielding little in the way of "results." But the important thing—as in any friendship—is to keep at it and, ultimately, come to know and love the Other more deeply. And to let the Other come to know and love you more deeply.

CHAPTER SEVEN

God Meets You Where You Are

Ignatian Traditions of Prayer

IN THE LAST THREE chapters we looked at how a prayer like the examen can help us find God in our lives, and how we can "listen" to God in prayer and in daily life. But there are many other traditions of prayer besides the examen. So among those, what's the best way to pray?

GOD LOOKS AT ME,
AND I LOOK AT GOD

The answer is: whatever you are comfortable with. "God meets you where you are," as David said. No form of prayer is any better than another, any more than one way of being with a friend is better than another. What's better is what's best for you.

Here's a story David liked to tell on himself, about labeling different forms of prayer as "better" or "worse."

One weekend after he had returned from a post as a spiritual director at the prestigious Josephinum seminary in Ohio, David visited his mother, an elderly Irish-Catholic woman, at her home outside of Boston. He noticed that she was praying her Rosary, one of the oldest Catholic spiritual traditions. The Rosary is a set of beads of varying sizes, arranged in five groups of ten. The small beads remind you to pray a Hail Mary. ("Hail Mary, full of grace. The Lord is with thee. Blessed art thou amongst women. And blessed is the fruit of thy womb, Jesus. Holy Mary, Mother of God, pray for us sinners, now and at the hour of our death.") The large ones, the Our Father. There are also different events from the lives of Jesus and Mary to think about while you are praying each "decade," or set of ten.

The origins of the Rosary lie deep in the Middle Ages: lay men and women used the Rosary as a way of praying along with the nearby monastic communities, who themselves would move through the 150 psalms during the year. (Three times around the Rosary would mean 150 Hail Marys.) As Sally Cunneen writes in a book of essays called *Awake My Soul,* "When most Christians were illiterate and when books, including Bibles, were unavailable except in monasteries, a string of beads or seeds provided a simple means for the faithful to re-create their attachment to the events of the Gospel as they prayed the prayer that Jesus taught and, also, repeated the words of Gabriel and Elizabeth to Mary," that is, the Hail Mary.

After his experience as a spiritual director, David felt that this "simple means" of prayer that his mother enjoyed was, well, too simple. So he decided to teach his mother something about "real prayer," as he said.

"Why do you pray the Rosary?" he asked her.

"David, I've always prayed the Rosary," she said.

"But why?"

"Well, I enjoy it," she said.

Sensing that he was making little progress, David decided he would probe his mother's limited experience in prayer and teach her a "better" way to pray.

So he asked, "What happens when you pray the Rosary?"

"Well, I quiet myself down," she said. "And then I look at God, and God looks at me."

"That stopped me in my tracks!" David said with a laugh when he recounted that story. He saw that he had been wrong to prejudge his mother's spiritual experiences. Who knows what is going on inside of another person? He recognized the danger of privileging one way of relating to God over another. As St. Ignatius wrote, "It is dangerous to make everyone go forward by the same road."

David realized something else too. "For all of my training, she probably had a deeper relationship with God than I had!"

David used to tell that story to remind me that there is no right way to pray. But there may be a particular method of prayer that fits you more comfortably.

So let's talk about some ways of prayer that are most often considered part of the Ignatian tradition. At the end of the chapter I'll speak more broadly about other ways, but the following methods are those most closely associated with Ignatian spirituality.

As you read along, notice which ones you feel most drawn to. Perhaps God is calling you, through this attraction, to try one out. Perhaps in one of these practices, as David's mother would say, God could look at you, and you could look at God.

IGNATIAN CONTEMPLATION

Remember those five hypothetical Jesuits I mentioned in the first chapter? The ones who gave us four definitions of Ignatian spirituality? Well, if you asked those same five to describe the Ignatian tradition of prayer, chances are that they would first mention "Ignatian contemplation."

All prayer is contemplative. But here I'm using the term to describe a certain type of prayer, which also goes by the names "contemplation," "contemplative prayer," and "imaginative prayer." Though Ignatius didn't invent this kind of prayer, he popularized it by giving it center stage in his Spiritual Exercises, where he called it "composition of place."

In Ignatian contemplation you "compose the place" by imagining yourself in a scene from the Bible, or in God's presence, and then taking part in it. It's a way of allowing God to speak to you through your imagination.

This was one of Ignatius's favorite ways to help people enter into a relationship with God. And it flowed from his own experience in prayer. As David Fleming writes, while Ignatius was an excellent analytical thinker (even if he probably would not have thought of himself as an intellectual), the "mental quality of thought that drove his spiritual life was his remarkable imagination."

When I first heard about this method in the novitiate, I thought it sounded ridiculous. *Using your imagination? Making things up in your head? Was everything you imagined supposed to be God speaking to you? Isn't that what crazy people think?*

In one of my first conversations with David, I confessed my doubts, even disappointment, about "Ignatian contemplation." As he listened, he began to smile. I can still see him sitting in his easy chair with his cup of coffee at the ready. "Let me ask you a question," he said. "Do you think that God can speak to you through your relationships with other people?"

"Of course," I said.

"Through reading Scripture and through the sacraments?" Yes and yes.

"Through your daily experiences, and through your desires and emotions?" Yes, yes, and yes.

"Do you think God can communicate through what you see every day and hear and feel and even smell?" Of course.

"Then why couldn't God speak to you through your imagination?"

That made sense. Think seriously about your imagination, David said. Wasn't it a gift from God, like your intellect or your memory? And if it was a gift, why couldn't it be used to experience God?

This made sense, too. Using my imagination wasn't so much making things up, as it was trusting that my imagination could help to lead me to the one who created it: God. That didn't mean that everything I imagined during prayer was coming from God. But it did mean that from time to time God could use my imagination as one way of communicating with me.

So, how do you "do" Ignatian contemplation? Well, here's where we turn directly to the Spiritual Exercises for some help.

The Composition, by Imagining the Place

First, take a passage from Scripture that you enjoy. For those making their way through the Spiritual Exercises, it's the passage that is assigned for the day. For example, in the Second Week of the Exercises, you follow Jesus through his ministry: preaching, traveling, healing the sick, forgiving sinners, welcoming the outcasts, and so on.

One of my favorite stories from the Second Week is the storm at sea, which is contained in several Gospels. It's often helpful for people who are struggling with big problems in their lives—i.e., everyone.

In the version of the story in Luke's Gospel (8:22–25), the disciples are in a boat with Jesus, when a sudden squall comes up. (On the Sea of Galilee, this happens even today.) "The boat was filling with water, and they were in danger," writes Luke. Terror stricken, they ask Jesus, who is asleep, why he doesn't help them. "Master, Master, we are perishing!" they shout. Jesus awakes and "rebukes" the wind and the rain, stilling the storm with his word. Then he turns to them and asks, "Where is your faith?"

The disciples are stunned. "Who then is this," they say, "that he commands even the winds and the water, and they obey him?"

Ignatius invites you to enter into the scene by "composing the place" by imagining yourself in the story with as much detail as you can muster.

Your starting points are the five senses.

The first step, after asking for God's help in the prayer, is to ask yourself: *What do you see?* Assuming that you're imagining yourself on the boat (instead of imagining the scene from a distance, which is another option), you might picture yourself with some of the disciples around you, all of you huddled together on the little wooden boat.

There's plenty to imagine when it comes to your "imaginative sight." What might the boat look like? You might have seen photos of the "Jesus Boat," a fishing vessel from the time of Jesus that was recovered from the Sea of Galilee in 1986. It is a long wooden boat with slats set up for uncomfortable-looking seats. As you picture this, you might realize that it's crowded for the disciples on board, something you have never thought about before. By the way, you don't have to be an expert in ancient cultures, or an archaeologist, to do this kind of prayer. It doesn't matter if you don't know exactly what Palestinian boats looked like in the first century. "Your" boat could be a modern version.

What does the scene *outside* the boat look like? Part of the fear of sailing in the dark is not knowing what will happen next, whether a lightning strike will hit the mast, a wave will crash over the side, or an unexpected swell will capsize the craft. And at night it's hard to see the waves except when they are lit up by flashes of lightning. With only one of your imaginative senses—sight—you can begin to experience some of the fear that the disciples must have felt.

Then imagine seeing Jesus asleep in the boat. Even something as simple as noticing him sleeping might make you ask new questions about Jesus. For instance, you might realize that his being asleep shows not so much lack of care for his friends, or even ignorance of the possible danger, but simple fatigue after a long day. Jesus led an active life, you may realize, with people always clamoring for his attention and care. How could he not have been tired?

Your understanding of the fear of the disciples is now coupled with compassion for the humanity of Jesus, who, after all, had a physical body that tired.

It's one thing to read a Gospel story and simply hear the words "Jesus was asleep." It's quite another to imagine it, to see it in your mind's eye. You may gain new insight into the humanity of Jesus in a way not possible from reading it in a book, or hearing it in a homily, because it's *your* insight.

Next ask yourself: *What do you hear?* You might imagine not only the howling wind and the booming thunder, but also the sound of huge waves crashing over the side of the boat. Maybe you imagine the sloshing of water over the floorboards, and the fishing gear and nets clattering noisily on the deck as the boat lurches from side to side. Perhaps you hear the disciples' protests. Are they growing resentful of Jesus' indifference? Over the sound of the wind and the waves you hear some grumbling. Do their complaints grow louder as the storm intensifies? Do they shout over the thunder? Our own protests to God do the same in the face of violent storms in our lives.

From the Spiritual Exercises

Here is St. Ignatius using "composition of place," by imagining the Nativity scene. Notice the questions that he asks, and notice that he doesn't tell you exactly what to imagine but leaves it up to your imagination, where Ignatius trusted that God would be at work on a very personal level.

The composition, by imagining the place. Here it will be to see in imagination the road from Nazareth to Bethlehem. Consider its length and breadth, whether it is level or winds through valleys and hills. Similarly, look at the place or cave of the Nativity: How big is it, or small? How low or high? And how is it furnished?

With your imaginative sight and hearing, you have now begun to enter more fully into this scene. But you're not finished yet: you have a few more senses at your disposal.

What do you smell? Along with seawater washing into the fishing boat, you would smell . . . fish! (Or at least the residual smell from the day's catch.) Finally, in such close quarters with the disciples you would smell rancid body odor and perhaps even some bad breath.

None of these imaginative exercises asks you to picture anything weird or bizarre. All Ignatius suggests is trying to imagine—as best you can—what things *might have* been like. You also trust that, since you're trying to enter into this scene to meet God, God will help you with this prayer.

You still have two more senses left. Touch is one. *What do you feel?* Are you wearing homespun clothes? Maybe the material feels scratchy against your skin. If you're sitting in a boat during a storm, you're probably soaked, feeling cold, wet, and miserable, on top of being tired from traipsing around Galilee with Jesus all day.

Finally, *what do you taste?* For this particular meditation, this sense is slightly less important. But for others, like stories where Jesus and his disciples are eating and drinking—as during the wedding feast at Cana and the Last Supper—this is a key sense. But even here in the boat, you might imagine tasting the saltwater spray.

Now that you have used your senses and "composed the place," you have the scene set. At this point you can just let the scene play out in your mind, with you in the picture.

But it's not just something to "watch." "You do not merely imagine the event as though you were watching it on film," Joseph A. Tetlow, S.J., writes in *Making Choices in Christ*. "You enter into the scene, letting it unfold as though you were part of it, standing warm in the temple or ankle-deep in the water of the Jordan."

Let the story play out in your imagination with as little judging on your part as possible. Let yourself be drawn to whatever seems most attractive or interesting. For example, if you notice the disciples more than Jesus, try not to judge that as inappropriate or wrong. While you're in the meditation, allow God to lead you through your imagination.

Pay Attention!

Afterward take note of what happened within yourself while you were involved in the story. As with any kind of prayer, there are many things that could be revealed: insights, emotions, desires, memories, feelings, as we discussed in the last chapter.

God desires to communicate with you all the time, but when you *intentionally* open yourself up to God's voice, you can often hear it more clearly. To use the metaphor of friendship, it is similar to saying to a friend, "You have my undivided attention." Ignatian contemplation enables us to hear more easily, or differently, and to recognize something that might otherwise be overlooked.

Opening Ourselves

Though intended by Ignatius to help one enter into events from the life of Christ, Ignatian contemplation can be used by all religious traditions to help you appreciate what John J. English, S.J., describes in his book *Spiritual Freedom* as "sacred events."

In Ignatian contemplation we form the habit of losing ourselves . . . in sacred events of great significance. After some initial practice, we learn how to stay with the scene and its actions, to relax in the presence of those who speak and move, and to open ourselves without reserve to what occurs, so that we may receive a deep impression of the event's mysterious meaning.

Insights, for example, are common in Ignatian contemplation. Whenever an insight would come up in my prayer, something that was clearly new, something that was clearly a fruit of the prayer, David would say, "Pay attention!"

For instance, let's say you notice how terrified the disciples are—not only by the storm, but by something more surprising: Jesus' display of power. His miracles could have been frightening to this band of Galileans. Though you may have heard this story dozens of times, perhaps you realize in a new way that watching the sea stilled by your friend would have been astonishing, amazing, exciting—and frightening.

You've just received an insight into the life of the disciples: it may have been frightening being around Jesus. Maybe you've heard about "fear of God." It is a natural enough reaction. "Who then is this, that he commands even the wind and the water, and they obey him?" they say afterward. For the first time, you feel not only the excitement behind that statement but also the fear. Then you wonder if they ever talked about their reaction with Jesus. What would Jesus have said in reply?

That might be as far as that insight goes—which is terrific. If you get a deeper insight into Scripture, it will help deepen your faith. But often the insight might lead to an insight about *your own life*. It might prompt you to ask yourself, *Where am I afraid of God?* Are there places where you've seen signs of God's presence but have been afraid to admit this—because you're afraid of God's power? Sometimes it's frightening thinking about God's taking an interest in your life. Is fear preventing you from a deeper relationship with God?

Just as common in contemplative prayer is a more emotional reaction, which can be surprising, revealing, and clarifying. The easiest way to explain this is to take something that happened to me when praying about this passage just a few months ago.

Swamped!

Recently I traveled to California to make the Spiritual Exercises, the first time since the novitiate over twenty years ago. It was part of the very last stage of my formal training as a Jesuit. (Yes, you read that correctly: the complete training of a Jesuit priest, which continues after ordination, may sometimes take over twenty years.)

In any event, during the Second Week that precise passage came up. To be honest, I thought, *The storm at sea? Been there, prayed that.* I couldn't imagine any surprises in store. But the God of Surprises had other ideas.

As I prayed about the storm at sea, there were no insights, few desires, little emotion, scant memories, and hardly any feelings. But I knew not to be frustrated. Prayer is often dry, and, at least on the surface, little seems to be going on.

The next day, I returned to the scene in my imagination. As soon as I climbed into the boat, a word popped into my head: *swamped.* The boat was taking on water during the violent storm, being swamped, and the disciples were terrified.

Swamped was the word I used frequently with friends to describe my daily life. I was forever racing among a variety of projects and often felt overwhelmed. Consequently, I had started to wonder if it was time for a change—time to either ask for a new job or change the way I was working.

You've probably felt this way at some point in your life. Many of us—parents of small children, overworked business executives, harried teachers, busy students, stressed-out priests—feel swamped by life, pulled in a million different directions. You think: *I have to change the way I work or change how I am living.*

The next day my spiritual director encouraged me to return to the scene. Repetition is an important part of the Ignatian tradition of prayer. Ignatius thought it important to gain all the fruit you could from a particular prayer. "I should notice and dwell on those points where I felt greater consolation or desolation," he wrote in the Exercises.

When I returned, I imagined myself standing on the sunny shore of the Sea of Galilee, after the storm passed. Then I imagined telling Jesus how swamped I felt. Sitting on the beach and airing out my feelings felt freeing. What a relief to share this with Jesus.

Then, in my imagination, the boat that Jesus had saved slowly started to sink into the Sea of Galilee. I was relieved to watch it slip away—as if all of my worries were sinking with it. Maybe I was being invited to let that old life slip away.

Sometimes, as you might realize already, these contemplative prayers move beyond the outlines of the Gospel stories and bring you to unexpected places. Obviously there's nothing in the Gospels about the boat sinking! But that's not to say God can't work through this kind of imaginative prayer as well.

Then I imagined the two of us building a new boat, with brand-new, fresh-smelling wood. At the same time, I thought, I could also hoist the old boat out of the water and fix it. Maybe the old boat just needed a little mending: a little tar, a few new boards. Maybe my old life just needed a little mending, too.

In prayer, I asked Jesus how he was able to juggle everything, how he was able to handle all the demands on his time. An answer suggested itself: Jesus took things as they came and trusted that God was bringing things before him, rather than trying to plan everything. He also accepted the need to withdraw from the crowds sometimes.

By the close of the prayer, I realized that whatever boat I chose—the new one (asking for a new job) or the restored old one (changing the way I worked)—Jesus would be in the boat with me. I had nothing to fear. That insight gave me enormous peace. No longer did I feel swamped, because I realized that I had a choice in life. (In the end I chose to fix up the old boat.)

Not every contemplative prayer is so rich. Not every one brings insights or emotions. You might try several times before it feels like you're even *in* the scene. Over the past twenty years, I've logged many hours, struggling in vain to "compose the scene" to little apparent effect. That's not to say that nothing was happening, because spending time with God is always transformative. But not every prayer leads to noticeable fruit.

But sometimes it is rich. And I offer that personal experience not because it's important that I felt swamped, but to illustrate that from even the most familiar of Scripture passages, God can reveal unfamiliar things, if you are open to hearing them.

LECTIO DIVINA AND
THE SECOND METHOD

The second form of Ignatian prayer is similar to Ignatian contemplation. It goes by the name *lectio divina* or meditation. (As with "Ignatian contemplation," the same prayer often goes by many names, which causes no end of confusion.)

Lectio divina means "sacred reading." Like contemplation, it uses Scripture to draw you into a deeper relationship with God. Lectio relies on both the imagination and the intellect. It also differs slightly from Ignatian contemplation. But most types of prayer overlap, so there's no problem if you combine aspects of one with another.

When I first stumbled across the term *lectio divina,* I imagined elderly monks sequestered in noiseless rooms, silently turning the parchment pages of medieval manuscripts, as sunlight streamed through a stained-glass window, illuminating the words they were reading. While appealingly romantic, it seemed something that would remain far from my experience.

But after I entered the novitiate, David introduced me to this ancient practice in an accessible way. Monks and cloistered nuns still do *lectio divina,* but it is a practice available to even the busiest and most nonmonastic among us. Essentially *lectio divina* is the practice of encountering God through Scripture.

Like Ignatian contemplation, while this form of prayer was not invented by Ignatius, it is very popular among Jesuits. Ignatius calls it the "Second Method" of prayer in the Exercises. (In case you think we've overlooked the "First Method" in the Exercises, we haven't. The First Method is less a method of prayer than a preparation: you review the Ten Commandments, and so on, to see where you have sinned, and you then make amends to your life.)

Rather than telling you how *lectio divina* differs from contemplation, let me introduce the technique, and you'll be able to see some of the differences yourself.

The easiest way I've found to approach *lectio* was suggested by my New Testament professor, Daniel Harrington. He suggested breaking the process down into four steps.

Before you begin, of course, you select a specific passage from the Bible as the basis for your prayer. Let's use the story of Jesus preaching in the synagogue in Nazareth, as told in the Gospel of Luke (4:16–30).

At the beginning of his ministry, Jesus comes to his hometown and enters the Jewish synagogue to preach. He unrolls the Torah scroll and begins reading a passage from the Book of Isaiah. "The Spirit of the Lord is upon me," he says, quoting Isaiah. "He has sent me to proclaim release to the captives and recovery of sight to the blind." Then he boldly says to the assembly, "Today this scripture has been fulfilled in your hearing." Initially the crowd praises Jesus, astonished that the hometown boy is so learned.

But then he begins to criticize the group for its lack of faith, and says, "No prophet is accepted in the prophet's hometown." The crowd then turns on him. "They got up, drove him out of the town, and led him to the brow of the hill," where they intended to throw him off the cliff. Unperturbed, Jesus "passed through the midst of them and went on his way."

As with any prayer, you first ask for God's help. Now let's consider the passage using *lectio divina*.

1. Reading:
What Does the Text Say?

First, read the passage. What is going on? With most stories from the Old and New Testaments, this is clear. But not always. Here you might glance at the bottom of the page of your Bible, where the editors might have included explanatory notes. Bible commentaries, which offer explanations of unfamiliar words, practices, and traditions, will help you appreciate the context of the reading before you go on.

For example, here's what the *HarperCollins Bible Commentary* says about what Jesus is doing in the synagogue that day. "[Jesus] lives and works within his tradition. He regularly attends the synagogue and participates as all male members were permitted to do, by reading scripture and commenting. He follows the regular practice: stand to read, sit to comment." Now you know that Jesus was following the standard practice, which might inform your prayer.

When Jesus reads from the scroll, he reveals his identity and mission to his friends and neighbors. It must have been shocking for the people of the little town of Nazareth to hear one of their own say, "Today this scripture has been fulfilled in your hearing." In other words, I am the fulfillment of this scripture.

After initially finding his discourse pleasant, the crowd turns on Jesus, attempting to kill him. No wonder this passage is sometimes called "The Rejection at Nazareth."

2. Meditation:
What Is God Saying to Me Through the Text?

Now ask if there is something that God wants to reveal to you through this text. This is where your imagination may come to the fore, as you begin to meditate more deeply on the text.

Sometimes the passage might immediately connect with something in your life. For example, where do you feel called to be prophetic, even in the face of rejection? In the Gospel story, Jesus wanted to proclaim his message even though he probably suspected it would be controversial. Is there something in your life that calls for a similarly courageous stance?

This is where linkages with your life are important. Let's say you're praying about this story and recall a troubling situation at work: someone in your office is consistently being mistreated. You've long thought about defending her, though you worry about what it might mean for your career.

Why did you remember your friend during this particular prayer? As David would say, "Pay attention!" Recalling your friend while praying about Jesus' saying something controversial may not be a coincidence.

Here's a concrete example: A few years ago I came to my annual retreat perplexed. For the previous few weeks I had been thinking about a controversial issue in the church that I wanted to speak about but was worried about the reaction that it would engender. During the retreat my spiritual director recommended this story. As I prayed with this passage, I noticed Jesus' ability to speak the truth, and I felt an impassioned desire to be like Jesus, to speak the truth. Afterward I wrote in my prayer journal: "People in the congregation felt different things and had various reactions to Jesus. Some were horrified, some cheered, and some were afraid. But he did it *anyway!*"

The text conveyed the confident freedom of Jesus. It seemed that, through my reaction to the story, God was offering me some of that same confidence and freedom.

3. Prayer:
What Do You Want to Say to God About the Text?

Now it's your turn to speak to God. How does the text make you feel? What questions arise in your mind? What is your reaction? Pour it all out to God.

After meditating on this particular passage, you might find yourself fearful. If it means standing up for your friend at work, or standing up for yourself, this could be dangerous. You might worry, rightly, about being rejected, as Jesus was in his hometown.

On the other hand, you might feel emboldened by his confidence, and you may come to see that all prophetic gestures probably made the prophets frightened. Yet, like Jesus, all the prophets acted in the face of this fear, trusting in God. Maybe you feel a mixture of fear *and* confidence. This is the time to be honest with God about your feelings.

During my own prayer I felt frightened about speaking out. Being prophetic sounds romantic until you face an angry mob. Or even a few angry people. What would happen if I spoke out? Would people reject me?

The more I prayed about it, the more I returned to the same question: How was Jesus able to make such bold statements, knowing that people would probably reject him? Gradually I realized that not only did everyone in the synagogue know Jesus, but Jesus probably knew *them*. Most likely he could have anticipated their response—the same way that you can guess how your friends will respond if you say something challenging. So Jesus most likely anticipated their rejection. One reason he was able to speak out was because he was free, unfettered by worries of acceptance or rejection, perfectly embodying what Ignatius called "detachment."

> We ought not to be content with being hearers, but doers.
> —St. Aloysius Gonzaga, S.J. (1568–1591)

4. Action:
What Do You Want to Do Based on Your Prayer?

Finally, you act. Prayer should move us to action, even if it simply makes us want to be more compassionate and faithful. Entering into a relationship with God will change us, will make us more loving, and will move us to *act*.

Now that you've read the story of Jesus in the synagogue, have asked yourself what God is saying, and have spoken to God about your reaction, it's time to *do* something. Perhaps you resolve to be more courageous in standing up for that person at work. Or you decide to forgive someone who has hurt you. Or you feel that you still want to pray more about what to do. But let your prayer move you to real action.

In my case, the attraction to Jesus' freedom encouraged me to speak out about that issue. It was a difficult thing to do, and it provoked the ire of a few individuals, but I felt that I was trying to follow Jesus' example. That helped me through the tough times and gave me confidence. And, in the end, there was little to fear: no one threw me off the brow of any hill, literal or figurative.

Those are the four steps of *lectio:* read, meditate, pray, act.

ANOTHER, SLIGHTLY DIFFERENT, WAY of praying *lectio divina* is to dwell on a single word or phrase, and, as Ignatius said, "relish" or "savor" the text. For people who feel uncomfortable with imagery in their prayers, this works very well. And it works especially well with the psalms.

In this method you read the Bible passage meditatively, pausing on any word or phrase that seems meaningful.

This was something that greatly appealed to Ignatius. In his Second Method of Praying, he says that one should pause on words and phrases, "as long as meanings, comparisons, relish, and consolations connected with it are found."

Let's take Psalm 23, which begins with the phrase "The LORD is my shepherd." The next line reads, "He makes me lie down in green pastures." Perhaps you might find yourself drawn to meditate on what it would feel like to rest in that "green pasture." If you're a busy person—or feeling swamped—you might simply rest with God. Maybe all God wants to do in that prayer is to give you rest.

Or perhaps you read "green pastures" and find yourself unexpectedly sad and wonder why. Maybe you can't see any green pastures in your life. You could share your sadness with God and may feel a new closeness with the God who wants to console you.

Or you may feel joy. This might be the time to share with God your gratitude for "green pastures" in your life. Or maybe God is simply asking you to pay attention to those "green pastures" you've been overlooking. Your prayer may be one of gratitude. All this from a simple phrase in the psalm.

Ignatius stresses the need to relax during *lectio*. There's no need to rush and no need to look for any earth-shaking "results." Prayer is not about producing. Take your time. As Ignatius writes in the Exercises, we need to slow down:

> If one finds . . . in one or two words matter which yields thought, relish, and consolation, one should not be anxious to move forward, even if the whole hour is consumed on what is being found.

Pay attention to any phrase that repels you too. You might read about the "darkest valley," and feel fear. You want to rush over those words or even feel physically uncomfortable. You might be tempted to move on, but places of resistance may be precisely where God wants to meet you. *Resistance* is another fruit of prayer, like emotions, insights, and memories.

Resistance is often an invitation to pray or think more deeply about those feelings. *Why do I feel resistance?* Are you being called to be free of whatever holds you back from a deeper love of God? *Why am I frightened of those dark valleys?* Is it because you don't trust God to care for you? Perhaps you can recall dark times in the past where you *were* cared for—by friends, family, coworkers—and see God's hand in this too. Your attention to resistance can lead you to a new level of trust or self-knowledge.

This resistance always reminds me of massage. Every few weeks, because of some chronic pain, I visit a massage therapist. Often she focuses on a sensitive spot on my back. That spot needs attention because that's where the most "energy" is, as she says. It's an important spot to pay attention to.

It's similar in prayer. When you feel reluctant to pray about a particular topic, it may mean you are resisting looking at something urgent, or a situation or memory that needs to be attended to. Maybe God wants to comfort you in that place or release you from some unfreedom or "disordered attachment." That's the reason there's so much "energy" around those passages. In these moments, God offers us the chance to stop resisting and let ourselves be healed. And freed.

CENTERING PRAYER AND THE THIRD METHOD

A little theology will help our discussion of "centering prayer," which has become popular in Christian circles.

Like two great rivers, two traditions of prayer flow through Christian spirituality. One is called "apophatic" and the other "kataphatic." *Apophatic,* from the Greek word *apophatikos,* which means negative, is an approach to God that moves away from images, words, concepts, and symbols. It is more "content free." The underlying theology is that God is beyond our comprehension, beyond any mental images we might have, unknowable; and so one seeks to find God by emptying oneself of preconceived notions of the divine.

Harvey Egan, S.J., a professor of theology at Boston College, noted in *The New Dictionary of Catholic Spirituality* (Michael Downey, ed.) that this tradition is rooted in both the Old and New Testaments. In the Book of Exodus, God dwells in "thick darkness" (20:21) and appears to Moses as a "cloud" (34:5). Moses cannot see God's face when God passes, which is another way of expressing the divine "otherness." St. Thomas Aquinas said that one can only know *that* God is, not what God is. The best known writer on this stance is the (still anonymous) author of the fourteenth-century work *The Cloud of Unknowing,* who speaks more of what God is *not,* rather than what God is.

The other stream is kataphatic prayer, which comes from the Greek word *kataphatikos,* meaning "positive." This tradition seeks to experience God in creation and makes overt use of images, concepts, words, and symbols in prayer. Kataphatic prayer is more "content rich." The theology here is that we can begin to know God through all of creation.

This method is also firmly rooted in Scripture. The Old Testament stresses that God can be understood through his visible works—that is, the natural world. In Christian theology this is made even more explicit: God is known as a person. As Jesus says in the Gospel of John (14:9), "Whoever has seen me has seen the Father." And Aquinas—now arguing for the opposing side—says that although God is ultimately unknowable, we can seek God through the things that are "known to us."

St. Thomas might be accused of a certain duplicity—arguing both sides of the argument. But he's right in both cases: God can be known through his works (kataphatic) but not known fully (apophatic). Both approaches are authentic. Both have been used by believers over the millennia. Moreover, many find themselves using these two different approaches at different times in their lives.

You've probably guessed where I'm going: Ignatian contemplation, with its emphasis on the imagination, fits squarely in the kataphatic tradition. So does *lectio divina.*

Centering prayer, a practice that seeks to find God at the center of one's being without the intentional use of images, is closer to the content-free way. In a recent conversation, Father Egan said plainly, "Centering prayer is apophatic."

As a result, centering prayer is not often associated with Ignatian spirituality. Instead most people align it with Zen Buddhism or yoga. But there are clear echoes of centering prayer in the Spiritual Exercises.

At one point in the Spiritual Exercises, Ignatius talks about the "Third Method of Praying," which he describes as done "according to rhythmic measures." You take a single word (he suggests words from the Our Father) and concentrate on the word while breathing in and out. "This is done in such a manner that one word of the prayer is said between one breath and another," he writes. This Ignatian practice is remarkably similar to Zen prayer as well as to the more contemporary centering prayer.

But before going any further with comparisons, let's talk about what centering prayer is (rather than, apophatically, what it is not) and how it fits in with the Ignatian way.

Bear Me Away

Jesuits pray in many ways. Sometimes they compose their own prayers. Here is one from Pierre Teilhard de Chardin (1881–1955), the French paleontologist and theologian, asking for the grace to age well.

When the signs of age begin to mark my body
(and still more when they touch my mind);
when the ill that is to diminish me or carry me off
strikes from without or is born within me;
when the painful moment comes
in which I suddenly awaken
to the fact that I am ill or growing old;
and above all at that last moment
when I feel I am losing hold of myself
and am absolutely passive within the hands
of the great unknown forces that have formed me;
in all those dark moments, O God,
grant that I may understand that it is you
(provided only my faith is strong enough)
who are painfully parting the fibers of my being
in order to penetrate to the very marrow
of my substance and bear me away within yourself.

The three men most responsible for introducing centering prayer into contemporary Christian circles in the English-speaking world are John Main, M. Basil Pennington, and Thomas Keating. Main was an English Benedictine monk. Pennington was, and Keating is, an American Trappist monk, like Thomas Merton. Pennington wrote that the term *centering prayer* was inspired by Merton's use of similar phrases in his writings.

Pennington and Keating wrote a brief book called *Finding Grace at the Center* along with Thomas E. Clarke, S.J. Before his death in 2005, Father Clarke, a quiet and gentle priest, resided at a small retreat house in a rural area north of New York City. He offers a concise introduction to the method: "Our theme is *the center*," he wrote, "the place of meeting of the human spirit and the divine Spirit, and, in that meeting, the place where the Christian at prayer meets the whole of reality, divine and human, persons and things, time and space, nature and history, evil and good."

Who can do that? I thought when I first read his words. But Tom's point is simple. Centering prayer is a move toward your center, where you encounter God. But it's not simple navel-gazing, nor is it simply about God and you alone. For any encounter with God will lead you to the rest of creation.

> God is within us and . . . we are in Him, and . . . this presence of God is a great motive of respect, confidence, love, joy, fervor.
> —St. Claude La Colombière, S.J. (1641–1682)

This simple framework may strike many people as suspicious. Initially, I was more suspicious of centering prayer than I had been about imaginative prayer. If Ignatian contemplation sounded ridiculous, meeting God within you sounded arrogant. Who was I to say that God dwelt within me? Some Christians also think centering prayer is suspect because it's "dangerously" close to Zen Buddhism and other Eastern practices. (The misguided idea that Christians couldn't learn anything from Eastern spiritualities was a great source of consternation for Thomas Merton.)

But the more I read about centering prayer, the more foolish my objections seemed—for the idea of God's dwelling within us is a foundational Christian belief. For one thing, most believers recognize conscience as the voice of God within. For another, multiple images of the indwelling God appear in the New Testament and in the early church. St. Paul said one's body is a "temple of the Holy Spirit," one place where God resides. St. Augustine wrote that God is *intimior intimo meo:* closer to me than I am to myself.

Centering prayer moves us to our center, where God dwells, waiting to meet us.

Three Steps

Father Pennington's essay in *Finding God at the Center* breaks down centering prayer into three steps.

> One: At the beginning of the prayer we take a minute or two to quiet down and then move in faith and love to God dwelling in our depths; and at the end of the prayer we take several minutes to come out, mentally praying the Our Father.

> "Faith," Father Pennington points out, "is fundamental for this prayer, as for any prayer." Moving to the center, you trust that you're moving toward the God who is *intimior intimo meo.*

> Two: After resting for a bit in the Presence in faith-full love, we take up a single, simple word that expresses our response and begin to let it repeat itself within.

In other words, you find a mantra or prayer word such as "love," "mercy," or "God" to help you focus. Don't concentrate on the meaning of the word. Rather, let the word anchor you in the presence of God. As the author of *The Cloud of Unknowing* says, "It is best when this word is wholly interior without a definite thought or actual sound."

Three: Whenever in the course of prayer we become aware of anything else, we simply gently return to the prayer word.

Distractions are unavoidable in prayer. Even Ignatius mentions them. ("I was disturbed by someone whistling," he once wrote, "but not so greatly disquieted.") The prayer word gently recalls you to the presence of God.

And that's it. Centering prayer is simple in theory. In practice, it can be difficult for beginners, especially if your life is packed with "content." The notion that you could meet God without "doing" anything may seem bizarre. But centering prayer is not about producing or doing or achieving. It's about being. Or rather, being with.

As Margaret Silf says, "In the eye of the storm is a center of perfect peace, where our deepest desire is embraced by God's own desire for us." Or to use Father Barry's analogy of friendship, centering prayer is like a long silent walk with a good friend. While you're not speaking to one another, there may be a deeper type of communication going on.

THE COLLOQUY

In Chapter Six, we touched on the idea of "speaking" with God by imagining God, or Jesus, in front of you. And I confessed that I've always found this a difficult way to pray. But for Ignatius it was an essential part of the Spiritual Exercises: he wanted you to come to know God, and Jesus. Conversation, or what he calls a "colloquy," was one way of doing this. For many people who travel along the way of Ignatius, this is the most enjoyable way to pray.

At the end of most meditations in the Exercises, Ignatius recommends that we imagine ourselves speaking to Mary, Jesus, and God the Father. At one point during the First Week, Ignatius asks us to speak with Jesus on the cross and ask ourselves, *What have I done for Christ? What am I doing for Christ? What ought I do for Christ?*

Sometimes this prayer has worked wonders for me. On a recent retreat, for example, I imagined standing before Jesus and asked myself, "What am I doing for Christ?" and started to grow angry. That anger was an obvious sign that something was happening deep down. "I'm doing way too much!" I complained to Jesus in prayer, and then listed all the unnecessary projects that I should have declined. And I felt Jesus say to me, *"I'm not asking you to do all that."*

Most of the colloquies in the Exercises are of a freer form, that is, they are not attached to specific questions like "What am I doing for Christ?" Often in the Second Week, when you are reflecting on the ministries and miracles of Jesus, a retreat director will ask you to imagine speaking to Jesus, or one of the disciples, to review what happened during the prayer. Ignatius recommends that you imagine speaking to God, doing so as "one friend speaks to another."

Colloquies can be simple. One Catholic sister whom I directed on a retreat spent four days sitting on a bench and imagining Jesus sitting beside her, while she told him what was on her mind. "Jesus and I had a great afternoon!" she said one day.

Again, what you "hear" in prayer needs to harmonize with your religious beliefs, what fits with your understanding of God, and what you know about yourself. In other words, *Does this make sense?* In time, you will be able to better discern what seems authentically from God.

OTHER FORMS OF PRAYER

This is not an exhaustive book on prayer. "By no means!" as St. Paul would say. But I don't want to leave you with the idea that those forms of prayer above are the only ways that Jesuits pray, or the only methods in the Ignatian tradition. Or the only methods recommended by other saints, theologians, or spiritual writers. So here are some very brief explanations of a few other ways to pray.

Communal prayer can happen in any group where participants are focused on God. For Catholics that includes the recitation of the Daily Office, as practiced by monastic communities and other groups; communal recitations of the Rosary; and the worship *par excellence:* the celebration of the Mass, called the "source and summit" of the church's life.

Other Christian denominations come together for Sunday services in which Scripture readings, songs, and preaching lift the congregation's hearts and minds to God. For Jews, the Friday evening *Shabbat* service reminds them of their covenant with God and their responsibilities to the community. For Muslims, the five-times daily call to prayer, which is often prayed privately, but many times in common, reminds them of their reliance on Allah, the Guide, the Restorer, the Gentle One.

Sometimes it's easy to forget that God meets us in groups, not simply when we're praying alone. "The funniest thing happened yesterday," said one young Jesuit recently. "I felt really moved during the Mass, almost to the point of tears." We both laughed at the tendency to overlook group worship as a way of interacting intimately with the Creator. Communal prayer is as much an occasion for the "Creator to deal directly with the creature," as Ignatius says, as is private prayer.

Rote prayer, like the Our Father, the Hail Mary, the Rosary, the Jewish *Shema* ("Hear, O Israel, the Lord is our God . . ."), and the psalms serve the believer in many ways. For one thing, they provide you with a ready-made template that is helpful when it is hard to find words to pray. Christians who pray the Our Father (or Lord's Prayer) know they are uttering words given to us by Jesus. It has been called the "perfect prayer," moving from praise to hope to petition to forgiveness. For another, rote prayers connect you with believers across the world. Rote formulas also help you lose yourself in prayer. As David's mother said about the Rosary, they can help you look at God, and God look at you.

Journaling is writing about your prayer or spiritual life. This method helps you both record and examine your prayer experiences, which are otherwise often dismissed as "just something that happened" or, more often, simply forgotten. Something in human nature works against remembering the fruits of prayer—for if we remembered all that we heard in prayer, we would have to change, and part of us recoils from that.

Dorothy Day, the cofounder of the Catholic Worker Movement, kept a spiritual journal for almost fifty years, which was later published as *The Duty of Delight* (edited by Robert Ellsberg). She pointed to another benefit of journaling, in an entry from 1950. "It is always so good to write our problems down so that in reading them over 6 months or a year later one can see them evaporate."

Interestingly, in their book *Birth: A Guide for Prayer,* Jacqueline Syrup Bergan and Marie Schwan, C.S.J., distinguish between keeping a diary of one's prayer and "meditative writing," where the writing itself is a prayer.

Meditative writing is like "writing a letter to one we love," Bergan and Schwan say. They offer three ways of doing this: writing a letter to God; writing down an imagined conversation between you and God; writing an answer to a question, like, "What do you want me to do for you?" and then writing the answer in God's voice. Meditative writing is useful for those who find it difficult to focus in prayer: it can free the mind of distractions and let God speak through the very act of writing.

Nature prayer is my term for finding God in meadows, fields, gardens, or backyards; or peering up at the night sky, walking along the beach, or joining in bird-watching expeditions, all the while searching for the divine presence. It can be a powerful way of connecting with God, something that I discovered when one woman challenged me with her style of prayer during a retreat that I was directing.

From Each Little Thing

Pedro Ribadaneira, one of the early Jesuits, wrote about his friend Ignatius's ability to find God in nature.

> We frequently saw him taking the occasion of little things to lift his mind to God, who even in the smallest things is great. From seeing a plant, foliage, a leaf, a flower, any kind of fruit, from the consideration of a little worm or any other animal, he raised himself above the heavens and penetrated the deepest thoughts, and from each little thing he drew doctrine and the most profitable counsels for instruction in the spiritual life.

"What was your prayer like yesterday?" I asked a middle-aged Catholic sister on retreat. "Well, I spent a long time hugging a tree." I had to suppress a laugh. Was she kidding?

"When I hugged the tree, I felt connected to the earth and to the beauty of God's creation," she continued. "Stretching my hands around its trunk made me feel grounded, connected to the earth, in a way that I never had. And here I was holding on to a living creature, which reminded me that God is continually creating." Her comments changed the way I look at that kind of prayer.

My busy life in New York City means that I have few opportunities to appreciate nature. The view from my window is an array of brick walls with a tiny sliver of blue sky, visible only if I crane my neck. So I treasure any time outdoors. One fall, I traveled to

Gloucester, Massachusetts, to direct a weekend retreat with Sister Maddy. The Jesuit retreat house is spectacularly situated only a few yards from the Atlantic Ocean. And only a few hundred yards from the house—separated from the ocean by a narrow spit of land—is a large, freshwater pond. To my mind, this is one of the most beautiful spots in the country.

On that Friday, however, I arrived in the dark of night, after a seemingly endless series of subways and trains that took me from New York to Boston to Gloucester. So I could see nothing of the retreat house's lovely grounds.

But in the early morning, when I stepped outside into the bright autumn sunshine, the view almost took my breath away. Near the retreat house were tall trees with red and orange leaves that stirred in the cool breeze. Above me was the vault of a brilliant blue sky. As I walked behind the retreat house, I saw fishing boats chugging around the bay, plowing through the steel-blue water. And though the air was filled with the calls of seagulls, ducks, and blackbirds, it seemed as if a silence filled my soul.

The colors, the smells, even the sounds, seemed ways of God comforting, calming, and consoling me.

Most of the men and women on retreat said the same. "How are you experiencing God this weekend?" I asked one man. "With all this!" he said, making an expansive gesture toward the window. At a talk that weekend, Sister Maddy told the story of her young nephew, who once stood on the rocks overlooking the Atlantic, taking in deep breaths.

"What are you doing?" said Maddy.

"Trying to take all this into me so I can take it home!" he said.

An Ignatian use of the imagination can aid us in nature prayer. (Ignatius himself used to gaze at the stars from the rooftop of the Jesuit headquarters in Rome.) Whenever I stand on a beach, I use the ocean as an image of a God who bears away my worries. With each wave that breaks on the shore and recedes, I imagine my fears and worries borne out to sea, to be received by God.

Music is another way to pray. "Who sings well prays twice," St. Augustine said. Ask any choir member or churchgoer who has felt lifted up during a worship service. Or ask a monk or nun who has chanted the psalms for years on end, until not only the words but the melodies become ways of expressing oneself to God. Sometimes the music itself can express what we are feeling better than words do. Lately, when I find it difficult to pray, I use a recording of the psalms, chanted by a monastery choir, whose songs pray for me when words do not come so easily.

Olivier Messiaen, the twentieth-century composer, once said that music serves for humanity as a conduit to the ineffable. When asked if a listener needed to have a spiritual experience to appreciate his music, Messiaen answered, "Not at all. But it would be the highest compliment to me as a composer if you had a spiritual experience because of hearing my music."

Work can be prayerful if done contemplatively. "Hands to work, hearts to God," as the Shakers used to say. Sometimes when I'm washing dishes or ironing or arranging the altar for Mass, I lose myself in the task and am reminded of doing small things with love.

But you have to be careful. Busy Jesuits (including me) sometimes say, half-mischievously, "My work is my prayer." This may mean our work leads us to God. Or it may be an excuse for not praying. Or it may mean we're doing neither wholeheartedly.

GOD COMMUNICATES WITH US in many ways. But prayer is a special time when God's voice is often heard most clearly because we are giving God our undivided attention. Whether in Ignatian contemplation, *lectio divina,* the colloquy, the examen, or any other practice, the "still small" voice can be heard with a clarity that can delight, astonish, and surprise you.

So when you pray, however you pray, and feel that God is speaking to you—pay attention.

CHAPTER EIGHT

The Simple Life

The Surprising Freedom of Downward Mobility

THAT'S PLENTY *ABOUT PRAYER* for now. I don't want you to think that the way of Ignatius is about nothing but hours and hours of prayer. Remember that one of Ignatius's ideals was the contemplative *in action*.

So after all that praying, let's stretch our legs a bit. Let's talk about how the way of Ignatius will affect your active life, your walking-around life.

And let's start with three ideas at the heart of the Ignatian vision that strike terror into the hearts of many readers: Poverty. Chastity. Obedience. It would be hard to find three more threatening words.

Everyone wants to avoid poverty, it would seem. Who wants to be poor? Doesn't everyone want to be as rich, or financially secure, as possible? Work hard and get ahead, right? That's the motivating force behind capitalism—Adam Smith's insight that by following self-interest the common good can be best served. The Protestant work ethic and the notion that God will bless those who work diligently with financial success are parts of the warp and woof of American culture. Poverty in this framework is not only something to be avoided, it is shameful.

Voluntary poverty, therefore, sounds absurd, almost un-American to many people.

And chastity? Who doesn't want sex? Sex is an extraordinary expression of love, and part of a healthy emotional life for most adults.

But we inhabit a culture where *everything* seems to be about having sex, preparing to have sex, or trying to get more sex: prime-time television, magazine ads, popular music, movies, and the Internet. You don't have to be a prude to admit that we live in a hypersexualized culture. In such an environment chastity is seen as a joke. Or just plain sick.

And obedience? It's seen almost as "ridiculous" as chastity. In a culture where people rightly celebrate the freedom to do, say, and be what they want, obedience is seen as mind control or, worse, slavery. As Kathleen Norris, author of *The Cloister Walk,* has written, obedience is viewed by many people as "desirable in dogs but suspect in people." Why would you let anyone tell you what to do or say or think? And if "Life, Liberty and the pursuit of Happiness" lies at the foundation of our political system, then obedience also seems un-American to many.

In a culture that celebrates money, sex, and freedom, a religious life of poverty, chastity, and obedience is not only irrelevant but a threat—to the economy, the social fabric, our political system, and an individual's well-being. All three should be soundly rejected, combated even, by any healthy adult. Right?

Well, not so fast.

Because those are precisely the values that St. Ignatius Loyola and the first Jesuits sought to embrace in the form of a lifelong vow to God.

Why would Ignatius do that? Why do Jesuits still do that?

WHY?

Ignatius did not invent the idea of poverty, chastity, and obedience. The "vowed life" was the longstanding tradition of Catholic religious orders like the Benedictines, Dominicans, and Franciscans centuries before the birth of Ignatius. (All Catholic priests and bishops are expected to live simply, but technically, only members of religious orders take formal vows of poverty.)

Why do members of religious orders do this? Let me give you just two reasons: one theological, the other logistical.

The theological reason is that members of religious orders are trying to emulate Jesus of Nazareth. While Jesus was probably born into the lower middle class, he lived his adult life like a poor man. ("The Son of Man has nowhere to lay his head," Jesus says in the Gospel of Luke, 9:58.)

Poverty.

And though Jesus could have gotten married, he chose not to. There are plenty of reasons to believe this statement, chief among them this: the Gospel writers mention almost every member of his family. ("Your mother and your brothers and your sisters are outside," says someone in Mark 3:32.) So omitting mention of his wife, if he had one, would have been unlikely.

Chastity.

And though Jesus could have done whatever he wanted to, he was obedient to his Father's will, even when it took him to the cross. ("Not my will, but yours be done," says Jesus in Luke 22:42.)

Obedience.

Jesus was poor, chaste, and obedient. This is the main reason that members of religious orders make these vows: in imitation of Christ.

The second reason is more logistical. The three vows help with the daily life of the religious community. Poverty means that we own nothing of our own, but all things together. This makes community life simpler and encourages unity. Chastity means that we're not married, and so we can devote more time to those with whom we minister. Obedience means that one person is ultimately in charge of things, which provides for clear-cut lines of authority. Each vow helps with the running of the community.

At this point I'll bet you're thinking, *Big deal.* Or maybe, *So what?* Or even, *Maybe I should skip this chapter!* You're thinking, *I'm not in a religious order, and I have no intention of living out poverty, chastity, or obedience. What does this aspect of Jesuit life possibly have to teach me?*

More than you think. In the next few chapters we'll deal with each of those "threatening" ideas and how they can help you lead a more satisfying life. First up: poverty.

THE CAUSE OF GREAT DELIGHT

Anthony de Mello was an Indian Jesuit priest renowned for his spiritual insights and, especially, his parables and stories. The author of many books on the spiritual life until his death in 1987, he was a popular lecturer within Catholic circles.

Some of de Mello's parables were drawn from Indian culture, others were his own creation, still others a sort of mélange. Here's one about a *sannyasi* (a wise man) that illustrates de Mello's outlook on wealth and poverty. As with many of his stories, it finds its inspiration in Eastern spiritualities but is quintessentially Ignatian. It's called "The Diamond."

> The sannyasi had reached the outskirts of the village and settled down under a tree for the night when a villager came running up to him and said, "The stone! The stone! Give me the precious stone!"
>
> "What stone?" asked the sannyasi.
>
> "Last night the Lord Shiva appeared to me in a dream," said the villager, "and told me that if I went to the outskirts of the village at dusk I should find a sannyasi who would give me a precious stone that would make me rich forever."
>
> The sannyasi rummaged in his bag and pulled out a stone. "He probably meant this one," he said, as he handed the stone over to the villager. "I found it on a forest path some days ago. You can certainly have it."
>
> The man gazed at the stone in wonder. It was a diamond, probably the largest diamond in the whole world, for it was as large as a person's head.

He took the diamond and walked away. All night he tossed about in bed, unable to sleep. Next day at the crack of dawn he woke the sannyasi and said, "Give me the wealth that makes it possible for you to give this diamond away so easily."

Poverty is a mystery for me. But not in the way you might think. The mystery is why more people don't choose to live more simply. I'm not suggesting that all people need to sell everything they own, beg for alms, let their hair and fingernails grow, and live in a cave, like Ignatius did after his conversion. (And which even he realized was excessive.) Rather, as de Mello's parable suggests, not being controlled by possessions is a step to spiritual freedom, the kind of freedom that most people say they want.

Poverty enabled Ignatius to follow the "poor Christ" of the Gospels, to free himself from unnecessary encumbrances, and to identify with the poor, whom Jesus of Nazareth loved. As such, it was a source of joy. In a letter to the Jesuits in Padua, Italy, in 1547, who were struggling with the demands of the vow, he wrote that poverty "is the cause of great delight in him who embraces it willingly." That surprising truth was something I discovered at the beginning of my Jesuit life.

THE RICH YOUNG MAN

After my eight-day retreat at Campion Center (when I thought about Jesus as a friend), I asked the Jesuits if I could enter the novitiate that same summer. Wisely, they counseled waiting for a year, until I had more experience of prayer and knew more about the Society of Jesus. Impatient, I asked them to reconsider. Eventually they agreed to let me commence the process, while cautioning that finding out so late meant I would have only a short time to quit my job, move out of my apartment, and prepare for the entrance date of August 28. So I embarked on the long process: undergoing several in-depth interviews, running through endless psychological tests, writing long essays, tracking down my baptismal records, and so on.

On August 15, the vocations director phoned to say that I had been accepted for entrance. "Is that what they mean by *getting the call?*" my sister asked dryly.

Immediately afterward, and even though this is not recommended, I started giving away all my possessions. (Most Jesuits wait until they take vows at the end of novitiate before they fully divest themselves of their possessions.)

My money and car went to my parents. My suits would sit in my parents' house in case the novitiate didn't work out. (I wasn't taking any chances.) The rest of my clothes went to Goodwill Industries, which would distribute them to the poor. My books went to friends who dropped by one sultry afternoon to scour my bookshelves. "I wish more of my friends joined religious orders," said one friend.

As I write this today, I can remember the initial burst of happiness I felt. How liberating it was! No more worrying about whether my suits were the proper shade of gray, my shoes the right brand, my ties the appropriate hue. No more worrying about whether I should rent an apartment or buy one. No more worrying about whether I needed a new this or a new that.

At Sunday Mass a few months before, the Gospel reading was of the "rich young man" who asks Jesus what is needed for eternal life. Its inclusion in the Gospels of Matthew, Mark, and Luke underlines its importance for the early Christians. When Jesus tells the man to follow the Ten Commandments, the man replies, in the Gospel of Luke, "I have kept all these since my youth" (18:21). Jesus can see that he is a good person. Mark's Gospel says Jesus "loved him" (10:21).

"There is still one thing lacking," says Luke's Jesus. "Sell all that you own and distribute the money to the poor, and you will have treasure in heaven; then come, follow me."

But as Luke writes, the wealthy man "became sad." He doesn't want to give up what he owns. The Gospel of Mark is more poignant.

"When he heard this, he was shocked and went away grieving, for he had many possessions."

That passage is often interpreted to mean the only way to get to heaven is to sell all you own. "How hard it will be for those who have wealth to enter the kingdom of God!" says Jesus in Mark. Consequently, this is a hard passage for many people to hear. A friend of mine once said, "I hate that story!" He felt that Jesus was making a ridiculous demand. "Who can do that?" he asked.

But as I see it, Jesus is not saying that one cannot own anything *at all* in order to be a good person. As St. Thomas Aquinas noted, "Possession of a few goods is important for a well-ordered life." Everyone outside of monasteries and religious orders needs some possessions in order to live.

Beyond the emphasis on a simple life, Jesus is showing his intuitive understanding of what was preventing the young man from growing closer to God. He has put his finger on what Ignatius would call the man's "disordered attachment." To another person Jesus might have said, "Give up your status." To another, "Give up your desires for success." Jesus was not simply inviting the young man to a simple life; he was identifying an unfreedom, and saying, "Get rid of anything that prevents you from following God."

As I unburdened myself that summer, I felt lighthearted. Now, as you can probably tell, there was some spiritual pride involved. (Spiritual pride is when you think, *Look how holy I am*.) But the joy had less to do with pride and more with the newfound feeling of being less burdened and more open to God.

Of course, I had to bring *some* things to the novitiate: I didn't appear naked at the front door. The day after "the call," the novice director phoned with a list of what items to pack: enough underwear and clothes for two years, a black clerical shirt, black pants, black shoes, and a few books if I wished. So it would be false to say that I gave away everything.

But the novitiate was a dramatically simpler lifestyle than the one I had been leading. Moving in with just a few clothes and a few books felt, well, simple. It's similar to what you may feel when you go on vacation with just one or two suitcases. You find yourself surprised that you can live with so little. You think, *Why can't I live like this all the time?* (As David would say, "Pay attention to that feeling.")

Few people can, or want to, live like members of a religious order. You have to clothe yourself, house yourself, and probably need a car to drive to work. If you have children, you need even more in order to care for and nurture them. The point is not that you have to give *everything* away, but this: the more you stop buying stuff you don't need, and the more you get rid of items you don't use, the more you can simplify your life. And the more you simplify, the freer you will feel, and be.

There are a few reasons for this.

First, possessions cost not only money but time. Consider the time you spend worrying about what you wear. You have to think about it, shop for it, buy it, clean it, repair it, store it, replace it. The same goes for your house, your car, your furniture, your television, your appliances, your computer, and your other electronic gadgets. The less you decide to buy, the more time you have for the things that matter more.

The second reason is less obvious. Our consumerist culture runs on comparisons. When I was working at General Electric, we employees were often told that clothes were an important part of our careers. "Dress for the job you want, not the one you have," my manager said. "Spend one week's salary on your shoes," said a friend. "Never wear a patterned tie with a patterned shirt," said a consultant at our annual Dress for Success seminar. The time spent comparing my wardrobe to those of my managers was considerable. So was the time spent comparing cars, apartments, furniture, and stereos. The less you buy, the less time you will spend comparing your stuff to your neighbor's stuff.

While visiting my sister and her family recently, I wore an old plaid short-sleeve shirt. My nine-year-old nephew said, "Uncle

Jim, that shirt was twenty years out of fashion twenty years ago!" I laughed and asked him where he had got that expression. He said he heard it on a cartoon. The impulse to buy, possess, and compare is inculcated early.

Third, the more things that society produces, the more we will want, or be encouraged to want, and the more unhappy we will be. In his book *The Progress Paradox*, Gregg Easterbrook sums it up nicely: "As ever more material things become available and fail to make us happy, material abundance may even have the perverse effect of instilling unhappiness—because it will never be possible to have everything that economics can create." Freeing yourself from the need to have more and more means that you may, paradoxically, be more satisfied.

Unrelieved Competition

John Kavanaugh, a Jesuit moral theologian who writes frequently on questions of the consumerist culture, has this to say about the corrosive impact it has on us and, specifically, on families, in his book *Following Christ in a Consumer Society:*

In my own discussions with parents and their children concerning the problem of family stress and fragmentation, I know of no other force so pervasive, so strong, and so seductive as the consumer ideology of capitalism and its fascination for endless accumulation, extended working hours, the drumming up of novel need fulfillments, the theologizing of the mall, the touting of economic comparison, the craving for legitimacy through money and possessions, and unrelieved competition at every level of life.

The Ladder

One of the best short analyses of the consumerist world in which we live is an article by Dean Brackley, S.J., that appeared in the journal *Studies in the Spirituality of Jesuits* in 1988. It was one of the first things I read in the novitiate. Father Brackley was uniquely qualified to write on the topic, having lived and worked with the poor in the South Bronx. A few years later he would move to El Salvador to replace one of the Jesuit priests assassinated as a result of their work with the poor in that country.

His article was called "Downward Mobility," a phrase borrowed from the Dutch priest Henri Nouwen. Brackley compares the way of the world, which can be summarized as "upward mobility," to the vision of Ignatius in the Spiritual Exercises, which invites us to detachment and freedom.

This drive to acquire, this constant striving toward "upward mobility," is at first driven by something healthy: our longings.

All of us have a natural longing for God. But, as Brackley notes, the consumer culture often tells us that we can satisfy this longing through money, status, and possessions. Sound crazy? Just think of the television commercials that promise happiness if you only buy one more thing.

How does the process work? Here is a summary of Brackley's twelve steps, with some added comments of my own. See if any resonate with your own experiences.

1. The consumer culture is primarily *individualistic,* with people pursuing private goals over more communal ones. In a competitive environment, it's everyone for himself or herself.

   This does not mean that personal goals are negative *per se.* Individual pursuit is the basis of the capitalist system, arguably the most efficient economic system for the production and distribution of goods. The danger, however, is becoming interested solely in your own well-being, unconcerned with those outside of your family, friends, and local community.

2. People are tempted to alleviate feelings of insecurity by having or *consuming*. We try to fill our emptiness with things, rather than with God or with loving relationships. Without this impulse the advertising industry would probably collapse: it exists to manufacture the desire for things.

3. This individualism and consumerism leads to the *ladder* as the dominant model for the culture—with some people higher up than others. Some are on the top, others on the bottom.

4. Individuals show their *status* through certain social symbols—job titles, possessions, credentials, and so on. One's personal worth depends on one's wealth or job.

   That's why discussing salary is perhaps the biggest taboo in social settings: it's the quickest way of ranking people and is society's prime measure of our worth. Finding out someone else's salary instantly makes you see the person in a certain light. If the other person makes less than you, you may see him as "less than." If he makes more, you may be jealous and see yourself as "less than." Most other conversational topics are welcomed among friends—family problems, illness, death—but, even there, salary is taboo, because of its inherent power.

5. Gradually, you *interiorize* these external measures. You judge yourself on your job, your salary, on what you "produce."

   Now, all of us are called to act, to do, to work. But when you judge yourself solely by these measures, you become a "human doing" rather than a "human being."

   Also, if you're not higher on the ladder or moving up that ladder, you feel inferior to others. In your desire to belong, the climb up the ladder becomes even more urgent.

6. At the top of the ladder is *the mythical figure*—the celebrity, the rich man or woman, the model. At the bottom is the "loser"—the unemployed, the refugee, the homeless.

It becomes easier, therefore, to ignore the poor. They are an implicit threat to the system, since they remind us that the ladder does not work perfectly. We think, *What if that were me?* That thought gives more urgency to the climb away from the "losers."

7. Under these conditions *competition* becomes the guiding force of social life. Your security is not enhanced, but threatened, by others' success. As Gore Vidal once wrote, "It is not enough that I succeed. Others must fail."

8. One's security depends on *climbing*. As Brackley notes, not everyone intent on upward mobility is arrogant or power hungry. But even the compassionate are forced to confront the dangers and risks of the ladder. You are tempted to ask not "Is this right?" but "Is this best for me?"

9. The social model is therefore not simply a ladder but a *pyramid,* in which whole groups band together against threats from above or below. Divisions are formed not just between persons but between groups.

10. Not everyone can be on top. So those on top work to *maintain* their positions and keep those on the bottom in place. Power often is exercised to keep the lower groups dependent or disorganized or ignorant.

11. Social class, race, gender, sexual orientation, education, physical appearance, and other factors help to define the pyramid. This leads to *further divisions.*

12. Finally, competition between the groups breeds not trust and cooperation but *fear,* mistrust, and, I would add, loneliness.

You may not agree with all of those factors. But, overall, Brackley's model well describes the consumerist world in which many of us live.

The constant drive for upward mobility, to maintain our positions, takes time and energy. So why not set at least *some of this* aside and be free of it? This is what Ignatius meant when he said that poverty, a kind of simple lifestyle, a "downward mobility," a setting aside of some of those values described above, "is the cause of great delight" for those who embrace it. Simple living is not a punishment, but a move toward greater freedom. So let's see what the way of Ignatius can teach us about simple living.

SENSIBLE SIMPLICITY

Here is how Ignatius begins his treatment of poverty in the *Constitutions:* "Poverty, as the strong wall of the religious institute, should be loved and preserved in its integrity, as far as this is possible with God's grace." It's essential.

Ignatius's outlook on simple living was formed by his own experience. After his conversion experience in the family castle, one of his first acts was to lay down his knightly armor before a statue of Mary and divest himself, as far as possible, of all his worldly goods at the Benedictine monastery of Montserrat.

> On the Eve of the feast of Our Lady, in March, at night, in the year 1522, he went as secretly as he could to a beggar—and stripping off all his garments, he gave them to the beggar; he dressed himself in his chosen attire and went to kneel before the altar of Our Lady.

This is a wholehearted response to Jesus' invitation to the rich young man in the Gospels. For Ignatius this was a clear way to follow Christ. His response also patterned itself on the practices of other religious orders, especially the one founded by his hero, St. Francis of Assisi. As John O'Malley notes in *The First Jesuits,* "The Franciscan influence upon him, direct or indirect, is nowhere more palpable than in this emphasis on the surrender of material goods."

Later, in a touching scene, a man races up to report to Ignatius what later happened to the same beggar:

As he was gone about a league from Montserrat, a man who had been hurrying after him, caught up to him and asked if he had given some clothes to a beggar, as the beggar affirmed. Answering that he had, tears flowed from his eyes in compassion for the beggar to whom he had given the clothing—in compassion, for he realized they were harassing him, thinking that he had stolen them.

Afterward, Ignatius spent almost a year in seclusion in the small town of Manresa, where he prayed, begged for alms, and fasted. His poverty was extreme.

He begged alms at Manresa every day. He did not eat meat nor drink wine, even though they were offered to him. . . . Because he was very fastidious in taking care of his hair as was the fashion of that time (and his was very handsome), he decided to let it go its way according to nature without combing or cutting it.

He even decided to follow the example of a saint, unnamed, who went for days without food in order to obtain a particular favor from God. Ignatius does this and finds himself "at the extreme limit, so that he would die if he did not eat." He grows despondent, even suicidal.

Gradually he realizes such severities would not only endanger his health but also prevent him from doing the work he wanted to do. As O'Malley writes, "Ignatius's personal experience fairly early persuaded him that too severe an understanding of 'actual poverty' hindered his attempts 'to help souls,' and later he and his colleagues in the Society saw even more clearly the impracticability of such an understanding for the institution they were founding."

Years later, for example, Ignatius insisted that the Jesuits in training take adequate care of their health in order that they might be able to carry on their work. "A proper concern with the preservation of one's health and bodily strength for the divine service," he writes in the *Constitutions,* "is praiseworthy and should be exercised by all."

This is why the Ignatian approach to a simple life has been helpful to so many. It does not ask you to become a half-naked, twig-eating, cave-dwelling hermit. It simply invites you to live simply. It is a sensible simplicity. A moderate asceticism. A healthy poverty.

For Ignatius, poverty was not an end in itself. It was: first, a means of identifying with the "poor Christ"; second, a way of freeing oneself up to follow God more easily; and third, a way of identifying with the poor, whom Jesus loved. Overall, poverty was "apostolic," making Ignatius available for God's work.

All these things combined to make poverty a critical part of his spirituality and, ultimately, a powerfully life-giving force for him and his followers. As André de Jaer, a Belgian Jesuit and spiritual director, notes in his book *Together for Mission,* "Beginning as a search for ascetical feats, it quickly matured into a desire to place complete confidence in God alone. When he began to compose the Spiritual Exercises . . . he relied on his own experience to write what might be helpful to others."

RICHES TO HONORS TO PRIDE

The other reason that Ignatius valued poverty is that he noticed the subtle way that the climb up the ladder can lead you away from God.

In the Second Week of the Spiritual Exercises comes one of the central images in Ignatian spirituality. It is called the Two Standards. Here Ignatius asks us to imagine two "armies" arrayed for battle under two different flags or "standards." On the one side is that of Satan; on the other, that of Christ. In this meditation the influence of Ignatius's career as a soldier is seen quite clearly.

The purpose of this meditation is to help us understand the workings of human nature. Through vivid imagery that may be foreign to some modern sensibilities, Ignatius offers a way to appreciate what most of us do not find foreign at all—the battle within ourselves to do the right thing.

From as early as his conversion, Ignatius was able to recognize what moved him toward God (the consolation he felt when he thought of serving God) and what moved him away (the dry feelings that attended his plans to seek fame). The discerning person, Ignatius believed, could distinguish between those two forces and make the right choices. In Ignatian spirituality this is called "discernment of spirits."

Battle, therefore, is a key metaphor for Ignatius. He believed in the presence of evil in the world, and not simply as a vague impersonal force, but as a personified entity—Satan, who is always at work trying to move us away from God. The Exercises refer to whatever moves us toward God as the "good spirit," and what pulls us away as "the enemy" or "the enemy of human nature."

Lately I've been suggesting to people J. R. R. Tolkien's *The Lord of the Rings* trilogy—either the books or the films—as a way of understanding what Ignatius had in mind: on one side, the army of the evil wizard Saruman and his awful Orcs; on the other that of the noble Frodo and his trusty Hobbit, human, and elvish companions. The *Harry Potter* series—again, either the books or the films—is another contemporary illustration of this kind of battle: on the one side, Voldemort and his evil minions; on the other, Harry and his stalwart friends.

But you need not understand things precisely as Ignatius did to profit from Ignatian spirituality. In his book *The Discernment of Spirits,* Timothy Gallagher, O.M.V., helpfully sums up the concept of the "enemy" as "those interior movements that would pull us away from God."

More important than this battle imagery is understanding the way that the two sides operate. In the Two Standards, Ignatius asks us to imagine Christ calling people to his side, to a simple life, renouncing the desire for honors, and desiring a life of humility. In other words, Christ invites us, as he did with the rich young man, to enjoy a life free of attachments.

Ignatius then invites us to imagine Satan advising his "uncountable devils" on how to ensnare men and women *through* attachments. This same clever literary technique—advice from an experienced devil to his younger counterpart—was used, centuries later, by the British writer C. S. Lewis in his book *The Screwtape Letters*.

The enemy works like this, says Ignatius: first by tempting people to desire *riches,* which leads to *honors,* which often leads to an overweening *pride,* the gateway to a gamut of sinful behavior. As any Jesuit will tell you, the shorthand phrase is "riches to honors to pride."

The process is insidious because riches and honors are seductive. I know this from personal experience.

From the Spiritual Exercises

Here is Ignatius speaking about the progressive dangers of not living simply, in the *Spiritual Exercises.* In the section known as the Two Standards he asks us to imagine Satan giving advice to his minions about how to tempt human beings to pride:

First they should tempt people to covet riches (as he usually does, at least in most cases), so that they may more easily come to vain honor from the world, and finally to surging pride. In this way, the first step is riches, the second is honor, and the third is pride; and from these three steps the enemy entices them to all the other vices.

Over the past few years, I've published several books and have written articles for newspapers, magazines, and Web sites. Consequently, I've been invited to speak in a variety of places as well as on radio and television. Overall, I'm happy that others find my writing helpful, especially since the work of a Jesuit is supposed to "help souls." The more people who read books about the spiritual life the more chance that at least a few more souls will be helped.

Speaking on television and radio is also valuable not only because it helps sell books, and therefore helps more souls, but because you can talk about God with millions of people—more than I could in a Sunday homily. (It's also fun.) John Courtney Murray, an American Jesuit theologian who worked as adviser to the Second Vatican Council, once said that the Jesuit should explain the world to the church, and the church to the world. Working with the media is one way of doing this.

But there is a danger. Even though I try not to let this go to my head, all those things—books, articles, media appearances—are what the larger culture considers as "success." They are one example of what Ignatius meant by "riches."

In the wake of these occasional successes comes praise from family, friends, acquaintances, and even strangers. Those are the "honors" that Ignatius talks about. And while I have been grateful for the compliments, something else was at work. Something insidious.

After experiencing some success, I began to notice within myself a creeping sense of entitlement. *Why do I need to sign up to celebrate Mass in our community? I'm busy! Why should I have to empty the house dishwasher? I have important things to do!*

Though I never acted on these feelings, I was saddened to discover them within me, especially after knowing the Exercises. My spiritual director smiled and said, "Riches to honors to pride!" Even though I've been a Jesuit for over twenty years, I'm still subject to the same temptations that everyone else is.

It was a potent reminder not only of my own humanity, and the

A Major Concern

Ignatius knew that ecclesial honors could lead Jesuits to become proud. An appointment as bishop or cardinal brought great riches and honors to the person and to his family, and so one was eagerly sought, particularly in Ignatius's day. This is one reason that there are so many restrictions in the *Constitutions* on Jesuits' becoming bishops and cardinals. Here is an amusing anecdote about an early Jesuit, Francis Borgia (yes, of *that* Borgia family) and the efforts, in 1552, to make him a cardinal. It is from the journals of Juan de Polanco, an early Jesuit, and uses the term "Ours" to refer to Jesuits. The last line is my favorite.

> Ours were freed from a major concern . . . for a rumor had made its way throughout the city [Valencia, Spain] regarding Father Francis Borgia and the cardinalatial dignity; the word was that he had been forced to accept it under pain of mortal sin. But when they received letters from Rome informing them that Father Ignatius had forestalled this business, their concern was changed to consolation. This was the reaction of Ours everywhere, though some of the blood relatives of Father Francis received the news with different emotions.

need to be vigilant, but also of Ignatius's keen insights into the love of "riches" of all kinds, as well as into the "good spirit," the "enemy," and plain old human nature.

BRING ON POVERTY?

The most popular joke about Jesuit poverty is this: A first-year novice is visiting a large Jesuit community during a big celebration of the feast day of St. Ignatius Loyola, on July 31, usually an occasion for grand dinners. The novice spies the immense dining room, the tastefully appointed tables, the flower vases, and the filet mignon ready on the table and announces, "If this is poverty, bring on chastity!"

No one laughs harder at that joke than Jesuits. Jesuit poverty is meant to be a true poverty that helps us to identify with the "poor Christ." It's also meant to be "apostolic," something that frees us for work. The early Jesuits were diligent in their following of poverty, preferring the worst lodgings, the worst food, and the worst dress in order to more closely follow Jesus.

But contemporary Jesuit living arrangements can sometimes be quite comfortable, at least in the United States. In Jesuit communities in some colleges and high schools, for example, as many as fifty Jesuits might live under the same roof. This means certain practical arrangements are unavoidable: large living rooms and dining rooms (to accommodate so many men), a cook and a kitchen staff (especially in houses with elderly Jesuits), several washing machines (try juggling one washing machine among fifty men), and sufficient amounts of food.

To the outside eye this institutional life can look lavish. Some Jesuits ruefully call these "full-service" communities. To the inside eye as well. Every Jesuit community tries to live simply, but in the midst of plenty, sometimes it's hard to feel that you're doing so. In other words, Jesuits are often in the same boat as everyone else when it comes to a simple lifestyle: they must strive to live simply—sometimes in a culture of plenty.

"You take a vow of poverty," said an unemployed friend. "But I live it!" It's a fair critique. With everything owned in common, our most basic needs—food, clothing, shelter—are provided for.

It's also an inaccurate critique. A vow of poverty means living very simply on a limited budget. Our monthly stipend for personal needs and expenses, which we call our *personalia,* is modest (in my novitiate it was $35). No Jesuit owns a car or house. All income—salaries, donations, gifts, royalties on books—is given to the community.

We must request permission for long trips, as well as money needed for expensive items like eyeglasses, a new suit, or a new coat, which are not covered by our *personalia.* That permission is sometimes not given. After working in Nairobi for a year, some lay friends asked if I could join them on a week's vacation on the coast of the Indian Ocean, in a student hostel, which would cost $100. The Jesuit superior told me it was out of the question. When I tried to convince him otherwise, he chuckled. "It's not a question of whether or not I think it's a good idea, Jim," he said. "We simply can't afford it."

Compared to some—affluent Americans—we live extremely simply. Compared to many—the destitute around the world—we do not live so simply. Still, every Jesuit priest and brother desires to be as free of possessions, to love poverty, and to live as simply as he can, as Ignatius intended. As one of my spiritual directors told me, "The vows allow you to live simply. How simply is up to you."

Fortunately, besides Ignatius, I have had many role models in this regard—"living rules," as I mentioned in the first chapter, men whose lives serve as models for their brother Jesuits. Many of them are revered specifically for their simplicity.

For several years I lived with an older Jesuit named John. Wise, clever, and compassionate, he was a living rule if there ever was one. In the style of his own training, which had taken place in the 1940s and 1950s, he used to call me "Mister." "Good morning, Mister!" he would say over breakfast. The week after my ordination he greeted me with, "Good morning, Father!"

One day, while still a "Mister," I knocked on John's door to ask him to hear my confession. His room was simplicity itself: a threadbare carpet, nothing on his walls but a few framed photos, a crucifix nailed above a rickety wooden kneeler, ancient plastic-covered chairs, and low-wattage lightbulbs.

Then I spied his bed, a single. Without any headboard, it was nothing but a box spring and a mattress perched atop a rickety metal frame. But what caught my eye was the yellow bedspread. An inexpensive polyester spread barely covering the mattress, it looked ancient, thin nearly to the point of transparency, faded in color; it was the most meager bedspread I could imagine.

"Father," I said, "I think it's time for a new bedspread."

"Mister," he said with a laugh, "that *is* the new bedspread!"

Guiltily, I remembered that just the week before I had asked for money for a new bedspread (which I really didn't need). My visit reminded me that for Jesuits, there is little that we really *need* in terms of material goods.

Voluntary poverty can also be a goad to help the truly poor. As the early Christians used to say, the extra coat hanging in your closet does not belong to you; it belongs to a poor person.

Jesuits who work directly with the poor—here and abroad—often seem more able to embrace a poverty that is closer to what Ignatius probably intended for his men. Part of this is because of the limited resources in those countries. But part of it has to do with the experience of living with the materially poor themselves, from whom Jesuits learn more about real poverty than they can even from the Spiritual Exercises. Closeness to the poor offers insights into why Ignatius called poverty something "which should be loved as a mother." This is something I learned when I worked in East Africa.

GAUDDY, AGUSTINO, AND LOYCE

Midway through my Jesuit training, my provincial superior sent me to Nairobi, Kenya, to work with the Jesuit Refugee Service, an organization founded in 1980 by Pedro Arrupe, then the Order's superior general.

The Jesuit Refugee Service (JRS) is part of the Society of Jesus' efforts to work with the poor, a central part of Christian discipleship since the time of Jesus. In the Gospel of Matthew, Jesus reminds his disciples that the test of a good disciple is not how often he prays, or what church he goes to, but how he treats "the least of these who are members of my family," that is, the poor (Matt. 25:40).

The "corporal works of mercy" (including feeding the hungry, clothing the naked, and visiting the prisoner) have always been at the heart of Christian service. Many of the most well known saints are known specifically for their work with the poor, from St. Francis of Assisi to Mother Teresa. Ignatius was no different in his desire to heed the call to care for the "least."

From the beginning, working with the poor was a focus of the Jesuits' mission, rather than simply founding schools, which is often thought to be the case. And, by the way, the original purpose of the schools was not simply to educate youth and help them in their development of character, but also to serve the common good. The early Jesuits hoped that the graduates would "grow up to be pastors, civic officials, administrators of justice, and will fill other important posts to everyone's profit and advantage," as Juan de Polanco, Ignatius's secretary, wrote.

After the Society was approved by Pope Paul III in 1540, Jesuits began visiting hospitals and prisons, ministering to the dying, and working with orphans, reformed prostitutes, and the children of prostitutes. And when famine, flood, or the plague broke out, the Jesuits quickly organized to provide direct physical or financial assistance to victims.

Of course, other religious orders engaged in charitable work, too; it is simply part of the Christian life. What was unusual about the Jesuits was what John O'Malley calls the "explicit articulation" of those charitable works as an essential element of the new order.

"In a few instances," O'Malley writes in *The First Jesuits*, "this commitment attained heroic dimensions." In 1553 the Jesuits remained almost alone in their willingness to minister to the sick during a plague in Perugia, Italy, with several Jesuits dying as a result. Aloysius Gonzaga, one of the earliest Jesuit saints, took ill and died after ministering to plague victims in 1591. He was twenty-one.

In all these works they were not only following the Judeo-Christian tradition of service, but also Ignatius's dictum that "love ought to manifest itself more by deeds than by words."

My own job in Kenya was to help the refugees who had settled in the sprawling slums of Nairobi start their own businesses so they could support themselves and their families. Much of the work consisted of visiting the refugees in their small shacks, which often contained nothing more than a mattress, a kerosene lantern, a cooking pot, some boxes, and a few plastic pails to hold water and food.

This kind of poverty—in which human beings are unable to satisfy their basic needs—is not something to which Jesuits, or anyone, aspires. Dehumanizing poverty is something that many Jesuits spend their entire lives combating, whether through direct work with the poor or advocacy on their behalf. The Jesuit goal of *voluntary* poverty in imitation of Christ is different from the *involuntary* poverty that is a scourge for billions across the globe.

But the two are inextricably connected: living simply means that one needs less and takes less from the world, and is therefore more able to give to those who live in poverty. Living simply can aid the poor.

Entering into the lives of the poor also encourages simple living. You see how the poor are able to manage with so little. How they sometimes live with greater freedom. How they are often more generous with what they have. And how they are often more grateful for life than the wealthy.

Learning About Poverty

Pedro Arrupe, the Jesuit superior general from 1965 to 1981, had a sense of humor even about serious topics. Two young American Jesuits once showed up at the Jesuit headquarters in Rome. Father Arrupe asked what assignment had brought them there. They explained that they were on their way to India to work with the poor, as part of their training. Afterward Arrupe said to an assistant, "It certainly costs us a lot of money to teach our men about poverty!"

When I think about the ways in which the poor teach us, I remember some of the refugees I knew in Kenya. One had the wonderful name of Gaudiosa, which means "joyful" in Latin. Gauddy, as everyone called her, was a Rwandese refugee. She had settled in Nairobi in the 1960s with her family, a victim of the Hutu-Tutsi conflict that had long plagued her homeland.

She was also a talented seamstress who, the year before I arrived, had received a grant from JRS to purchase a single sewing machine. From that modest beginning, she and several other Rwandese women built a flourishing tailoring business called the Splendid Tailoring Shop.

One day Gauddy dropped by our office. At the time, we had just decided to open a shop—called the Mikono Centre—for refugees to market their wares. And I was trying to interest priests and members of religious orders in purchasing the handicrafts made by the refugees.

Gauddy and I discussed making liturgical stoles for priests with *kitenge,* a colorful cotton fabric used in Rwandese dresses and shirts. For a talented seamstress, a stole is an easy venture: just two long pieces of cloth sewn together in a V shape. Stoles, I suggested, might be big sellers to visiting Western priests as well as to missionary priests working in local parishes. And Gauddy always had plenty of leftover *kitenge* in her shop.

Gauddy's *kitenge* stoles flew off our shelves; we could barely keep them in stock. When I ordered twenty more in the first week, Gauddy folded her hands in her lap, bowed her head, and said, "God is good."

"Yes," I said, but why did she think so?

"Why?" Gauddy laughed and clapped her hands, evidently surprised that I would ask such a ridiculous question. "Brother Jim!" she exclaimed. "God is helping me get rid of this leftover *kitenge*. God is giving me money for making these stoles, which are so easy to make. God is giving me this business for my shop, and for my ladies. Surely you can see that God is very, very good!"

As with many refugees, Gauddy's thoughts, in good times and bad, turned to God. Perhaps I would have eventually discerned God's hand, but Gauddy saw God *immediately*. She typified the relationship that many refugees had with God. To use the analogy of friendship, Gauddy had placed herself closer to God, and so was a better friend to God than I was.

Another friend was a Mozambican wood-carver named Agustino. We first met on a busy street corner in Nairobi, where Agustino was sitting on a piece of cardboard, carefully carving his beautiful ebony and rosewood statues and trying to sell them to passersby. When I asked if he wouldn't rather sit under a tree outside the Mikono Centre and sell to more customers, he readily agreed and showed up at our shop the very next day. He has worked there ever since.

One morning Agustino showed me with great enthusiasm an enormous three-foot-tall sculpture carved from a single piece of ebony. It was called the "tree of life" and depicted men working in the fields, women nursing children, and children playing. Though beautifully made, the price was very high. I doubted we could sell it in our shop, and told him so.

After Agustino tried unsuccessfully to convince me to buy it, I agreed to take the piece on consignment. "Will you pray that it sells?" Agustino said. Yes, I said, I would. But I had doubts: it was too big and too expensive. We lugged the heavy piece of wood inside and set it atop one of our display tables.

A few minutes later, a woman in a green Land Rover pulled into our driveway, walked into the shop, spied the enormous sculpture, and promptly bought it—for a few hundred shillings more than our asking price.

"See?" said Agustino. "Your prayers were answered."

When seeking help, Agustino's first recourse was to ask God. When expressing gratitude, his first instinct was to praise God. He relied on God more than I did.

In later conversations it became clear that his trust had something to do with his poverty: his daily life had a precariousness that reminded him of his fundamental reliance on God, something that the more affluent often take for granted. Agustino seemed to be a close friend of God, too. Many of the poor, at least in my experience, evince this quality.

God meets us where we are. And the poor are often already close by.

Still, overly romanticizing the poor is a danger. Not all are cut from the same cloth. Not all are religious. Not all are believers. Even talking about "the poor" is problematic. Gauddy and Agustino are not so much members of a vague sociological group called "the poor" as they are individuals.

Nonetheless, the refugees with whom I worked were, in general, more ready to rely on God and more ready to praise God than I was.

This gratitude made many of them more generous, too. One afternoon I visited Loyce, a Ugandan woman to whom we had given a grant for a single sewing machine. She lived outside of Nairobi in a wooden shack in a largely rural area. Upon entering her dimly lit home, I found that Loyce had prepared an elaborate meal: roasted peanuts, vegetables, and even meat, a rarity for her. It must have cost a week's earnings. I was stunned by her generosity. Loyce gave, as Jesus said of a poor widow in the Gospels, "out of her poverty" (Mark 12:41–44).

Not every refugee was as generous as Loyce. So again, it's wrong to generalize. But my experience with many of the refugees points out what happens when you refuse to take things, or people, for granted, and when you are able to take stock of your blessings. Your gratitude increases.

God is good, as Gauddy said.

Every time these things happened in Kenya, I thought of a line from Scripture that had long baffled me. "The Lord hears the cry of the poor." It was also a line from a popular contemporary hymn we sang in the novitiate. But *why* would the Lord hear the cry of the poor in particular? Why wouldn't God hear the cry of *everyone*? It seemed partial. So did the line from the Psalms, "The Lord is near to the brokenhearted" (34:18). Why?

In Kenya I found an answer. In many of our lives a great deal comes between us and God: concerns about status, achievement, appearance, and so on. Less stood between the refugees and God. Overall, they were more aware of their dependence on God. So, like Gauddy, they praised God in good times; like Agustino, they called on God when they were in need; and like Loyce, they expressed gratitude with generosity.

The poor place themselves close to God, the poor have less between them and God, the poor rely on God, the poor make God their friend, and the poor are often more grateful to God. And so God is close to them. This is one reason why Ignatius asked the Jesuits to love poverty "as a mother."

DOWNWARD MOBILITY?

Here's what you might be thinking: *Those are inspiring stories about Gauddy and Agustino and Loyce, but what do they have to do with me? Do you expect me to live like a refugee?*

In general, whenever I speak about living more simply, people's reactions tend toward extremes. They fall into two categories.

1. Are you out of your mind? I can't give up everything I own—that's ridiculous! (That's the most common response.)
2. I feel guilty when I think about how much stuff I have that I don't need. When I think about the poor, I feel awful. But there's no way I can live simply. It's impossible for me to change. (This is closer to the response of the "rich young man" in the Gospel of Matthew.)

The two responses display (1) anger and (2) despair.

Both responses block us from freedom. If we dismiss the insights that come from the poor and reject the invitation to simplicity by saying, "I can't live like that," then these insights and invitations will never make a difference in our lives. Making the message unattainable also makes it easier to reject. Likewise, when we wallow in guilt and decide that it's impossible to change, we are subtly letting ourselves off the hook, excusing ourselves from change.

Both responses mean that freedom cannot take hold.

The invitation to live a simple life does not mean giving up everything you have. Surrendering all your possessions is the right path for only a very few people, mostly those who choose to live in common with others. We're not meant to live exactly like Gauddy or Agustino or Loyce. But the opposite of their situations—that is, a total immersion into our consumerist culture, which tells us that we can only be happy if we have more—is a dead end.

Nor does the invitation to a simple life mean you have to feel bad about yourself. But, from time to time, it's good to feel the sting of conscience. Ignatius said the voice of conscience sometimes feels like the "drop of water falling onto a stone," a sharp feeling that awakens you to reality. If you feel guilty about how much stuff you have, perhaps this is an invitation from God to give some of it away, to live more simply.

But it is an invitation to freedom, not to guilt. The turn to a simple lifestyle frees us, reminds us of our reliance on God, makes us more grateful, and leads us to desire "upward mobility" for everyone, not just for the few. Ultimately, it also moves us closer to the forgotten and outcast, something at the heart of the ministry of Jesus of Nazareth, and a theme frequently mentioned in the Old Testament. It reminds us that people like the refugees of East Africa, people you may never meet, are part of our lives. As Dean Brackley writes in "Downward Mobility,"

> This vision reveals a fundamental equality of all human beings that overshadows all differences. In other words, the outcast has the potential to shatter my world. When I can identify with the outcast, allowing her to come crashing in on my world, the ladder collapses, at least for me, exposed as a colossal fraud. The superiority of the great dissolves together with the inferiority of the small. If only for a moment we all appear naked and on an equal footing. This crucial experience shows that identifying with the outcast enables us to identify with *everyone*. I can say, "These people are all just like me."

So, as it turns out, Gauddy, Agustino, and Loyce have a lot to do with you.

But How Do I Do It?

That still raises the question, How can you live simply? Given that you're not called to give up everything, how can you simplify your life and respond to the invitation to live with less stuff coming between God and you?

Let me suggest three steps, of increasing difficulty. Then a challenge. In all these things, trust that God will help you along this path, because it's a path to freedom, which God desires for you.

First, get rid of whatever you don't need. It's the obvious first step to simplifying. What should you do with all that stuff? Well, once again, the extra coat you're not using doesn't belong to you; it belongs to the poor. Call a local church, shelter, or clothing distribution center.

But some friendly advice: don't give your junky stuff to the poor—toss that out. During the novitiate, I worked in a homeless shelter in Boston for several months. One day I handed one fellow a tattered orange corduroy jacket. "Ugh," he said, "I wouldn't wear that!" Initially I thought, *He should be grateful.* Then, as if reading my mind, he said, "Would *you* want to wear it?" No, I wouldn't. The poor deserve decent clothes, just like you do.

Second, distinguish between wants and needs. Is it "nice to have" or "need to have"? Do you "need" a bigger television or the latest phone or the newest computer? Or is it something you want because your friends just bought one or because you've seen it advertised? It's difficult to resist the desire to have what friends have and what marketers say you need, but again, turning these things down leads to freedom.

Think of it like a diet. Hard as it is, you feel better if you avoid unnecessary calories. You'll also feel better if you avoid unnecessary purchases—lighter, healthier, freer. Go on a buying diet.

Third, get rid of things you think you need, but can actually live without. This goes beyond things you *know* you don't need into things you believe you need but can, in a pinch, forego. This is something I still find difficult, even after twenty years living under a vow of poverty. But I'm always happier after I've walked this path. After a friend cared for my father during his final illness, I gave her a treasured possession: a multicolored quilt given to me by some of the refugees in East Africa, which I had used on my bed. It was hard to give it away, but every time I see my friend, and remember her great kindness, I'm glad I did so.

Finally, here's a challenge: *get to know the poor.* That's difficult for some of us, since we are sometimes trained to ignore them, view them as lazy, or fear them. But finding opportunities to volunteer in a soup kitchen or homeless shelter (and finding appropriate and safe ways for your children to do so as well) will introduce you to people like Gauddy, Agustino, and Loyce in your own community. You will soon come to know them not as "the poor," but as individuals with their own stories.

They will have often suffered much, and it may, initially, be hard to be around them, but they can also teach you a great deal about gratitude, about perseverance, and about being close to God.

POVERTY OF SPIRIT

Many poor men and women instinctively turn to God: like Gauddy during times of joy or like Agustino during times of hope. One reason is that they live another kind of poverty that often accompanies material poverty: the radical understanding of dependence on God, called "poverty of spirit."

Poverty of spirit is an overlooked concept within many spiritual and religious circles. "Blessed are the poor in spirit" is the first saying in St. Matthew's account of the Sermon on the Mount (5:3–12). But for many believers, those words are just as mysterious as they were when Jesus first uttered them. If you ask a practicing Christian if he should be charitable, he will say yes. If you ask if he should be poor in spirit, he might say, "Huh?"

Perhaps not surprisingly, I first came into contact with real poverty of spirit in East Africa, but in a roundabout way.

Though I had looked forward to going to Nairobi, once I arrived I felt a crushing loneliness, since I was cut off from friends in the States, worried that I couldn't endure two years in East Africa, and concerned about picking up some rare tropical illness. (Before I left, my doctor gave me a pamphlet that helpfully pointed out all the exotic diseases I could contract while there.)

On top of that, I was first assigned to a job that consisted largely of paperwork. Had I come to Kenya to push papers? In a few months,

I would begin my work with the small businesses, the best job I've ever had, but at the time, life was both boring and lonely.

During this low ebb, my Jesuit formation director sent me a book to encourage me: *Poverty of Spirit,* by Johannes Baptist Metz, a German Catholic theologian.

Metz speaks of poverty of spirit as the inherent limitations that every human being faces in daily life. It is the spiritual awakening that comes with knowing not only the talents and gifts given us by God, which fill us with a grateful confidence, but also our limitations. Poverty of spirit means accepting that we are powerless to change certain aspects of our lives. "We are all members of a species that is not sufficient unto itself," he writes. "We are all creatures plagued by unending doubts and restless, unsatisfied hearts."

Poverty of spirit also means accepting that everyone will face disappointments, pain, suffering, and, eventually, death. Though this should be obvious to anyone who has thought seriously about life, Western culture often encourages us to avoid, ignore, or deny this essential truth—we are limited, finite, physical: human. And part of being human is that we sometimes suffer and are often powerless over what happens to us, to others, and to the world around us. Accepting this means moving closer to poverty of spirit.

Unlike the material poverty that brings misery to hundreds of millions of our fellow human beings and which I saw daily in Nairobi, spiritual poverty is something to be *sought.* And I don't romanticize material poverty: I have stepped over filthy streams of sewage and noisome piles of rotting garbage, eaten with poor refugees in drafty hovels, and seen all manner of physical deprivations and illness. Such poverty cannot be romanticized.

Poverty of spirit is different: it is a life-giving goal.

Poverty of spirit is another way of speaking of humility. Without it, we resist admitting our reliance on God, are tempted to try to make it on our own, and are more likely to despair when we fail. And since spiritual poverty recognizes our fundamental reliance on God, it lies at the heart of the spiritual life.

"Thus poverty of spirit is not just one virtue among many," writes Metz toward the end of his book. "It is the hidden component of every transcending act, the ground of every 'theological virtue.'"

THE THREE DEGREES OF HUMILITY

Ignatius put a premium on poverty of spirit. In the Spiritual Exercises, following the meditation on the Two Standards, he offers the framework of the Three Ways of Being Humble, also known as the Three Degrees of Humility.

In his book *Draw Me into Your Friendship*, David Fleming, S.J., describes Ignatius as laying out a spectrum of humility, in which we are encouraged to choose the greater degree, and so more closely follow Jesus. George Aschenbrenner, S.J., describes the three degrees in *Stretched for Greater Glory*, as "three ways of loving."

The First Degree is one in which you would always be obedient to "the law of God" by leading a moral life. Here you would do nothing to cut yourself off from God. You want to do the right thing. Aschenbrenner says, "This amounts to loving someone so much that you would go to whatever trouble may be involved to respond to that person's [in this case, God's] explicitly stated desire."

The Second Degree is one in which, when presented with an option for a choice in life, you strive to be free of wanting the choice that would bring wealth, honor, or a long life. It's the classic example of Ignatian "indifference" or "detachment." Not only will you do the right thing, you will be free to *accept* whatever life presents. In this stage, says Fleming, "the only real principle of choice is to do the will of God." You are detached and strive never to turn away from God. "This degree of love," writes Aschenbrenner, "goes beyond the first and presumes the freedom of indifference."

The Third Degree, the "most perfect" way, is one in which you actually *choose* the more humble way, in order to be like Christ. You desire so much to follow him that, as Fleming writes, "his experiences are reflected in my own." In other words, you choose to be poor and even rejected as Jesus was. Aschenbrenner notes, "Here the desire to imitate has become an eagerness to share . . . the whole being and condition of the Beloved."

Is this masochistic? Another confirmation of those stereotypes about how "sick" Christianity is? Only if it's misunderstood. The Third Degree of Humility does not seek poverty or rejection for its own sake, but as a way of identifying with Christ and as a way of freeing oneself from an exaggerated self-interest. The friendship analogy is useful: when your friend is suffering, are you willing to suffer with him?

The Third Degree is an often unattainable goal for me: most days I feel I can barely make it to the Second Degree! But it's an important one, because it helps to move us toward freedom from disordered attachments that keep us from following God. As Brian Daley, S.J., noted in an article called "To Be More Like Christ," this kind of humility makes us ready to be "as free as possible from our ingrained self-centeredness, as full a realization as possible of Jesus' concrete call to each individual to be a disciple in his image."

What Do You Believe?

Many Jesuit jokes play on our (supposed) struggles to be humble. One has a Jesuit, a Franciscan, and a Dominican dying and going to heaven. They are ushered into God's throne room, where God is seated on an immense, diamond-encrusted gold chair. God says to the Dominican, "Son of St. Dominic, what do you believe?" The Dominican answers, "I believe in God the Father, Creator of heaven and earth." God asks the Franciscan, "Son of St. Francis, what do you believe?" The Franciscan says, "I believe in your son, Jesus, who came to work with the poor." Finally God turns to the Jesuit and from his great throne asks, "Son of St. Ignatius, what do you believe?" The Jesuit says, "I believe . . . you're in my seat!"

BLESSED ARE THE POOR IN SPIRIT

Poverty of spirit does not take away joy in life. Quite the contrary. It is the gateway to joy, because it enables us to surrender to ultimate reliance on God, which leads to freedom. "Paradoxically, then, we are truly rich," writes Fleming, "with an identity that only God can give and no one can take from us."

Reliance on God may sound like a recipe for laziness, as if you needed to do nothing on your own. But the reality is the opposite. It is a practical stance that reminds you that you can't do everything. Many things are not within your power to change. Some things, outside of your control, need to be left to God. Spiritual poverty frees you from the despair that comes when you believe that you can rely only on your own efforts.

This insight can free you from a popular temptation these days: workaholism and messiahism. It's easy to imagine that you are indispensable, that everything depends on you, that you must do everything. Diligence can degenerate into a subtle form of pride. "Look how busy I am—I'm so important!" Or "Everything depends on me!" Poverty of spirit reminds you that there is only so much that you can do.

Or as my spiritual director said when I complained about having too many tasks to do, "There is a Messiah, and it's not you!"

Over and over in Kenya, I was invited to relinquish my desire to fix everything and to solve everyone's problems, not only because it was impossible, but also because that impossible task would have paralyzed me with despair. Moreover, it flew in the face of reality. Refugees given grants for sewing machines would return home and find that their homes had been torched by jealous neighbors. One man, a Ugandan cattle farmer named John, did everything necessary for success: located a plot of land, found the right type of cattle, and bought the correct kind of feed. John had done everything right. But he was forced to cease his business when a drought struck, which parched the land, killing the grass that fed his cows. I remember standing with him outside his farm when he asked, "What will I do now?"

I had no answer. I could not make it rain. I could not find him water in a parched land. All I could do was give him an additional grant to tide him over and pray with him for a change in weather. Poverty of spirit is a reflection of reality: we are often powerless to change things.

A Deep Sense of Humor

Let me have too deep a sense of humor ever to be proud.

Let me know my absurdity before I act absurdly.

Let me realize that when I am humble I am most human, most truthful, and most worthy of your serious consideration.

—Daniel Lord, S.J. (1888–1955)

Spiritual poverty also means freedom from the need for constant motion, constant work, and constant activity. It encourages you to say *no* from time to time, since you know that you can't do everything, please everyone, show up at every gathering, telephone every friend, and counsel every person in need. It means accepting that you cannot do everything at home, in your workplace, or in your church. It saves you from being a "human doing" instead of a "human being."

Ironically, our generous desire to do everything, care for everyone, and make everyone happy can lead to our becoming less attentive and more distracted, which does no one any good. Saying *no* to one thing means saying *yes* to another thing. Saying *no* to one more responsibility you cannot possibly assume means saying *yes* to greater attentiveness to what is already before you.

Poverty of spirit, then, is not a road to sadness; it is a path to freedom. It is not some mystical dogma that only the saints can follow; it is the simple acceptance of reality. Reminding you of your fundamental reliance on God, it is a stance that enables you to be more grateful for the blessings that come from God, because you know how precious they are. This is why Jesus calls the poor in spirit "blessed." Or in the original Greek, "happy."

Let me end with a story from Pedro Arrupe, the former superior general who did so much to invite the Jesuits to work with the poor. It beautifully encapsulates the Ignatian insights into simple living, poverty, and poverty of spirit.

WHAT A CONTRAST

Father Arrupe was known for his love of the poor. He once told the story of visiting some Jesuits working in a desperately poor slum in Latin America. During his visit, he celebrated Mass for the local people in a decrepit building; during the liturgy cats and dogs wandered in and out freely. Here's what happened after the Mass, in Arrupe's own words, taken from a book of interviews called *One Jesuit's Spiritual Journey:*

When it was over, a big devil whose hang-dog look made me almost afraid said, "Come to my place. I have something to give you." I was undecided; I didn't know whether to accept or not, but the priest who was with me said, "Accept, Father, they are good people." I went to his place; his house was a hovel nearly on the point of collapsing. He had me sit down on a rickety old chair. From there I could see the sunset. The big man said to me, "Look, sir, how beautiful it is!" We sat in silence for several minutes. The sun disappeared. The man then said, "I don't know how to thank you for all you have done for us. I have nothing to give you, but I thought you would like to see this sunset. You liked it, didn't you? Good evening." And then he shook my hand.

As I walked away I thought, "I have seldom met such a kindhearted person." I was strolling along that lane when a poorly dressed woman came up to me; she kissed my hand, looked at me, and with a voice filled with emotion said, "Father, pray for me and my children. I was at that beautiful Mass you celebrated. I must hurry home. But I have nothing to give my children. Pray to the Lord for me; he's the one who must help us." And she disappeared running in the direction of her home.

Many indeed are the things I learned thanks to that Mass among the poor. What a contrast with the great gatherings of the powerful of this world.

CHAPTER NINE

Like the Angels?

Chastity, Celibacy, and Love

HERE'S HOW ST. IGNATIUS Loyola famously begins—and famously ends—his discussion of chastity in the *Constitutions*.

> What pertains to the vow of chastity requires no interpretation, since it is evident how perfectly it should be preserved, by endeavoring therein to imitate the purity of the angels in cleanness of body and mind. Therefore, with this presupposed, we shall now treat of holy obedience.

When I first read that passage in the novitiate, I said to David Donovan, "That's it? Did I miss the rest of his discussion on chastity?"

"No," he laughed. "That's it!"

As John O'Malley notes in *The First Jesuits*, while Ignatius and the early Jesuits offered reflections about chastity elsewhere, for the most part it was understood that the vow was "clear-cut and needed no explanation."

So, according to Ignatius, Jesuits should observe chastity like the angels. And angels were popularly believed to have no sexual organs!

Sixteenth-century Christians, including Ignatius and the early Jesuits, understood sexuality in a vastly different light than we do. First of all, there was a heightened emphasis on chastity as a way to spiritual "purity," as Ignatius wrote. The ideal Christian should strive for the purity of Jesus, Mary, and the saints (and the angels). And purity included chastity. Peter Favre, one of the first Jesuits, made this connection early in his life: "When I was about twelve years of age," he wrote, "I went into a field where from time to time I helped to guard [his family's] flocks, and there, full of joy and with a great desire for purity I vowed perpetual chastity to our Lord."

That's a poignant image—Peter Favre surrounded by wildflowers, the sun overhead, ardently making a youthful vow to God. But few people would encourage that kind of promise today. For one thing, purity doesn't mean refraining from sex. Purity flows from a pure heart, and there are plenty of married men and women who have pure hearts. For another, what twelve-year-old (then or now) has an adequate understanding of sexuality to make a lifelong vow of chastity? But Favre lived in a different time.

Members in religious orders were also willing to go to extremes to encourage chastity, or as they would say, to "safeguard" it. Late in life Favre made another promise: never "putting my face" close to anyone—male or female, young or old, as a way of further preserving his chastity. St. Aloysius Gonzaga, a young nobleman-turned-Jesuit, maintained "custody of the eyes," which meant never looking a woman in the face—including his mother!

On the other hand, St. Ignatius Loyola, whom Peter Favre knew and Aloysius Gonzaga revered, enjoyed the warm friendship of a great many women, for whom he served, through letters or in person, as a valued spiritual director and counselor. As the authors of *The Spiritual Exercises Reclaimed* note, many of his women friends returned the favor by supporting Ignatius and his new religious order, particularly in terms of finances. Two women—Isabel Roser and Juana, the regent of Spain—even took vows as Jesuits. "A more accurate picture reveals Ignatius not as a solitary figure," the authors write, "but as a relational one; these relationships included specific women."

This complicated history leads to some provocative questions:

Can religious chastity teach us anything? Can St. Ignatius's ideas about chastity teach us anything? Can men who lived in a world where sexuality was considered dangerous—even evil—teach us anything about healthy, loving relationships?

You won't be surprised when I say that the answer to all these questions is: yes.

But you might be surprised when you find out that the answer has less to do with abstinence and purity and more to do with love and friendship. Because chastity is about love.

CHASTITY? CELIBACY?

Chastity is the most difficult thing to explain about life in a religious order. It inevitably conjures up the stereotype of the hateful, cold priest or the repressed, bitter nun—out of touch with their own sexuality, closed off to the world of love and human relationships, as well as rigid, cold, spiteful, and maybe a little cruel. And crazy, too.

In the wake of the sexual-abuse crisis in the Catholic Church, in which chastity was seen by the general public as a contributing cause, the vow of chastity engenders more suspicion than ever. Now it is seen as not only crazy, but unhealthy, sick, and—something that would have astonished sixteenth-century Christians—dangerous.

Popular thinking runs along three lines:

1. Chastity is unnatural; it tries to shut down a natural part of life and thus leads to unhealthy behaviors.
2. Chastity is unhealthy; therefore religious orders attract unhealthy people.
3. Chastity is impossible. No one can keep that vow with any integrity or honesty, so anyone who says he or she is celibate must be lying.

Before I continue, I should explain that despite their common usage there is a difference between chastity and celibacy. It's a bit complex, so bear with me.

Strictly speaking, chastity refers to the proper and loving use of our sexuality, something that everyone is called to. In his book on human sexuality, *In Pursuit of Love,* Vincent J. Genovesi, a Jesuit professor of moral theology, quotes another author who says that living as a chaste person means that our "external expressions" of sexuality will be "under the control of love, with tenderness and full awareness of the other." Summing up the work of another theologian, Genovesi calls chastity "honesty in sex," where our physical relationships "truthfully express" the level of personal commitment we have with the other. In other words, the goal of chastity is receiving and giving love.

The Catholic Church believes that everyone—married, single, vowed, ordained, lay, or clergy—is called to *this* kind of chastity, where your physical relationships express the degree of personal commitment, where you make the proper use of your sexuality, and where your sexuality is guided by love and care for the other person. Most people would agree with those general ideas: love, commitment, honesty, and care in our sexual relationships.

Celibacy is different. Technically, it is the restriction against marriage for members of the Catholic clergy. For instance, Jesuits take a *vow of chastity* after their novitiate, but priests make a *promise of celibacy* at their ordination.

Celibacy is a canonical (church law) requirement that could, theoretically, be lifted by the Catholic Church. During the first half of church history, no restrictions existed against marriage, and many priests were married men. As the Rev. Donald Cozzens writes in *Freeing Celibacy,* not until the twelfth century did clerical celibacy become the norm for the entire Western, or Latin, church. We know, for example, that St. Peter was married, since the Gospel of Mark speaks of his mother-in-law (1:29–31). Today there are many married Catholic priests: priests of the Eastern rites, or branches, of the

Catholic Church, and priests from other Christian denominations who convert to Catholicism but stay married. Even among Catholics, chastity and celibacy are confused, used improperly, and assumed to mean the same thing. Moreover, the spirituality surrounding both celibacy and chastity for priests and members of religious orders is similar. Sometimes people talk about "religious chastity," to distinguish between the chastity that everyone is called to and the kind that religious orders live.

Confusing, isn't it?

So here's what I'm going to do. Hereafter I'm going to talk about chastity in the way that most people understand it, that is, refraining from sex because of a religious commitment. More important, I'm going to describe what a life of religious chastity can teach you—even if you're having sex every day.

LOVING CHASTITY

Back to the old stereotype of the cold, rigid, bitter, hateful priest or nun. The irony is that some of history's most loving persons—those whom even nonbelievers admire—were chaste. Think of St. Francis of Assisi or Mother Teresa. Would anyone say they did not love? And by now you know that St. Ignatius Loyola was a compassionate, generous, and loving man.

Better yet, think of Jesus of Nazareth, who most serious Scripture scholars agree (for a variety of reasons) never married. Does anyone doubt that Jesus was a loving person?

Whenever I hear that stereotype of the cold priest, I always wish I could introduce people to all the loving priests, brothers, and sisters I've known, men and women who lead lives of loving chastity and who radiate love.

I wish you could meet my friend Bob, who, despite some chronic medical problems, worked for many years at a hardscrabble Native American reservation in South Dakota and now works as a spiritual director and art therapist in Boston. Few Jesuits are more loving or more beloved. Bob is small in stature with an outsized laugh: when you're watching a funny movie in a theater with him, his booming laughter turns every head in the audience.

The Native Americans with whom he worked first named him "Little Man with Big Laugh." "But that name didn't take," he explained once. "So they call me Holy Eagle with Gentle Voice instead."

Bob is one of the best listeners I've ever met. People naturally feel comfortable talking with Bob, perhaps because they sense, through his physical limitations, that he understands what it means to suffer and still find joy in life. Several times when I've come up against a thorny personal problem, Bob has listened intently, completely focused on my words. This is a form of chaste love.

Or I wish I could introduce you to Tim. During our graduate theology studies, Bob, Tim, and I lived together in the same Jesuit house in Cambridge, Massachusetts. Tim is a quiet, hardworking, studious fellow who was assigned to work as pastor of an inner-city parish in Chicago after he finished his studies. During the summer when I was recuperating from major surgery in Chicago (where I had that revelation on the operating table), Tim gave me a great gift.

Despite his busy schedule as a pastor, he drove to see me at a Jesuit community in Evanston, about an hour's drive away, every day. For two weeks Tim dutifully visited me, got me to laugh, took me for a drive, fixed me a meal when I was unable to, and talked to me about what I was experiencing. We weren't all that close during the time we lived together; we were after that summer. His generosity—quiet, unobtrusive, selfless—was a form of chaste love.

And I wish you could meet Sister Maddy, my friend at the retreat house in Gloucester, Massachusetts. As I mentioned before, we first met when we were both working in East Africa. Maddy, a practical and hardworking sister with a quick smile and short-cropped hair, worked with two other American sisters in a remote part of Tanzania and ran a girls' school in a remote village called Kowak. For their

Fall in Love

This meditation from Pedro Arrupe, S.J., may be his most famous piece of writing. There's just one problem: no one has been able to find it in any of his letters or speeches. One of his advisers, Vincent O'Keefe, S.J., told me it was most likely copied down by someone at a conference and circulated. And, said Father O'Keefe, it's just the sort of thing Arrupe would say.

Nothing is more practical than finding God, that is, than falling in love in a quite absolute, final way. What you are in love with, what seizes your imagination, will affect everything. It will decide what will get you out of bed in the morning, what you will do with your evenings, how you will spend your weekends, what you read, who you know, what breaks your heart, and what amazes you with joy and gratitude.

Fall in love, stay in love and it will decide everything.

vacations, the three sisters would come to our little Jesuit community in Nairobi. Maddy is a terrific cook who would relax by preparing colossal Italian meals for our community—so everyone involved looked forward to her vacation. After two years in Tanzania, she had a serious medical condition that forced her to leave the sisters and students at Kowak. A few years later she was able to return for a proper good-bye.

Since then, Maddy and I have directed many retreats together. Because of some physical limitations, Maddy has a difficult time navigating the sprawling grounds of the retreat house, but, even with freezing temperatures and two-feet-high snowdrifts, her joyful spirits are undimmed and her laughter unabated. A few years ago I signed up for a retreat at Gloucester and discovered that she was to be my director. Having a close friend as a director, I thought, would be odd. "Well, I'm going to treat you like I would treat any other director," I told her.

She laughed her hearty laugh. "And I'm going to treat you like any other retreatant!"

Maddy proved to be an astute director, who helped me through a difficult period in my life—negotiating artfully between the responsibilities of a spiritual director and those of a friend. Among other things, Maddy's hard work for her students in Tanzania and her patient listening to those at the retreat house in Gloucester are a form of chaste love.

Each of these friends—Bob, Tim, and Maddy—who all vowed chastity, show love in a variety of ways. Each reminds me of one of St. Ignatius Loyola's sayings, from the Exercises: "Love ought to manifest itself more by deeds than by words."

CHASTITY IS ABOUT LOVE

One of the main goals of chastity is to love as many people as possible as deeply as possible. That may seem strange to those used to defining chastity *negatively*—that is, as not having sex. But this has long been the tradition of the church. Chastity is another way to love and, as such, has a great deal to teach everyone, not just members of religious orders.

Chastity also frees you to serve people more readily. We're not attached to one person or to a family, so it's easier for us to move to another assignment. As the Jesuit *Constitutions* says, chastity is "essentially apostolic." It is supposed to help us become better "apostles." Like all the vows, chastity helps Jesuits to be "available," as Ignatius would say.

So chastity is about both love *and* freedom.

Chastity (remember I'm talking about religious chastity) is not for everyone. Obviously, most people are called to romantic love, marriage, sexual intimacy, children, and family life. Their primary way of loving is through their spouses and children. It is a more focused, more exclusive, way of loving. That is not to say that married couples and parents do not love others outside their families. Rather, the main focus of their love is God and their families.

For the person in a religious order, the situation is the opposite. You vow chastity to offer yourself to love God and make yourself available to love as many others as possible. Once again, this is not to say that married and single men and women cannot do this. Rather, this is the way that works best for *us*.

Chastity is also a reminder that it is possible to love well without being in an exclusive relationship and without being sexually active. In this way, the chaste person can serve as a signpost in our hypersexualized culture, where loving someone may be confused with hopping into bed. Thus chastity can help us to refocus our priorities: the goal of life, whether single, married, or religious, is to love.

Who is more loving? The head-over-heels-in-love couple with an active sex life; the committed middle-aged couple who have sex less frequently due to the demands of family life; or the tender elderly couple who, because of illness, are not sexually active at all? Who is more loving—the married man who loves his wife or the single woman who loves her friends? Who is more loving—the celibate priest or the sexually active wife?

The answer is: they are all loving. In different ways.

By the way, chastity doesn't lead to unhealthy behavior. The sex-abuse crisis in the Catholic Church was, as I see it, more about a small percentage of psychologically unhealthy men who should have never been admitted into seminaries or religious orders in the first place, and some bishops who should have never shuttled them from one parish to another, than it was about chastity per se.

Chastity also takes practice. You don't become a perfect husband or wife on the day of your wedding. Nor do you understand your chastity completely on the day of your vows. It takes time to grow into your vows in an integrated way. That's one reason for novitiates and seminaries—they function almost like an engagement, to see if this way of life is right for a person.

"What about lust?" a friend asked recently. Well, the chaste person still has his (or her) head turned by an attractive person and still longs for sex. We're human, after all. But when that happens, you remind yourself of a few things. First, it's natural. Second, the life you've chosen does not allow that. And third, if you're completely overcome with a constant desire for sexual intimacy, then something may be missing in your affective life. What is it? An intimate relationship with God in prayer? Fulfilling friendships? Satisfying work? Where might you be not responding to God's love in your chaste life? Because the chaste person not only makes a vow of chastity but also believes that God will help him in this.

Chastity also helps other people feel safe. People know that you've made a commitment to love them in a way that precludes using them, or manipulating them, or spending time with them simply as a means to an end. It gives people a space to relax. As a result, people can often feel freer with their own love.

A few years ago, as I mentioned, I worked with an acting troupe in New York City that was developing an Off-Broadway play on Jesus and Judas. Initially, I aided the playwright with his research for his play and met with the actor playing Judas. Eventually I was invited to work with the director and the cast.

For many hours we sat around a huge table in an Off-Broadway theater talking about the Gospels, about Jesus, and about sin, grace, despair, and hope. "Why did Judas betray Jesus?" "Why did the apostles run away after the crucifixion?" "Was Jesus in love with Mary Magdalene?" These spirited conversations were different from those I have with Catholics, who often feel (me included) that Catholics have all the answers already.

And here was a group of people inhabiting a world foreign to my own: the theater. When we began, they didn't know me at all, so I wondered how they would react to a Jesuit priest. But since they knew I was celibate, they knew I wasn't there for any other reason than to help them. Probably as a result, some felt comfortable sharing some intimate details of their lives with me—someone they barely knew—opening up during times of sorrow and celebrating during times of joy.

Their trust was a gift that helped me, in a sense, fall in love with all of them. Whenever I entered the dressing room, I was usually surrounded by smiling faces and plenty of hugs.

As in other situations, I realized I was there not just to give love but to receive it. When the show closed, I recognized that I was also called not to *hold on* to their love. While I hoped that some of us would remain friends afterward (and we have), I knew I couldn't "possess" anyone's love. It had to be freely given and freely received.

That's another lesson of chastity: love cannot be owned.

My friend Chris, a Jesuit brother who works in New York City, said it's similar for school teachers. "It's just like when a school year ends," he said at the time. "You have to love freely and be loved freely, but you have to remember that you can't hold on to it." As Jesus said after the Resurrection, "Do not hold on to me."

This may be one of the greatest gifts that the chaste person can offer: showing not only that there are many ways to love, but that loving a person *freely*, without clinging to him or her, is a gift to both the lover and the beloved. Often we are tempted to think that loving someone—a spouse, a boyfriend or girlfriend, or even just a friend—means clinging to them, which is a subtle form of ownership. But love means embracing the poverty of not owning the other.

So chastity might be able to teach the world about a free way to love and a loving way to be free.

Is It Possible?

But is religious chastity really possible, with any degree of healthiness, integrity, or honesty?

With God's help it is. So let me talk briefly about my own experience with chastity, which I hope might offer you some insights into your own life of loving and being loved.

A few months into my novitiate, David told me that at some point as a Jesuit I would fall in love and that others would fall in love with me. I was horrified!

His response was memorable. "If you don't fall in love from time to time," he said, "there's something wrong with you." He went on to explain: "It's both human and natural. The question is: what do you *do* when you fall in love?"

Priests, and men and women in religious orders, have to accept the possibility that they will fall in love. If you hope to be a loving man or woman, you will run the "risk" of falling in love. Jesus, as a fully human person, also opened himself up to that possibility—when he offered his heart to others and opened himself to receiving their love.

Despite what you might read in popular novels, Jesus was not secretly married. It is pretty clear from the New Testament that Jesus of Nazareth remained unmarried throughout his life. (As I wrote earlier, the Gospel writers speak freely about Jesus' brothers and sisters. Not mentioning a wife—if he had one—would be strange.) But Jesus, in his humanity, was as prone as anyone to falling in love and having others fall in love with him. His response was to love others both chastely and deeply.

What happens when a member of a religious order falls in love? He must choose. Either he finds that he cannot live his vows and must leave the order, or he must reaffirm his commitment to his vows. This is somewhat similar to the situation for a married person who falls in love with someone other than his or her spouse, said David. In both cases, you remind yourself of your commitment and take the right steps to honor it.

David was right. Not long after the novitiate I fell in love. The depth of my love and the passion I felt was unexpected, overwhelming, and confusing. For a few months I believed that this was the person with whom I could spend the rest of my life. It was both wonderful and terrible. Wonderful because I was in love and being loved. Terrible because continuing with the relationship would mean leaving the Jesuits.

In the midst of the turmoil, I met with my spiritual director. He listened to my story and then said nearly the same thing as David had. "Falling in love is part of being human, perhaps the most human thing you could do. It shows that you are a loving person. That's a wonderful thing for anyone." He paused. "But you have to decide what you want to do now. You are free to leave the Jesuits and pursue this relationship, or you are free to honor your commitment and end the relationship."

After prayer, spiritual direction, and conversations with friends, I saw that though I had fallen in love, my overpowering desire was to remain committed to my vows. Leaving seemed appealing at times, but when I looked back over the years I saw how happy I was as a Jesuit. Also, I knew that I had flourished when living a life of chastity—not having one exclusive relationship, but many.

Like Ignatius, who sat on his sick bed and "discerned" his feelings about two paths in life, when I thought of leaving the Jesuits, I felt despair, frustration, and disquiet. When I thought of staying, I felt peaceful, hopeful, and uplifted. "Well *that* sounds clear enough!" said a close friend at the time. "You do believe in all that Ignatian stuff, don't you?"

Falling in love enabled me to grow in wisdom about the heart and the head. It also furnished me with some insights into the human condition that have helped when counseling others. It helped me to become more, in a word, human.

Moreover, it helped me see that we are often presented with competing desires in life. In Ignatian spirituality we are asked to discern which is the greater desire, or the "governing desire." Competing desires do not negate the choice that you have made: they simply make it more real. What married person does not occasionally feel the same? Who doesn't feel the occasional pang of regret over a life-changing decision? The key is understanding your governing desire, as well as honoring your original commitment.

Chastity is not easy. The more loving you are, the more likely it is that you will fall in love, and the more likely it is that others will fall in love with you.

The life of religious chastity can also be lonely. No matter how many friends you have, how close you are to your family, how supportive your religious community is, and how satisfying your ministry is, you still have to face an empty bed at night. There is no one person with whom you can share good news, on whose shoulder you can cry, or on whom you can always count for a hug after a hard day. Single, divorced, or widowed men and women know this feeling too.

Charles M. Shelton, S.J., a professor of psychology at Regis University in Denver, put it this way in a recent conversation: "Whenever I speak to young Jesuits about chastity, I begin by saying that chastity means you will never be the most important person in anyone's life. First, their faces get quizzical and then a number start to evince concern. After a few moments, I ask them if it's okay that they'll never be the most important person in someone's life. Finally, I say that even if it is okay now, for every Jesuit there comes a time when this realization is felt acutely. It's a good springboard to discuss the reality of the vow."

Ultimately, as Shelton says, the vow becomes not something that you do, but something deeper. "In the novitiate, if someone asked me why I don't have sex, I might have said, 'Because it violates the vow.' Now I would say, 'That's not who I am.'" Married couples also may relate to that last statement. In the movie *Moonstruck,* when a married woman is propositioned by a friendly man her own age, she declines by saying, "I know who I am." It's about integrity and commitment.

Finally, says Shelton, there needs to be something "special" about chastity. Shelton, for example, is a chaplain for two sports teams at the university—soccer and baseball. That means spending time with the students, taking an interest in who they are and what they do, going to the games, and getting to know their families. These things take up time that he would rightfully want to give to his family, were he married.

"But there is something more," he says. "I've come to realize that I wouldn't trade those moments, and the enduring relationships that have been forged after the students graduate, or the times that I've been available to a student in crisis, for a life with a wife and kids. Chastity provides me with something I couldn't have if I were married, and which means just as much. This is what I would call 'special' for me." He describes it in the same way that married couples might speak of their love: a special gift.

How Can I Love Chastely?

At this point you still might be saying to yourself, *So what? So what if that's how chastity works for a Jesuit?* Or, more bluntly, *Sex is an enjoyable part of my life, so what does chastity have to do with me?*

Well, the insights of religious chastity can help you even if you're not a Catholic priest or in a religious order—namely, as a reminder that there are ways other than sex by which you can give and receive love. My friends Maddy, Bob, and Tim, all of whom live chastely, showed me love through their actions at different points in my life. These ways can be as valuable, meaningful, and important as a sexual expression of love.

Religious chastity means that you love people outside the context of a romantic relationship. And, if you think about it, that covers most people in your own life. If you're single, widowed, or divorced, it covers everyone; if you're in a committed relationship (married, engaged, etc.), it covers all but one person. So the insights of chaste love are more relevant to your life than you might at first think.

So how can you love chastely in your own life?

Let me suggest five brief ways based on Ignatius's dictum that love shows itself more in deeds.

First, *listen compassionately.* As I mentioned, my friend Bob (Holy Eagle with Gentle Voice) is a good listener. A few years ago, he helped me work through a difficult personal problem by listening first. But real listening is an art. Before Bob even said one word, he listened to my entire story, for almost an hour, with great concentration. Without true, compassionate, attentive listening the next steps—advice, counsel, comfort—will fail, because you haven't taken the time to understand the other.

Compassionate listening is also an important way of making someone feel respected and loved. Often we are embarrassed by our problems, especially when we feel that we are in some way responsible for them. Having someone listen even to our most mortifying mistakes reminds us that we are loved in the midst of our struggles, which is always a welcome gift.

Listening in joyful times is important, too. Letting someone you love share good news with you—even if it relates to a part of her life that is unfamiliar to you—can magnify her own joy.

Second, *be present*. As Jesuit novices, when we were working as hospital chaplains we were taught that a "ministry of presence," simply being with another person, is an important part of pastoral care. While there is often little that you can do for a sick person, you can be with him or her.

This is frequently the case when loved ones are going through a hard time: often, since we can't solve their problems, the most loving thing we can do is just be with them. As Woody Allen said, "Ninety percent of life is just showing up." Something similar may hold true for chaste love. When Tim visited me every day during my long recuperation in Chicago, his quiet presence helped me on the road to recovery and did something else, too: it made me feel his affection more than any phone call or card could.

Third, *do something practical*. Sometimes, on the other hand, you need to *do* something beyond listening or being present. When Maddy went to Tanzania, she helped to build a school and teach young girls living in a remote area. When she came to our community in Nairobi, she cooked her famous Italian meals for us. She did something practical that helped people in a concrete way and in doing so expressed her love. Again: "Love ought to manifest itself more by deeds than by words."

Here's a good question to ask: *What active ways of chaste loving can be part of my life?* How about: Help your elderly mother clean her house. Drive a sick friend to the hospital. Babysit for a stressed young couple. Take a friend out to dinner even if it's not her birthday or a special event. Write a letter to someone whom you know is lonely. Drop someone a note on his birthday and tell him why you value his friendship. These are all ways of loving.

Fourth, *love freely.* One of the hardest parts of love is this: allowing the other to love you as he or she can, not as you want to be loved. Have you ever caught yourself thinking that your beloved *should* do this or that? If she really loved me, you say, she would do this. We often expect the beloved to be completely focused on our needs. But your beloved may not be able to do precisely what you want. Now, in some marriages partners may have to ask each other to more closely attend to their needs. Still, *demanding* this (whether you say it aloud or just believe it) essentially takes away a person's freedom. It can cheapen and even destroy loving relationships.

A few close friends of mine, for instance, aren't very good at "keeping in touch." They've always been that way—with me and others they love. It's simply the way they are. Accepting them as they are means not only trusting in their love, but respecting how they choose to love.

Giving people the freedom to be who they are is a form of love. It says, "I love you for who you are, not for who I want you to be." This reverences the person God created.

Fifth, *forgive.* Even those who love us most will occasionally hurt us. Perhaps they say something needlessly harsh, perhaps they disappoint us with a thoughtless action, perhaps they even betray us. Can you forgive them? Some of the unhappiest people I've ever met are those who refuse to forgive a spouse or a family member and find themselves trapped in a world of bitterness and recrimination.

Forgiveness releases the other from the trap of guilt and can also help to release you from your own anger. It is never easy, but in the end it is an act of love that heals both the forgiver and forgiven. That may be one reason why Jesus of Nazareth stressed it so often in his ministry of love.

Sixth, *pray*. Ask God to help those you love. Ask God to be close to them. Most of all, ask God to allow you to see others the way God does.

It may sound strange to hear these simple things described as acts of love. Yet they are ways of expressing love in a chaste way. And, by the way, like any act of real love, these actions can be difficult. "Love in action is a harsh and dreadful thing compared to love in dreams," wrote Fyodor Dostoevsky.

And when loving becomes hard, it helps to know that God desires for you to be loving and is always with you as you do so.

Such chaste ways of loving can help those who are not in a committed relationship and who fear they might not be able to live a loving life recognize that they can lead lives of love and intimacy. While their actions are not sexual, they can be among the most powerful signs of love that one can give.

Also, for those who feel trapped in relationships that seem to be *only* about sex, these insights about chastity remind us that love is much fuller than simply sexual intercourse, as wonderful as that is.

Finally, these insights can help those who are leading healthy and sexually fulfilled married lives by reminding them that love can take many forms. The insights of chastity can enrich all of us, whether or not we make a vow to live that way of life.

Now, you may have noticed that many of the things being said about love can be said about friendship. And here is another area where the experiences of the chaste person are useful for everyone. Because the one who lives his or her chastity in a healthy way in a religious community is also the one who deeply values friends.

Friendship is essential for the healthy Jesuit. And for the healthy single person. And for the healthy married person. For everyone. So let's talk about an underappreciated part of the spiritual life: friendship.

CHAPTER TEN

More by Deeds Than by Words

Friendship and Love

SOME PEOPLE CLING TO the idea that being a member of a religious order means you don't have to care about real-life human relationships. The thinking goes like this: since we spend all of our time in prayer, we never have to relate to any actual human beings and never have to deal with any interpersonal problems. And we're thought to be solitary types unconcerned with something as commonplace as friends.

But overall, Jesuits have a lot of experience developing friendships. First, as chaste men, we cannot enjoy the intimate sexual relationships that married men and women can. So besides relying on our friendship with God, our families, and our communities, we count on the love of close friends, both men and women.

Second, Jesuits move around frequently, sent from job to job, and place to place. Over the course of the past twenty years as a Jesuit, I've lived in Boston, Jamaica, New York, Boston again, Chicago, Nairobi, New York again, Boston again, and New York again. Each move meant discovering and rediscovering friends. Despite stereotypes people have about celibacy, Jesuits have to grow in the ability to make and keep close friendships. And we value them greatly.

Single, divorced, and widowed people know about this. A single friend of mine was once asked by her company to move far away. Her manager said, "You're single. You don't have any kids. Moving will be easy for you." But precisely since she didn't have a husband or children as a built-in and portable support system, she didn't want to leave, because she would be leaving her *only* supports behind—her friends. They were her primary source of love and affection.

Another stereotype is that we Jesuits don't know much about human relationships since we're so "Christian." My brother-in-law once said, "It must be nice to live in a place where no one argues."

"What do you mean?" I asked.

"Well," he said, "isn't it sort of illegal for Jesuits not to be nice to one another?"

That sums up the common thinking about religious communities: they're full of holy people who always get along. To that I say, "Ha!"

So the third reason we have become proficient in friendship is that living in a religious order means living with actual human beings who have competing interests and strong opinions. Over time you become adept at dealing with various kinds of personalities. Until my brother-in-law got to know some real-life Jesuits, he remained convinced of our superhuman goodness.

SUNTNE ANGELI?

It reminded me of a story, perhaps apocryphal, about the American Jesuits in the 1860s who were planning a new theology school for young Jesuits in rural Maryland, in a town called Woodstock. Huge numbers of men were then entering seminaries and religious orders, so the building would have to be vast.

The Jesuit provincial worked diligently with architects to draw up plans for the complex, with hundreds of rooms for the Jesuit priests, brothers, and scholastics (those in training); classrooms; an immense dining room; and an ornate chapel. No detail was left out. After poring over the blueprints, the provincial mailed the plans to the Jesuit headquarters in Rome.

A few months later the drawings were returned with a single Latin phrase scrawled on the bottom of the blueprints: *Suntne angeli?*

Which means, "Are they angels?"

The architects had left out the bathrooms.

No, we are not angels. And that extends beyond our use of bathrooms. We can be short-tempered, shortsighted, and just plain short with one another. (As an aside, the architect quickly tacked on two tall towers for the bathrooms. Years later, a visiting nun wrote a poem that praised the Jesuits' doing their thinking "in the white towers," which was probably true.)

Jesuit community is a great blessing. The men with whom I've lived for the past twenty-one years are joyful, prayerful, and hard-working—and so different from one another. As the saying goes, "If you've met one Jesuit, you've met one Jesuit!" One friend is a gerontologist who enjoys fly-fishing. Another is a prison chaplain who keeps pet ferrets. Another is a former political consultant who sings in piano bars. All enrich my life with their insights, inspire me with their faith, and challenge me to become a better person. After twenty-one years as a Jesuit, I couldn't imagine my life without my Jesuit friends. Whenever I think of Jesus' promise to his disciples that anyone who follows him will receive a "hundredfold" of what-ever he has given up, I think of my Jesuit friends.

But community life can be a challenge. One Jesuit thinks we aren't living simply enough. Another thinks we're living too simply. One thinks that if you find someone's wet clothes in the community washing machine, you should put them in the dryer. That's common courtesy, he says. Another is angry when you do just that with his clothes: "You've shrunk my cotton shirts!"

More seriously, as in any human environment, resentments creep into communities, grudges intensify, and relationships become cold. One friend joked that his friends used to speak of the "Ice House," the fictional Jesuit residence for the coldest men of the province. "But we always debated," he said. "Who would be the superior? Who was the coldest?"

The seventeenth-century Jesuit saint John Berchmans, who died at age twenty-two, before finishing his Jesuit training, said,

Vita communis est mea maxima penitentia. Some Jesuits translate that as "The *common life* is my greatest penance." That is, the common life of all men and women is difficult enough. But most Jesuits believe it's more accurately translated as, "Life *in community* is my greatest penance." (On the other hand, as Avery Cardinal Dulles once remarked about Berchmans, "I wonder what the community thought of *him!*")

Like any group—a family, a business, a parish—a Jesuit community can be the source of both joy and grief. Living peacefully with others and maintaining healthy friendships requires a great deal of love, patience, and wisdom.

But that's a challenge for everyone—not just Jesuits. All of us are called to live compassionately with one another and maintain healthy friendships with love, patience, and wisdom. None of us are angels.

So given our common desires for love and friendship, and our common human shortcomings, what does the way of Ignatius and the traditions of the Jesuits say about love, friendship, and human relationships?

THE PRESUPPOSITION

The Spiritual Exercises begins with good advice. In what he calls his Presupposition, Ignatius says that we "ought to be more eager to put a good interpretation on a neighbor's statement than to condemn it."

Always give people the benefit of the doubt. What's more, says Ignatius, if you're not sure what a person means, you should, says Ignatius, "ask how the other means it." Ignatius placed that crucial advice at the beginning of the Exercises to ensure that both the spiritual director and the retreatant don't misunderstand each other. Each presupposes that the other is trying to do his or her best.

This wisdom is applicable not simply for spiritual direction. It's a key insight for healthy relationships within families, in the workplace, and among friends. And while most people would agree with it, in principle, we often do just the opposite. We expect others to judge us according to our *intentions,* but we judge others according to their *actions.*

> Beware of condemning any man's action. Consider your neighbor's intention, which is often honest and innocent, even though his act seems bad in outward appearance.
>
> —St. Ignatius Loyola

In other words, we say to ourselves, *My intention was good. Why don't they see this?* But when it comes to other people, we often fail to give them the benefit of the doubt. We say, "Look what they did!"

The Presupposition helps us remember the other person's intention, which helps ground relationships in openness. You approach every interaction with an open mind and heart by presuming—even when it's hard to do so—that the other person is doing his or her best and isn't out to get you.

The Presupposition also helps to release you from grudges and resentments. It makes it less likely that you will approach a thorny relationship in terms of a battle. Rather than steeling yourself for another confrontation with your enemy, which takes a great deal of energy, you can relax.

Sometimes the other person *is* out to get you—for example, in a contentious office environment. Few people are *angeli.* But that doesn't mean human interactions should be approached as battles. Instead of preparing for war, you can set aside your armor. This may help the other person feel better able to deal with *you*—because most likely you are part of the problem. The Presupposition steers you away from anger and so provides the other person with the emotional space needed to meet you on more peaceful territory. It may even invite him or her to change.

My mother once told me that at her local supermarket worked a checkout clerk who had a "mean look and a grumpy disposition." None of the other clerks liked her. My mother remembered something her own mother had told her, another version of the Presupposition: "Be kind to everyone, because you never know what problems they have at home." So my mother decided to shower the grumpy clerk with kindness and made it a point to talk with her whenever she could. In time, the woman softened. "I discovered," said my mother, "that her mother, whom she cared for, was ill and that she herself had neck problems after a car accident." You never know what problems people might have.

The Presupposition also helps *you* stay open to change, growth, and forgiveness. Peter Favre, one of the first Jesuits, spent many years interacting with the new Christian denominations of his age. In that era Catholics and Protestants were intensely suspicious of one another. For many Protestants, Catholics were "papists," Rome was "Babylon," and the pope was the "Antichrist." For Catholics, Protestants were simply heretics.

Favre adamantly refused to let those beliefs close his heart, which was extraordinary for the time. "Remember," he wrote to a Jesuit asking for advice, "if we want to be of help to them, we must be careful to regard them with love, to love them in deed and in truth, and to banish from our souls anything that might lessen our love and esteem for them." That is an astonishing comment in an era of bad feelings.

My favorite quote from Favre on the matter is even simpler: "Take care, take care never to shut your heart against anyone."

Openness will not cure every relationship, but it can provide an opening for change, and it certainly won't make things any worse. The Presupposition can make healthy relationships healthier and unhealthy relationships less unhealthy.

IGNATIUS AND HIS FRIENDS

With his prodigious talent for friendship, Ignatius enjoyed close relations with a large circle of friends. (That is one reason for his enthusiasm for writing letters.) Indeed, the earliest way that Ignatius referred to the early Jesuits was not with phrases like "Defenders of the Faith" or "Soldiers of Christ," but something simpler. He described his little band as "Friends in the Lord."

Friendship was an essential part of his life. Two of his closest friends were his college roommates, Peter Favre, from the Savoy region of France, and Francisco de Javier, the Spaniard later known as St. Francis Xavier.

The three met at the Collège Sainte-Barbe at the University of Paris, then Europe's leading university, in 1529. By the time they met Ignatius, Peter and Francis were already fast friends who shared lodgings. The two had studied for the previous few years for their master's degrees; both were excellent students. And both had heard stories about Ignatius before meeting him: the former soldier was a notorious figure on campus, known for his intense spiritual discipline and habit of begging alms. At thirty-eight, Ignatius was much older than Peter and Francis, who were both twenty-three at the time. And Ignatius's path to the university was more circuitous. After his soldiering career, his recuperation, and his conversion, he had spent months in prayer trying to discern what to do with his life.

Ultimately, he decided that an education was required. So Ignatius went to school, taking elementary grammar lessons with young boys and, later, studying at the universities of Alcalá and Salamanca. His studies provide us with one of the more remarkable portraits of his newfound humility: the once-proud soldier squeezed into a too-small desk beside young boys in the classroom, making up for lost time.

Several years later, he enrolled at the University of Paris, where he met Favre and Xavier. There, in Favre's words, the three shared "the same room, the same table and the same purse."

Ignatius's commitment to a simple life impressed his new friends. So did his spiritual acumen. For Favre, a man troubled all his life by a "scrupulous" conscience, that is, an excessive self-criticism, Ignatius was a literal godsend. "He gave me an understanding of my conscience," wrote Favre. Ultimately, Ignatius led Peter through the Spiritual Exercises, something that dramatically altered Favre's worldview.

This happened despite their very different backgrounds. And here is one area where Ignatius and his friends highlight an insight on relationships: friends need not be cut from the same cloth. The friend with whom you have the least in common may be the most helpful for your personal growth. Ignatius and Peter had, until they met, led radically different lives. Peter came to Paris at age nineteen after what his biographer called his "humble birth," having spent his youth in the fields as a shepherd. Imbued with a simple piety toward Mary, the saints, relics, processions, and shrines, and also angels, Peter clung to the simple faith of his childhood. Ignatius, on the other hand, had spent many years as a courtier and some of them as a soldier, undergone a dramatic conversion, subjected himself to extreme penances, and wandered to Rome and the Holy Land in pursuit of his goal of following God's will.

One friend had seen little of the world; the other much. One had always found religion a source of solace; the other had proceeded to God along a tortuous path.

Ultimately, Ignatius helped Peter to arrive at some important decisions through the freedom offered in the Spiritual Exercises. Peter's indecision before this moment sounds refreshingly modern, much like the indecision of any college student today. He wrote about it in his journals:

Before that—I mean before having settled on the course of my life through the help given to me by God through Iñigo—I was always very unsure of myself and blown about by many winds: sometimes wishing to be married, sometimes to be a doctor, sometimes a lawyer, sometimes a lecturer, sometimes a professor of theology, sometimes a cleric without a degree—at times wishing to be a monk.

In time, Peter decided to join Ignatius on his new path, whose ultimate destination was still unclear. Peter, sometimes called the "Second Jesuit," was enthusiastic about the risky venture from the start. "In the end," he writes, "we became one in desire and will and one in a firm resolve to take up the life we lead today." His friend changed his life. Later, Ignatius would say that Favre became the most skilled of all the Jesuits in giving the Spiritual Exercises.

Ignatius would change the life of his other roommate, too. Francisco de Jassu y Javier, born in 1506 in the castle of Javier, was an outstanding athlete and student. He began his studies in Paris at the age of nineteen. Every biographer describes Francis as a dashing young man—with boundless ambition. "Don Francisco did not share the humble ways of Favre," wrote one.

Francis Xavier was far more resistant to change than Peter Favre had been. Only after Peter left their lodgings to visit his family, when Ignatius was alone with the proud Spaniard, was he able to slowly break down Xavier's stubborn resistance. Legend has it that Ignatius quoted a line from the New Testament, "What does it profit them if they gain the world, but lose or forfeit themselves?" As John O'Malley writes in *The First Jesuits,* Francis's conversion was "as firm as Favre's but more dramatic because his life to that point had shown signs of more worldly ambitions."

It is impossible to read the journals and letters of these three men—Ignatius the founder, Xavier the missionary, and Favre the spiritual counselor—without noticing the differences in temperaments and talents.

In later years Ignatius would become primarily an administrator, guiding the Society of Jesus through its early days, spending much of his time laboring over the Jesuit *Constitutions*. Xavier became the globe-trotting missionary sending back letters crammed with hair-raising adventures to thrill his brother Jesuits. (And the rest of Europe, too; Xavier's letters were the equivalent of action-adventure movies for Catholics of the time.) Favre, on the other hand, spent the rest of his life as a spiritual counselor sent to spread the Catholic faith during the Reformation. His work was more diplomatic, requiring artful negotiation through the variety of religious wars at the time.

Alike in Spirit and in Love

Francis Xavier writes from India, in 1545, to his Jesuit friends in Rome, expressing love for his faraway friends:

> God our Lord knows how much more consolation my soul would have from seeing you than from my writing such uncertain letters as these to you because of the great distance between these lands and Rome; but since God has removed us, though we are so much alike in spirit and in love, to such distant lands, there is no reason . . . for a lessening of love and care in those who love each other in the Lord.

Their letters reveal how different were these three personalities. They also make it easy to see how much they loved one another. "I shall never forget you," wrote Ignatius in one letter to Francis. And when, during his travels, Xavier received letters from his friends, he would carefully cut out their signatures and carried them "as a treasure," in the words of his biographer Georg Schurhammer, S.J.

The varied accomplishments of Ignatius, Francis, and Peter began with the commitment they made to God and to one another in 1534. In a chapel in the neighborhood of Montmartre in Paris, the three men, along with four other new friends from the university—Diego Laínez, Alfonso Salmerón, Simon Rodrigues, and Nicolás Bobadilla—pronounced vows of poverty and chastity together. Together they offered themselves to God. (The other three men who would round out the list of the "First Jesuits," Claude Jay, Jean Codure, and Paschase Broët, would join after 1535.)

Even then, friendship was foremost in their minds. Laínez noted that though they did not live in the same rooms, they would eat together whenever possible and have frequent friendly conversations, cementing what one Jesuit writer called "the human bond of union." In a superb article in the series *Studies in the Spirituality of Jesuits,* titled "Friendship in Jesuit Life," Charles Shelton, the professor of psychology, writes, "We might even speculate whether the early Society would have been viable if the early companions had not enjoyed such a rich friendship."

The mode of friendship among the early Jesuits flowed from Ignatius's "way of proceeding." For want of a better word, they did not try to *possess* one another. In a sense, it was a form of poverty. Their friendship was not self-centered, but other-directed, forever seeking the good of the other. The clearest indication of this is the willingness of Ignatius to ask Francis to leave his side and become one of the church's great missionaries.

It almost didn't happen. The first man that Ignatius wanted to send for the mission to "the Indies" fell ill. "Here is an undertaking for you," said Ignatius. "Good," said Francis, "I am ready." Ignatius knew that if he sent Francis away, he might never see his best friend again.

So did Francis. In a letter written from Lisbon, Portugal, Francis wrote these poignant lines as he embarked. "We close by asking God our Lord for the grace of seeing one another joined together in the next life; for I do not know if we shall ever see each other in this. . . . Whoever will be the first to go to the other life and does not find his brother whom he loves in the Lord, must ask Christ our Lord to unite us all there."

During his travels, Francis would write Ignatius long letters, not simply reporting on the new countries that he had explored and the new peoples he was encountering, but expressing his continuing affection. Both missed each other, as good friends do. Both recognized the possibility that one would die before seeing the other again.

"[You] write me of the great desires that you have to see me before you leave this life," wrote Francis. "God knows the impression that these words of great love made upon my soul and how many tears they cost me every time I remember them." Legend has it that Francis knelt down to read the letters he received from Ignatius.

Francis's premonitions were accurate. After years of grueling travel that took him from Lisbon to India to Japan, Francis stepped aboard a boat bound for China, his final destination. In September 1552, twelve years after he had bid farewell to Ignatius, he landed on the island of Sancian, off the coast of China. After falling ill with a fever, he was confined to a hut on the island, tantalizingly close to his ultimate goal. He died on December 3, and his body was first buried on Sancian and then brought back to Goa, in India.

Dear Brothers

So that I may never forget you and ever have a special remembrance of you, I would have you know, dear brothers, that for my own consolation, I have cut your names from the letters which you have written to me with your own hands so that I may constantly carry them with me together with the vow of profession which I made. . . . I gave thanks first of all to God our Lord, and then to you, most dear Brothers and Fathers, for the fact that God has so made you that I derive such great consolation from bearing your names. And since we shall soon see each other in the next life with greater peace than we have in this, I say no more.

—St. Francis Xavier, from the Malacca Islands in 1546,
to his Jesuit friends in Rome

Several months afterward, and unaware of his best friend's death, Ignatius, living in the Jesuit headquarters in Rome, wrote Francis asking him to return home.

FRIENDSHIP AND FREEDOM

One important insight we can take from the friendships of the early Jesuits—especially between Ignatius, Francis, and Peter—has to do with the complex interplay between freedom and love.

Friendship is a blessing in any life. For believers it is also one of the ways God communicates God's own friendship. But for friendship to flourish, neither the friendship nor the friend can be seen as an object to be possessed. One of the best gifts to give a friend is freedom.

This is a constant motif in the lives of the early Jesuits. A more selfish Ignatius would have kept Francis in Rome, to keep him company and to give him support, rather than allowing his friend to follow his heart. Shelton suggests in his article "Friendship in Jesuit Life" that the early Jesuits found their friendships to be a "secure base," a safe place that enabled them to enjoy their lives and complete their work, rather than worry about the relationship too much.

What does this have to say to you? After all, you're not going to lead a life remotely like those of Ignatius, Peter, or Francis. Still, we can sometimes find ourselves wanting to possess, control, or manipulate our friends as well as our spouses or family members.

How many times have you wondered why your friends weren't "better" friends? And how many times did being a "better" friend mean meeting *your* needs? How often have you wondered why your friends or family members don't support you more? How often have you worried whether you were being a good friend? These are natural feelings. Most of us also know the heartache of seeing friends move away, or change, or grow less available to us.

So how were Ignatius, Francis, and Peter able to be such close friends and be free at the same time?

Often I've had to remind myself that my friends do not exist simply to support, comfort, or nourish me. A few years ago, one of my best friends told me he was being sent to work in a parish in Ghana, in West Africa.

Matt was well prepared for his work in West Africa. Twice during his Jesuit training he had spent time in Ghana, living in a remote village with poor fishermen and their families and helping out at a small parish, all the while learning the local languages. Later, during graduate studies in theology, when we lived in the same community, Matt tailored some of his courses for his work in West Africa.

Matt told me how excited he was to be returning to Ghana, now as a priest. Knowing how seriously he had prepared for this work, and how much he loved Ghana, I should have been happy for him. Instead, selfishly, I was sad for myself, knowing that I wouldn't see him for a few years. Sadness is natural for anyone saying good-bye; I would have been a robot if I hadn't felt disappointed.

Still, it was hard to move away from wanting Matt to remain behind—to meet my needs. It was the opposite of the freedom that Ignatius and Francis had shown, which valued the good of the other person. It was an example of the possessiveness that can sometimes characterize and, if left unchecked, damage relationships. Needed was Ignatian freedom and detachment.

William Barry, the Jesuit spiritual writer, is also a trained psychologist. Recently I asked him about this tendency to possessiveness in friendship. "You need close friends, but you don't want to cling to them out of a desire to keep them around you," he said. "But this would be true for anyone, not simply for Jesuits." He, too, pointed to the early Jesuits as models. "Francis Xavier has such a deep love for his friends, and yet this doesn't keep him from volunteering and never being seen again."

Another story that illustrates this freedom comes from the seventeenth century, when Alphonsus Rodríguez, the doorkeeper at the Jesuit College in Majorca, Spain, became friends with another Jesuit, Peter Claver.

Alphonsus had come to the Society of Jesus by a circuitous route. Born in 1533, he was the second son of a prosperous cloth merchant in Segovia. When Peter Favre visited the city to preach, the Rodríguez family provided hospitality to the Jesuit. Favre, in fact, prepared the young Alphonsus for his First Communion, an important rite of passage in the church.

At twelve, Alphonsus was sent to the Jesuit college at Alcalá, but his father's death put an end to his studies; he was forced to return home to take over the family business. At twenty-seven, Alphonsus married. He and his wife, Maria, had three children, but, tragically, his wife and children all died, one after the other. Heavy taxes and expenses led Alphonsus to the brink of financial ruin; many biographers depict him as feeling like a failure. In desperation he called on the Jesuits for guidance. The lonely widower prayed for many years to understand God's desires for him.

Gradually Alphonsus found within himself the desire to become a Jesuit. At thirty-five, he was deemed too old to begin the long training required for the priesthood and was rejected for entrance. But his holiness was evident to the local provincial, who accepted Alphonsus into the novitiate as a brother two years later. The provincial is supposed to have said that if Alphonsus wasn't qualified to become a brother or a priest, he could enter to become a saint. He stayed for only six months before being sent to the Jesuit school in Majorca, in 1571, where he assumed the job of porter, or doorkeeper.

Each time the doorbell rang, as I mentioned, Brother Alphonsus said, "I'm coming, Lord!" The practice reminded him to treat each person with as much respect as if it were Jesus himself at the door.

In 1605 Peter Claver, a twenty-five-year-old Jesuit seminarian, met the humble, seventy-two-year-old Alphonsus at the college. The two met almost daily for spiritual conversations, and in time Alphonsus encouraged Peter to think about working overseas in "the missions." The prospect thrilled Peter, who wrote to his provincial for permission and was sent to Cartagena, in what is now Colombia, to work with the West African slaves who had been captured by traders and shipped to South America. For his tireless efforts to feed, counsel, and comfort the slaves, who had endured horrifying conditions, Peter would earn the sobriquet *el esclavo de los esclavos,* the slave of the slaves.

St. Peter Claver, the great missionary, was later canonized for his heroic efforts. St. Alphonsus Rodríguez was canonized for his own brand of heroism: a lifelong humility.

Alphonsus and Peter met every day to build up their friendship. But this did not prevent Alphonsus from encouraging Peter to volunteer for work in South America. Alphonsus gave Peter not only the gift of friendship but freedom, just as Ignatius, Peter, and Francis gave to one another.

SOME BARRIERS TO HEALTHY FRIENDSHIP

Given the centrality of freedom in relationships, it is not surprising that in his study on Jesuit friendship, Charles Shelton, the Jesuit psychologist, lists *possessiveness* as the first barrier to healthy friendship. Your friend may not be able to reciprocate the level of your feelings, given that his attention may be somewhere else, say, on a pressing family or work situation. The other person may also move to another town or city or may be less able to spend time with you, say, because of marriage or a new child. All these things may increase your sense of possessiveness and animate a desire to control the other.

Part of friendship is also giving the other person the freedom to grow and change. The desire for friendship should not overshadow the friend. But, as Father Barry noted in a conversation, there is another side to that desire for freedom. "The danger is that because people will move, or leave, or even die, you are tempted not to give your heart to people."

Father Shelton's cautionary list of other pitfalls is helpful not simply for Jesuits, but for anyone interested in healthy relationships. *Overactivity* is one area where friendships founder because people are too busy to keep up with one another. One simply loses touch. Happily, I am blessed with many friends, and since I don't have the responsibilities of a marriage, I have more time to keep up with them. For married couples, though, the burdens can be overwhelming, and cherished friends may fall away.

Married people reading this might think, *How am I supposed to balance all the responsibilities of marriage* and *keep up with my friends?* The point here is not to add burdens, but to relieve them. Marriages can never fully provide for all the emotional needs of a couple. Nor were they designed that way: in the past, marriages presumed the nurturing support of an extended family and the wider community. Friends are needed even for married couples. Healthy friendships outside a marriage help husbands and wives in their own relationship.

You Must Remember This

Some of the best advice from Jesuits on human relationships comes in earthy ways. When John O'Malley was a Jesuit novice, an older priest told him three things to remember when living in community: *First, you're not God. Second, this isn't heaven. Third, don't be an ass.* Had I followed those guidelines earlier, I could have saved myself years of self-induced heartache.

Overactivity is an important consideration when it comes to a healthy approach to work, which we will look at in a coming chapter. For now, suffice it to say that when work is so overwhelming that you are unable to sustain friendships, your life becomes impoverished, though you may be working to get richer.

On the other hand, as Shelton points out, is the danger of *excessive emotional involvement*. Here the tendency is to focus too much on the friendship, focusing obsessively on the feelings that arise and analyzing every slight and comment. Clinginess smothers friendship and repels the most generous of friends. A healthy relationship is like a flame that gives off light and warms both friends: it can be extinguished for lack of attention but smothered by too much attention.

Competition is another danger. In a culture where people are often defined by what they do and how much they make, the temptation to compete can be overwhelming. Shelton asks if your friend's success is a threat to your own sense of self-worth. If it is, maybe it's time to consider the blessings in your own life more carefully.

Envy, I would add, is equally poisonous. You can move away from that by being grateful for the blessings in your own life (the examen can help) and by realizing that everyone's life is a mixed bag of gifts and struggles. If you doubt that, just talk to your friends about their problems.

Shelton next calls attention to *complaint-driven* relationships, where getting together becomes an excuse for carping. In situations like this, the world begins to take on a dark cast. Complaining spreads like a virus through conversations until everything seems useless, and both parties end up bitter and despairing. Shelton also warns against *impairing relationships,* which encourage unhealthy or destructive behavior, like alcoholism or drug abuse.

In both these cases you need to ask if the friendship is healthy. If not, can you discuss the situation? Or do you have to move away from the friendship for your own health? One of my spiritual directors once asked me bluntly, "Is being with your friend good for your vocation?"

Still, an essential part of love is maintaining what you could call the *difficult friendship.* The story of Simon Rodrigues, one of Ignatius's friends, will show what I mean.

A SPECIAL LOVE

One of the early Jesuit companions was a trying person. Simon Rodrigues, a Portuguese student in Paris, was one of the six friends who pronounced vows of poverty and chastity with Ignatius in Paris in 1534. After the founding of the Society of Jesus, Rodrigues was asked by Ignatius to assume the important position of overseeing all the Jesuits in Portugal.

But, as William Bangert notes in *A History of the Society of Jesus,* Rodrigues soon "evidenced an instability and recalcitrance that pushed Ignatius almost to the brink of dismissing him." The man was an inveterate complainer and excessively permissive with the Jesuits under his care; as a result, the Jesuits in Portugal were increasingly in disarray.

In time, Rodrigues also became the confessor to King John III of Portugal and took up residence in the royal court—while still functioning as Jesuit provincial. Word spread that Rodrigues was scandalizing others, as he could not live without the "palaces and pomp of the world," as one contemporary wrote.

How did Ignatius respond to his difficult friend?

Rather than angrily berating him, Ignatius wrote his old friend several letters and asked Simon to correspond more frequently so that he could help him with his problems. But Ignatius was also serious about his role as superior general; in response to the growing crisis, he relieved Rodrigues from his post in December of 1551 and sent him to Spain. Unfortunately, Rodrigues's behavior continued to be a source of embarrassment, and Ignatius was forced to call him back to Rome.

This must have been a painful time for even someone as balanced as Ignatius: one of his most trusted confidants had failed. Ignatius may have felt let down by a friend. Or embarrassed at the trust he placed in him. Or angry at Simon's intransigence.

Yet Ignatius treated his friend with dignity, remembering the Presupposition and giving him the benefit of the doubt. In the letter relieving Simon of his post in Portugal, Ignatius mentions not Simon's shortcomings and problems—which both knew—but the burden that was placed upon Simon as provincial and how it "does not seem proper to hold you any longer in these labors." After asking Simon to return to Rome, Ignatius wrote compassionately of his desire to maintain his friend's good reputation and provide for Simon's future. There is not an ounce of recrimination in his generous letter.

Moreover, says Ignatius, he treasures Simon's friendship. If he loves the other Jesuits, he says, he feels an even greater affection for his first companions, "particularly toward you, for whom, as you know, I have always had a very special love in the Lord." It is a remarkable letter that shows how well Ignatius understood the value, and challenges, of friendship and love.

We all have friends or family members who find themselves in trouble, who disappoint us with self-destructive behavior, or who seem incapable or unwilling to change, despite the best efforts of those who love them. These periods may last for a few weeks, a few years, or a lifetime. In these situations we are called to be special friends and to not only encourage them to lead healthy lives, but also to extend to them our "special love," as Ignatius did with Simon Rodrigues.

And if you think your relationships are too complicated for this, remember Ignatius had to deal with a devilishly complex situation—having to balance the following: his responsibility for the Jesuits in Portugal and Spain; his duty toward those with whom they worked in their schools and churches; his need to remain in the good graces of the king of Portugal; his desire to uphold the reputation of the Society of Jesus; and his wish to be kind to one of his oldest friends.

Ignatius was able to navigate these waters because of his "way of proceeding." To begin with, Ignatius, who was, after all, the author of the Presupposition, gave Simon the benefit of the doubt, trying to see things from his point of view. Second, he was honest without being insulting. Third, he was reasonable about what would work and what wouldn't, making decisions and taking actions that would be painful for himself, and that even might lead him to be misunderstood. Fourth, he understood the absolute centrality of love. Fifth, he was "detached" enough to know that he might not be able to change his "difficult friend." Eventually, according to *The First Jesuits,* Rodrigues came to accept the wisdom of Ignatius's actions.

Ignatius had a talent for friendship because he had a talent for charity, honesty, reason, love, and detachment.

UNION OF HEARTS AND MINDS

Just as I was writing this chapter, I got a phone call from a good friend. Dave was a mathematics professor before entering the Jesuits and is also one of the most organized and hardworking people I know. And one of the kindest, too—I don't think I've ever heard him say an uncharitable word about another person. During philosophy studies in Chicago, we lived in the same community. (The wall between our two rooms was so thin that we also, unavoidably, heard each other's phone conversations, and therefore we had few secrets!)

But as with many Jesuit friends, my days of living near him are over for now. Since Dave works in Chicago, we rarely see each other.

After I told Dave that I was working on this chapter, I asked him, "What do you think it takes to keep a good friendship?"

"Staying in contact is most important," he said. Times when distance or overwork diminish one's ability to maintain friendships are when one needs to be diligent about keeping in touch. And, said Dave, the times when you are most tempted to neglect friendships, which can move you toward loneliness, are precisely when you most need to care for yourself by nourishing those relationships.

Even with the hurdles of distance and time, deep friendships can be sustained. "Like most people who have known each other well, we have a commonality that enables us to reconnect," said Dave. "So the distance is not so much a problem."

Ignatius referred to this as a "union of hearts and minds," in which Jesuits could be united in a common purpose, and as companions, even though many miles apart. That's a good goal for any friendship: the union of hearts and minds.

After Dave's providential phone call, I decided to call a few other friends, men and women who are well versed in Ignatian spirituality to ask them what the way of Ignatius taught them about friendship and love.

Many insights dovetailed with Father Shelton's article on friendship, in which he offers not only some things to avoid, but also some positive tips on what leads to healthy friendships. Let's look at some of Shelton's recommendations and also some of my own friends' wisdom.

Shelton begins by saying that good friends *know about one another's lives*. That sounds obvious, doesn't it? But a friendship can become one-sided. Sometimes you see your friend or a family member as existing to serve your needs—say, as psychologist or life coach—forgetting the need to take an active interest in the other person's life. There has to be both giving and receiving. "Love consists in a mutual communication between the two persons," wrote Ignatius in the Exercises. "Each shares with the other."

Sister Maddy, my friend from Nairobi and Gloucester, also pointed to that dynamic—but wanted to emphasize the receiving. "You have to let your friend be a friend to *you*," she said. "Sometimes it's more difficult to receive." She quoted one of her favorite sayings: "A friend knows the song in my heart and sings it to me when my memory fails."

When I asked Bill, president of a high school in Portland, Maine, if I could identify him as one of my oldest Jesuit friends, he laughed. "Say *longest,* not oldest!" Bill and I entered the novitiate the same year and have gone through over twenty years of Jesuit training, so we know each other well. He's an easygoing, affable fellow with plenty of friends.

For Bill the "work" of friendship includes taking initiatives. "It's easy to say you want to see one another," he said, "but just as easy to let things slide. Friendships can die through attrition if you don't take the initiative."

Paula, a longtime friend from graduate school who studied alongside many Jesuits, is a lively but soft-spoken woman. Ten years after finishing her theology degree, she is now married with two young children and works as a campus minister at a Jesuit university in Cleveland, Ohio. She laughed when I asked about sustaining good friendships.

"You mean with Jesuits or with others?" she said. "Because friendships with Jesuits require a special set of strategies!"

More seriously, Paula pointed to "intentionality" as a key element. She asks, "Are there core values that go beyond the situation that brought you together? Was it only a great college friendship, or is it deeper? Are you able to talk about meaningful areas of your lives?"

Paula agreed with Shelton's warning against possessiveness, even—and she surprised me by saying this—in a marriage. She appreciated this in terms of Ignatian spirituality. "The Principle and Foundation of the Spiritual Exercises," she said, "talks about not being attached to any one thing or person. And that includes your spouse."

"When I first heard about being 'detached' from my husband, I thought it was ridiculous!" Paula explained. "But as I got older, I realized that as wonderful as the relationship is, it can't be more important than my relationship with God, because one day it will end. You cannot be utterly dependent on anyone and look to only one person to fill all your needs. Because, eventually, they won't be able to." She often shares that insight with college students who are inclined to make their girlfriends or boyfriends the center of their lives.

Does putting God at the center mean that you have less love available for your spouse? "Oh no," she said immediately. "If God is at the center, there's always room for others. In fact, there's more room."

In his article Shelton noted that a good friend is also able to *share his true feelings* and listen to the other's feelings, even when it may be uncomfortable. A good question to ask is, *Whom do I trust enough to freely share any negative feelings with?* In other words, with whom can I be honest?

That starts with being honest with yourself. One of my closest friends is George, who entered the novitiate the year before me. Today he is a prison chaplain in Boston. George offered some rich insights into how Ignatian spirituality can help with friendship.

"Since Ignatian spirituality helps us to be honest with ourselves, it also invites honesty in our relationships with friends," said George. "My friends are those with whom I can be myself: they know my baggage and limitations. They also appreciate my strengths—perhaps more than I do. And when I think of the Ignatian idea of 'sinners loved by God,' it easily translates into 'sinners loved by friends.'"

This means looking at both ourselves and our friends compassionately. "Having more compassion for myself," says George, "allows me to have more compassion for friends."

> It is a great help to progress to possess a friend who is privileged to point out to you your failings.
> —St. Ignatius Loyola

Like George, each of my friends made explicit connections between Ignatian spirituality and friendship. Bob is president of a Jesuit high school in Jersey City, New Jersey. He's an excellent listener and, as a result, an excellent friend. Bob reflected on the link between friendship and the Ignatian understanding of desire.

"From an Ignatian standpoint, God interacts with a person on a direct basis," Bob said. "And the way this often happens is through our friends. So friendship, in both its support and challenges, is one of the main ways we discover God. We discover who we are as loved individuals, and we discover that in our friends."

That desire for friendship comes from God, he said. "It's a desire to discover what's going on with someone else. And it's the desire for the infinite, which comes from God, and the desire to participate with the infinite, which is ultimately satisfied by God, who is our friend."

One way Jesuits cultivate friendships is through a practice called "faith sharing." The practice may provide hints about how you can build an honest relationship with your friends.

LISTEN MUCH

Every Sunday night in the novitiate our community gathered for "faith sharing," which meant speaking to one another about our spiritual lives: where we had experienced God in our daily lives and what our prayer was like.

There were two rules. First, everything was confidential. Second, no comments were allowed after someone spoke, unless it was a question asked to clarify something.

The first rule made sense. The second seemed ridiculous. Early on, when people expressed their struggles, I wanted to say, "Why not try this?" If someone said he missed his old life, I wanted to say, "Me, too." If someone talked about being lonely, I wanted to say, "Knock on my door." I couldn't understand why the novice director wanted us to be silent.

Gradually I realized: it was so we could listen.

Listening is a lost art. We *want* to listen, we want to *think* we're listening, but we are often so busy planning what we're going to say in response or what advice we're going to give, that we fail to pay attention.

As Gerry, our novice director, explained, there was ample time in the novitiate to console, to counsel, and to advise. The practice echoed one of Ignatius's lesser-known sayings: "Speak little, listen much." We were also told that keeping everything strictly confidential made people feel more relaxed.

Gradually I grew to love faith sharing. When my fellow novices, as well as Gerry and his assistant, David, shared about how they had experienced God in the previous week, I was fascinated. What a wonder to see how complicated these men were and how much they were all trying to grow in holiness, trying to be better men, better Jesuits.

It's Listening!

Jesuits aren't always good listeners. One of my favorite Jesuit stories might sound apocryphal, but I know the two men involved!

One was a wise and elderly priest, renowned for his spiritual-direction skills. The other was my friend Kevin, who was at the time a novice. The two met at a Jesuit gathering. The priest said, "So, Kevin, where are you from?" Kevin said, "Boston."

Then Kevin decided to ask this revered spiritual director an important question. "Father," he said, "what would you say is the most important part of spiritual direction?" The priest answered, "That's easy, Kevin. It's listening. You have to be a good listener. Listening is the key to being a good spiritual director." Kevin said, "Thanks, Father. That's really helpful."

And the priest said, "So, Kevin, where are you from?"

After a few weeks, I became not only amazed at how God was at work in their lives, but also more tolerant of their foibles. When one novice was short-tempered, I remembered that he had been dealing with a difficult situation in his family. When another was sullen, I remembered that he was dealing with an intractable problem in his ministry. The way they related to the world was colored by their own experience. It helped me to remember the Presupposition, and give them the benefit of the doubt.

My friend Chris is a Jesuit brother who worked for several years in the vocation office, helping to recruit and screen candidates to the Society of Jesus. Chris has a wide circle of friends—both Jesuit and otherwise. In our discussion on friendship and love he pointed out the value of listening, and he adverted to faith sharing.

"For a long time," said Chris, "I've known that faith sharing is critical." He offered an example why: "Early on, I lived with a Jesuit community member whom I found, well, difficult. Knowing his struggles from faith sharing was helpful because it is harder to dismiss or judge another person when you know he's struggling."

Listening attentively and compassionately to my fellow novices also helped me feel less crazy. Until then, I assumed that everyone led healthy and integrated lives. Except me—or so I thought. Faith sharing was the first time I grasped that everyone's life is a full measure of joy and suffering. And that all of us are more complex than our surface appearance indicates.

> We should be slow to speak and patient in listening to all. . . . Our ears should be wide open to our neighbor until he seems to have said all that is in his mind.
> —St. Ignatius Loyola

Listening also made me better able to celebrate with my friends. When a novice who was having personal problems experienced some healing, I was more able to rejoice with him, since I knew what he had been through.

Most of us don't have the time to do faith sharing, or any kind of sharing, with our friends for an hour every week.

But the concept may provide important lessons for developing loving relationships within families and maintaining good friendships. First, before you start to console or advise or sympathize, really listen. Second, try to listen without judging. Third, the more you know about your friend, the easier it will be to understand, sympathize, console, and even forgive your friend. Fourth, the more you can share honestly, the greater will be your ability to say challenging things. Fifth, the more you listen and understand his or her life, the more you will be able to celebrate with your friend over joys.

In these simple ways you will deepen your relationships, your conversations, and your compassion for your friends, and you'll begin to develop real intimacy, where, as St. Francis de Sales says, "Heart speaks to heart."

HUMILITY AND FRIENDSHIP

James Keenan, S.J., a professor of moral theology, once wrote that compassion is the willingness to enter into the "chaos" of another person's life. But even the best of friends sometimes avoid getting involved in the chaos of another life. You might feel overwhelmed by a friend's problems or frustrated that you can't fix or solve things for him or her. You might find yourself unconsciously pulling away from friends or family members who are facing job stress, marriage or relationship problems, serious illness, or even death. What happens when you feel you can't help someone?

This is when you are often called not to do but to be. To remember that you are not all-powerful. Shortly after I entered the novitiate, for example, two friends of mine had an explosive argument and stopped talking with each other. I confessed to David, my spiritual director, how frustrated I felt that I wasn't able to get them to reconcile. Consequently, I felt like a failure. And a bad Jesuit. It was driving me crazy.

"Shouldn't a Jesuit be able to do all this?" I asked.

"Where did you get that idea from?" he asked.

"Well," I said, "that's what Jesus would do. Jesus would help them to reconcile. Jesus would get them to talk to each other. Jesus would work until there was peace between them, right?"

"That's true," David said. "Jesus would probably be able to do all of that. But I have news for you, Jim. You're not Jesus!"

We both laughed. Not because it was silly, but because it was true. In some of the most painful moments in the lives of friends and families—illness, divorce, death, worries about their children, financial problems—we usually cannot work miracles. Sometimes our efforts do effect change, but sometimes they do not.

Paradoxically, admitting your own powerlessness can free you from the need to fix everything and allow us to be truly present to the other person, and to listen. A cartoon in the *New Yorker* had one woman saying testily to her friend, "There's no point in our being friends if you won't let me fix you."

Humility doesn't apply just to the way you relate to your friends, but to *you*. Besides not being able to solve all of your friends' problems (and recognizing that your friends won't be able to solve yours), admitting your own shortcomings is critical if you want to nurture healthy relationships. In other words, you need to both apologize and forgive.

Over the years I've done many thoughtless things to people. I've gossiped about them, suspected the worst about them, and tried to manipulate them into doing what I wanted them to do. On these occasions I've found it necessary to seek forgiveness, something that is at the heart of the Christian message. Just as often, they have come to me to ask for forgiveness.

Sinfulness exists within any human setting, Jesuit communities included. So in any human setting, apology and forgiveness are always needed. Seeking forgiveness is difficult and, since it goes against our ego-driven desires to be right all the time, is always an exercise in humility.

Almost always people have forgiven me and the friendship has grown stronger. But on one or two occasions, the person has not. Here I find it helpful to pray for the person and always be open to reconciliation, but also remember, once again, that just as I cannot force another person to love or even like me, I cannot force another person's forgiveness.

HEALTHY FRIENDSHIPS

Let's return to some of Father Shelton's tips for healthy friendships and see if you can find insights for your own relationships with friends and family.

Without *honesty,* he says, a friendship will wither and die. William Barry provided a concise description of how this happens. "It's difficult to be honest," he told me recently, "but when something painful happens—for example, the other person is sick or dying, of if you're angry for some reason—if you can't talk about it you become more and more distant. And if there's something that you're holding onto, then eventually you can't talk about anything. And pretty soon, you haven't got a friend."

Being *open to challenge,* Shelton notes, is not just something that we expect to do *for* our friends; it is something to expect *from* our friends. Can you accept the occasional challenge from your friends—that you have acted selfishly and may need to apologize from time to time?

"There are two difficulties in being honest," my friend Chris said. "One is when you know your friend doesn't want to hear something. The other is when *you* don't want to say it—especially when you know you're at fault. But it's important to be humble about admitting our own wrongdoing or faults."

Friends also *wish the good* of the other. That goes for members of the same family who want to love one another. Ignatius gave Francis Xavier the freedom to be the person he was called to be, even if it was half a world away from Ignatius. It also means celebrating the times when the other person does well or succeeds.

Jesuits can sometimes be competitive. In many instances this is a good thing: natural competitiveness spurs us to greater achievement. St. Ignatius Loyola, in effect, was being "competitive" with St. Francis and St. Dominic when he lay on his sick bed and thought, "What if I should do this which Saint Francis did and this which Saint Dominic did?" Without a healthy sense of competition in Ignatius, there would be no Society of Jesus. But as Ignatius grew older, he gave up the darker side of ambition and even wrote rules into the Jesuit *Constitutions* designed to limit and moderate unhealthy ambitions and competition among Jesuits.

Competition is usually present among friends, siblings, neighbors, coworkers, or anywhere two or three are gathered, to borrow a line from the Gospels. During my philosophy and theology studies, some competitiveness was healthy. Whenever I saw my organized friend Dave, who always kept his notes neatly collated in pristine blue binders, start studying a few days before a test, I knew it was time for me to study. Dave's industriousness prompted me to do a better job.

But too much competition is poisonous. The competitiveness that leads to wishing ill for the other is the beginning of the end of friendship.

Father Shelton lists one more aspect to a healthy friendship. You have to learn when to maintain a *discreet silence*. Sometimes our friends or family members don't need our advice. Or at least not right at that moment.

My friend Steve, *another* president of a Jesuit high school, this one in New York City, agrees. Steve has many friends, thanks to his ebullient good humor and his preternatural ability to remember birthdays, names of spouses, and even names of pets. His friends know to expect comments like, "Isn't today your mom's birthday?"

Steve talked about discretion in friendships: "I'm very direct and like to get to the point," he said, "and I like to have the kinds of conversations that get to the heart of things, especially in the middle of a busy life. But you also have to be discreet: learning when to bring something up, or file it away for a better time—a time when it would be good for *the other* to hear it, not necessarily for you to say it."

To Shelton's recommendations, I would add a few more. First, friends give one another freedom to *change*. The person that we knew a few years ago, in high school, college, at work, or in the novitiate, may have changed utterly. It's important not to force the person to be who he or she was years ago—besides, it's impossible. This is part of the freedom we can give to our friends. And to spouses, too. One married friend recently told me, "Probably the biggest killer of marriages is the lack of freedom to grow and change."

Second, friendship is *welcoming*. It welcomes others and is not exclusive. That sounds reasonable enough, doesn't it? But for Jesuits "exclusive" is a loaded word.

Throughout much of the twentieth century, some Jesuit superiors inveighed against "particular friendships." Too much "exclusivity" or "particularity" among young Jesuits was thought to lead to, or foster, overly close bonds and perhaps encourage gay men to break their vows of chastity. Jesuit superiors discouraged exclusive relationships by requiring that during recreation periods, when novices strolled the novitiate grounds, there should always be at least three men in any group. *Numquam duo, semper tres,* went the oft-quoted Latin saying: Never two, always three.

This attitude reflected the general misunderstanding about homosexuality (that is, the wrongheaded notion that gay men couldn't live celibately or enjoy close friendships with one another). More important, it reflected a general misunderstanding about friendship. Having a very close friend is a blessing, not a curse.

But there was a healthy insight here that we should not overlook: Jesuit superiors recognized that too much exclusivity in friendships could lead men to become isolated and separate from the larger community. When a friendship turns in on itself and excludes others, it becomes less healthy, sometimes prone to obsessive attention, building up unrealistic expectations, and causing frustration on both sides.

You might ask yourself a few questions to guard against an unhealthy "exclusivity." Do you hesitate to welcome other people into your friendship? Are you jealous when your friend spends time with other friends? Do you feel that the person needs to always be available to you? If your answers are yes, then you may need to remind yourself that your friend does not exist simply to be your friend.

This is true for your friendship with God, too. As Maureen Conroy, R.S.M., says in *The Discerning Heart*, "As we grow in mutual relationship with God, we want to share with others our life-giving love." Our friendship with God is not exclusive, but inclusive—welcoming.

Third, friendships need to be leavened with *humor*. One of the most important parts of friendship is simply having fun, enjoying oneself, and having a good laugh—all elements of a healthy psychology and spirituality. Friendships are fun—a word you don't hear much in spiritual circles—and part of fun is humor and laughter.

So good friends remind you not to take yourself with such deadly seriousness. My friend Chris was once listening to me bemoan some insignificant problem. After a few minutes of complaining, I said, with mock seriousness, "My life is such a cross!"

Without missing a beat, he said, "Yes, but for you or for others?" It was a great one-liner that helped to put things in perspective. When I get too focused on my own problems, I like to remember Chris's light—but meaningful—joke. Humor helps us to deflate our overblown egos.

Fourth, friends need to *help* one another. It's not all about conversation, sharing, and listening! Sometimes your friend needs you to *do* something: visit him in the hospital, help him move a sofa, babysit his children, lend him some jumper cables, give him a ride to the airport. This is part of the fundamental work of *helping souls* and is part of everyone's call. As David Fleming writes in *What Is Ignatian Spirituality?*, "Helping does not require extensive training and a fistful of academic degrees."

GROWING IN GRATITUDE

So far the type of friendship that I've described sounds almost utilitarian: friends should do *these* things and avoid *those* things in order to produce *this* kind of friendship. But a friendship, indeed any loving relationship, is not a machine designed to produce happiness. Perhaps a better metaphor is flowers in a beautiful garden. Unless you're a bee, the flowers are not there to *do* something for you, as much as to be enjoyed.

That brings me to the final part of our discussion: gratitude.

The way of Ignatius celebrates gratitude. *The Spiritual Exercises* is crammed with references to expressing gratitude for God's gifts. "I will consider how all good things and gifts descend from above," he writes in the Fourth Week, "from the Supreme and Infinite Power above . . . just as the rays come down from the sun." The examen, as we've mentioned, begins with gratitude. For Ignatius, *ingratitude* was the "most abominable of sins," indeed "the cause, the beginning and origin of all sins and misfortunes."

When I asked Steve about friendship, the first thing he mentioned was finding gratitude during the examination of conscience. "When I think about friendship, the first thing that comes to mind is finding God in all things," he said. "That surfaces during my examen, when frequently God directs me to things that *God* thinks are important—rather than what I might be focusing on. Often that turns out to be friends and interactions with other Jesuits—in even the simplest of ways: a random comment in a corridor or a homily from another Jesuit. The examen helps me to be more mindful of, and more grateful for, my friends."

Paula noted wryly that while everyone will *say* they are grateful for their friends, the examen makes it easier to focus on that gratitude. "The examen *always* helps in friendships and in family relationships," she said, "because it helps with gratitude." For Sister Maddy, even days when friends aren't present are occasions for being grateful for them. "Every night during my examen, I remember my gratitude for friends—even if I've not been in contact with them on that particular day. I'm grateful for them wherever they are."

Paul, the rector of a large Jesuit community in Boston, said that gratitude was the most neglected part of friendship. For many years, Paul was in charge of training young Jesuits in Boston and Chicago. He has a lifetime of experience in counseling others in their spiritual lives. "One of the most important parts of friendship is living in gratitude for the gift, and growing into that kind of gratitude," he said.

Paul noted that one common problem in Jesuit friendships stemmed from a lack of gratitude. Without gratitude, you take friendship for granted. "You forget that it takes a little effort. And the small things matter: making time to call, staying in touch. If people can name a friendship and can appreciate it, they are more inclined to work at it."

True friendships are hard to come by, Paul said, and they take work. And patience. "There are a small number of people who, for whatever reason, easily make and keep friends. But the vast majority of the human race has to ask for friendship and be patient in waiting for it to come. When we imagine friendships, we tend to imagine things happening instantly. But like anything that's rich and wonderful, you grow into it."

This chapter may have helped you to find ways to strengthen or deepen your appreciation of relationships with family and friends. But what about those readers for whom talk of friendship just reminds them of their loneliness? If this is where you are, you can still enjoy God's friendship in prayer, seeing how God is active in your work, your reading, your hobbies.

Still, what can we say to those who long for a good friend?

It would be wrong to downplay the pain of loneliness: I have known many lonely people whose lives are often filled with sadness. Perhaps one thing I could suggest is to remain open to the possibility of meeting new friends and not move to despair, trusting, as much as you can, that God wants you someday to find a friend. The very desire for friendship is an invitation from God to reach out to others. Trust that God desires community for you, though that goal may seem far away.

"For those who wonder why it's not happening faster in their lives," Paul said, "I think that it's more important to love and take the first step. And it also may seem that most people have to spend their lives giving more than receiving."

"But at the end," Paul said, "even with all the work that is involved, even if you only find one friend in your whole life, it's worth it."

CHAPTER ELEVEN

Surrendering to the Future

Obedience, Acceptance, and Suffering

ST. IGNATIUS WAS CRYSTAL clear about the place of obedience in the life of a Jesuit. Here's how he began his discussion of the vow in the *Constitutions,* in a section called "What Pertains to Obedience."

> All should strongly dispose themselves to observe obedience and to distinguish themselves in it, not only in the matters of obligation but also in the others, even though nothing else be perceived except an indication of the superior's will without an expressed command.

In other words, we Jesuits should be distinguished by our obedience so that even the *indication* of a superior's intention should be enough reason to act. What's more, we should receive the command from the superior "as if it were coming from Christ," since we are practicing obedience out of love of God. We should be ready to set aside anything we are doing—even being "ready to leave unfinished any letter"—once we know what the superior wants.

Most people find that impossible to fathom. To quote the writer Kathleen Norris again, most people see obedience as "desirable in dogs but suspect in people." Many even find the term *superior,* the term for the head of a religious community, freakish. Rick Curry, a Jesuit friend, once ran into a psychiatrist who lived in the same building where Rick kept an office. At the time, Rick was in an elevator with another Jesuit. Rick introduced him. "This is my superior," said Rick.

After his superior left the elevator, Rick's friend said, "I wish you wouldn't *say* things like that!"

Rick said, "What things?"

She said, "He's not your superior! You're every *bit* as good as he is!"

Rick laughed and explained to her what the term meant.

Let me do some explaining, too, about the vow of obedience, before we move on to how the Jesuit experience with obedience might help you in your everyday life.

OBEDIENCE AS LISTENING

Obedience was a normal part of religious life in the days of Ignatius. Once his tight-knit band of friends decided to become a religious order, it would have been unthinkable to arrange things in any other way. It has always been, and remains, part of almost every Catholic religious order.

The word comes from the Latin *oboedire,* which includes the root for "to hear." Obedience means hearing or listening. As with the vows of poverty and chastity, obedience is designed to help us follow the example of Jesus, who listened to, and was obedient to, God the Father.

Men and women in religious orders believe that God is at work not only through their own daily lives and prayer, but also through the decisions of their superiors, who are also trying to decide the right course of action. We believe that God's Spirit is at work through the decisions of the superior who is, like the Jesuit under his care, trying to "listen" to God.

That doesn't mean that the superior arrives at his decisions alone. Superior and Jesuit together try to discern God's desires. When a Jesuit is about to be "missioned" to a particular work, the superior is attentive to the Jesuit's own desires, since he knows—and the reader knows by now—that this is one way that God's desires are made known. This is what the founder of the Jesuits intended.

The Jesuits William Barry and Robert Doherty note in *Contemplatives in Action: The Jesuit Way* that Ignatius's insistence on individual discernment is surprising when you consider how hierarchical and authoritarian were the circles in which Ignatius moved—courts of kings and nobles, the military, the academy, the church. Nonetheless, they write, "Ignatius also expected that God's will could be made manifest through the experience of the men themselves."

How does a superior know a man's desires? Through a practice called the "account of conscience." Once a year the provincial meets with each Jesuit under his care to discuss his work, his community life, his vows, his friendships, and his prayer. Afterward the superior has a clearer idea of the Jesuit's interior life and so is better able to mission him.

After a decision is made, if a Jesuit feels that he has not been adequately listened to, he can return to the superior and appeal. This is known as "representing." If that fails to satisfy, the Jesuit can appeal to a higher authority—all the way up to the superior general. But in the end—unless it is a matter of conscience—the Jesuit is bound by his vows to obey. After prayer, conversation, and discernment, even if you think it's a poor decision, you must accept it.

Crafty Jesuits

Jesuits are supposed to be clever—if not crafty—when it comes to obedience. One joke has a Jesuit feeling guilty about one of his bad habits. He asks his superior, "Father, may I smoke while I pray?" The horrified superior says, "Certainly not!" He relates the story to another Jesuit who has the same habit. After pondering the matter, the second Jesuit asks, "Father, may I pray while I smoke?" "Of course!" says the superior.

Or, as the apocryphal Jesuit superior is supposed to have said, "I discern, you discern, we discern, but I decide!"

Since around the 1960s, Jesuit superiors have recaptured Ignatius's original notion that not only is God at work through a man's desires, hopes, and talents, but also that a person will flourish more in a job he enjoys. Most Jesuits teaching in a university, for example, have spent years preparing for their work and are happy to use their academic training—and their superiors are happy to send them there. But attentiveness to a man's desires and talents has long been part of Jesuit discernment. "If people among us [show] a zeal and aptitude for a particular work, say foreign missions," wrote the English Jesuit Gerard Manley Hopkins in 1874, "they can commonly get employed on them."

Following the will of one's superiors is usually a joyful experience, as one feels that one's desires and the needs of the larger community are aligned. But there are times when you are asked to go somewhere that you would not choose on your own. Or do something that you would rather not do.

Many readers who have a problem accepting this aspect of obedience may have an easier time accepting a more practical reason: someone needs to be in charge. Managing a worldwide religious order, as Ignatius did, required one person, one ultimate authority, to guide the work. So the vow of obedience is always, as are the other vows, "apostolic," that is, it helps us to carry out our assignments more effectively.

Actually, I'm always surprised by the number of people who scoff at obedience in religious orders yet live it religiously in their own lives. Many people who work in professional settings report to a manager who gives directives that they would often not choose on their own. When I worked for General Electric, I saw many longtime employees transferred to faraway locations, yet they would never think of complaining because they were so devoted to the company. These decisions are seen as necessary to achieve the organization's goals—as are decisions in a religious order.

And having spent six years working in corporate America, I can say that in the Jesuits you have *more* say in these matters than in the corporate world. Your religious superior believes that your own desires, insights, and conclusions are valuable, whereas with management in the business world this is sometimes not the case.

In addition to the standard vows of poverty, chastity, and obedience taken by members of religious orders, Ignatius asked many Jesuits to profess what is called the "fourth vow." That special vow relates to the pope. At the close of his training, a Jesuit promises "special obedience to the sovereign pontiff regarding the missions."

What was the thinking behind this vow? Worldwide mobility. Ignatius saw the fourth vow not so much focused on the person of the pope (though he expected his men to have profound respect for the pope), but flowing from an understanding that the pope knew where the needs were the greatest, by virtue of his overall knowledge of the universal church. "The vow assumed," writes John O'Malley in *The First Jesuits,* "that the pope had the broad vision required for the most effective deployment in the 'vineyard of the Lord.'"

"It's a vow to be a missionary, to be 'on mission,' to 'travel to any part of the world,'" said Father O'Malley in a recent letter.

The will of Ignatius was clear: a Jesuit's obedience was a hallmark of religious life. But besides the efficient running of a religious order, what are some other benefits of obedience?

Poverty frees you to live simply and frees you from worry about material possessions. Chastity frees you to love people freely and move around more easily. Obedience is about freedom, too. It frees you from excessive self-interest, careerism, and pride and allows you to respond more readily to the larger needs of the community. Rather than wondering, *What's the best way for me to get ahead?,* obedience asks you to trust that your superiors, who presumably have a better idea of larger needs, will be able to answer another question: What's the best use of this man's talents, given the needs of the community?

Obedience frees you for that kind of service.

How does this work in practice? If you asked most Jesuits about obedience, they would talk to you about experiences in being missioned, or sent to a new work. The reason that St. Francis Xavier went to "the Indies" and St. Isaac Jogues to "New France" was not simply because they wanted to go, but because they were *missioned* there. Their vow of obedience gave their work the added dimension of being under the care of God. Like all Jesuits, they trusted that their work was as close as they could possibly come to following God's desires—since it flowed from their desire to serve God and was confirmed by their superior. In short, they believed that God took their vows as seriously as they did, because the actual vow is made to God, to whom all Jesuits are obedient.

WITH AS MUCH LOVE AND CHARITY AS POSSIBLE

How does obedience play out in the everyday life of a Jesuit? Do superiors simply order you around the house, or arbitrarily send you on far-flung assignments?

The answer is different than it would have been a few decades ago. In the past, American Jesuits sometimes found out their assignments not during a conversation with their superiors but when the yearly list of assignments (called the *status,* pronounced in the Latin way) was posted every July 31, the Feast of St. Ignatius Loyola.

One elderly Jesuit told me a story about a province *status* that was posted in the late 1950s. He scanned the list and saw, to his puzzlement, that he had been assigned to teach chemistry. Well, he thought, there is clearly a mistake. Not only had he never taught chemistry—he had never even studied chemistry. He realized what must have happened: there was another Jesuit with the same last name who had majored in chemistry in college. That Jesuit had been assigned to teach English—what my friend had studied. So my friend made an appointment with the provincial to "represent."

"Father Provincial," said the young Jesuit. "I think you've made a mistake."

When my friend told me this story, he interrupted himself, roared with laughter, and said, "Well, that was the *last* thing *he* wanted to hear!" Annoyed by the young Jesuit's presumption, the provincial said that there had been no mistake: he was assigned to teach chemistry in one of the province's high schools.

"What did you do?" I asked.

"I taught chemistry for a year," he laughed. "And you know what? I got pretty good at it, too!" It was a misuse of power that my friend handled with grace.

Some Jesuits have nursed longstanding grudges about the bad decisions of superiors. The first editor of *America* magazine, on the fiftieth anniversary of his ordination, stood up before a group of Jesuits, friends, and family and boldly announced, "All I have ever accomplished in the Society of Jesus has been despite my superiors!"

During much of the twentieth century, the emphasis was placed more on the superior's than the individual's discernment. But since the Second Vatican Council, when religious orders were asked to revisit the original spirit of their orders, Jesuits have reappropriated this essential piece of Ignatian wisdom: the Spirit works through everybody. Today decisions come after a long process of conversation and prayer.

But what would happen if you *still* don't agree? Well, you can "represent" and explain your reasons one last time. In the rare instance when a serious dispute arises, a superior might order you to accept his decision "under obedience." In that case, the challenge is to find a sense of peace and to trust that God is at work even in decisions with which you don't agree.

Underneath these decisions is the superior's responsibility to pray to discover God's desires and to carry out his decisions with love for the Jesuit. As Barry and Doherty write, "The practice of obedience in Jesuit governance, obviously, is not supposed to be authoritarian and arbitrary. . . . Ignatius wants superiors to act with love, even when they must do something painful for another." For example, asking a man to do something he would rather not do.

That includes the most painful choice of all—the decision to dismiss someone from the Jesuits. Indeed, Ignatius carefully outlined the steps to be taken after the decision is made to ask someone to leave. This particular example of a compassionate superior could be profitably used by the corporate world.

First, said Ignatius, the superior should ensure that the man is able to leave the house with the respect of his peers, without any "shame or dishonor." Second, the superior should send him away "with as much love and charity for [the community] and as much consoled in our Lord as is possible." Third, he should "guide him in taking up some other good means of serving God, in religious life or outside . . . assisting him with advice and prayers and whatever . . . may seem best."

Ironically, this no-nonsense to-do list is among the most touching of all of Ignatius's writings. The gentle heart of Ignatius is revealed more openly than anywhere else in the *Constitutions*. Ignatius sees even this wrenching decision under the governance of love. (Compare that with the way firings and layoffs are sometimes handled in the business world.)

All Jesuits understand the goals of obedience. But there are times when, even with that understanding, it remains a challenge. Let me tell you two brief stories about that.

Two Stories About Obedience

Strange as it may seem today, Robert Drinan, S.J., was for many years a member of the U.S. House of Representatives, serving a congressional district in Massachusetts. In the late 1960s his prayer and discernment led Drinan, at the time a law professor at Boston College, to conclude that entering political life would be the best way to effect lasting change in society, and he received the approval of his superiors to run for office. Drinan served until 1981 and became famous for being the first member of Congress to call for the impeachment of President Richard M. Nixon in 1973, in light of his actions during the Vietnam War.

But in time the Vatican decided that priests should not be involved in political life so directly. So Pedro Arrupe, the superior general of the Society of Jesus, being obedient to *his* superior—Pope John Paul II—ordered Drinan not to run for reelection in 1980. Drinan's comments at a press conference were striking. Here is a Jesuit relinquishing his important work and—most important—trusting in the obedience that he had made at his first vows.

> I am proud and honored to be a priest and a Jesuit. As a person of faith, I must believe that there is work for me to do which somehow will be more important than the work I am required to leave. I undertake this new pilgrimage with pain and prayers.

Afterward Bob became a popular law professor at Georgetown University and a distinguished author of many articles and books on international human rights, respected by those inside and outside religious circles. In later years, before his death in 2007, he was criticized for some of his writings on abortion. (And I disagreed with him on this myself.) Still, I always respected him as someone who showed what it meant to trust that God was at work even in painful decisions.

A few decades earlier, another prominent Jesuit, the theologian John Courtney Murray, confronted a similar order. A tall, erudite man who, one Jesuit said, "entered a room like an ocean liner," Murray was a brilliant scholar who once appeared on the cover of *Time* magazine. But his renown did not prevent him from accepting a hard decision from his superiors.

In the 1950s, a group of talented theologians, including Murray, were "silenced" by Vatican officials and their own religious orders. Murray, a theology professor at the Jesuit's Woodstock College in Maryland, had written extensively on the question of church and state, proposing that constitutionally protected religious freedom, that is, the freedom of individuals to worship as they pleased, was in accord with Catholic teaching. The Vatican disagreed, and in 1954, Murray's superiors ordered him to cease writing on the topic. One Jesuit recalled seeing Murray quietly returning all the books on the topic to the library of Woodstock College.

A few years later, however, Francis Cardinal Spellman, the powerful archbishop of New York, saw to it that Murray was named an official *peritus,* or expert, at the Second Vatican Council. There the previously silenced Murray would serve as one of the architects for the Council's "Declaration on Religious Freedom," which drew on Murray's earlier, banned work and clearly affirmed religious freedom as a right for all people. Toward the end of the Council, John Courtney Murray, along with other scholars who had been silenced, was invited to celebrate Mass with Pope Paul VI, as a public sign of his official "rehabilitation." Murray died a few years later, in 1967.

Maybe you're reading about those two Jesuits and thinking, *That's ridiculous!* or *Why didn't Drinan continue with his political career?* or *Why didn't Murray write what he wanted to write?* Indeed, some Jesuits have decided that they cannot abide by their vows and have left to say or do what they feel they must.

What enabled men like Drinan and Murray to accept these decisions was the trust that God was somehow at work through their vow of obedience. Through their vows, offered freely to God, they believed God would work even if their superiors' decisions seemed illogical or unfair or even foolish.

The stance is similar to the seriousness with which couples take their marriage vows during rocky times. Often in marriages, unhealthy, hurtful, or destructive situations must be confronted and changed. But through it all, the couple trusts that though their marriage is turbulent (or seemingly dead) and seems to make little earthly sense, their vows remain a sign of God's covenant with them, a symbol of the sacredness of their commitment and a reason to trust that God will see them through. The vows are part of one's relationship with God, and one trusts that God will fulfill his part of the deal.

The vow of obedience rarely leads to situations that are so painful. Most of the time the vow is easy, and most Jesuits begin their new missions with alacrity. And even in cases when they don't agree with the wisdom of the decision at the moment, the wisdom is often appreciated in retrospect, sometimes many years later.

At one point in my formation, as I had mentioned, I fell in love. It happened in East Africa, not long before I was about to continue on to theology studies. At the time I had completed all the necessary paperwork and had been accepted into a graduate theology program, as my peers had been.

When I told my provincial, in a phone call, about how confusing it had been to fall in love and that it had briefly caused me to call into question my vocation, he decided that it would be better to delay my theology studies for another year.

It was a crushing disappointment. For one thing, my friends knew I had already been approved for theology studies. My provincial's decision meant that I would have to admit the delay. Mostly, I worried, was this a sign that I was being asked to leave the Society? Had I failed the Jesuits?

It was the closest I ever came to leaving the Jesuits. Why stay if I can't do what I want to do? Why stay in the face of embarrassment? Why stay if the Jesuits didn't (seemingly) want me? This was how I falsely interpreted things: after all, the provincial had said not a word about my leaving.

Confused, I met with my spiritual director, a prayerful and kindhearted Jesuit. George spent many years as a science teacher and late in life had rediscovered the Spiritual Exercises. At age seventy, he accepted a new assignment at the Jesuit retreat house in Nairobi, where I saw him for spiritual direction every month. He was an avuncular man with snow-white hair, a broad smile, and an affinity for royal blue cardigans. Simply being in his presence was a balm for my spirit. There were few people I respected more.

Or was more grateful for. Once, when I contracted mononucleosis and was too ill to leave my community, George drove an hour from his retreat house to give me spiritual direction at my home. "I'm making a house call!" he said cheerfully. We spent the afternoon sitting under a palm tree in the backyard of the Jesuit community.

After I spoke to my provincial, I had a worry more serious than mononucleosis: my future as a Jesuit. The next day I drove from the retreat house and told George the bad news. How could I accept the provincial's ridiculous decision? What would I tell my friends and family, and especially my Jesuit friends, all of whom knew I was ready to begin theology studies? Was it a sign to leave the Jesuits?

George patiently led me through all the good things that had happened during my time in Kenya. The Jesuit Refugee Service had helped scores of refugees start their own businesses—we had sponsored woodcarvers, painters, basket makers, and dairy farmers; the refugees had set up tailoring shops, bakeries, carpentry shops, even a few Ethiopian restaurants and a chicken farm. After a year we opened up a small shop to market some of the refugee handicrafts. In the first few months the shop had made $50,000 for the refugees. Over the previous two years I had made many friends among the refugees and had given and received so much love. And my prayer as a Jesuit had been rich and satisfying in Kenya. George even reminded me of that consoling spiritual experience on the little hillside, on the way home from work, and of feeling I was in the right place.

"How can you doubt your vocation after this?" said George.

But I was adamant. The provincial's decision was a sign that I should leave the Jesuits. Looking back, it seems clear that I was rapidly moving away from God and into despair, leaping from a delay in my training to leaving the Jesuits completely. The "enemy," as Ignatius said, was at work—working on my pride and quickly moving me to despair and a rash decision.

"Jim," said George, "how do you see your Jesuit formation?"

I didn't understand him at all. Then he said something that changed my idea of the spiritual life.

"Is this just a series of hoops to jump through?" he asked. "Is it a ladder that you are climbing to get ahead?" He paused.

"Or is this how God is forming you?"

Embarrassed, I admitted that I had seen my formation as a series of hoops to jump through in order to reach the big goal: ordination. I still saw it more like work (where the goal was a promotion) or school (graduation). But maybe something bigger was going on. Maybe I really was being "formed" by God.

With George's help I recognized something: the joy I experienced as a Jesuit for the previous two years had been real; I was called to be a Jesuit in the midst of all of that, and so I was also called to accept the provincial's decision. God's hand, so hard for me to see, must be at work. So I decided to stay.

After a few more conversations, the provincial assigned me for one year to a new task: to work at *America* magazine.

The provincial's "bad" decision led me to my writing career. If it hadn't been for his decision, which I vehemently opposed, you wouldn't be reading this book. In retrospect, I can see how different my life would have been had I not been faithful to my vow of obedience.

Years later, I saw the former provincial at a Christmas gathering of Jesuits. By this point we were friends. But I had never talked with him about that time in Kenya.

"You know," I said, "you were right all those years ago."

"About what?" he said.

"About delaying my theology studies," I said. "Looking back, I can see that I wasn't ready. I was too unsettled and confused, and I wouldn't have been able to enter into theology studies or think about ordination. Plus that year at *America* really changed my life. So, in retrospect, you were right."

I expected him to say that now, with the benefit of hindsight, he could finally see the wisdom of his choice. Instead he laughed.

"Jim," he said good-naturedly, "I knew I was right even then!"

The Reality of the Situation

So Jesuits make a vow of obedience. Big deal, right? You're probably asking what this has to do with you. You're most likely not in a religious order or planning to join one. You're probably never going to "vow obedience" to anyone—unless it's in a traditional marriage ceremony, which is a different kind of "obedience" anyway. You may think that those stories about Jesuit obedience are ridiculous. In short, you may still believe that obedience is "desirable in dogs but suspect in people."

It may be hard to see how this aspect of Jesuit spirituality relates to your life. Poverty and chastity have more obvious applications: Poverty gives insights into the freedom of the simple life. Chastity offers perspectives on how to love freely and be a good friend. But what about obedience?

Well, obedience is something that everyone has to face in the spiritual life. Because whether you're in a religious order or not, you'll find yourself having to surrender to "God's will" or "God's desires" or just God. But not in the way that you might think.

Often when we think about God's will, we think of trying to figure it all out. What is God's will? What am I supposed to do? One of the themes of this book has been the Ignatian model of "discernment," in which your desires help to reveal God's desires for you. We look for signs of those desires in our lives.

But there is a danger: We might overlook the fact that God's "plan" often doesn't need much figuring out or discernment.

Sometimes it's right in front of us. And that's what one of my Jesuit heroes realized in a labor camp in the Soviet Union.

At the beginning of the book, I mentioned the story of Walter Ciszek, the American-born Jesuit priest who had been sent by his superiors to work in Poland in the late 1930s. (Speaking of obedience, he had volunteered.) Originally hoping to work in the Soviet Union itself, Ciszek found it impossible to gain entrance and ended up in an Oriental Rite church in Albertin, Poland. When the German army took Warsaw in 1939, and the Soviet army overran eastern Poland and Albertin, Ciszek fled with other Polish refugees into the Soviet Union, hoping to serve there (in disguise) as a priest.

In June 1941, Ciszek was arrested by the Soviet secret police as a suspected spy. He spent five years in Moscow's infamous Lubianka prison and then was sentenced to fifteen years of hard labor in Siberia. In addition to his forced labor, he served as priest to his fellow prisoners, risking his life to offer counseling, hear confessions, and—most perilously—celebrate Mass.

> We said Mass in drafty storage shacks, or huddled in mud
> and slush in the corner of a building site foundation. . . . Yet
> in these primitive conditions, the Mass brought you closer
> to God than anyone might conceivably imagine.

Ciszek wouldn't return to the United States until 1963. By then many Jesuits assumed he was long dead. And why wouldn't they? The Society of Jesus sent out an official death notice in 1947. But toward the end of his captivity, Ciszek was suddenly and surprisingly permitted to write letters home. Only then did family and friends learn of his "rebirth."

After a complicated diplomatic exchange was worked out with the help of President John F. Kennedy, he returned to the United States on October 12, 1963, coming directly to the Jesuit community of *America* magazine in New York. Thurston Davis, S.J., the editor-in-chief at the time, wrote in the next week's issue, "In his green raincoat, grey suit and big-brimmed Russian hat he looked like the movie version of a stocky little Soviet member of an agricultural mission."

Ciszek settled down to work on the story of his time in Russia, called *With God in Russia,* detailing the extreme conditions in which he lived—his sudden capture by the Soviets, the grueling interrogation, the long train ride to Siberia, the wretched prison camps, and his eventual release into the Russian population as an ex-convict under surveillance. The book, still in print, was a huge success. But a few years later he realized that the book he really wanted to write was the story of something else: his spiritual journey. That book is called *He Leadeth Me.*

Ciszek wrote that he wanted to answer the question everyone kept asking: "How did you manage to survive?" His short answer was "Divine Providence." The full answer is his book, which shows how he found God in all things, even in a Soviet labor camp.

In one of the most arresting chapters of the book, Ciszek describes a startling epiphany about what it means to follow "God's will."

For a long time, as he toiled in the labor camps, he had been wondering how he would be able to endure his future. What was God's will? How was he supposed to figure it out? One day, along with another priest friend, he had a revelation. When it comes to daily life, God's will is not some abstract idea to be figured out or puzzled over or even discerned. Rather, God's will is what is presented before us every day.

> [God's] will for us was the twenty-four hours of each day: the people, the places, the circumstances he set before us in that time. Those were the things God knew were important to him and to us *at that moment,* and those were the things upon which he wanted us to act, not out of any abstract principle or out of any subjective desire to "do the will of God." No, these things, the twenty-four hours of this day, were his will; we had to learn to recognize his will in the reality of the situation.

This truth was so freeing that Ciszek returns to that theme again and again in his book. This recognition sustained him through many years of hardship, suffering, and pain.

> The plain and simple truth is that his will is what he actually wills to send us each day, in the way of circumstances, places, people, and problems. The trick is to learn to see that—not just in theory, or not just occasionally in a flash of insight granted by God's grace, but every day. Each of us has no need to wonder about what God's will must be for us; his will for us is clearly revealed in every situation of every day, if only we could learn to view all things as he sees them and sends them to us.

What is Ciszek's response to the question of how he survived? Obedience to what life has placed before him. "The challenge lies in learning to accept this truth and act upon it," he writes. This is something that everyone experiences: our lives change in ways we cannot control.

Now, when life changes for the better, acceptance is no problem! You meet a new friend. You get a promotion at work. You fall in love. You learn that you'll soon become a mother or a father or grandmother or grandfather. In these cases acceptance is easy. All one needs to do is be grateful.

But what happens when life presents you with unavoidable or overwhelming suffering? This is where the example of the Jesuit approach to obedience may be helpful. What enables a Jesuit to accept difficult decisions by his superior is the same thing that can help you: the realization that this is what God is inviting you to experience at this moment. It is the understanding that somehow God is with you, at work and revealed in a new way in this experience.

Let me be clear: I'm not saying that God wills suffering or pain. Nor that any of us will ever fully understand the mystery of suffering.

Nor that you need to look at every difficulty as God's will. Some suffering *should* be avoided, lessened, or combated: treatable illnesses, abusive marriages, unhealthy work situations, dysfunctional sexual relationships.

Nonetheless, Ciszek understood that God invites us to accept the inescapable realities placed in front of us. We can either turn away from that acceptance of life and continue on our own, or we can plunge into the "reality of the situation" and try to find God there in new ways. Obedience in this case means accepting reality.

SURRENDERING TO THE FUTURE

This point was driven home a few years ago by my close friend Janice, a Catholic sister. Sister Janice was one of my professors during graduate theology studies at the Weston Jesuit School of Theology in Cambridge, Massachusetts, and was a beloved figure among the students. A member of the French-founded Religious of Jesus and Mary, Janice, small in stature, with short gray hair and a cheerful demeanor, taught church history and Christian spirituality. At the end of my second year of studies, at my diaconate ordination, she met my parents, with whom she became fast friends.

A few years after theology studies ended, my family got the disastrous news that my father had cancer. As I mentioned earlier, he had fallen in a parking lot, which alerted his doctors to a problem. Tests showed that lung cancer had traveled to his brain, and he would have to begin chemotherapy and radiation treatments immediately.

When I heard the news, I froze. How could I do what it seemed God was now asking—help my mother in Philadelphia, accompany my father in what might be his last months, and continue my regular day-to-day work?

Besides these new responsibilities, I was dealing with something else: a sadness beyond anything I had ever experienced. My father had moved from job to job in the previous few years, never finding happiness at work. And that image of him collapsed in a parking lot in the dark, in the rain, seemed infinitely sad. It seemed certain that his future would be even sadder.

At one point I confessed to Janice my fear of facing all of this. "I know that I have to step on this path," I told her, "but I don't know if I can."

Janice said, "Can you surrender to the future that God has in store for you?"

Those words helped me to understand obedience in daily life. It was the acceptance of what life put in front of me, the "reality of the situation," as Ciszek said. For most people, obedience is not being sent away to work in a foreign land. It is stepping onto the path of daily life and continuing on it.

Everything Is Precious

Those who have abandoned themselves to God always lead mysterious lives and receive from God exceptional and miraculous gifts by means of the most ordinary, natural and chance experiences in which there appears to be nothing unusual. The simplest sermon, the most banal conversations, the least erudite books become the source of knowledge and wisdom to these souls by virtue of God's purpose. This is why they carefully pick up the crumbs which clever minds tread underfoot, for to them everything is precious and a source of enrichment.

—Jean-Pierre de Caussade, S.J. (1675–1751),
The Sacrament of the Present Moment

There is a choice involved: instead of acceptance, you can avoid plunging into the "reality of the situation." You can hold it at arm's length and see it as a distraction from life, rather than life itself. You tiptoe on the path, walk gingerly along its edges, or avoid it completely.

Janice's advice enabled me to step onto the path on which God was inviting me to walk. This is something of what Walter Ciszek realized: obedience came in accepting what was presented to him at that moment. The eighteenth-century French Jesuit Jean-Pierre de Caussade wrote two entire books on that topic: *The Sacrament of the Present Moment* and *Abandonment to Divine Providence*. "Once we grasp that each moment contains some sign of the will of God," he said, "we shall find in it all we can possibly desire."

My father died in a hospital bed nine months later, losing his battle with brain and lung cancer. A few days before his death Janice took a six-hour train ride all the way from Boston, stayed overnight in a nearby convent, and spent two hours talking with my father as he lay in his hospital bed—an unforgettable act of charity and love.

My father's death opened up a bottomless well of sadness in me. Yet I was able to preside at his funeral Mass and preach about his life, which was a very human one, full of joy and sorrow. In the end, I was grateful that I was able to help my mother, accompany him, and even continue my daily work as a Jesuit. And I couldn't have done any of that if I had resisted stepping on that path.

FINDING GOD
IN THE MIDST OF SUFFERING

This raises an essential question in the spiritual life: How do you find God in suffering? But that in turn raises another difficult question: Why do we suffer? This is a question we need to reflect on briefly before we move on to what Ignatian spirituality has to say about it.

The immense question, Why do we suffer? or the "problem of evil," has bedeviled theologians, saints, mystics—all believers—for thousands of years. How could a good God allow suffering?

First, we have to admit that no one answer can completely satisfy us when we face real suffering—our own or that of others. The best answer may be, "We don't know."

Second, we may have to admit that we believe in a God whose ways remain mysterious. In an article in *America* magazine, Rabbi Daniel Polish, author of *Talking About God,* put it succinctly. "I do not believe in a God whose will or motives are crystal clear to me. And as a person of faith, I find myself deeply suspicious of those who claim such insight."

Polish goes on to quote Rabbi Abraham Joshua Heschel: "To the pious man knowledge of God is not a thought within his grasp." This is the greatest challenge of faith, says Polish, "to live with a God we cannot fully understand, whose actions we explain at our own peril."

Third, while there are no definitive answers to the question of suffering, and while we may never fully understand it, there are some time-honored perspectives offered by the Jewish and Christian traditions, which have helped believers as they move through periods of suffering and pain.

During theology studies I took a fascinating course called "Suffering and Salvation," taught by Daniel Harrington, the New Testament scholar I mentioned earlier. In that course, later adapted into a book called *Why Do We Suffer?,* Father Harrington looked at the traditional explanations presented in Scripture. None answers the question and each may, in fact, raise more questions. Yet, taken together, they can provide, as Harrington wisely says, "resources" for the believer.

So our class read in the Old Testament the psalms of lament, the Book of Job, passages in the Book of Isaiah about the "suffering servant;" excerpts from the New Testament about the passion and death of Jesus; as well as meditations on the meaning of the Cross in St. Paul's writings.

We studied the main approaches to suffering found in Scripture: Suffering is a punishment for one's sins (or an ancestor's sins). Suffering is a mystery. Suffering is a kind of purification. Suffering enables us to participate in the life of Jesus, who himself suffered; likewise, the Christ who understands suffering can be a companion to us in our pain. Suffering is part of the human condition in an imperfect world. And suffering can enable us to experience God in new and unexpected ways.

A few of these perspectives I have found, at best, wanting; at worst, unhelpful. For example, the notion that suffering is a punishment from God makes no sense in the face of innocent suffering, especially when it comes to terrible illness or a natural disaster. Can anyone believe that a small child with cancer is being punished for his or her "sins"? It is a monstrous image of a vengeful and cruel God.

Jesus himself rejects this image of God in the Gospel of John, when he comes upon a man who has been blind since birth (9:2). His disciples ask him, "Rabbi, who sinned, this man or his parents, that he was born blind?"

Jesus replies, "It was not this man who sinned, or his parents, but that the works of God might be made manifest in him" (v. 3). And he heals him.

But many of these traditional biblical and theological resources have been of inestimable help in my own life during different periods of suffering. One incident stands out, not for its severity, but for its durability, because it continues today. And the insights that I learned still provide me with some perspective.

At the beginning of theology studies, I began to experience shooting pains in my hands and wrists. Initially I figured it would subside, but after a few weeks I found myself in near-constant pain, incapable of typing, barely able to write, and slowly losing the ability to do simple things like turning a doorknob or holding a pen.

After six months of visiting all sorts of doctors—internists, neurologists, orthopedic specialists, even hand specialists—I was given a generic diagnosis: repetitive strain injury. Stop typing immediately, my doctor said, lest you risk further injury. By the way, he said, it's probably incurable.

In desperation I visited a host of holistic healers: massage therapists, chiropractors, acupuncturists, even a man who would be accurately called a Catholic faith healer, who prayed over me in his office. Nothing worked.

In time, I learned to manage the pain: stretching, exercise and massage, along with setting limits on typing, seemed to work. The pain continued through theology studies and beyond—in fact, I still have it and am limited in my daily writing.

A few years after theology studies, when I was working at *America* magazine, I started to grow increasingly frustrated about my admittedly minor but nonetheless painful condition. Why would God do this? What was the sense of a writer who couldn't write? What was the point? One day I confessed my frustration to my spiritual director, named Jeff.

"Is God anywhere in this?" he asked.

"No!" I said. How I had grown to hate that question. I tried to find God in all things, but this seemed baffling. The pain prevented me from typing papers during theology studies and complicated my work as a writer and editor at the magazine. Why would God prevent the work that I was missioned to do? So I glumly admitted to Jeff that I couldn't find God anywhere in this situation.

"Really?" he said. "Nowhere?"

Then, almost despite myself, I started to recount how the illness had changed me. Since I could only type for a short period of time each day, I told Jeff, I was more grateful for what I was able to write, because I knew that it was only thanks to God's grace and the gift of health, even if temporary. I was more careful about what I wrote too. Perhaps I was becoming more patient, too, since I couldn't do everything at once. And I was less likely to get a swelled head, since I couldn't talk about the grandiose plans I had for future writing. And I was more aware of others with physical limitations and with far graver illnesses. Maybe I was becoming more compassionate.

Jeff smiled. "Anything else?"

"I'm more conscious of how much I rely on God," I said, "since I can't do anything on my own. I'm less likely to forget about my poverty of spirit."

Jeff laughed. "But God isn't *anywhere* in this?"

Suddenly I realized where God was. That's not to say I was happy about my situation or would have chosen it, that I didn't want it taken away, or even that I completely understood it.

But I did see *some* signs of God, many of which were part of the traditional Christian perspectives on suffering. That it was okay, and even healthy, for me to lament these things before God, as many of the psalms do. That it was indeed mysterious, something I might never understand, like Job's questions in the Old Testament, but that I could still be in relationship with God. That I could try (but would sometimes fail) to emulate the patient way that Jesus faced suffering. That Jesus, who had suffered intensely in his life, could be, through my relationship with him, someone who understood my trials, small though they may be. That suffering could open up new ways of experiencing God. Most of all, that God had been with me in this, and small signs of resurrections became apparent only when I accepted Walter Ciszek's "reality of the situation."

In vulnerability, in poverty of spirit, in brokenness, we are often able to meet God in new ways—perhaps because our guard is down and we are more open to God's presence. This is not the "why" of suffering, but it can sometimes be part of the overall experience.

But my suffering is very small. When I was in East Africa, I met refugees whose brothers and sisters had been murdered before their eyes. I knew a woman in Boston who had been confined to a hospital bed for over twenty years. And recently a close friend's young wife was suddenly diagnosed with an inoperable brain tumor, and, after returning from the hospital, I wept at home for the two of them, and

I saw in an instant how little I had ever suffered compared to them and others. My suffering is very small.

Moreover, my suffering is not yours. Nor is my own perspective of suffering. Just as every believer must find a personal path to God, so must he or she find a personal perspective on suffering. And while the collective wisdom of the religious community is a great resource, the platitudes and bromides offered by otherwise well-meaning believers as quick-fix answers are often unhelpful. Sometimes those easy answers short-circuit the process of deeper individual reflection.

Believers are rightly suspicious of easy answers to suffering. My mother once told me of an elderly nun who was living at a retirement home with my ninety-year-old grandmother. One day the woman's religious superior came to visit. The elderly nun began to speak about how much pain she was enduring. "Think of Jesus on the cross," said her superior. The elderly nun replied, "Jesus was only on the cross for three hours." Easy answers can do more harm than good.

My friend Richard Leonard, an Australian Jesuit, recently wrote about his experience with such facile answers in his book *Where the Hell Is God?*

Richard's family has been touched with great suffering. His father died of a massive stroke at the age of thirty-six, leaving his mother to care for Richard, then two, and his siblings. At dawn on Richard's twenty-fifth birthday, his Jesuit superior woke him to summon him to the phone for an urgent call from his mother. His sister Tracey, a nurse working at a healthcare facility for aboriginal people, had been involved in a terrible car accident. When Richard and his mother reached the hospital, their worst fears were confirmed: Tracey was a quadriplegic. Through tears, Richard's mother began to ask him questions about suffering that put his faith to the test. Richard called it "the most painful and important theological discussion I will ever have in my life."

"Where the hell is God?" his mother asked.

Seedtime, Not Harvest

Alfred Delp, S.J., a German pastor and writer, was executed by the Nazis in 1945 for his opposition to Adolf Hitler. He was an unlikely martyr, headstrong in his youth, but now composed while facing death. In jail, he wrote this about his fate:

> One thing is gradually becoming clear—I must surrender myself completely. This is seedtime, not harvest. God sows the seed and some time or other he will do the reaping. The one thing I must do is to make sure the seed falls on fertile ground. And I must arm myself against the pain and depression that sometimes almost defeat me. If this is the way God has chosen—and everything indicates that it is—then I must willingly and without rancor make it my way. May others at some future time find it possible to have a better and happier life because we died in this hour of trial.

Richard's answer to his mother was, in essence, that God was with them in their suffering. "I think God is devastated," said Richard. "Like the God who groans with loss in Isaiah, and like Jesus who weeps at his best friend's tomb, God was not standing outside our pain, but was a companion within it, holding us in his arms, sharing our grief and pain."

Besides the idea that suffering sometimes opens us to new ways of experiencing God, this is the theological insight that I find most helpful in times of pain: the image of the God who has suffered, the God who shares our grief, the God who understands. Much as you instinctively turn to a friend who has already gone through the same trial you are facing, you can more easily turn to Jesus, who suffered. "For we do not have a high priest who is unable to sympathize with our weaknesses," as the Letter to the Hebrews says (4:15).

Richard takes a dim view of those who offer glib answers. "Some of the most appalling and frightening letters," he writes, came from "some of the best Christians I knew." Tracey must have done something to offend God, some said. Others suggested that her suffering was a "glorious building block . . . for her mansion [in heaven] when she dies." Others wrote that his family was truly "blessed," because "God only sends crosses to those who can bear them." Or, more simply, that it is all a "mystery" that simply needed to be accepted, almost unthinkingly.

Richard rejected these answers in favor of a hard look at the reality of suffering, one that only comes with the long struggle to engage in an "intelligent discussion about the complexities of where and how the Divine presence fits into our fragile and human world."

When we are suffering, our friends will naturally want to help us make sense of our pain, and they will often offer answers like the ones Richard described. Some answers may work for us. Others may leave us cold or even be offensive. But, in the end, each of us must grapple with suffering for ourselves. And while our religious traditions provide us with important resources, ultimately, we must find an approach that enables us to confront pain and loss honestly with God.

Suffering is a mystery for most believers, but it is one that we should engage with all our minds, hearts, and souls. And the way of Ignatius can help us do so. Let me suggest how.

SOME IGNATIAN PERSPECTIVES
ON SUFFERING

The Ignatian worldview accepts and highlights the traditional insights of Scripture and the Christian tradition. But it personalizes those insights by inviting you to meditate deeply on the life of

Christ, to ponder how God might accompany you in your pain, and to develop new insights for yourself.

The reality of suffering is highlighted in one of the first sections of the Exercises, called the Principle and Foundation. Ignatius, after outlining the purpose of life for human beings ("to praise, reverence, and serve God our Lord, and by means of doing this to save their souls"), reminds us to strive for indifference to all created things. That means not shrinking from accepting sickness, poverty, dishonor, or even a short life. Through a variety of meditations, Ignatius reminds us that life will often present us with hardships: this is assumed in the Exercises, as it is assumed in the Christian tradition.

Indeed, two of the most famous meditations in the Exercises incorporate some traditional Christian approaches on suffering. At the beginning of the Second Week, which focuses on the life of Christ, Ignatius asks retreatants to meditate on what he terms the Call of the King. In this meditation we are asked to imagine a charismatic leader asking us to follow him or her.

First we are asked to imagine "a human king" calling us to work alongside him. These days monarchical imagery can leave some people cold. The idea of following, say, Richard the Lion-Hearted into battle may not be as appealing today as it was in the time of Ignatius. As a result, many spiritual directors suggest imagining something closer to a modern hero or heroine: I chose Thomas Merton on my first long retreat and Mother Teresa on the second.

Imagine, suggests Ignatius, your hero asking you to follow him or her. Imagine how exciting it would be to receive a personal call from your hero inviting you to join in a great adventure. Most people, were they actually called personally by their heroes—Martin Luther King, Jr., Mahatma Gandhi, Dorothy Day, Mother Teresa, Pope John Paul II, the Dalai Lama—would immediately say *yes*. But your hero reminds you that you need to do exactly what he does, eat the same food, wear what he wears, work where he works, no matter how difficult.

Next Ignatius invites us to imagine Jesus calling us to work beside him. If we were excited by the prospect of a hero calling us, "how much more" would we want to follow Jesus. But, says Ignatius, we need to be content to experience what Jesus experiences. "Therefore, whoever wishes to come with me must labor with me, so that through following me in the pain he or she may follow me also in the glory."

The Call of the King reminds you, as the Gospels do, that the Christian life will always involve some suffering—something that Ignatius, Walter Ciszek, and all the saints understood.

It also implicitly highlights the image of a Jesus who fully understands what human suffering is, and this image can help us feel less alone when faced with pain.

Jesus' suffering, by the way, does not simply mean his Passion. During his life in Nazareth, he would have fallen ill like any person of his time, endured poverty, and felt sorrow over the death of friends and family—particularly Joseph, his foster father, who most likely died before Jesus' crucifixion. During his ministry, he endured physical hardships as he traveled around the countryside, encountered rejection from religious authorities, and probably felt a loneliness about a mission that, after all, no one else could fathom. Jesus understood the human condition. These are new insights that one gains by imaginatively meditating on his life.

Later in the Second Week, Ignatius presents the Two Standards, which we mentioned in Chapter Eight, in our discussion of "riches to honors to pride." Here are two sides of a titanic battle between good and evil arrayed against each other. "The supreme commander of the good people is Christ our Lord . . . the leader of the enemy is Lucifer." In the Ignatian worldview, there is a battle raging within ourselves between the attractions to do good and to do evil. But Ignatius trusts in the Christian belief that the forces of good will ultimately overpower those of evil.

Moreover, the Two Standards reminds you that while the life-giving choice is clear—choosing Christ—it will involve some suffering, specifically "poverty," "reproaches," and "contempt." Ignatius says that if you want to emulate Christ, you will want to be more like him and will therefore choose a more difficult path.

The notion of choosing a harder path appears several times in the Exercises. The logic goes like this: If I want to follow Jesus, then I will choose to become like him. And if becoming like Jesus means accepting hardships, then I will *seek* those things, assuming that this is not against God's will.

Like the rest of the Exercises, none of this makes sense without understanding the goal of following God. The person who hopes to emulate Christ in his suffering (remember the Third Degree of Humility) does so not because he desires suffering for its own sake or because suffering is a good or because he wishes to punish himself, but rather to be more like his hero, Jesus, who chose to accept the suffering that was placed before him.

This may be the hardest part of Ignatian spirituality to understand—choosing the more difficult route. But for many believers it is freeing, for in doing so, they can emulate their leader and follow him along the same road he trod and experience freedom and joy: the freedom that comes with being detached from excessive self-interest and the joy that comes with following your hero.

Where Ignatius helps us to understand suffering in a unique way lies in his invitation to imagine the suffering of Christ through imaginative prayer. This constitutes the bulk of the meditations for the Third Week of the Spiritual Exercises. Suffering is a mystery to be pondered within the context of a relationship between God and you, and some of this can be done in prayer, especially by meditating on the experiences of Jesus of Nazareth.

In the Third Week the retreatants imagine themselves following Jesus of Nazareth through the Last Supper, to his trials in the garden of Gethsemane, his arrest and beating, the rejection by Peter, his crucifixion, his suffering on the cross, and his death. "Consider what Christ our Lord suffers," Ignatius writes, "or desires to suffer, according to the passage being contemplated."

The retreatant tries to accept the invitation to be with Christ in these meditations. We ask for empathy with the suffering Christ. At one point Ignatius asks us to pray for "sorrow with Christ in sorrow; a broken spirit with Christ so broken; tears; and interior suffering." We are to be present with Jesus as he suffers, something that is difficult for most of us who find it difficult to face suffering that we cannot fix or take away.

David Fleming writes that it is as if Jesus is saying to us, "Let me tell you what it was like, what I saw, and what I felt. . . . Just stay with me and listen."

A Willing Acceptance

Because of their intense desire to follow and identify with Christ, while some Jesuit saints did not actively seek out martyrdom for its own sake, they welcomed it when it was inevitable. They saw it as the ultimate offering of themselves to God, their ultimate obedience. While this spirituality may be difficult to understand, it was the chief way that the martyrs approached the dangers they faced. In the seventeenth century, St. Isaac Jogues and his companions were martyred by the Iroquois during their work among them. This notion of acceptance appears again and again in many of their letters written home. Here is Isaac recounting the last day of René Goupil, who was a lay companion of the Jesuit.

Upon the road he was always occupied with God. His words and the discourses that he held were all expressive of submission to the commands of Divine Providence, and showed a willing acceptance of the death which God was sending him. He gave himself

as a sacrifice, to be reduced to ashes by the fires
of the Iroquois. . . . He sought the means to please
[God] in all things, and everywhere.

Before his death in 1642 René Goupil took vows as a Jesuit. A
few days later he was killed, gruesomely. His body was hidden
by the Iroquois in a deep ravine, and Isaac was only able to
locate his skull and a few bones. Jogues himself was martyred four years later. At the National Shrine of the North
American Martyrs in Auriesville, New York, the ravine is
untouched, overgrown with grass, St. René's body still lost.

Christ is the example *par excellence* of the one who "surrendered
to the future" that God had in store, as Sister Janice said; who accepted the "reality of the situation," as Walter Ciszek said; who
was "obedient to the point of death," as St. Paul said. By meditating
imaginatively on his life, we can gain insights into what it means to
"accept" and what happens when we do and how God can bring new
life out of even the darkest situations.

Moreover, by entering into the scene, you often gain a highly
personal perspective on suffering, one that even the greatest theologians cannot offer. As David Fleming notes in *What Is Ignatian Spirituality?* this kind of prayer "makes the Jesus of the Gospel *our* Jesus."
It helps us to understand better Jesus' sufferings and our own.

Here is Fleming on what people may learn during these meditations:

Our third week meditations also teach us how difficult acceptance is. When we cannot change a situation, we are tempted
to walk away from it. We might literally walk away; we are too
busy to sit with a suffering friend. Or we walk away emotionally; we harden ourselves and maintain an emotional distance.
We might react to the Gospel accounts of Jesus' passion and

death this way. They describe something terrible and horri-
bly painful, yet we might shield ourselves from the pain. We
know the story of the Passion. Ignatius wants us to *experience*
it as something fresh and immediate. We learn to suffer with
Jesus, and thus learn to suffer with the people in our lives.

In the end, we learn that Ignatian compassion is essentially our loving presence. There is nothing we can do. There
is little we can say. But we can *be* there.

And remember the simple technique of the "colloquy," in which
you speak to God in prayer "as one friend speaks to another"? When
meditating on the Passion, retreatants often feel moved to speak
with Jesus about their own suffering. "Seeing" Jesus' suffering is a
reminder that, for the Christian, we are accompanied by a God who,
even if he does not—for whatever mysterious reason—take away our
pain, understands it, since he lived as a human being. During the
times of the worst anguish in my life it has been this prayer that has
most consoled me: speaking with the Jesus who knows suffering.

Let me give you a brief example from my own experiences with
the Exercises, as a way of illustrating our discussion, not because my
experience is normative or even important, but because talking about
suffering demands, I believe, a personal narrative. It's also a chance
to share how Ignatian contemplation can often help you meet God
in ways that are personal, intimate, and surprising.

JESUS OF LOS ANGELES

Recently, I made my second thirty-day retreat at a Jesuit house in
Los Angeles. It would be only the second (and maybe the final) time
that I would make the full Spiritual Exercises. Even though I was
guarding against too many expectations, I was still worried about
"performing" and producing amazing results in prayer, placing upon
myself expectations about what I needed to "do" in prayer, rather
than leaving it up to God.

If you're thinking to yourself, *After twenty years, you should have known better,* you're right!

The Long Retreat was part of the final stage of Jesuit formation, coming almost twenty years after I first entered, and I would be making the retreat with some old friends from novitiate, philosophy, and theology studies.

It seemed easy to enter into the First Week of the Exercises, with its emphasis on being "loved sinners," and more so into the Second Week, which focuses on the earthly ministry of Jesus. Since the Pacific Ocean was not far from the house, I took to running on the beach every other day. Entering into the Gospel passages where Jesus called his disciples by the seashore was a breeze: I had been there just a few hours earlier.

As I approached the Third Week and began to meditate on the last days of Jesus, prayer continued to go smoothly. Insights, memories, emotions, feelings, and desires came during each meditation.

Meditating on Jesus in the garden of Gethsemane, for example, opened up new insights about acceptance, obedience, and what types of temptations Jesus might have faced. When confronted with the possibility of rejection, Jesus may have felt the temptation not to offend anyone with his preaching and thereby avoid his fate. That is what you might call the temptation to accommodation. When faced with opposition, he may have experienced the temptation simply to wipe out his opponents—either through human means (like encouraging his disciples to rise up in furious rebellion) or through divine means (which may be what his followers expected): the temptation for annihilation. Finally Jesus may have felt tempted simply to leave his ministry behind and avoid the path that God was laying out, in favor of a more conventional life: the temptation for abandonment.

Accommodation, annihilation, and abandonment. How often are we tempted to avoid suffering like this? We can accommodate by not fully accepting the reality of suffering—for example, by not entering into the lives of loved ones in pain, but staying safely on the sidelines. We can annihilate by destroying the invitations into the suffering of friends and families—by casting out anyone from our lives who brings us face-to-face with pain. We can abandon by ignoring our responsibilities in the face of suffering.

Yet Jesus accepts the "reality of the situation."

Finally I saw Jesus jailed in Pilate's dank cell, weeping. In my imagination Jesus wept not simply for himself and his upcoming physical torment, but because of something else: the loss of his great project. How many times have you hoped for some great thing, dreamed wonderful dreams, or planned for something joyful, only to have those plans completely dashed?

In my prayer, Jesus remembered all the times he had preached, all the people he healed, all those who had gathered around him— ready to start something new, ready to make great changes, ready to bring joy to the world. As he sat in his cell, all that now seemed lost. His great work, on which he had spent years, seemed over. His friends, on whom he had lavished his love, had deserted him. His project had, seemingly, failed.

More Than Ever

Pedro Arrupe wrote this prayer after a stroke and in the wake of some struggles with the Vatican. It was part of his farewell address to the Jesuits at the General Congregation who had gathered to elect his successor as superior general, in 1983. By this point Arrupe was unable to speak. These words had to be read aloud for him.

More than ever I find myself in the hands of God. This is what I have wanted all my life, from my youth. But now there is a difference; the initiative is entirely with God. It is indeed a profound spiritual experience to know and feel myself so totally in God's hands.

Jesus believed in his course and trusted in his Father, but how could he not be sad? Perhaps in his dark moments—or so I imagined in prayer—he may have wondered if it was all worth it. So Jesus wept.

For Christians, these are points of entry into the life of Jesus: in times of sadness and loneliness and dejection in your own life, you can connect with the human experience of Jesus and, perhaps more important, Jesus can connect with you.

Now let me share with you something quite personal, and quite explicit, as a way of illustrating what can sometimes happen in these Third Week meditations, while contemplating suffering.

Curiously, all the meditations I just mentioned came and went with little feeling. "Very unemotional," I wrote in my journal. When I recounted this to my retreat director, an elderly Jesuit named Paul, it was also with scant feeling. Paul, an experienced spiritual director, listened intently. Then he said, "I think you're blocking something."

"I'm not blocking anything," I told Paul. "I've told you everything I've experienced."

Paul was surprised that so little feeling surrounded these meditations, and he encouraged me to return to Jesus' Passion. This time, he said, sit in the tomb where Jesus has been laid. Ask for the grace to be free of anything that keeps you from being closer to God. Is there anything of you that needs to "die" in that tomb?

When I grudgingly returned to prayer the next day, something surprising happened. Imagining myself sitting in the tomb, I saw Mary, dressed from head to toe in black, sitting silently beside me. And I asked God to free me of whatever was burdening me.

All at once I was aware of the burdens in life that I wanted to set down in that tomb. All the things I had unconsciously kept bottled inside during the previous few weeks—things I didn't want to examine since they might disturb the equanimity of the retreat, things I didn't want to take out of the "box," as David Donovan would say—poured out. Loneliness for one. Not the loneliness of being friendless, but the existential loneliness of religious life: the loneliness of chastity. (Single, divorced, and widowed men and women know this loneliness.) Tiredness for another. Not the tiredness of everyday life, but what seemed like the continuous stress of two, three, or even four jobs at a time. (Parents know this tiredness, too.)

So I told Jesus: "I am lonely and tired." Expressing this brought forth what Ignatius called the "gift of tears."

Immediately I saw myself at the foot of the cross in as vivid a prayer experience as I've ever had. Just that day I had finished a book called *The Day Christ Died,* by Jim Bishop. In it, Bishop notes that Roman crucifixes were probably elevated not far off the ground, and here in my mind's eye was the base of the cross—squarish, boxy, rough. At eye level were Jesus' feet nailed to the cross.

I imagined looking up at Jesus' face. And he said deliberately, *"This is your cross. Can you accept it?"*

I knew what I was being asked to accept. Loneliness and tiredness are the lot of most people, not just Jesuits. But both are still "crosses." Could I accept the "reality of the situation"? Could I surrender to the future that God had in store for me?

"Can you accept it?" I imagined Jesus saying.

I knew what the answer should be, but I wanted to be honest.

"I don't know," I said with many tears.

"Do you want to follow me?" he said.

"Yes, but show me the rest," I said.

After the meditation ended, I was wrung out. Now, these kinds of intense prayer experiences are not so common to me. (Mostly, my prayer is calm and not quite so vivid. Like most everyone else's, it is rich at times, dry at others.)

The next day I returned to the scene and asked Jesus once again to show me the rest: in other words, the Resurrection. And I realized sadly that I would have made a poor martyr—asking for evidence of "new life" before accepting my cross. Though I knew not to compare myself to the Jesuit martyrs, I seemed already to have failed. I felt cast down.

At noontime I walked into the dining room where someone had put on a CD from the movie *Out of Africa*. The music transported me back to my years in Kenya. An hour later in the chapel, I was awash in memories of my time in East Africa and pictured myself standing with Mary, still clad in black, on the grassy hillside I loved near the Jesuit Refugee Service office, the place where I had felt great consolation years ago, a place that still symbolized great freedom and joy for me.

Together Mary and I walked through the places where I had worked during my two years in Nairobi: through the little shop we had started for the refugees, through the dimly lit refugee houses, through the wide grassy paths that I would take returning from work, through the sprawling slums where the refugees lived. I saw their bright faces, I could hear their East African accents, and I could feel their warm affection.

This is a nice resurrection, I thought. But was this all there was? Was this enough for me?

Then, all at once, Jesus was standing beside me, radiant and joyful in his dazzling white robe. This was something I hadn't needed to imagine: it simply appeared in my mind. Jesus reached out his hand and said, *"Follow me!"* The two of us returned to the same places, one by one, now with him holding my hand. It was a vivid reminder that he had been with me throughout my stay.

Jesus appeared in the place where I had felt the freest in my life. It was a surprising, personal, and intimate way to experience a resurrection. For, in a flash, it dawned on me that only by accepting the loneliness and tiredness was I able to experience what I had found in Kenya. God seemed to be saying, *"Yes, you must accept the loneliness and the tiredness, but here is what awaits you when you do. Here is what happens when you say* yes. *And you know this from experience. Here is the new life."*

This experience was a reminder of how helpful Ignatian prayer can be, offering a moment that is at once personal, meaningful, transformative, and even difficult to communicate to others. It was also a reminder of why spiritual direction is helpful—without Paul's guidance I would have simply avoided entering into this passage.

Since that time I've not feared the loneliness or overwork as much. It is part of what I'm asked to accept about my life. But I also know that acceptance means that I can often see signs of new life. The cross leads to resurrection.

All this leads back to obedience. God sometimes asks each of us to accept certain things that seem at the time unacceptable. Unbearable. Even impossible. For me it was loneliness and tiredness. For another it might be terrible illness. For another, the loss of a job. For another, the death of a spouse. For another, a stressful family situation.

This doesn't mean you court those things or that some things should not be changed. "Don't work even *longer* hours because of your retreat!" said my friend Chris after the retreat. Rather, some struggles in life are unavoidable. And, at least in my own life, embracing them may sometimes lead to new ways of finding God.

This small insight may pale in the face of whatever suffering you are experiencing. But it has helped me in my life, and I wanted to share it with you, and I hope it might help you during tough times.

The insight goes by many names: accepting the "reality of the situation," as Walter Ciszek would say; surrendering to "the future that God has in store," as Sister Janice would say; taking up "your cross daily," as Jesus would say. Acceptance. Abandonment. Humility. Poverty of spirit. Finding God in all things.

All of them are talking about the same thing, and all these words and phrases point to one word, a word that may have seemed so strange at the beginning of the chapter and yet which lies at the heart of this life-giving path: obedience.

CHAPTER TWELVE

What Should I Do?

The Ignatian Way of Making Decisions

PROBABLY THE HARDEST DECISION I've ever had to make as a Jesuit was the decision to stay or leave after being delayed for theology studies. I had made a lifelong vow to God, but life somehow seemed to be pulling me away from that original commitment. (The decision seems an easy one now, but like many such choices, it didn't seem so at the time.) And I knew it would be a life-altering choice. Fortunately, my spiritual director was adept at what we Jesuits call "discernment."

Discernment is the overall term for the decision-making practices outlined by Ignatius in the Spiritual Exercises. A Jesuit superior is considered good at discernment not only when he takes seriously the need to pray over each decision, but also when he understands the specific Ignatian techniques of coming to a good decision.

As I mentioned in the last chapter, Jesuits believe that when decisions are to be made, especially concerning assignments, a good process is essential. We also believe that if the superior and subject are both seeking to hear God's voice, then we can rely on God's help in the process itself. Thus, even when Jesuits are sent where they would rather not go, their disappointment is tempered if the discernment has been careful. Likewise, when they find themselves going where they *want* to go, if the discernment seemed shallow, there may remain a nagging doubt over whether the decision was made properly.

Our techniques for making decisions come mainly from the practices outlined in the Spiritual Exercises. Ignatius, assuming that those experiencing the Exercises were reaching a turning point in their lives, includes some superb techniques for making good choices, which we will look at in this chapter. The way of Ignatius will help you answer the question, "What should I do?"

Ignatius's practical ways of making a choice have proven of great use to millions who have walked along his way. They can seem abstract, so I'll use some real-life examples to illustrate what Ignatius was talking about.

INDIFFERENCE

Before entering the decision-making process, Ignatius asks us to try to be "indifferent." In other words, try to approach the decision-making process as freely as possible. "I beg of you, my Lord, to remove anything that separates me from you, and you from me," as Peter Favre wrote.

"Indifference" is easily misunderstood. When most people hear that word, they think not of being free, but of being bored or uninterested. Several years ago an anguished young man, just engaged, came to me with a problem: he wasn't sure if he should continue with the wedding as planned; he was torn over whether he was ready to make a lifelong commitment. Obviously a painful dilemma. During our first conversation I said, "Well, first you have to start with indifference."

"Indifference!" he said. "This is my *life* we're talking about!"

What Ignatius meant by indifference was freedom. The freedom to approach each decision afresh. The ability to be detached from one's initial biases and to step back, the willingness to carefully balance the alternatives. An openness to the working of God in one's life. George E. Ganss, S.J., one of the modern translators of the *Spiritual Exercises,* wrote that indifference means

> undetermined to one thing or option rather than another; impartial; unbiased; with decision suspended until the reasons for a wise choice are learned; still undecided.

Ganss concludes with what I conveyed, less eloquently, to the young man thinking about postponing his wedding. "In no way does it mean unconcerned or unimportant. It implies interior freedom."

Every major decision carries some baggage. The question, "Should I marry this person?" or "Should I go on with my wedding plans?" may have in the background your fiancé(e) or your parents or your best friend pressuring you to get married. Or not to change your plans.

But while advice from friends and family can help us arrive at a good decision, Ignatius asks us to begin the decision-making process as impartially as possible. That bit of common sense is often forgotten.

To use a famous Ignatian image, one should try to be like the "pointer of a balance." If you've ever seen an old metal scale, like the ones used in old-time butcher shops for weighing meats, you'll remember a metal arrow that points straight up—to zero—when the scale is empty and perfectly at rest. There's nothing weighing on either side.

This is what Ignatius means. When we begin to make a decision, we should emulate that metal pointer—not leaning in one way or another. You don't want to imitate the unscrupulous butcher who sticks his thumb on the scale to fudge the weight. That's cheating. Starting off by assuming that you should decide one way or the other is cheating yourself out of a good choice.

Indifference in decision making is hard to achieve. The fellow planning his marriage found himself in the midst of a serious emotional crisis where indifference seemed nearly impossible. But it is an important goal. Like all things in the spiritual life, while you try to move toward it and strive to be as free as possible, indifference is a result of God's grace.

IGNATIUS GETS A HAIRCUT

Many of Ignatius's famous practices for making good decisions came from his own life. The earliest example, as I mentioned, was the insight he received when he was reading the life of Christ and the lives of the saints. After Ignatius thought about emulating the saints, he was filled with peace. When he thought about doing more worldly things (impressing "a certain lady"), he felt dry. Slowly he came to see that this was one way that God was leading him.

Ignatius realized that if you act in accord with God's desires for you, you will naturally feel a sense of peace. That insight—that following God's invitation leads to peace—is a central part of Ignatian discernment. If you are in accord with God's presence within you, you will feel a sense of rightness, of peace, what Ignatius called "consolation." It is an indication that you're on the right path.

Conversely, feelings of spiritual "desolation," which Ignatius describes as movements to "disquiet from various agitations and temptations," signal that you're on the *wrong* path. The thoughts and feelings that spring from consolation and from desolation are contrary to one another. One leads you to the right path, the right action, right relationship with God; the other in the opposite direction.

From the Spiritual Exercises

Since spiritual consolation and desolation are central to Ignatian discernment, let's look at Ignatius's original definitions. By consolation he means not only feelings that cause a soul to be "inflamed with love" for God, and even shed tears for the love of God, but also

every increase in hope, faith, and charity, and every interior joy which calls and attracts one toward heavenly things and to the salvation of one's soul, by bringing it tranquility and peace in its Creator and Lord.

By desolation, Ignatius means feelings that are "contrary" to consolation, that is obtuseness of soul, turmoil within it, an impulsive motion toward low and earthly things, or disquiet from various agitations and temptations. These move one toward lack of faith and leave one without hope and without love. One is completely listless, tepid, and un-happy, and feels separated from our Creator and Lord.

These feelings, which Ignatius knew from his initial conversion, as well as from years of prayer afterward and his spiritual direction of countless persons, enable us to discern which choices will help lead us closer to God.

This basic element of Ignatian discernment is rooted in the experiences of Ignatius, as well as his observations about how God worked in the lives of others. David Lonsdale, who teaches spiritu-ality at Heythrop College in London, addresses discernment in his book *Eyes to See, Ears to Hear*. Discernment, says Lonsdale, is about the "spiritual interpretation and evaluation of feelings, and particu-larly with the direction in which we are moved by them." Michael Ivens, S.J., in *Understanding the Spiritual Exercises,* points out that this is "recognizing the action in human consciousness of the Holy Spirit." David Fleming calls it "decision-making by a loving heart."

Discernment has a practical end. It is not simply a way to try to find God's will; nor is it a way just to move closer to God in prayer. Discernment helps to decide what is the best way to *act*. It isn't simply about relationship with God alone; it is about living out your faith in the real world. Ignatius was a results-oriented mystic.

And, as a practical man, he was not averse to changing his mind in the face of new data.

Not long after his conversion, as I mentioned, he retired to a dank cave outside a town called Manresa. With characteristic en-thusiasm, Ignatius decided that in order to throw off his former vanity, he would take the opposite tack. The formerly vain person would no longer care for his appearance, letting his hair grow wild and refusing to cut the nails on his fingers and toes. The former elegant courtier must have presented a fearsome sight.

A few months later he reverses his decision. What happened? He concluded that his austerity was doing little to help him with his ultimate goal of "helping souls." Even though he had adopted this penance for a good reason, he abandoned it to accomplish his goals. The reasons are hard to discern: he may have felt his bizarre appearance would repel others. But whatever the motivation, he wrote, "He gave up those extremes that he had formerly practiced."

Thereafter he would follow a path of moderation, toning down the severe religious penances popular in his day. Years later, he counseled Jesuits against undertaking similarly austere practices if they prevented working efficiently. In the *Constitutions* he advised Jesuits to be moderate in all things and maintain their health: eat healthy food, get good exercise, and have the proper rest in order to carry out their work. "A proper concern with the preservation of one's health and bodily strength for the divine service is praiseworthy and should be exercised by all," he said, quite sensibly.

A seemingly minor decision about cutting his hair was among the first of many times when Ignatius would weigh the pros and cons of a course of action and also realize the need for constant evaluation and reevaluation.

Years after his conversion, while celebrating Mass, he frequently felt overcome with emotion, often to the point of tears. But this became so physically taxing, with tears affecting his vision, that he resolved for a time to give up his Masses to regain his health, in order that he might work better. Discernment for Ignatius frequently meant changing course.

Ignatius was "indifferent" enough to learn from his experiences. The ascetic pilgrim who neglected his health could, with great freedom, change course and later counsel Jesuits to care for their own health. And one of the greatest mystics in Christian history could curtail his own time in prayer and counsel Jesuits against excessive prayer lest it take them away from their work. Reaching your goal, Ignatius realized, sometimes means changing paths. Sometimes it even means turning around.

One of his earliest companions, Jerónimo Nadal, wrote that even when it came to planning the direction of the Society of Jesus, "He was gently led where he did not know."

A final aside before we look at his decision-making practices: for Ignatius all mature choices are between "goods." In other words, you don't consider something manifestly evil. So the question, "Should I punch my boss in the face because he's a jerk?" is not worth considering. Nor is: "Should I chop down my neighbor's maple tree if it keeps dropping those stupid leaves on my lawn that I have to rake up every Saturday?" Both are obviously bad choices, and justified though you may feel in wanting to make them, they are not the choices that Ignatius feels should be under consideration. (Then again, Ignatius was his own boss, and he never lived in the suburbs.)

Some matters aren't up for grabs. If you've already made an "unchangeable" decision, according to Ignatius, you should stick with it. Commitments are honored. And if you've made a "changeable" decision for good reasons and you're comfortable with it and there's no reason to change things, don't bother making a new decision.

So I don't come to my annual retreats with the question, "Should I stay a Jesuit priest?" Now and then I may seek more clarity, and I may even be tempted to think about leaving once in a while. (Or, as my friend Chris jokes, you might be tempted to "think about thinking about leaving.") But it's not something that requires a decision. Ignatius would say: Don't waste your time. You've already made a commitment.

Also, if you've made a good decision and suddenly feel downcast, it's not a sign to reconsider. Let's say you have decided to be a more generous person and will forgive someone against whom you've had a grudge for many months. So you speak with your friend. If your forgiveness doesn't seem to heal the relationship immediately, it does not mean you should stop being a forgiving person. "When you have made a good decision to serve God better and after a while go into desolation, you should not change the decision; it's hardly a good spirit moving you," writes Joseph Tetlow in *Making Choices in Christ*. "When you are feeling down, you would do well to pray a little more and increase the help you give to others."

On the other hand, if you've made a changeable decision in a *bad* way, you can revisit it. You might want to "make it anew in a properly ordered way," says Ignatius. If you've made a poor decision that can still be changed, why not take a fresh look at things?

In the Exercises, Ignatius lists three "times" of making a decision, which could also be described as three situations in which we find ourselves facing a choice. Now the following discussion may seem tricky at times, and you even might find yourself initially a little baffled by some of the terminology and the various steps. That was my first reaction when I was introduced to these practices as a novice.

But don't worry. Perhaps because he came from a military class, or needed to manage a large religious order, Ignatius liked things marshaled in an orderly fashion. As a result, the Spiritual Exercises are full of lists, most of which come in twos and threes. The Two Standards. The Three Degrees of Humility. The Three Times of Making a Decision. Sometimes it feels less like prayer and more like algebra.

And don't worry if you get confused in the following discussion over what time you're in, or what method you're using. More important is finding some techniques, or combination of techniques, that work for you, that fit. Eventually, if you practice enough, you'll find that the techniques will become second nature.

You'll find something else about his techniques for decision making: they work.

THE THREE TIMES

The First Time

Occasionally there is no question about what to do. This is decision making in the First Time. Your decision comes, says Ignatius, "without doubting or being able to doubt."

One example: You've been searching for a job in a particular city with a particular company, starting at a particular time. After months of interviewing, you land the job. You are elated at your good fortune and sure it is the right move. You accept the new job immediately with barely a thought.

Ignatius compares the First Time with the story of St. Paul being blinded by a heavenly light and hearing the voice of Jesus. No doubt here. Paul was asked to go into Damascus, and he did so.

Recently an actor told me of falling in love with acting in high school. He decided on his career after his first play, never looked back, and never regretted his choice. "I loved acting so much that it hurt," he said. That was that. The First Time.

In their book *The Spiritual Exercises Reclaimed,* the three authors give a marvelous example of the First Time, from a woman known by one of the writers:

> I've spent the past twenty years putting my husband through school, and then the kids. I was happy to be taking the kids to Little League, but now it's time for *me.* There is a community college close, and my son just got his driver's license, so there is no need to be carting him to after-school sports. I'm going to school now. It's the right time and the right thing to do. I just know it.

In all these cases a decision was made, and though someone might not compare his or her experience with St. Paul's, it could not be doubted. In a sense, the answer comes as soon as the question is asked.

The eventual decision to enter a religious order was something like that for me. In an earlier chapter I mentioned returning home one night after work and stumbling upon a documentary on Thomas Merton, which led me to enter a religious order. Looking back, it was a decision made in the First Time.

At the time I was working for General Electric in Stamford, Connecticut, in human resources. When I arrived at my apartment one night, which I shared with two friends, it was nearing 9:00 p.m. After changing out of my business clothes, I rummaged around the refrigerator for some leftovers, popped a plate of old spaghetti in the microwave, sat down in front of the television, and started flipping through the channels.

Presently, I stumbled upon a documentary about a Trappist monk I had never heard of. All sorts of people—musicians, writers, scholars—appeared on screen to testify to the influence that he had in their lives. The program detailed Thomas Merton's long process of conversion, from lonely boy to rebellious college student to aimless grad student to brand-new Catholic to, finally, Trappist monk. But the most arresting part of the show was not the story, but the photographs of Merton. His face radiated a kind of serenity that was unknown to me and that called to me.

The next day, I tracked down and began reading Merton's autobiography, *The Seven Storey Mountain*. When I finished the book late one night, it dawned on me that I wanted to do what Merton had done in the 1940s: leave behind a life of confusion and join a religious order. (Little did I know that life in a religious order is not free of confusion.) Over time I learned more about the Jesuits, the religious order that seemed to suit me best.

Still, though the desire to join a religious order was born on that evening, I resisted it. It would take two years before I was able to see it with absolute clarity. After I buried myself once again in work, the thought of entering religious life lay dormant in my soul, like a seed ready to sprout—as soon as it received some water.

Eventually someone—a psychologist I was seeing because I was so stressed at work—watered that seed. He asked me a question that helped me to name my desire. One day I was complaining to him about my job. It wasn't satisfying, wasn't enjoyable, and wasn't something I could see doing for more than a few more years.

Finally he said, "What would you do, if you could do anything you wanted to do?"

The answer came as if it had been waiting there all my life. "That's easy," I said. "I would become a Jesuit priest!"

And he said, "Well, why don't you?"

"Yeah," I said, "why *don't* I?"

The path to the Jesuits suddenly became clear. While I knew little about the Jesuits, and even less about the application process, I knew for sure that I wanted to join up immediately. It was a real *Aha!* moment. As with St. Paul, it was as if "something like scales" fell from my eyes. As Ignatius says, I neither doubted nor was able to doubt. Everything fell into place and a few months later I entered the Jesuit novitiate. It was the best decision I've ever made and also one of the few occasions when I experienced making a decision in the First Time.

The Second Time

The Second Time is less clear. It is not love at first sight. It's not like being bowled over by clarity à la St. Paul. It's less of an *Aha!* moment. It requires some deliberation.

In the Second Time you may not be completely sure, at least initially. Contrary forces and desires seem to pull you one way or the other. To return to our career example, you have found a job with a good salary, but it's not starting at the right time. Or it's the right salary but the wrong job. While the decision may not be clear initially, in time, after you think about it, talk about it, and pray about it, the decision gradually becomes clearer. You find yourself moved toward taking the job.

At this point, says Ignatius, it's good to meditate on which option gives you the greater consolation. Ignatius asks you to look at the "motions" within you as a sign of God's helping you with your choice. For people trying to discern God's hopes and dreams for their lives, the presence of God will be reflected primarily through consolation.

Consolation, again, is the sense of God's presence and those interior feelings that lead to peace, tranquility, and joy. Here, in a time of decision, consolation is a sense of peace and of rightness of the choice. Consolation leads you to feel encouraged, confident, and calm in your decision.

For many years I wondered about the connection between making a good decision and feeling consolation. It seemed almost superstitious. Does God zap you with consolation, like a magic trick, to help you make the right choice?

No. As David Lonsdale writes, we feel peace about a particular decision when it is "coherent with" God's desires for our happiness. Ignatius understood that God works through our deepest desires. When we are following that path to God, things seem right. Things feel in synch because they *are* in synch.

Lonsdale's explanation of consolation is superb. The main feature of feelings of consolation is that "their direction is toward growth, creativity and a genuine fullness of life and love in that they draw us to a fuller, effective, generous love of God and other people, and to a right love of ourselves."

The flip side of consolation is desolation. By this Ignatius means anything that moves you toward hopelessness. You are agitated or restless or, as Ignatius says, "listless, tepid, and unhappy." These feelings mean you are moving away from a good decision.

Ignatian discernment means trusting that God will speak to you through these spiritual experiences about the choices you are considering. As Fleming writes, our hearts will gradually tell us which choices are moving us closer to God. All this is based on the belief that God does move our hearts and that we can grow in our sensitivity to God's voice within us.

While recovering from his wounds at Pamplona, Ignatius felt consolation when he thought about following the saints. When he thought about impressing "a certain lady," he felt desolation. Gradually he realized that these were ways that God was calling him to the best course of action. These are the kinds of feelings that you weigh in your prayer during the Second Time.

The Discerning Mother

Here's a joke about discernment: A woman asks her local priest for advice. "Father," she says, "I have a little boy who is six months old. And I'm curious to know what he will be when he grows up."

The priest says, "Place before him three things: a bottle of whiskey, a dollar bill, and a Bible. If he picks the bottle of whiskey, he'll be a bartender. If he picks the dollar bill, a business man. And if he picks the Bible, a priest." So the mother thanks him and goes home.

The next week she returns. "Well," said the priest, "which one did he pick: the whiskey, the dollar bill, or the Bible?"

She says, "He picked all three!"

"Ah," says the priest, "a Jesuit!"

Besides praying about decisions and examining whether you feel a sense of consolation, there is another practice that can be used during the Second (and Third) Times. It is imagining living with each choice for a set period of time and seeing which choice gives you a greater sense of peace.

For a few days, act as if you were going to choose one alternative. Though you've not made the choice, *imagine* that you have, and move through your day as if you had made the decision already. Try the decision on, like a new sweater. How does it make you feel? Do you feel at peace or agitated? Then, for the next few days take the opposite tack. How does that make you feel?

This is a powerful tool. Normally our minds move restlessly from one alternative to the other, jumping like a nervous grasshopper from one blade of grass to the next, never giving ourselves sufficient time to consider either alternative. But after imaginatively living with one course of action, and then the other, certain things will come to mind that you may not have noticed before. Advantages and disadvantages become more evident with time. In a sense, you'll see the consequences of the decision before you make it. At the end of the process, ask yourself which option gave you the most peace? Then trust your feelings and make the decision.

But discernment, as Fleming notes, is not simply a matter of feeling peaceful. You must carefully assess what is going on inside of you. "Complacency and smugness about a decision can masquerade as consolation. At times, desolation can be a timely sense of restlessness pointing us in a new direction." Honesty about what you are really feeling, and why, is paramount.

When it comes to making decisions, the First and Second Times present relatively few difficulties. The First Time is crystal clear. The Second Time may be less clear at first but, after prayer and consideration, becomes clear enough through these feelings of consolation and desolation and leads to what Ignatius calls "sufficient clarity and knowledge."

The Third Time

For many people, the most common decision-making situation is the Third Time. You find yourself with two or more good alternatives, but neither one is the obvious choice. There is no *Aha!* moment. There is little clarity in prayer.

"The soul," says Ignatius, "is not being moved one way and the other by various spirits." And this murky time is where the clearly defined practices of St. Ignatius may be the most helpful. His techniques may also give you something unexpected: calm. Recently a young man who comes to me for spiritual direction said that simply knowing these techniques made him feel less overwhelmed by the prospect of having to make a big decision.

For the Third Time, Ignatius provides two methods. Let's use a familiar example: whether to buy a new house or stay in the small apartment where you live. As anyone who has made that decision knows, that kind of move is notoriously complex—raising issues that are both economic and emotional.

The First Method is based on reason. Once again, start with indifference. You should be inclined neither to move one way or the other, despite the agonizing you may have done over this decision already.

This is a key insight. We cannot freely consider a decision if we have already made it, or have made it by default. "I am not more inclined or emotionally disposed toward taking the matter proposed rather than relinquishing it," writes Ignatius, "nor more toward relinquishing it rather than taking it. Instead, I should find myself in the middle, like the pointer of a balance."

In this First Method, Ignatius gives us six steps:

First, put before yourself in prayer the choice: in this case, buying a house or staying in your apartment.

Second, identify your ultimate objective, which for Ignatius is the desire to please God, as well as the need to be indifferent.

Third, ask God for help to move your heart toward the better decision.

Fourth, make a list, either in your head or on paper, of the possible positive and negative outcomes of the first option. Then make a list of the possible positive and negative outcomes of the second option.

The house hunter would list the benefits of buying a new house: more space, more freedom to do what you want with the place, the money now going for rent will go to ownership, and so on. Then list the negative aspects about buying a new house: you assume a mortgage and will have to tend the property, mow the lawn, worry about repairs, and so on.

Then think about the alternative. What are the positives? Remaining in your apartment would mean you wouldn't have to spend time moving, you would feel comfortable in your old place, and you could keep to your familiar daily schedule. What about the negatives? Rent increases, cramped surroundings, noisy neighbors.

The First Method reminds us that no decision leads to the perfect outcome. Each outcome is a mixed bag. Listing the positives and negatives frees you from the idea that a good decision means choosing perfection.

Fifth, now that you have your lists, pray about them and see which way your reason inclines. Eventually you will come to a choice that brings some peace. But there is a further step.

Sixth, ask for some sort of confirmation from God that this is the right decision.

Confirmation should be sought in every decision. And Ignatius *expected* that one will experience confirmation of the "rightness of our choice," as Lonsdale says. This may mean the experience of consolation as described above, or simply the feeling of being at peace with yourself and God. A poor choice would more likely lead to feelings of desolation or agitation, as if we had somehow taken a wrong turn. As Michael Ivens notes, "We pray for confirmation in order to be as sure of doing God's will as it is given us to be; and to counter the tendency in us to opt for hasty closure."

Ivens reminds us that we should be satisfied with whatever confirmation we receive. Even if it's simple. "This may in the end be simply the negative confirmation that nothing comes up to call our decision into question."

That's not to say that a good decision won't stir you up. If you decide to move, there will be lots to do. And everyone feels some buyer's remorse. You may feel some anxiety as you think about all the responsibilities a new house entails. But if, deep down, you feel consolation, you feel peace, you feel you're headed in the right direction, it's probably a good choice.

Sometimes confirmation comes in a more dramatic way. Sometimes the clarity might even make you smile. My longtime friend Chris was thinking of leaving his old job as an investment manager in a large corporation. He had been offered a new position at a midsize university, his alma mater, managing their investment portfolio. Chris had come to the brink of accepting the new job, but something seemed to hold him back.

The morning he had to give his decision to the university, he turned on his computer. Chris is a faithful member of the United Church of Christ and reads an online devotional each day, a short reflection on Scripture and faith. This morning he flipped on his computer and went to the devotional Web site that he turns to every morning. The heading for that day was: Time to Leave.

Maybe the Lord has sent this message into your life at this time to give you one more encouragement to obey his leading you to let go of something safe and follow him into something bigger and better, but largely unknown.

Chris had his confirmation. He laughed when he recounted the story and said, "Isn't it nice when God is direct?"

But most of the time God is not so clear. So be content with what confirmation God gives you.

Confirmation also needs to be found *outside of you*. It's not just about how you feel or even the feeling of "rightness." In Jesuit life, if you make a decision and the superior does not reach the same decision, you can say that ultimately it was not confirmed. For most people the confirmation also comes from testing it out.

Here's an example: Let's say you've decided to confront your manager about his tirades at work. You've carefully discerned that you will speak to him during your annual job performance evaluation. But on that very morning you discover that your boss is in a foul mood and has just exploded in anger at a coworker. It doesn't seem like your decision to confront him today has received confirmation. But it may be as simple as waiting a few days. Just because you've discerned doesn't mean that you shouldn't look to reality for some real-life confirmation. As one Jesuit said, "Trust your heart but use your head, too."

All this does not mean that you've made a bad choice. It may simply be time to discern again based on the new data. This is the pattern of "reflection-action-reflection" that Jesuits teach their students. You reflect on a decision, act on it, see what happens, and then reflect on that experience, leading to another decision, propelling you ahead. This is part of being a "contemplative in action," someone who is always reflecting on his active life, as Ignatius did.

Now, you might say that the First Method is an obvious way of making a Third Time decision. "Big deal—a list of pros and cons!"

But Ignatius highlights a few steps that we normally ignore when making a choice.

First, he reminds us of the value of indifference. Many times we enter into a decision with our minds already made up, or too concerned about how others will judge our decision. Try to avoid both traps.

Second, the First Method is more concerned with reason than emotion. This helps to remove the tremendous anxiety that normally surrounds a major decision. Emotions are critical when making a decision. But often we are so emotional about a big decision that while we *know* that making a list is the sensible thing to do, because of all the emotional stress we never do it! The First Method reminds us of the value of reason.

Third, Ignatius reminds us that each course of action will be imperfect. Every solution has positive and negative aspects. As a Jesuit friend likes to say, "There are pros and cons on both sides." This helps us avoid the trap of seeking the "perfect" outcome.

Using lists in decision-making is common. What Ignatius adds to this approach is indifference, praying over the list, seeking confirmation, and trusting that God is part of the process, because God desires your happiness and peace.

Sometimes the First Method can be difficult. One man told me that with all these lists, he found this too analytical, too much like "processing data," as he put it. That's okay, I told him, because Ignatius has another method for you.

The Second Method relies less on reason and more on imagination. It employs some creative techniques to help us think about the decision in a fresh way. Remember, Ignatius was flexible. Here he offers a variety of ways for making a decision, depending on a person's psychological makeup—some rely on prayer, some on reason, some on the imagination. Once again Ignatius shows us his keen understanding of human nature.

First, he suggests you "imagine a person whom I have never seen or known," and *imagine what advice you would give to this person* regarding the same decision you are facing. This can help free you from excessive focus on *yourself.*

A few years ago, for example, I felt obliged to speak out about a controversial issue in the church. The only problem was that my Jesuit superior told me that he didn't want me speaking out. It was a difficult situation: my integrity pulled one way, and my vow of obedience another. If I went with my integrity, I would have to disobey my superior. If I obeyed my superior, I would have to compromise my integrity.

Coming to a good decision seemed impossible. In prayer I was drawn to the figure of Jesus courageously preaching the truth. At other times I imagined Jesus reminding me about my vow of obedience. My emotions failed to lead me to a clear answer: on the one hand, I felt the desire to speak out; on the other the desire to be a good Jesuit. My reason also failed to lead me to a clear answer: on the one hand, you should speak the truth. On the other hand, you should keep your vows.

In the midst of my confusion I remembered the Second Method. So I imagined someone in my situation: a Jesuit who felt obliged to speak out, but wanted to follow his vow of obedience. Instantly it became clear what I would say to him, as I was freed from focusing on *myself.*

In my imagination, I advised this hypothetical person that he needed to seek the approval of his superiors, even though it might take years. In this way he would be honest, trying to say what his conscience impelled and also faithful to his vows as a Jesuit. After I had finished with that prayer, I felt a tremendous burden lifted. The Second Method had freed me to see clearly. I knew what I had to do, because I knew what *he* had to do.

Second, says Ignatius, you can imagine yourself *at the point of death.* That sounds morbid, I know. It is also clarifying. Think of yourself on your deathbed, far in the future, and imagine asking yourself: what should I have done?

It's easy to see why this is so effective. Often we choose something that is more expedient *now,* the easier course, which we know might be a decision that we will regret. The old saying that no one on his deathbed ever said, "I wish I had spent more time at the office," captures some of this insight.

Third, we can imagine ourselves at the *Last Judgment.* Which choice would we want to present before God?

To use our earlier example of the house hunter, no one is going to be scolded by God for staying in an apartment rather than buying a house! But, particularly with moral choices, this method can help to focus on the demands of faith.

For example, perhaps you're deciding whether to accept a new job, with a higher salary, but one that means you will spend dramatically less time with your family. You might imagine God, at the end of your life, being sad over that decision.

Let me add an additional suggestion to those of Ignatius, a *fourth* technique: *imagine what your "best self" would do.*

You probably have an idea of the person you would like to become, the person you think God is calling you to be or, likewise, your "best self," "authentic self," or "true self." For me, it's a person who is free, confident, mature, independent, and loving. Can you imagine your best self, the person you hope to become one day? As you consider your decision, ask yourself: *What would my best self do?* Sometimes the insight will come all at once—you think, *if I were a freer and more loving person, I would obviously choose this option.*

Making decisions with that fourth technique may seem odd at first. That is, acting as if you were your best self may feel unfamiliar. But, eventually, by acting that way, you will help yourself move in the direction of actually being your best self. As Gerard Manley Hopkins wrote, a person can "act in God's eyes what in God's eye

The Discerning Mule

In his autobiography Ignatius tells the hair-raising story of one of his earliest, and most misguided, discernments. Soon after his conversion, Ignatius met a man traveling along the road, who insults the Virgin Mary. The hotheaded Ignatius is furious and begins to decide whether or not to kill him. He comes to a fork in the road, and reasons that if his mule follows the same path as the blasphemous man, that will be a sign from God, and he will kill the man. "He felt inclined," writes Ignatius of himself, "to stab him with his dagger." Fortunately for everyone involved, the mule picks the other road. When telling this story to a group of young Jesuits, one provincial drew laughs by saying, "And ever since then, asses have been making decisions in the Society of Jesus!"

he is." Making decisions as if you were your best self will help you become your best self.

THE RULES FOR DISCERNMENT

In addition to these methods and practices, Ignatius lists what we could call "helpful hints" for making big decisions. He also shows how to recognize when the "enemy of human nature" is at work and when the "good spirit" is at work in your choices.

You might be tripped up again by the antiquated terms that Ignatius uses. Make no mistake: Ignatius believed that the "good spirit" is the Spirit of God leading us to a healthy and holy life. The "evil spirit" or the "enemy," in Ignatius's worldview, is the spirit of Satan. That's what I believe, too, though I don't necessarily think of Satan as having horns and hooves. (Then again, who knows?)

Another way to think of this is to see those feelings that pull us away from God as opposing the Spirit of God. Or to distinguish between what is "of God" and what is "not of God." Most of us feel that pull between good and evil, healthy and unhealthy, selfish and generous, in our lives. Ignatius casts this in terms of a battle and, through a variety of means, helps us to identify which spirit is at work. Timothy Gallagher, O.M.V., in *The Discernment of Spirits* says: "Ignatius recognizes that when we seek to embrace God's love and follow God's will according to the full truth of our human nature, we will encounter something inimical to this seeking; we will be faced with an *enemy*."

But no matter how you imagine evil operating, the way that the "enemy" *works* within people is instantly identifiable and seems to have certain traits that make it recognizable. However you understand it, you'll see that here, especially, Ignatius is a worthy match for Freud or Jung in his canny understanding of the human psyche. "Smart guy," a psychologist once said of Ignatius after I described some of these insights.

These tips, called Rules for Discernment, are not so much tech-niques like those above, but insights.

Let me share the ones that I have found the most useful.

The Drop of Water

If you're going from one bad thing to another, on a downward path, the enemy will encourage you to continue. The enemy "makes them imagine delights and pleasures of the senses, in order to hold them fast and plunge them deeper into their sins," says Ignatius. So if you're engaging in sinful behavior, the evil spirit will make you feel *good* about those things. If you're engaged in some sleazy business scheme, the evil spirit will say, *"Oh, just keep going. Don't worry. Imagine all the money you'll make. No one will find out. Everyone's doing it. You deserve it. Everything will be fine."*

In the 1940 Alfred Hitchcock movie *Rebecca,* based on a Daphne Du Maurier novel, there is a marvelous scene in which Mrs. Danvers, the wicked servant of the house (played by Judith Anderson), is peering out a window alongside Mrs. de Winter, the new wife of the master of the house. The jealous servant despises the new wife and has succeeded in making her life in the house miser-able. Lonely and forlorn, the new Mrs. de Winter gazes at the ground below her, as Mrs. Danvers encourages her to kill herself.

"You have nothing to live for, really, have you?" she purrs. "Look down there. It's easy, isn't it? Why don't you? Why don't you? Go on . . . go on . . . don't be afraid."

That's the way the evil spirit works: encouraging us to continue our bad thoughts or bad actions, moving us backward. *"Go on,"* it says. *"It's easy, isn't it?"*

For persons on the downward path, the *good* spirit acts in the opposite way. Here you feel the sting of conscience "with remorse," says Ignatius. If you're stealing money from your company, you will feel a jolt in your conscience, saying, in essence, *"Wake up! You're doing something wrong!"* That's the good spirit at work.

Here Ignatius famously uses a homey metaphor: the drop of water. For those going from bad to worse, the evil spirit feels like a drop of water falling on a *sponge:* soothing, calming, encouraging. Or as Ignatius says, "delicate, gentle, delightful." But the good spirit in these cases is like the drop of water falling on a *stone:* startling, hard, even loud. "Violent, noisy, and disturbing," says Ignatius. As my friend David would say, "Pay attention!"

By the way, when we are going from bad to worse, the startling drop of water on a stone can come both interiorly and exteriorly: it can take the form of hardnosed advice from a friend, who jolts us out of spiritual complacency.

For those moving in the opposite direction—which is most of us—trying to lead a good life, striving to go from good to better, the feelings are *reversed.* In this case the good spirit is like the drop of water on the sponge; the bad spirit the drop of water on the stone.

Let's say you've decided to volunteer at a soup kitchen. In this case, the good spirit gently encourages you on this good path. Here, says Ignatius, the good spirit will "stir up courage and strength, consolations, tears, inspirations, and tranquility. [The good spirit] makes things easier and eliminates all obstacles, so that the persons may move forward in doing good." You will feel consoled, inspired, and buoyed up as you think of volunteering and moving along a loving path.

The enemy will move you in the other direction, acting like the drop of water on the stone. *Uh oh!* you think suddenly, *I've never done anything like this! It's too hard!* Frequently this comes as a sudden, disorienting fear. It is characteristic of the evil spirit, says Ignatius, to "cause gnawing anxiety, to sadden, and to set up obstacles. In this way he unsettles these persons by false reasons aimed at preventing their progress."

Why do good and evil spirits work in opposite ways depending on the state of one's soul? Here's Ignatius's homey explanation: "The reason for this is the fact that the disposition of the soul is either similar to or different from the respective spirits who are entering.

When the soul is different, they enter with perceptible noise and are quickly noticed. When the soul is similar, they enter silently, like those who go into their own house by an open door."

Another discernment dyad I like to use is what-ifs and if-onlys. For the person trying to do good, the evil spirit discourages you with what-ifs and if-onlys. Let's say that you've started to volunteer at a local shelter. Suddenly you have a frightening thought: *Oh no! What if I get sick working with all of those poor people? What if one of them attacks me? What if the staff thinks I'm too inexperienced?* Those what-ifs lead to a dead end. The enemy proposes only the worst about the future, which is unknowable. That's the evil spirit causing "gnawing anxiety," and it should be avoided.

If-onlys focus our worries on the past. You might be derailed by thinking, *If only I had started this years ago! If only I hadn't wasted so much time! If only I had thought about the poor earlier!* The evil spirit is causing "gnawing anxiety," this time centered on the past. That's a dead end as well: the past cannot be changed. Ignore that feeling, too.

Sometimes what-ifs and if-onlys can help us dream, or they can move us to sorrow for our sins. But when they move you toward fear, prevent you from moving ahead in healthy ways, lead to dead ends, and "cause gnawing anxiety," they are most likely not coming from God.

Finally, you might look carefully at the "pushes" and "pulls," too. One of my spiritual directors, Damian, said that when you feel pushed to do something—*I should do this, I should do that*—out of a sense of crushing and lifeless obligation or a desire to please everyone, it may not be coming from God. David Donovan used to call this "shoulding all over yourself." (Read it aloud and the pun becomes obvious.)

God's "pulls," on the other hand—gentle invitations that beckon in love—feel different. Sometimes an obligation is an obligation, and you need to do it in order to be a good and moral person. But be careful your life is not simply one in which you only respond to shoulds or pushes that may not be coming from God.

No Changes in Desolation

Another tip: "During a time of desolation one should never make a change," says Ignatius. Why not? Because when you are feeling distant from God and experiencing desolation (gnawing anxiety, etc.), you are more inclined to be guided by the evil spirit. When feeling abandoned by God, you are more likely to say, "This is useless!" and change course. Or ask despairingly, "What's the use?" and give up. Don't do it. To allow yourself to be led by desolation, says Michael Ivens, is to be drawn into "downward momentum."

This makes sense, doesn't it? If someone told you that he was miserable, couldn't think straight, and was completely despairing, would you say that this is a good time for him to make a big decision? Of course not. He's not thinking clearly. "Don't make decisions when you're freaking out," is another way of saying it. You're more likely to be guided by unhealthy motives. Yet people do that all the time—out of desperation. Resist that urge.

What's more, says Ignatius, when you are in desolation you should do the following: pray and meditate even more; embark on further self-examination; remind yourself that you're not all-powerful; and try to be patient. Likewise, when you find yourself in a state of consolation, you might "store up new strength" for the future, like a smart squirrel storing up nuts for the winter. This is where keeping a journal is helpful; when you're feeling distant from God, you can look back on times when God felt close. (It can also remind you to stick with the good choices you made.)

My Bad Decision: A Case Study

Let's take an example of the "drop of water" and "making decisions in times of desolation" and see how those two insights work together. For that, I want to tell you about one of the worst decisions I've ever made. (That is quite a contest, by the way.)

One morning I came into our refugee center in Nairobi and discovered that someone had stolen our cash box, filled with tens of thousands of shillings (hundreds of U.S. dollars), equivalent to almost a week's revenue for our handicraft shop. Furious, I summoned our staff—two refugees and two Kenyan locals—told them how betrayed I felt, and demanded that the malefactor confess immediately. Each of them vehemently denied any wrongdoing.

Infuriated, I drove to each of their houses to search for the cash box, a gravely insulting act in East African culture—in any culture. (As I said, Jesuits are not angels.)

For a few days I tried to pray about a course of action. But I was too angry. Every time I sat down to pray, I sprang up again and paced around my bedroom. Rather than focus on God and the movements of my soul, all I did was fume about this betrayal. (In my selfish state, I was angrier about someone betraying me than about the loss of funds for the refugee projects.) Though my Jesuit friends counseled patience, I ignored them and grew increasingly intent on punishing someone. So I was closing out God and my friends, on a downward path, inviting desolation, and isolating myself from two ways that God communicates: prayer and friends.

Finally, someone advised that the best way to rectify this was to sack all of them. Fire them. Send a message to everyone that stealing will not be tolerated, he said. *Yes!* I thought gleefully. That would make things so easy. Here the evil spirit was *encouraging* me, like the drop of water on the sponge. *"Go on,"* it said. *"It's easy, isn't it?"*

So I fired everyone. How unjust that was—to punish each of them for the sins of only one. It was a wretched scene. All four wept and begged me to keep them on: each was already teetering on the edge of utter poverty. Our stormy meeting made me weep with frustration after they left the office and briefly made me wonder if I was doing the right thing. But I forcibly suppressed those feelings.

Afterward I proudly told everyone what I had done—what a big man I was to stand up to those thieves!

The next morning I awoke with a start: What had I done? And I recognized this alarm bell as my conscience. I had gone from bad to worse, from anger to vengeance, from pride to injustice. And I saw—with a shock—that I had made a terrible mistake. It was the drop of water on the stone, "violent, noisy, and disturbing," trying to wake me up. Trying to get the attention of my conscience.

Like Ignatius did in many cases, I changed course. Over the next few weeks, I hired back two of the employees, found another one a new job, and started to provide financial support for the last person (the one who was probably the culprit). In the end, I sought forgiveness and reconciled with each of them. Once I had done this, I felt a sense of peace.

What would Ignatius say? Well, I had made a poor decision in a time of desolation. The evil spirit had encouraged me along the wrong path, but fortunately the good spirit had woken me up "with perceptible noise." And after I had changed course, I felt consolation, the confirmation of a good decision.

Three Ways the "Enemy" Works

We've talked about Ignatius's worldview, with its images of the good spirit and the bad one. You still may find that antiquated, but he had a flawless understanding of the specific ways in which—take your pick—the "enemy," the "evil spirit," or, if you prefer, our "worst selves" are at work in our lives. And he identifies three main ways.

Over the past twenty years as a Jesuit, this has been the part of Ignatian spirituality that has been easiest for me to see in action. And once you're familiar with it, you'll begin to see it in yourself.

These are the three primary ways that the evil spirit works, slightly adapted from Ignatius's Rules for Discernment.

First, the enemy conducts himself like a *spoiled child*. In this case the child is "weak when faced by firmness but strong in the face of acquiescence." Frequently we find ourselves beset by what feels like a child within us. You think, *"I want this! And I want it now!"* Like a child screaming for another candy bar. If this overwhelming want is for something unhealthy, selfish, or even immoral, then it is important to recognize this for what it is. If part of you wants to jump into bed with another office worker, even though you're both married, and you hear that babyish, demanding, petulant voice over and over in your head, you're hearing this voice of the spoiled child. *"I have to have sex with her, and I have to have it now!"*

What's the antidote? Do what you would do with a spoiled child: put your foot down on those temptations. You'll find it effective. "The enemy characteristically weakens, loses courage, and flees with his temptations when the person engaged in spiritual endeavors stands bold and unyielding."

Pity the parent who gives in to the spoiled child who keeps demanding more and more. And pity the person who doesn't put his foot down with these kinds of selfish wants. The married man (or woman) who continually listens to that childish voice that says, *"I have to have sex with that person!"* risks falling into a devastating choice. If you begin to "fear and lose courage," as Ignatius says, the temptations will only intensify. So put your foot down!

Second, the enemy acts like a *false lover*. Essentially, the enemy would prefer that temptations, doubts, and despairs be kept secret, which only makes things worse for the person.

Ignatius compares the enemy to a "scoundrel" who tries to "remain secret and undetected." In a colorful passage he compares the enemy to a man intent on seducing a good wife away from her husband. (Let's hope Ignatius was not speaking from an earlier experience!) The scoundrel wants his "words and solicitations" to remain secret, lest the husband finds out and puts things right.

In the same way, he writes, "When the enemy of human nature turns his wiles and persuasions upon an upright person, he intends and desires them to be received and kept in secrecy. But when the person reveals them to his or her good confessor or some other spiritual person . . . he is grievously disappointed. For he quickly sees that he cannot succeed."

What's the antidote here? Bring everything out in the open—all those negative feelings and temptations and urges to do wrong or to despair or to move away from God. Bring them out of that "box," as David would say. Talk about them with a friend you trust, a counselor, or a spiritual director. You'll see how those temptations, which seem so powerful when hidden within, quickly lose much of their power when they're brought into the light of day.

How often this happens in spiritual direction! Someone seems to be dancing around some uncomfortable topic, something he is afraid of revealing, precisely because he knows that once it's out in the open he will be challenged to recognize how unhealthy it is.

Once it's revealed, the unhealthy urge, decision, or tendency can be examined, healed, or rejected. When a young Jesuit is tempted to break his vows in any way, for example, he often suppresses the desire to talk about his struggles with his superior or spiritual director, and the frustrations and fears and secrecy and problems only deepen.

"The devil never has greater success with us than when he works secretly and in the dark," said Ignatius. Or, as members of Alcoholics Anonymous say, "You're only as sick as your secrets." As an aside, the spiritual director of Bill Wilson, one of the founders of A.A., was Father Edward Dowling, a Jesuit, which may explain why some of Ignatius's insights may sound familiar to recovering addicts.

Finally, the enemy acts like an *army commander*. This is my favorite image, and one that most likely draws on Ignatius's military background. The army commander knows exactly where our weak spots are and targets them. The army commander, when preparing to attack a castle, makes his camp, carefully studies his target's weaknesses and strengths, and then attacks at the weakest point.

In the same way the evil spirit "prowls around" (1 Pet. 5:8) and studies where we are weakest, where we are most likely to be tempted, *even in good times.* "There he attacks and tries to take us," writes Ignatius. In other words, the evil spirit will attack where you are most vulnerable. Is your pride your weak spot? In that case, when all is going well in your life, the evil spirit will try to attack you there. "When the devil wishes to attack anyone," Ignatius wrote elsewhere, "he first of all looks to see on what side his defenses are weakest or in worst order; then he moves up his artillery to make a breach at that spot."

Let's say you've just started to care for your aging parent, a generous act. Little by little, others start telling you how noble you are. Then you start to think, *I'm doing a good deed.* So far, so good. But the army commander is looking for a way to get in. So, little by little, you move from *I'm doing a good job* to *I'm such a good person.* And from there to *I'm so holy.* And finally to *I'm much holier than everyone else.* You become self-righteous, proud, and arrogant. From there you may start to judge, condemn, and even hate others who are not as "holy" as you.

What happened? You may wonder, *How did I get here?* The evil spirit has succeeded in finding your weak point and is winning the battle.

What's the best defense against this? Shore up the weak parts of your spiritual castle. Pay special attention to the ways that you are tempted at your weak points, and work against those tendencies.

In time you'll be able to predict the ways you'll be tempted. For me, the temptations usually come in two ways: feeling lonely or worrying about my physical health. In the month before my ordination, for example, I found myself consumed with sexual desire. Then, just a week before, I ended up with a horrible virus, which plunged me into despair. It was almost comically easy to see how my weakest points were open for attack. So I shored up those points of my life, by making sure I spent time with my close friends and by reminding myself that health wasn't the most important thing in life, and, on the day of my ordination, I marched happily up the aisle.

In time you'll get to recognize those feelings. You'll get to *know* when you're being tempted to go down the wrong path.

The Angel of Light

That brings us to another Ignatian insight: the evil spirit can masquerade as the good spirit. That sounds like something out of a cheesy horror movie, but it's a clearheaded insight into human nature. Simply put, it means that things that *seem* good to us can take a dramatically wrong turn and mask something darker. The evil spirit, says Ignatius, "takes on the appearance of an angel of light."

Let's take the case of a father who decides that he is going to pray more. He thinks he is doing this to be more contemplative and more loving as a husband and father. But perhaps his motives are not so pure. Perhaps unconsciously he wants to escape from his family. Gradually he becomes so consumed with his desire for prayer that he starts neglecting his wife and his children. Soon he grows bitter and resentful whenever his precious time in prayer is interrupted. "Get out!" he yells to his children, "I'm praying!" The evil spirit has subtly taken on the guise of the good spirit to draw the person into an attitude of bitterness.

Ignatius puts it this way: "[The evil spirit] brings good and holy thoughts attractive to such an upright soul and then strives little by little to get his own way, by enticing the soul over to his own hidden deceits and evil intentions."

John English, a Canadian Jesuit, notes in *Spiritual Freedom* that the evil spirit can also use the pretext of a person's beginning to live a spiritual life, and then suggesting, *"Well, now, everything is dependent on God, so let's just take it easy."* English writes that people "become lazy, wallow in discontent, and abandon" their enthusiasm for love and service.

This is a subtle experience. When it happens, says Ignatius, we should examine the ways that we were led by the evil spirit, in order to guard against this in the future. This is a good practice whenever we recognize how we've been led down this backward path.

In time, after putting these insights into practice, you'll begin to know, really know, when you're being led down the wrong path, because you will have the experience of having gone down that path. In the movie *The Matrix,* which stars Keanu Reeves as Neo, an average man invited to see the radical truth of his world, there is an illustration of just that kind of knowledge—of knowing the wrong path from experience. In one scene Neo is riding in a car with a woman who already knows the truth about Neo's world. (Suffice it to say, this is a simple rendition of a devilishly complex plot.) Reluctant to accept her invitation to a new life, Neo opens the car door, ready to return to his former life. He peers down a dark rainy street. The woman counsels him not to choose that path. He asks why not.

"Because you have been down there, Neo," she says. "You know that road. You know exactly where it ends. And I know that's not where you want to be."

It's a good illustration of discernment. If you know that the path will lead you to a bad end, why take it? (By the way, the woman's name in the movie is Trinity.)

By examining the ways that we have failed in the past, we'll be better able to make good choices and lead happy and satisfying lives, nourishing our true selves and resisting our more selfish tendencies. We'll be able to take the right paths and end up where we want to be.

SAYING *YES* TO EVERYTHING

One final comment about discernment: making good choices means accepting that even the best decisions will have drawbacks. Often, though, we believe that if we make the right choices, there will be no downside. Then, when we live out that choice and discover its drawbacks, we grow discouraged. A newly married man realizes how much freedom he has relinquished—he can no longer enjoy beers with his buddies as often as he used to. A newly married woman can't hang out with her girlfriends as frequently. They start to doubt the good decision to marry.

Good decisions mean a wholehearted *yes* to both the positives and negatives that come with any choice. Saying *yes* to entering the Jesuits, for example, did not mean saying *yes* only to the positives—Ignatian spirituality, the loving Jesuit friends, the exciting work, the warm communities, the wonderful people with whom I'd minister, the intellectual stimulation. It also meant saying *yes* to the negatives—occasional loneliness, frequent overwork, problems in the church, and so on.

Every state of life, every decision, includes some pain that must be accepted if you are to enter fully into those decisions, and into new life. "All symphonies remain unfinished," said Karl Rahner. There is no perfect decision, perfect outcome, or perfect life. Embracing imperfection helps us relax into reality. When we accept that all choices are conditional, limited, and imperfect, our lives become, paradoxically, more satisfying, joyful, and peaceful.

All this points us to the unconditional, unlimited, and perfect One to whom we say *yes:* God. All of our decisions should be focused on this reality. "Our only desire and our one choice," said Ignatius, "should be this: I want and choose what better leads to God's deepening his life in me."

Ignatian discernment, as I mentioned at the beginning of this chapter, may seem complicated—with its definitions of consolation, desolation, and confirmation, not to mention the Three Times and the Two Methods, as well as the spoiled child, the false lover, and the army commander.

But at heart it is simple. Ignatian discernment means trusting that through your reason and your inner life, God will help to draw you to good decisions, because God *desires* for you to make good, loving, healthy, positive, life-giving choices. So find whatever works for you, whatever draws you closer to God, and whatever helps you make good decisions. Most of all, trust that God is with you as you choose your paths in this life.

CHAPTER THIRTEEN

Be Who You Is!

Work, Job, Career, Vocation . . . and Life

WHEN I FIRST MET John, he was already a revered Jesuit spiritual director in New England. A ruddy-faced man in his seventies with a snow-white beard, John was a friendly presence at the Eastern Point Retreat House in Gloucester, Massachusetts.

John was one of those unruffled people in whose presence you always felt calmer. My spiritual director in Africa, George, who had helped me in my struggle with obedience, was like that as well. So was Joe, the elderly priest living in our novitiate whose refrain was "Why not?" If I were upset about anything, just a few minutes with any of these older men would make it seem as if any problems were manageable.

Why is that? First, thanks to their advanced age, they had experienced much and now possessed a wealth of wisdom—and compassion. Second, because each was a spiritual director and had spent years immersed in Ignatian spirituality, each grew to embody the lessons of the way of Ignatius—compassion, generosity, and, especially, freedom.

And they knew who they were. After decades of formation, retreats, prayer, and spiritual reading, and after facing the natural struggles of life, they knew themselves and understood their place in creation. They radiated a sense of peace.

One day at the retreat house, John gave a homily on the idea of vocation. That day the Gospel passage was the one in which Jesus asks Bartimaeus, the blind beggar, "What do you want me to do for you?" John was talking about how our desires help us to find our vocations; they help us to be who we are.

At the end of his homily John neatly summed it all up with a saying he heard from an old gentleman living in the Deep South: "You gotta be who you is and not who you ain't!" he said, letting out a rumbling laugh. "Because if you ain't who you is, then you is who you ain't. And that ain't good!"

CALLED

In the last chapter we talked about making decisions according to the way of Ignatius. We talked about good everyday decisions. Now let's talk about two big decisions:

1. What should I do?
2. Who should I be?

In other words, let's talk about vocation. Let's look at how Ignatian spirituality helps us know what we're meant to *do* in life and become the persons we are meant to *be*. To quote John's friend, let's look at how the way of Ignatius helps you to "be who you is."

Vocation is a word that is easily misunderstood. In some Catholic circles to "have a vocation" still means being "called" to the priesthood or religious life. Some Catholics used to think that a *real* vocation was confined to those two areas, while the rest of life's choices—getting married, being single, being a parent, working as a doctor or lawyer or businessperson, and so on, were "less than."

That's a holdover of an older theology that placed the lives of priests, sisters, and brothers above those of married and single laypeople. In Sunday school my class was once given a little drawing to color. On the top of the sheet was written the word *Vocations*. On the left side was an image of a married couple. Under that image it said,

Good. On the right side was an image of a priest and a nun. Underneath it read, *Better.*

But ever since the Second Vatican Council in the early 1960s, which stressed the "universal call to holiness," Catholics have been reminded that everyone has a vocation. This is something that we could have easily learned from other Christian denominations: their churches have always sought the active participation of the lay members and have placed comparatively less emphasis on ordained ministries. Everyone has a vocation.

The root meaning of the word points to this. It has little to do with ordination or religious orders. It comes from the Latin *vocare,* "to call." A vocation is something you're called to.

Vocation is different from work or a job or even a career. You could say that work is the labor required to do a task. A job is the situation in which you do it. A career is the long-term trajectory or pattern of many jobs. But vocation is deeper than each of those concepts.

Recently I spoke with Chris Lowney about this. He is the author of *Heroic Leadership,* a book that uses the insights of Ignatius and applies them to organizations. Lowney is a former Jesuit who worked in the corporate world and so brings a wealth of experience to these topics. How did he see those terms?

"Work, career, vocation," he said, considering the question. "There are some problematic ideas attached to those terms. *Work* tends to be construed as work for pay, but work is any purposeful activity, so it's helpful to have a broader concept of work. *Career* tends to mean that you study for a profession that you do for the rest of your life. But for many people that's not true any longer. In the modern sense, a career is less about a workplace, or even a specific profession, and more about how you develop your skills and talents."

What about vocation?

"People tend to associate *vocation* with a specific work, job or career," he said. "The Protestant reformers talked about a general calling to become holy people, and a specific calling to different kinds of ministries and work, which is more accurate."

Vocation overarches our work, jobs, and career and extends to the kind of person we hope to become. It is what we are called to do, and who we are called to be. But how do we discover our vocations?

In the past few chapters I spoke briefly about my own vocation, which was jumpstarted when I saw a television documentary about the Trappist monk Thomas Merton. That led me to read his book *The Seven Storey Mountain,* which led me to contact the Jesuits, which led me to read more about their training program, which led me to consider entering, which led me to apply, and which ultimately led the Jesuits to accept me.

But how did this happen? Through desire. At each juncture I was drawn by a desire, an attraction or interest to that life. This is one primary way that we discover what we are meant to do and who we are: desire.

The easiest way to think about this is to use a familiar example: marriage. Most believers would readily agree that God calls a married couple together. Even if they don't understand marriage as a sacrament, as Catholics do, most people would say that God has, in some way, drawn the two together. This happens in part through a wide variety of desires. A man and woman are drawn together in desire—physical, emotional, spiritual—and discover their vocations as a married couple. This is one way God draws these people together, and how the call to marriage manifests itself.

Desire works in a similar way in the lives of those drawn to specific professions. Accountants, writers, physicians, artists, lawyers, and teachers, among others, discover an attraction for their work, perhaps by hearing about those careers at an early age, meeting people in those lines of work, or reading about people in those professions. They find their vocations through their natural longings. Desire works the same in the lives of the saints, drawing each of them to different types of service in the church.

Let me give you an example outside of the seminary, novitiate, or convent. When I was working at General Electric, one of my peers loved reading business journals in his spare time. Where for me the job was something I did to support myself, he liked nothing better at the end of a long day than settling down with the *Wall Street Journal.* "How can you read that after work?" I once asked.

"Are you kidding?" he said. "I *love* this stuff!"

Working in corporate finance was just a job for me; for him it was a real vocation. It flowed from a clear desire—an attraction to the business world, a desire to immerse himself in it and succeed. It was also an early indication that I might not be in the right place myself: for those who will succeed are those who love what they do, who find in it a real vocation.

As we've seen in previous chapters, desire is an essential element in the spiritual life. That's why Ignatius asks you to pray for what you desire at the beginning of each prayer in the Spiritual Exercises. The very first exercise includes the invitation "to ask God our Lord for what I want and desire." It's also why William Barry writes, "Retreat directors, I believe, do their most important work when they help their directees to discover what they really want."

God calls each of us to different vocations. Or, rather, God plants within us these vocations, which are revealed in our desires and longings. In this way God's desires for the world are fulfilled, as we live out our own deepest desires. Vocation is less about *finding* one and more about having it *revealed* to you, as you pray to understand "what I want and desire."

Desire, of course, has a bad reputation in religious circles. But selfish wants are not what Ignatius is talking about. As Margaret Silf notes in *Wise Choices,* "There are deep desires and there are shallow wants."

One way to distinguish between deep desires and shallow wants, and to more fully understand our vocations, is to reflect on what you are drawn to over the long haul. You can use the techniques of the examen to look at where you've been drawn. You may ask yourself,

What desires have lived long in my heart? What do I most enjoy doing? What are my dream jobs?

> Latent and sometimes locked within each human heart is a dream waiting to be born.
> —Jacqueline Syrup Bergan and Marie Schwan, C.S.J.,
> *Birth: A Guide for Prayer*

If your job requires you to hunch over a desk crunching numbers but you have long dreamt about working more closely with people one on one, your desire may point to your true vocation. Maybe you're meant to work in human resources or counseling. Conversely, if you're a harried teacher who dreams of doing something more solitary, your desire may point to your vocation. Maybe you're meant to be a writer—or, if that is impracticable, maybe to spend *some* time writing. Recently a friend told me that he had started to volunteer in a prison as a lay chaplain, though his current work is as a financial manager in a large corporation. His volunteer work gives him enormous reserves of joy and energy, and he grew enthusiastic just talking about it. You could see the elation in his face as he discussed his volunteering.

Sometimes an image may help you uncover such desires. Let me suggest one that has helped me over the years.

When I was in elementary school, our science teacher once asked our class to visit a nearby stream and draw out a glass of water, whose contents we would bring into class to peer at under a microscope. But before we could use the microscope, said our teacher, we would need to set the glass on a windowsill overnight: the water needed to clear. Plunging a glass directly into a pond will bring up all sorts of dirt, leaves, and twigs. Even after a few hours the water will still be cloudy. But if you let it *settle,* things become clearer.

Can you sit with yourself and let some of the dirt, leaves, and twigs of your life—your selfish wants—settle down so that things will be clearer? Or here's another watery image: think of skimming things from the surface of your soul, getting rid of what is preventing you from seeing clearly, seeing what lies deeper down.

I was astonished to run across this precise metaphor—which I thought was my own!—in *A Time to Keep Silence,* published in 1953 by the British travel writer Patrick Leigh Fermor, who visited the La Grande Trappe, the original Trappist abbey in Normandy, France. In his secluded cell, he wrote, "the troubled waters of the mind grow still and clear, and much that is hidden away and all that clouds it floats to the surface and can be skimmed away; and after a time one reaches a state of peace that is unthought of in the ordinary world."

Likewise, can you wait for something to *surface?* Sometimes when your glass is still, something will rise up from the bottom, a small bubble, a little leaf or even a tiny fish. Maybe this is what God wants you to see. Can you let your dreams and desires rise to the surface?

Also using the analogy of the stream, David Lonsdale reminds us in *Eyes to See, Ears to Hear* that often what is most important is not on the surface of the stream. "The surface of a fast-flowing river is often broken by waves and eddies in which the water seems to rush off in all directions and even contrary to the main flow; while underneath all this busyness there is a constant, steady current which can be felt more strongly below the surface where the river is deepest."

Looking back on your life, to see where you've been drawn, can also lead to the uncovering of desires. Or you can take an opposite tack: the question that enabled me to see my vocation looked *ahead* not backward. After months of wondering about the Jesuits, the psychologist asked me to imagine a brand-new life *without* thinking about the past. "If you could do anything you wanted," he asked, "what would it be?" That forward-looking question surfaced an answer that was buried under a lot of life's sediment. When the glass cleared, the answer rose to the surface.

What would your answer be to that question? And is there a realistic way to move at least a little closer to the answer?

A less metaphorical way to think about these questions is by using some of the key images from Ignatian discernment that we looked at in the last chapter: Imagine yourself on your deathbed. Imagine yourself before God. Imagine giving advice to someone in a similar situation.

Try These Questions

Using Ignatian themes, Margaret Silf asks you to consider the following questions, when asking, "What do you really want?" This is from her book *Wise Choices:*

Now take a look at the deeper level of desiring: Is there something you've always wanted to do but never managed? What are your unfinished dreams? If you had your life over again, what would you change? If you only had a few months to live, how would you use the time? If a significant sum of money came your way, how would you spend it? If you were granted three wishes, what would they be? Is there anyone, or anything, for whom you would literally give your life?

Take time to ponder one or more of these questions. The responses you make to yourself—provided they are honest answers and not just the answers you feel you *ought* to give—will be pointers to where your deepest desires are rooted.

Look closely, taking time to reflect on what you find. There may be patterns in your desiring that help you more fully understand who you are.

Like any desires, these must be tested. Just because I desire to be an opera star doesn't mean that I can be one, especially if I cannot sing! This is where the Ignatian goal of confirmation enters, as we discussed in the last chapter. You need to look not only at your desires, your prayer, and the fruits of your discernment, but also at the "reality of the situation."

So you reflect on your desires in terms of your everyday life. As Chris Lowney told me, "Sometimes people are given guidance that is too romantic when it comes to career or vocation. These ideas of 'follow your bliss' or that your calling is 'where the world's deep need and your deep hunger come together' can be misleading. These notions are valuable, but that's not the only ingredient in figuring out what to do. Every decision has to do with interests and needs but also circumstances and talents."

Vocation is not simply about one's desire or one's idea of the world's needs, but also a reality that sometimes does not exactly conform to our desires. Trust your heart, but use your head.

"I might feel drawn to be a baseball player, but there's no way!" said Lowney. "That's operative in all kinds of areas. Maybe you can't throw the equivalent of a fastball in teaching. Decisions like that factor in our talents, needs, interests, and circumstances, and in all those things, not just in our desires, are God's fingerprints. Feeling good about those things is one important piece of data, but so is the fact that I can or cannot do it. Those should be equally seen as God's fingerprints."

A SPIRITUALITY OF WORK

Even if you have a good idea of your vocation, you may still have a hard time finding God at work—whatever it is. What does the way of Ignatius have to say about finding God on the job?

Before entering the Jesuits, I spent six years in a large corporation, so I know something about the "real world." But when I entered the Jesuits, I didn't stop working! During my formation I worked in a large hospital in Cambridge, Massachusetts; taught in an inner-city school in New York; managed a shop and microfinance operation in Nairobi for two years; and worked as a chaplain in a prison in Boston.

And for the last ten years I've worked at a weekly magazine, a professional workplace that includes meetings, deadlines, budgets, job evaluations, and an eclectic mix of colleagues with a wide variety of personalities and temperaments that sometimes gives rise to differences and disputes. And even though Jesuits don't have to worry much about salary increases, downsizing, or climbing the corporate ladder, Jesuits are expected to work hard.

Like the vast majority of those in the workforce, I try to be a good employee, a good colleague, and a good manager. So, in many respects, my situation may not be so different from your own. And through the lives of my non-Jesuit friends, who work in a variety of professions, I try to keep up with the challenges of other sectors of the working world. In short, I think I have a good idea of the challenges of living a spiritual life on the job.

And there are many. Living a spiritual life in the working world has grown increasingly challenging as more and more demands are placed on employees. So here are what I observe to be the main challenges of maintaining a spiritual life from nine to five—and some perspectives, using some of the Ignatian practices we've been discussing.

Finding Time for God and You

Nine to five? More like 24/7! Time is at a premium for most people in the workforce. Despite vaunted increases in productivity and technology (anyone remember how the personal computer was going to lead to four-day workweeks?), the amount of time demanded by companies from their workers has only increased. Round-the-clock markets; round-the-clock financial news; and round-the-clock access with e-mail, cell phones, BlackBerrys, and laptops often translate into round-the-clock work. Moreover, decreasing job security and increasing numbers of dual-career households mean more stress and less time for married couples and parents.

So the first challenge: how can you make space for a life of prayer and worship?

When I recently asked some friends about this, a few suggested that the only way to do this is to sacrifice time at work. "It's a conscious choice," said one friend who works in a large corporation. While he found it difficult, he said he could avoid what he called the "trap of constant work" only by sacrificing some upward mobility and choosing to spend time with his family and on his spiritual life. Otherwise, he said, one's life becomes informed solely by work, and without the nourishment of either individual or communal prayer, one's spiritual life slowly atrophies.

But while my friend is a busy man with a growing family, he is also successful financially and can afford to sacrifice a bit of upward mobility. It's more difficult for those struggling to make ends meet: the single mother working two jobs or the underpaid employee desperate to earn a better living for his family and hang on to his health insurance, both stretched to the limit.

A few years ago I co-edited a book with Jeremy Langford called *Professions of Faith,* in which we asked various Catholics to reflect on their work. Amelia Uelmen, a former corporate lawyer who now teaches at Fordham University in New York, wrote, "By far the biggest challenge in legal practice at a large firm is not the lack of openness to conversations about social responsibility. It is insisting on the necessity of maintaining the balanced life that enables one to hang on to this kind of perspective."

Time is a problem for those in the working world—or for any busy person. Here the examination of conscience can be extremely helpful. For those overwhelmed by time demands, the examen, requiring only ten to fifteen minutes a day, can be a spiritual lifesaver.

One friend, a busy investment adviser with three children, does the examen at his desk in the morning, thinking back over the events of the previous day. If he's too busy in the morning, he does *lectio divina* at lunch, closing his door for a few minutes to immerse himself in the readings for the day.

Balancing work and prayer, the active and contemplative, was essential to the early Jesuits. And still is. One of our recent General Congregations wrote that Jesuits need to be "undividedly apostolic and religious." The connection between work and worship "needs to animate our whole way of living, praying and working." Work without prayer becomes detached from God. Prayer without work becomes detached from human beings.

Overwork is a danger for Jesuits for the same reasons that it is for everyone. First, we grow distant from God, the foundation of our lives; second, we grow frustrated when things do not go as planned, since we can overlook our reliance on God; third, we spend less time with friends or families and begin feeling isolated; and fourth, we begin to believe that we are what we do, and so at the end of our lives when we have little "to do," we feel worthless.

For those who find it absolutely impossible to carve out time—like parents of young children or those juggling two or three jobs—the goal of being a "contemplative in action" is especially relevant. Can you maintain an awareness of the presence of God around you?

Ignatius not only made time for prayer; he maintained a contemplative attitude throughout the day. One of his earliest companions, Jerónimo Nadal, wrote this about his friend: "In all things, actions and conversations he contemplated the presence of God and experienced the reality of spiritual things so that he was likewise in action contemplative (a thing which he used to express by saying: God must be found in everything)." Ignatius's way is an invitation for those who feel that they are disappointing God if they cannot find time to pray during extremely stressful times in their lives.

As David Lonsdale notes, "Time set aside for contemplation is one way of being contemplative; but a full involvement in a busy life can also be another way, and people who are 'contemplative in action' learn to find God in both these different ways according to what they decide is needful and possible."

Finding God Around You

In the first chapter I mentioned one of the best pieces of advice I've ever received. "You can't put part of your life in a box," said David Donovan, my spiritual director. In Ignatian spirituality nothing is hidden away; everything can be opened up as a way of finding God. "God must be found in everything," as Nadal noted, summarizing Ignatius.

When you're in a job you enjoy, that's easy. The work itself becomes a way to find God: the emotional, mental, and sometimes physical satisfaction that comes with the labor is a way of experiencing God's joy and God's desire to create alongside you. One of the main characters in the 1981 movie *Chariots of Fire,* about competitors in the 1924 Olympics, is a Scots minister who is also a runner. When asked why he runs, he says, "When I run, I feel [God's] pleasure." That's as good a description as any about living out a vocation. The work itself is pleasurable.

Clearly some people are able to find God in their work. But what if you're stuck in a career that feels stale, a job that doesn't seem like a vocation, or work you don't enjoy? Let's be realistic: some people cannot follow what they believe are their vocational paths for a variety of reasons—financial constraints, family demands, educational restrictions, physical limitations, or a tight job market. How might they be able to find God, using the Ignatian tradition?

Let me suggest this: by trying to find God in all things, not just the work itself. First of all, *through the people around them.* This is perhaps the easiest of routes.

When I was in high school and college, to earn money for tuition I worked in a variety of summer jobs, where I met many people who detested their work. For a few summers, I took on the typical summer jobs for an adolescent boy in the 1970s—delivering newspapers, mowing lawns, washing dishes and busing tables in a series of restaurants, caddying, and working as a movie theater usher. But one job taught me more about miserable work than all the rest combined.

The summer after my freshman year at college I worked three jobs. In the evenings I worked as an usher at a local movie theater; on Saturdays and Sundays I worked as a waiter in a small restaurant; weekdays I worked on an assembly line in a local packaging plant. That last one was easily the worst job I've ever had. But I counted myself fortunate to get it—since it paid more than either of the other two jobs.

Here was my schedule: Up at 6:00 a.m. for a shower. Wolf down some cereal. Stand at the front door waiting for a friend to pick me up, since I had no car. By 7:00 I was expected to be "on the line," standing in front of a deafening, room-sized machine that shoved pills into boxes and disgorged the filled boxes onto a rapidly moving conveyor belt.

My job was to take the smaller boxes that came shooting off the line and put them into bigger boxes, and then cover them with plastic shrink wrap. Farther down the line, another person packed them into bigger boxes. Finally someone loaded them onto a wooden pallet. At the head of the line, workers tore huge sheets of "blister packs" of pills and loaded them into the hopper, which poured them into the belt.

I hated it. Everyone hated it. Every ten minutes I checked the clock on the wall to see how much closer lunchtime was. After lunch, I watched the clock and prayed for (or at least anticipated) the end of the shift at 4:00. At lunchtime some of the college-age workers smoked pot in the trash-filled parking lot to relieve the boredom. And at least once a week someone threw a wooden ruler into the machine to shut it down temporarily; then we all took a break while someone called the repairman. That was the high point of the week. But for the rest of the time everyone was miserable.

But surprisingly, three women on the line laughed almost the entire day. Having worked in the plant for several years, they knew one another and spent the day chatting about their children, their husbands, their homes, and their plans for the weekend. Gradually they drew me into their circle, where conversation focused mainly on how much we hated the job. By summer's end they were ribbing me about all sorts of things: how slow I was, how young I was, how skinny I was, how much dust got in my hair, and, especially, how afraid I was of sticking my hand in the machine to fix it when it jammed. (The metal gears could easily rip a finger off.) "Is you a man or is you a *mouse?*" one would tease.

They hated their jobs but loved one another.

Since that time, I have worked in several places where people may not have enjoyed their work but enjoyed one another. Celebrating birthdays, sharing interests in television shows, socializing outside of work, consoling one another on losses, trading photos of children and grandchildren—these are ways of connecting on an often intimate level. This important facet in the workplace often goes overlooked in discussions of the spirituality of work: finding God in others even in the midst of a crummy job.

The second way that one might find God in the midst of a difficult job is by understanding that your job is directed toward a *larger goal*. Something similar often happens with those caring for small children or elderly parents: you may not like the physical labor required, you might recoil from cleaning up vomit or changing soiled diapers, but you know it is for an important purpose. In a way you see this part of the job as a means to an end.

When I was starting out in the corporate world, I worked with one man who was notable for his loathing of his job. After decades in the accounting department, he was laid off. During his last week he lamented his layoff but admitted that he never once enjoyed his work. As a recent college graduate with starry-eyed ideals about the company, I was horrified. Though I knew assembly-line workers who hated their jobs, this was corporate America—where I expected people would be happier, more fulfilled.

"So how did you make it?" I asked him.

He pulled out his wallet and flipped it open. "With this," he said quietly, and showed me a picture of his family, a wife and children. With that gesture, he showed me the reason for his labors.

This doesn't make a job itself any more pleasant. There is a *New Yorker* cartoon that shows Egyptian slaves hauling massive stone blocks to build a pyramid. One says to the man beside him, "Oh, stop complaining! It's an honor to be associated with an enterprise of this magnitude." Some jobs are just awful. And sometimes it's necessary to leave the job. But sometimes it's impossible to do so.

Even in the midst of unpleasant jobs, however, it may help to focus on larger goals. This is not to minimize how rotten some jobs are, but, for some people, the uniting of one's work to a larger goal can invest their labor with meaning. The believer can also unite his work with a larger good that *God has in mind,* for example, caring for his children or providing for his family.

Even for Walter Ciszek, the Jesuit sentenced to work in a Soviet concentration camp, being forced to build worker housing was more tolerable when he imagined the end results. Though he wasn't helping his family, he told his friends in the labor camp that he was doing something important:

I tried to explain that the pride I took in my work differed from the pride a communist might take in building up the new society. The difference lay in the motivation. As a Christian, I could share in their concern for building a better world. I could work as hard as they for the common good. The people who would benefit from my labors would be just that: people. Human beings. Families in need of shelter against the arctic weather.

The third way to find God may be to act as a *leaven* in unhealthy work situations. In the Gospel of Matthew (13:33), Jesus reminds his disciples that they are to be like "leaven" in the world, the tiny bit of yeast that helps the bread to rise. A small agent of change can alter situations dramatically. Though trapped in a job that paid terrible wages, the women on that factory line nonetheless helped one another meet the day with some happiness.

If you find yourself in a dehumanizing situation, you may find some sense of purpose knowing that you are acting against these tendencies and helping to better the environment, even if in a small way.

During the time of the Protestant Reformation, Peter Favre regularly found himself confronted with Catholics who said virulent things about the Reformers (and vice versa). "If we want to be of help to them," he wrote of the Reformers, "we must be careful to regard them with love, to love them in deed and in truth, and to banish from our soul any thought that might lessen our love or esteem for them." His journals show that every day Peter prayed for a long list of those on the opposite side of his theological divide. Peter was able to act as a leaven in the midst of a difficult "job."

Finding Time for Solitude

Whether commuting during rush hour, relaxing at home in the evenings or weekends, or even traveling on vacations, growing numbers of working men and women are never far from e-mail or without their cell phones. The sight of someone nervously pressing a phone against her ear as she races to catch a cab is a common one in many cities, as is the sight of a traveler desperately punching out another e-mail on his laptop as he waits for the next flight home in a crowded airport.

While these gadgets are terrific for keeping us in touch with our work and our families and friends, they pare away the few remaining moments of solitary time we have left—for reflection, silence, and inner quiet. Where is the time for "recollection," as spiritual writers say?

So the second challenge: How can the working person balance the need to be "connected" with the need for solitude, a requirement of a healthy spiritual life?

Sometimes it seems as if we can no longer stand to be alone or "out of touch." But without some inner silence, it becomes harder to listen to those desires that we spoke of. It is difficult to listen to the "still small" sound, as the First Book of Kings (9:12) describes God's voice. If your eyes are glued to your BlackBerry and your ears stopped up by your iPod, it's hard to hear what might be going on inside you. Cutting back on these gadgets and not answering every single e-mail and phone call right away may lead to a measure of calm.

"Deep calls to deep," says Psalm 42 (v. 7). But what if you can't hear the deep?

Solitude and silence also enable us to connect on a deeper level with others, for we are put in touch with the deepest part of our-selves—God. And in coming to know God, we are better able to find God in others and are freed of our loneliness. So sometimes you have to disconnect to connect.

Likewise, if you're completely absorbed in the electronic world, obsessively checking e-mail and constantly returning phone calls, it becomes impossible to experience the quirky surprises in the world around us. The examen allows us to not only grow more aware of God in the past, but also, as we practice this discipline, in the present. But if you're *always* connecting with friends, you might miss out.

The other day I was walking through a park in New York City. Racing across Union Square to an appointment, I stumbled on a pair of grungy young men; one was playing an accordion, the other a violin. Their music was a sprightly, lively, intricate, intoxicating type of Eastern European folk music. Mesmerized, I stopped to listen to the furious melodies and rising and falling rhythms. A little crowd gathered around, and I noticed that we were in the middle of the weekly open-air farmers' market, with vendors carefully laying out fresh fruits, vegetables, and flowering plants for all to see.

As I listened to these two skinny guys, one with long dreadlocks, the other with a scraggly beard, I smelled something unusual—fresh peaches—from behind me. What a glorious moment: the music, the sunshine, the crowd, the shoppers at the market, and the smell of ripe peaches.

Just then someone cut through the rest of the crowd: a woman punching her BlackBerry and listening to her iPod. She knifed through us and rushed away. She had missed the entire experience, since she was entirely absorbed in her own world.

Ignatius on "Overloading"

In 1547 a group of young Jesuits at a school in Coimbra, Portugal, were trying to outdo one another in over-the-top religious practices. Ignatius cautions against doing too much, by use of some homey metaphors: "Let your service be a reasonable service," he calmly counsels the Jesuits.

> First . . . God is not really served in the long run, as the horse worn out in the first days does not as a rule finish the journey. . . . Second, gains that are made with this excessive eagerness are not usually kept. . . . Third, there is the danger of being careless about overloading the vessel. There is danger, of course, in sailing it empty, as it can then be tossed about. . . . But there is also danger of so overloading it as to cause it to sink.

Solitude also includes caring for one's physical health. Giving yourself the gift of solitude may mean allowing yourself time for rest and exercise, necessary ingredients for a healthy life. This may include, as we mentioned in our discussion of "poverty of spirit," saying *no* to things that you cannot do. Saying *no* to some nonessentials and avoiding the constant rush that sometimes characterizes our lives (including my own) is a way of saying *yes* to a more balanced way of living.

In his *Constitutions,* Ignatius places a surprising emphasis on the need to attend to a "proper concern with the preservation of one's health." In a section called The Preservation of the Body, he shows an understanding of the need for a balance among work, prayer, and rest, based on his own early experience, when he favored extreme penances that damaged his health. Ultimately, he recognized the need for moderation. "With a healthy body, you will be able to do much," he wrote to his friend Teresa Rejadell.

For Ignatius, the requirements for a healthy life for Jesuits include maintaining a "regular" schedule, and caring for "food, clothing, living quarters, and other bodily needs." He recognized the need for exercise, even for sedentary Jesuits:

> Just as it is unwise to assign so much physical labor that the spirit should be oppressed and the body be harmed, so too some bodily exercise to help both the body and the spirit is ordinarily expedient for all, even for those who must apply themselves to mental labors.

These ways of self-care are to be "exercised by all." It is a warning against overwork.

In his perfectly named book *CrazyBusy: Overstretched, Overbooked, and About to Snap,* the psychiatrist Edward M. Hallowell notes that pathological overwork may not simply reflect the real demands on our time, but may mask underlying problems. Overbusyness, he suggests, acts as a kind of high and also serves as a status symbol. We may also fear being left out if we slow down; and we avoid dealing with some of the realities of life—poverty, death, global warming—

by frantically running from task to task. And, he suggests, we may not know how *not* to be busy.

Having regular times for prayer and solitude, and a mixture of work and rest, even in the midst of a busy life, is an important step on the way to becoming a contemplative in action. This does not mean that you have to be lazy. Far from it. But the possibility for contemplation grows slimmer if you are always stressed out, frazzled, or ready to collapse from fatigue.

Working (and Living) Ethically

When I studied business ethics as an undergraduate at the Wharton School, most of the textbook cases were of the black-and-white variety, with simple answers. Would you give a bribe to someone who demanded one? (No.) Would you pollute the environment with nasty chemicals? (No.) Would you discriminate on the basis of race or sex? (No.)

When I entered the business world, I was surprised to learn how much subtler most ethical dilemmas are and how rarely they are framed in black-and-white terms.

This is not to say that the black-and-white dilemmas never arise. A good friend of mine, an accountant, was once asked by a manager to falsify some figures on a report. He refused politely, and the manager saw that he was wrong and apologized.

Subtler problems are more common. How, for example, do you respond when you discover that you work in a corporation where moral values are not always paramount? During my time in human resources, I was asked to confront a manager who was planning to fire a longtime employee. That employee had just received an incentive award for outstanding performance. Finding it bizarre that we would suddenly fire one of our top-performing employees, I told the manager it was a bad idea.

"I don't care," he said. "I want him out. I don't like him."

I reminded him that this middle-aged employee had been with the company for twenty years and had always done a good job and, also, that disliking someone was not a valid reason for dismissal. None of that mattered, I was told. Finally, I said in desperation, "Have some compassion. The guy's got a family." The executive's answer was short and memorable. "To hell with compassion!" he said. (He used even stronger language.) Fortunately, his boss over-ruled him, and the employee stayed, but the episode left me with a sour taste for the company.

So the third challenge for the working person is: how can you stay true to your moral, ethical, or religious values?

For many people, this means consciously searching for a company whose values are congruent with their values. A friend who manages investments for a multinational corporation told me that he was glad the values he prized—integrity, honesty, rectitude— were precisely what was valued in his world of long-term investing. "If you're dishonest, your reputation and therefore effectiveness will suffer," he explained.

But what happens when you work in an environment where, say, compassion is not valued or, worse, is ignored? Finding work in a new company or a different position in your current workplace may not be feasible or even possible.

Part of the solution may lie in maintaining Ignatian detachment from the unhealthy values of the workplace. If you work in an environment that prizes aggressive or downright mean behavior, you need not be aggressive or mean. (Religious institutions are not entirely immune to these sorts of behaviors.) Often a superior level of work can overcome the perceived need to participate in activities that go against your moral grain. Talent can sometimes trump aggression and meanness.

You might also act, as mentioned above, as a leaven of change in an unethical environment, doing your part and hoping that your leaven may help to encourage change. "Never doubt that a small group of thoughtful, committed citizens can change the world," wrote the anthropologist Margaret Mead. "Indeed it is the only thing that ever has."

Likewise, you might be entirely unable to change anything yet still able to help others in their struggles. To take an extreme example, St. Peter Claver, the Jesuit who ministered to the slaves in seventeenth-century Cartagena, did not end the slave trade. But he was able to care for those who were trapped in that sinful system by distributing food and counseling to slaves on board the ships that had arrived in the center of the African slave trade in the New World.

In other words, one of the simplest ways we can find meaning in work is by being kind to those who are struggling—the mother working two minimum-wage jobs; the secretary beleaguered by her tyrannical boss; the underappreciated janitor. To put it in Ignatian language, can you see yourself as someone who could "help souls" at work?

Or you might consider it your duty to act prophetically by standing up against the injustice around you. Are there times when you need to gather up your courage to do the right thing? Here the believer remembers the duty to care for all of God's creatures, no matter where they are on the corporate ladder. The Christian remembers the call of Jesus to care for the "least of these" our brothers and sisters. The Catholic remembers the social encyclicals of the church that ask us to stand for the rights of the poor and marginalized. And the follower of the way of Ignatius remembers Third Degree of Humility, where you choose to stand with those who are persecuted.

You may need to sacrifice some upward mobility in exchange for a clear conscience, since most workplaces rarely reward the prophet. One lawyer friend put it bluntly, "I don't expect to make partner, because I don't play the games that others play, but I don't really want that; it's not good for me." If you are working in a corporation that prizes selfishness, you might have to choose between advancement and values. If you are more fortunate, you will be able to find a company whose values match your own.

Discerning your response to ethical questions can be aided by some Ignatian questions from the last chapter: What would you recommend to someone in a similar situation? What would you have wanted to do, from the vantage point of your deathbed? What would your "best self" do?

The Ignatian triad of "riches to honors to pride" can also shed some light here. Salary and wealth are the ultimate measures of value in our culture. That is one reason why salary is a taboo topic in most social gatherings. Once revealed, it brutally places people in a social hierarchy with one another.

So you have to be careful that the riches (a high salary) that lead to honors (the esteem of colleagues) do not lead to pride (the belief that you are better than others simply because your paycheck is bigger).

Remembering the Poor

Step into any airport bookstore today, and you'll see a section marked *Business* filled with books on how to get ahead. These books betoken a lively conversation among former CEOs, successful entrepreneurs, and business writers on how to be more successful, how to trounce your competitors, and how to stay on top, with the goal of more and more wealth.

But in those discussions one group is missing: the poor. For at least two reasons: First, their presence is a reminder of the inability of the capitalist system to provide for all, and so they represent a silent reproach to the capitalist "way of proceeding." Second, the material needs of the poor remind us of our responsibility to care for them. For both reasons, the poor appear, in the words of Pope John Paul II, as "a burden, as irksome intruders trying to consume what others have produced."

And increasingly they are obscured—by gated communities that shut out the nonwealthy, television shows that focus on celebrities, and slick ads for all manner of expensive consumer goods. Where are the poor? As Dick Meyer says in his book on American culture, *Why We Hate Us,* "We have used our affluence and abundance to build screens and false idols that obscure what matters most, what is authentic, what is unmediated." That authenticity includes the poor.

Thus, the final challenge: how to remember the need to care for the poor.

One of my friends, a corporate lawyer, told me he found three things that help: first, being grateful for what you have; second, helping out in a church community; and third, really stretching yourself when you give charitably.

Another goal might be to spend time with the poor. To get to know the poor one-on-one, rather than as objects of charity. And it is not only the poor who benefit; it is the more affluent, too, who discover one of the secrets of the kingdom of God: the poor are able to invite the wealthy to think about God in new ways, as the refugees did for me in Africa. As Jon Sobrino, a Jesuit who teaches theology in El Salvador, wrote in *The True Church and the Poor:* "The poor are accepted as constituting the primary recipients of the Good News and, therefore, as having an inherent capacity of understanding it better than anyone else."

THOSE ARE A FEW suggestions on living a spiritual life in the working world based on the way of Ignatius. Overall, it requires carving out time for both prayer and solitude, finding God around you, practicing a degree of detachment from some corporate values, and remembering the need for solidarity with God's poor.

HOW TO BRING YOUR BEST SELF TO WORK

There's an old Jesuit joke that says that the clearest sign of the presence of the Holy Spirit at work in the Society of Jesus is that, despite all the craziness and confusion, we're still here. Only God could do that!

That's a humble way of looking at our successes, and it reminds us that we are ultimately dependent on God for our future.

Willingness to trust in God's providence is what Pedro Arrupe had in mind when a journalist innocently asked him the question, "Where will the Society of Jesus be in twenty years?" Arrupe laughed and said, "I have no idea!" Like the church, the Society may be managed by human beings, but we believe that God ultimately guides us. And who knows where God will lead us in the future?

Still, there may be a few concrete reasons that can be adduced for the success of many of our ventures: Jesuits have a common mission; we try to work hard; we are available for many kinds of work; and we are inspired by the example of Jesus, as all Christians are, to accept whatever sacrifices are needed in pursuit of the common good.

Today you could add to that list of reasons another important one: Jesuits work with talented lay colleagues who share in the Ignatian vision. What's more, Jesuits often work *for* those lay colleagues who share our vision.

But there may be more specific aspects of "our way of proceeding" that have helped the Society of Jesus endure for over 450 years, ideas that may be useful to those in the business world. Chris Lowney's book *Heroic Leadership* has as its subtitle *Best Practices from a 450-Year-Old Company that Changed the World*. His book examines the characteristics of "our way of proceeding" that have helped the *Compañia de Jesús* flourish, and then he proposes some of those ideas as models of "best practices" for workers, managers, and corporations.

A former-Jesuit-turned-investment-manager, Lowney boiled down the list of the "Jesuit leadership secrets" to what he calls the "four pillars." They are self-awareness, ingenuity, love, and heroism.

Let's look at Lowney's four pillars, add a few more, and think about how they might be applied in the working world.

The first pillar is *self-awareness*. "Leaders thrive by understanding who they are and what they value," writes Lowney, "by becoming aware of unhealthy blind spots or weaknesses that can derail them, and by cultivating the habit of continuous self-reflection and learning."

By now this should be a familiar part of Jesuit spirituality. The way of Ignatius is designed to help us not only grow closer to God, but also understand ourselves—our strengths and our weaknesses—and whatever it is that keeps us from freedom. The examen, for example, continually invites us to reflect on what we've done, what we are doing, and what we will do. Part of Ignatian spirituality is that constant process of reflection, action, reflection.

This spiritual practice is applicable to the professional life. Good workers or leaders will be familiar with weaknesses and stumbling blocks that may derail them, can address those problems and also reflect on what motivates them to excellence.

Second, *ingenuity*. "Leaders make themselves and others comfortable in a changing world," writes Lowney. "They eagerly explore new ideas, approaches, and cultures rather than shrink defensively from what lurks around life's next corner. Anchored by nonnegotiable principles and values, they cultivate the 'indifference' that allows them to adapt confidently."

This is clearly seen in the life of Ignatius, who determined that the times demanded that his men should not be cloistered monks but rather "in the world." His indifference enabled him always to be adaptable and not overly concerned with incidentals.

That kind of ingenuity also finds expression in the lives of the great Jesuit missionaries. St. Francis Xavier, for example, used any possible means to spread the Gospel, including ringing a bell to attract attention and singing songs in native tongues.

Perhaps the most notable example of this ingenuity comes from Matteo Ricci, a sixteenth-century Italian Jesuit who immersed himself in the study of Chinese and donned the robes of the Mandarin scholar, as ways of presenting himself as a man of deep learning to the Chinese nobility. He wrote to his superiors:

> We have let our beards grow and our hair down to our ears, at the same time we have adopted the special dress that the literati wear . . . of violet silk, and the hem of the robe and collar and the edges are bordered with a band of blue silk a little less than a palm wide.

Soon Ricci's home became a gathering place for scholars and Chinese thinkers. "His high intellectual prestige," writes William Bangert in *A History of the Society of Jesus,* "was magnified by his more than twenty works in Chinese on apologetics, mathematics and astronomy, some of which have honored places in the history of Chinese literature."

Ultimately, Ricci's venture was scuttled after the Holy See disapproved of the Jesuits' acceptance of the notion that "ancestor worship" and veneration paid to Confucius in Chinese culture were compatible with Christianity. (Ricci saw them simply as respect paid to families and to one of the most important men in Chinese history, and, in his words, "certainly not idolatrous, and perhaps not even superstitious.") In time, Ricci would establish a Jesuit house in Peking, with the approval of the emperor, and by his death in 1610, twenty-five hundred Chinese had become Catholics.

These innovations flowed from the Jesuit emphasis on learning, the importance of which Ignatius understood from his own life, and ingenuity. Added to this was the Jesuit "indifference" to incidentals and their desire to try something new.

Ingenuity also means flexibility and adaptability: what works well in one place may not in another. Ignatius grew his hair long as a way of trying to be more ascetical. When he saw that this had little to do with his spiritual progress, he cut it. Ricci, on the other hand, realized that in order to be accepted at all, he would have to grow his hair. Ignatian flexibility can be a component for success in the modern workplace, too.

But of all the stories of Jesuit ingenuity, the one that delights me most is the largely forgotten history of Jesuit theater.

In the sixteenth and seventeenth centuries, Jesuit priests and brothers were well known throughout all of Europe for their expertise in producing immensely popular plays, mainly through their schools, which in many towns were the leading civic and cultural institutions. *The Catholic Encyclopedia,* for example, estimates that between 1650 and 1700 roughly one hundred thousand productions of Jesuit plays took place, some often staged for royal visits. In 1574 one play performed in Munich transformed almost the entire town into an elaborate backdrop, with one thousand actors taking part. At a performance in seventeenth-century Vienna, the audience was so vast that police from neighboring towns had to be called to keep the surging crowds in check.

What distinguished the Jesuit theatrical productions was their ingenuity: the creative use of scenery and staging, including intricately designed backdrops, realistic props, and complicated mechanical devices. René Fülöp-Miller in *The Power and Secret of the Jesuits,* writes:

> On every conceivable occasion, the Jesuit producers made divinities appear in the clouds, ghosts rise up and eagles fly over the heavens, and the effect of these stage tricks was further enhanced by machines producing thunder and the noise of winds. They even found ways and means of reproducing with a high degree of technical perfection the crossing of the Red Sea by the Israelites, storms at sea, and similar difficult scenes.

For added measure, Jesuits either invented or perfected the screen known as the scrim, a modern-day theatrical mainstay, as well as the trap door. (The next time you see someone disappear through a trap door, remember Jesuit ingenuity!)

Lowney's third quality of heroic leadership is *love*. "Leaders face the world with a confident, healthy sense of themselves as endowed with talent, dignity, and the potential to lead. They find exactly these same attributes in others and passionately commit to honoring and unlocking the potential they find in themselves and in others. They create environments bound and energized by loyalty, affection, and mutual support." Lowney contrasts the way of Ignatius with that of his near contemporary, Niccolò Machiavelli, who counseled that "to be feared is safer than to be loved."

The clearest indication of this comes from Ignatius's instructions for the director of novices, often called the most important man in the province. The person must be not simply a man who can give young Jesuits "loving admonition," but—most striking—someone whom all the novices "may love" and to whom they may "open themselves in confidence." At the very beginning of Jesuit training, Ignatius wishes to instill a sense of love to engender the confidence needed to help young men progress.

How different this was from my own experience in the working world. Occasionally it seemed that it was precisely the angry, mean-spirited, and foul-mouthed people who rose to the top. (My workplace was by no means normative: most people in the working world are caring, decent, and compassionate.) Still, imagine my surprise when I observed that Jesuits seemed to grow *kinder* as they assumed roles in governance. This not only fostered a sense that I wanted to be like them, but also that I would gladly follow them.

In the *Constitutions,* Ignatius emphasizes the overarching value of love during each stage of Jesuit training, beginning with the novitiate. And he includes it in the qualities required for a good superior general, to which he devotes several pages. (Many Jesuits at the time believed that Ignatius was unconsciously describing himself.) The superior general needs to be closely united with God, says Ignatius, from whom "charity toward all his neighbors should particularly shine forth . . . and in a special way toward the members of the Society; likewise a genuine humility which will make him highly beloved of God our Lord and of human beings."

Look at the words from Ignatius that we've quoted just in the last few paragraphs: *loving, love, charity, beloved.* Ignatius intended the Society to be a loving and supportive place. Isn't it obvious that a loving and supportive environment where everyone's talents and skills are respected would be a good place to work? This goes for both religious orders and corporations.

Chris Lowney's final characteristic is *heroism.* "Leaders imagine an inspiring future and strive to shape it rather than passively watching the future happen around them. Heroes extract gold from the opportunities at hand rather than waiting for golden opportunities to be handed to them," he writes.

Lowney points to a letter to the Jesuit community in Ferrara, Italy, in which Ignatius counseled his superiors to "endeavor to conceive great resolves and elicit equally great desires." Once again, Ignatius highlights the place of desire, this time as a way of encouraging people in their dreams.

And big dreams, too. One of the few important characteristics of Jesuit spirituality that we haven't yet discussed is the elusive idea of the *magis,* from the Latin word for the "more" or the "greater." This complex notion is probably best addressed at this point in this book, after having discussed humility and spiritual poverty. The *magis* means doing the more, the greater, for God. When you work, give your all. When you make plans, plan boldly. And when you dream, dream big. But, as David Fleming recently wrote to me, the *magis* is comparative. The more, not the most. The greater, not the greatest. "Ignatius never works with superlatives," said Fleming. "When we want to do the best, we may get frozen. If we want to do what might be better, we are able to choose."

The *magis* does not mean you act foolishly or unrealistically. Nor do you do these great things for yourself or even for the glory of the Society of Jesus. Rather, you strive to do great things for God. Thus the phrase used by Ignatius as a criterion for choosing, which has become an unofficial Jesuit motto: *Ad Majorem Dei Gloriam*. For the greater glory of God.

Built into the Ignatian way, then, is the desire for the *magis*. Ultimately, "eliciting great desires" and inviting people to think big is the seed for accomplishing great things for God.

One historical example of the *magis* in action served as the inspiration for the 1986 movie *The Mission*. Perhaps the most well-known film based on the Society of Jesus, *The Mission* starred Jeremy Irons, Robert De Niro, and Liam Neeson as priests and brothers working in the Jesuit Reductions of seventeenth-century South America. During that time, Jesuit priests and brothers began to gather the native peoples, often the target of ruthless slave traders, into organized villages. The term "reductions," *reducciones,* comes from the desire to "reduce" the sprawl of the local settlements into a smaller area as a way to protect them from slave traders and more easily introduce them to Christianity.

"We have worked hard to arrange all this," wrote the real-life Roque Gonzalez, S.J., in 1613, of his work with the Guaraní peoples, "but with even greater zest and energy—in fact with all our strength— we have worked to build temples to Our Lord, not only those made by hands but spiritual temples as well, namely the souls of these Indians."

In these villages, scattered throughout present-day Argentina, Bolivia, and Paraguay, the Jesuits taught a variety of crafts, leading to an unprecedented flowering of indigenous Christian art, inspired by the European Jesuits but creatively translated into the artistic idiom of the local peoples. In *A History of the Society of Jesus,* William Bangert describes a typical village in its heyday:

From a central plaza, pointing north, south, east and west
and built of the material of the area, even stone and adobe,

spread the homes of the people, who sometimes numbered up to 10,000. Close by stood the assembly of workshops with tools for carpentry, masonry, metal work. Behind the homes stretched the fruit orchards, the pasture land for cattle, and the farms which provided wheat, rice, sugar cane, and cotton. In the church, the noblest edifice of all and the center of community life, the Indians, instructed in the dignity of the liturgy and inspired by the beauty of the altar, sang their hymns and played musical instruments. . . . To establish such vibrant centers of faith . . . the Jesuits brought, in addition to the sacraments and the word of God, their skills as metallurgists, cattle raisers, architects, farmers and masons.

Some of these immense stone churches, or their ruins, located deep in the jungles of South America, are popular tourist attractions today; others still serve as working parishes for the local peoples, who follow the faith introduced to their ancestors three centuries ago. Here is a clear legacy of the *magis:* people who were, in difficult circumstances, trying to do the more, the greater, the better for God and for God's people.

The *magis* also lies behind more unsung achievements: the high-school teacher who spends hours painstakingly grading exams; the college campus minister driving a bus filled with boisterous students on a service trip to Appalachia; the priest who carefully guides a couple through the preparation for their wedding. This way of fulfilling the *magis* may be less dramatic than, say, the Jesuit Reductions, but no less important.

But by no means is the *magis* confined to the accomplishments of Jesuits or members of religious orders or priests. *Anyone* who dreams of doing great things for God can live out the *magis*—whether you are a father caring for your young child, a middle-aged woman nursing your aging parent, or an inner-city teacher working overtime to tutor a needy student. Great works are often quiet works.

In addition to Lowney's four pillars for organizations, institutions, and businesses, I would add three more to this list of "best practices" for a more specific group: believers in the working world.

The first is *an appreciation of the dignity of work*.

One of the most overlooked aspects of Christian spirituality is the fact that Jesus worked. And I don't mean simply preaching, healing the sick, and performing all those miracles, like stilling the storm, turning water into wine, and raising the dead. I mean something that took place earlier in his life.

We know almost nothing about the time in Jesus' life between the ages of twelve and thirty. All the Gospel of Luke has to say is, "Jesus increased in wisdom and in years" (2:52). What was Jesus doing? Working. According to Luke, Jesus followed his foster father in his trade as a *tekton,* usually translated as "carpenter" but also as "craftsman." (Scholars say he may also have been what we would call today a "day laborer.") In his time this could have meant not only working with wood, which was scarce in the area, but also doing day jobs—building walls, hoeing fields, and so on. As a boy, he was probably apprenticed to Joseph in the carpentry shop at Nazareth. Because little is known about this time, it is often called Jesus' "hidden life."

Jesus was a craftsman and a businessman. Working as a carpenter would have meant selecting the right kind of wood, negotiating a fair price with his clients, traveling to different households and towns, and doing a solid day's work. It's not surprising that so many of his parables have to do with farmers, fishermen, farm managers, and day laborers. Jesus knew what it meant to work.

All work has dignity. No job, when done freely, is ignoble. Part of our Jesuit novitiate training was doing "low and humble tasks" in the house, like cleaning toilets, mopping floors, and washing dishes. Two of the greatest Jesuit saints, close friends we have already met, did those kinds of work: Alphonsus Rodríguez tended the door at the College in Majorca, Spain. His friend, Peter Claver, the "slave of the slaves," worked to exhaustion bringing food to the slave ships of Cartagena. No work done freely and with a good intention is undignified. And was Jesus any less the Son of God when he was doing manual labor?

Understanding the dignity of work comes when we realize that we are, as theologians say, "cocreators" with God. In the Spiritual Exercises Ignatius asks us to imagine ourselves "laboring" with God and God "laboring" on our behalf. We work with God to build a better world. And God sees the fruit of our labor, even if others cannot. Think of Joseph, the carpenter who taught Jesus his craft, a man given no lines to say in the New Testament and whose life remains almost completely hidden. Through his silent work he was able to help fashion, as the Jesuit theologian John Haughey says, "the instrument most needed for the salvation of the world."

Joseph's work was of supreme importance—even though others may not have seen this at the time. How similar this is to the many millions of people who do hidden work today: spending long hours working to put their kids through school; taking on an extra job to save money to care for an elderly parent or relative; working to exhaustion scrubbing floors, doing multiple loads of laundry, and spending hours over a stove for their families. Even if their efforts are hidden from others, they are seen by the One whose gaze matters most.

Here's a parable about this that I like: An elderly stone-carver was working in a medieval cathedral on a marble statue of a saint. He spent many days carefully carving the intricate folds of her dress, on the back of the statue. First he used a large chisel, then a smaller one, and then sanded it down with great care. Another stone-carver noticed what he was doing and realized that the statue would be placed in a dark niche, its back facing the wall, his friend's handiwork hidden. "Why are you doing that hard work?" his friend asked. "No one will see it."

"God will," he said.

The Dignity of Work

Karl Rahner, the German Jesuit, spoke of the value of hidden work—in a meditation called "Why Become or Remain a Jesuit?"

> I think of brothers I myself have known—of my friend Alfred Delp, who with hands chained [in a German prison for opposing Hitler] signed his declaration of final membership in the Society; of one who in a village in India that is unknown to Indian intellectuals helps poor people to dig their wells; of another who for long hours in the confessional listens to the pain and torment of ordinary people who are far more complex than they appear on the surface. I think of one who in Barcelona is beaten by police along with his students without the satisfaction of actually being a revolutionary and savoring its glory; of one who assists daily in the hospital at the bedside of death until that unique event becomes for him a dull routine; of the one who in prison must proclaim over and over again the message of the Gospel with never a token of gratitude, who is more appreciated for the handout of cigarettes than for the words of the Good News he brings; of the one who with difficulty and without any clear evidence of success plods away at the task of awakening in just a few men and women a small spark of faith, of hope and of charity.

The second Ignatian insight into work is *acceptance of failure*. While we should use our self-awareness, ingenuity, love, and heroism, there is no guarantee that we will always succeed. Accepting this—on the job, in the home, or in life—is an important way to embrace what Walter Ciszek termed the "reality of the situation" and understand our own humility and poverty of spirit.

One of the most powerful stories I've heard on this topic comes from Jim, a kind-hearted Jesuit brother from Kentucky, who taught social work at Loyola University in Chicago. Jim once told me the story of Carol, whom he met at a social-service center he founded at a parish in Los Angeles.

Carol, a former model who had fallen on hard times, visited the center one morning and met Jim. When she asked for a pair of jeans, he brought her to another volunteer, who led Carol into the clothes distribution room. A few minutes later, Jim heard a commotion. Carol was drunkenly running through the building, half-naked, with her pants falling off, complaining about her jeans and screaming expletives at the staff.

Jim took Carol outside and calmly explained that she was welcome but that she needed to remain sober. He offered her a cup of coffee and asked if she understood their "deal." She stared at him and said, "The coffee is cold. And you're mean!"

During Jim's three years at the center, Carol visited at least thirty times, sometimes drunk, sometimes angry, sometimes sober. When she was lucid, said Jim, her former beauty (both inner and outer) would shine forth, and she was full of humor and good insights. Over time he got to know Carol well: the two talked about her family, her background, her battle with alcoholism, and her soured career dreams.

Once, Jim got a call from her sister, asking if Jim had seen Carol lately. He hadn't. "You know, she considers your center her home, don't you?" she said.

After three years, Jim's work at the center came to a close. By way of wrapping things up, he tried to say good-bye to as many of the guests of the center as possible. On his last day, he walked to the post office to mail a package.

On his way, he saw Carol. She was with her "friend," a man who had physically abused her in the past. Jim said he "froze in his tracks." He thought about crossing the street to say good-bye but just stood there. Carol finally motioned to Jim with a slight wave and kept walking with her companion.

Jim recounted the end of the story for me recently in a letter. "I wanted to leave the parish on a 'high,' knowing that I had done good things and tried to help people in need. As Carol turned the corner and walked out of sight, my concern for her turned into tears streaming down my face. I was sad because I had hoped she would be on the path to a healthier and more whole life, and I was disappointed and frustrated because she was in the company of a man with whom she swore she wouldn't meet again, and I was angry at him for luring her back."

All Jim could do when he returned to the rectory was silently whisper good-bye to Carol. "As I sat on the rectory steps, I felt the only thing I could offer her were prayers for her happiness and well-being."

No matter how hard we work, there are some things we are powerless to change, and failure does not lie in laziness or foolishness or poor planning. Work can sometimes be a well of great suffering.

Men and women who are laid off suddenly, whose businesses collapse, who face failures in the workplace know this. The mystery of suffering invades the working world, and this insight must be an essential part of a spirituality of work: in some aspects we are powerless, and our efforts seem fruitless. Here the mystery of suffering comes to the fore.

But even work that seems fruitless on the surface can still be directed to God. In his novel *Exiles,* about the Jesuit Gerard Manley Hopkins, Ron Hansen includes a lovely passage from one of Hopkins's actual retreat journals. It is a prayer offering his work to God, though the writing itself might seem fruitless: "Also in some meditations today I earnestly asked our Lord to watch over my compositions that they might do me no harm through the enmity or imprudence of any man or my own; that He would have them as His own and employ or not employ them as He should see fit. And this I believe is heard."

Christian Failure

St. Francis Xavier died on a small island six miles off the coast of China, his ultimate destination in sight. Not having reached his goal, Xavier felt himself something of a failure. Here is Walter Burghardt, in his book *Saints and Sanctity,* reflecting on times of failure even after we have worked hard.

This is dreadfully difficult for a human being to accept— even for a Xavier. Just because I am trying to do God's work with every ounce of my being is no guarantee that my plans will prosper. There is no guarantee that an effective Christian apostle will not be cut down in his prime. . . . There is no guarantee that because you have given yourself to a Christian marriage, your oneness will be lasting . . . that because you love God deeply, you will not lose your job, your home, your family, your health. . . . There is no guarantee that because you believe, you will not doubt; because you hope, you will not despond; because you love, your love will not grow cold. There is no guarantee that a Xavier will reach China. In this sense there is a Christian frustration, a Christian failure. . . .

You do your Christian task as God gives you to see it; the rest, the increase, is in His hands. God still uses what the world calls foolish to shame the wise, still uses what the world calls weak to shame its strength, still uses what the world calls low and insignificant and unreal to nullify its realities. . . . In this sense, there is no Christian frustration and no Christian failure.

The third aspect is *reliance on God*.

St. Ignatius was a hard worker who nonetheless knew that everything he had accomplished was thanks to God. This attitude is freeing, since we recognize that we're not working on our own, we have a partner in our labors, and, moreover, we cannot do everything on our own. Jim's experience with Carol is a reminder of this: he couldn't "save" her. Relying on God brings both humility and freedom. As my spiritual director said, "There is a Messiah, and it's not you."

> God could do precious little if He could not sustain me one more day.
> —St. Claude La Colombière, S.J. (1641–1682)

Those are a few ways that the way of Ignatius can help you in your work, as you live out your vocation in the world.

But vocation is not just about working. It's also about being. It's not just about what you do, but, more important, who you are. So let's look at the question "Who should I be?"

BE WHO YOU IS!

Each of us is called to a unique vocation in life, based on the desires that God plants within us, as well as our talents, skills, and personalities. This is one reason why Ignatius speaks of a God who wants to enter into a deep relationship with us and of the Creator's dealing "immediately with the creature." God knows that our deepest desires are those that will bring joy to us and to the world.

But this is about more than just work, a job, or even a career. Vocation may have little to do with one's actual work. For the deepest vocation is to become who you are, to become your "true self," the person whom God created and calls you to be.

Part of this path is accepting that God loves us already. That God loves us *as we are*. Man or woman, young or old, wealthy or poor, we are all loved by God. No matter how you see yourself, God sees you as his beloved. Hard to believe? Then let me tell you a story about acceptance.

WONDERFULLY MADE

Rick Curry is a gregarious and quick-witted Jesuit who founded the National Theatre Workshop of the Handicapped. He also received his doctorate in theater studies (and is the one who introduced me to the history of "Jesuit theater"). Rick, who was born without a right arm, entered the Jesuits after high school. For a time he was an actor. The genesis of the National Theater Workshop came when Rick went to audition for a commercial.

When he met the casting agent in her office, she noticed his one arm and said, "Is this a joke? Who sent you?" And he said, "What do you mean? I'm here for the audition." And she said, "Oh please. Tell me who put you up to this. This is hysterical." She didn't see him as an actor, or barely a human being, but, quite literally, a joke. This convinced him of the need for a school for handicapped actors.

For many years his theater provided disabled actors for various auditions. Once, a casting director called and said, "We want a double amputee for a role in a television show." Rick asked, "Do you want someone without his arms or legs?" The casting director said, "I'm not sure. Does it matter?" And Rick said, "Well, it does to him!"

But I want to tell you another story about Rick. When he was a little boy, in the 1950s, the preserved right forearm of St. Francis Xavier came to Philadelphia. Strange as this may seem to non-Catholics, this relic is particularly well known: it's the arm that the Jesuit used to baptize thousands of people during his missionary days in Africa, India, and Japan.

Rick's first-grade teacher, a Catholic sister, thought it would be a good idea for Rick to see the arm—though she didn't expect there would be any sort of miraculous outcome. Neither did his mother, though she wrote a letter to permit Rick to be excused from class to see the relic.

But his Catholic-school classmates were praying hard for a miracle. Maybe Rick would be healed—and become like all the other children in his class. So when Rick's mother picked him up to drive him to the cathedral downtown, his class was thrilled.

A huge line wound up and down the aisles of the cathedral. Because of the crowd, officials announced that visitors would be able only to touch the reliquary, the glass box that held Francis's arm. You wouldn't be able to kiss the reliquary, as some pious Catholics had hoped. But when several priests saw the boy without a right arm, they said to his mother, "Oh, no, *he* can kiss it!" Rick, however, desired no such "healing."

So he kissed the glass case, but pressed the stump of his right arm against himself—hoping that it would not grow.

On his way back home, on the trolley car, he kept checking his arm. There wasn't any change. No miracle. When he returned to class, his classmates told him how disappointed they were. Perhaps, they said, he wasn't worthy of a miracle.

But someone else had a very different reaction. When he returned home that night, his sister Denise, who would later become a nun, was hiding behind the drapes of the living-room windows. She peeked out. When she saw Rick, she was delighted. "Oh great!" she said. "I'm so happy that nothing happened. Because I like you the way you are!"

This is the way that God loves us: as we are.

Rick never forgot that affirmation. It helped him to see his disability as a gift, as an entry into the humanity of others, and as a reminder of the call to be grateful for all of life. He told me recently that a disability was a negative "only to the extent that you absorb the negative impressions of others."

So maybe a miracle did happen that day.

Self-acceptance is the first step to holiness. But for many the path to self-acceptance can be arduous. Men, women, and children in ethnic or social minorities, with physical disabilities, with dysfunctional family backgrounds, with addictions, or those who feel unattractive, uneducated or undesirable may struggle for many years before accepting themselves as beloved children of God.

But the journey is essential. Many gay men and lesbians, for example, have told me that the real beginning of their spiritual path was accepting themselves as gay men and women—that is, the way that God has made them. Coming to see themselves in this way, and, more important, allowing God to love them as they are, not as society might want them to be, or think they should be, is an important step in their relationship with God.

"For it was you who formed my inward parts; you knit me together in my mother's womb," says Psalm 139. "I praise you, for I am fearfully and wonderfully made." God loves us as we are because that's how God made us. This is something of what the psalmist may have meant, and what Rick's sister meant, too.

COMPARE AND DESPAIR

The primary difficulty in accepting ourselves and valuing our individuality is the false belief that to become holy, or useful, or happy, we have to become someone else—or become perfect. The young mother who cares for her children may say to herself sadly, "I'll never be like Mother Teresa," when her vocation is to be a caring mother. The lawyer or doctor or schoolteacher who reads about St. Francis Xavier may say, "I'll never be like him." But they are not meant to be Mother Teresa or St. Francis Xavier, estimable as they were. They are meant to be themselves.

That means letting go of the wish to become someone else and remembering that your own vocation—not someone else's—is the path to happiness. You don't need to use anyone else's map to heaven, because God has already placed within your soul all the directions you need.

It also means joyfully accepting your own personality and dreams. One of the greatest bits of advice I've ever received was

What I Do Is Me

It took me many readings of this poem by Gerard Manley Hopkins before realizing how much it is about being who you are.

> As kingfishers catch fire, dragonflies draw flame;
> As tumbled over rim in roundy wells
> Stones ring; like each tucked string tells, each hung bell's
> Bow swung finds tongue to fling out broad its name;
> Each mortal thing does one thing and the same:
> Deals out that being indoors each one dwells;
> Selves—goes itself; myself it speaks and spells,
> Crying Whát I dó is me: for that I came.
> I say móre: the just man justices;
> Keeps grace: thát keeps all his goings graces;
> Acts in God's eye what in God's eye he is—
> Chríst—for Christ plays in ten thousand places,
> Lovely in limbs, and lovely in eyes not his
> To the Father through the features of men's faces.

from a Jesuit spiritual director. At the time (I'll keep this vague) I was working with an unpleasant person on the job. As time passed, I found myself simply *reacting* to him: becoming more guarded, more defensive, more cautious, more suspicious, as a way of protecting myself from his bad temper. My reactions were beginning to make me callous and hard. One day I confessed to my spiritual director, "I feel like he is forming me into something I don't want to be."

How often we feel this! Other people, or groups, or situations, we feel, are shaping us into something we wouldn't choose to be.

My director said, "Don't let anyone take from you the freedom to become who God wants you to be."

This means you, someone unique, someone loved by God.

The Almighty Artisan

A rough and unshapen log has no idea that it can be made into a statue that will be considered a masterpiece, but the carver sees what can be done with it. So many . . . do not understand that God can mold them into saints, until they put themselves into the hands of that almighty Artisan.

—St. Ignatius Loyola

It's easy to see this marvelous individuality in the lives of the holy men and women around us. So far in this book I've introduced you to many of my friends. Each of them is very different. John, my Jesuit friend from Gloucester, Massachusetts, was different from my first spiritual director, David. John was more relaxed and laid back; David, more energetic. John was happy to stay home and watch television at night; David was more of a social animal.

During our novitiate we took several personality tests, designed to help us understand how differently people interacted with the world. One series of tests was structured to determine whether we were extroverts or introverts. The result: I was the only extrovert in the house. That explained a great deal—for example, why after a house party I was energized, but the others were drained and needed to retire to their rooms to recharge. Or why they needed to process information before they spoke, rather than discussing something in order to understand what they were thinking. The tests helped me see that the others who approached life differently weren't wrong or misguided, but simply different. Or, more accurately, that *I* was different!

After we got the results, I grew discouraged. Was I going to be an inadequate Jesuit because I wasn't an introvert? Not at all, said David. The Society of Jesus needs extroverts also.

It's always difficult to avoid comparison with others and to think not only that they have it easier, but that they are somehow holier than you are. So you need to maintain a healthy tension between acceptance and desire. On the one hand, you honor the person God made—with your background, personality, talents, skills, and strengths. On the other, you allow God to move you in new directions, to change, to grow, and to discover who you are meant to be. God has created something wonderful in you, but God is still creating.

Much of my own journey to self-acceptance involved letting go of the need to be somebody else. Nobody in particular, just a feeling that I needed to be different. Early in the novitiate, I thought that being holy meant a suppressing of my personality, rather than building on it. Eradicating my natural desires and inclinations, rather than asking God to sanctify them. I knew that I wasn't a holy person, so therefore being holy must mean being a different person. Strange as it sounds, I thought that being myself meant being someone else.

> It is dangerous to make everyone go forward by the same road, and worse to measure others by yourself.
> —St. Ignatius Loyola

David kept reminding me that I didn't need to be like anyone else except me. "You do not have to change for God to love you," as Anthony de Mello said. It took a while for that to sink in. Besides a lingering sense that I wasn't worthy of being a Jesuit, there was envy involved. At various times in my life, especially when things were not going so well, I have been envious of other people. At heart, the envy boiled down to this: everyone else has it easier than I do. And so they are obviously happier than I am.

This is false. And dangerous, too. One tends to compare one's own life, which is always an obvious mixture of good and bad, with what one falsely perceives as the perfect life of the other. In this way, we minimize our own gifts and graces and maximize the other person's.

Ironically, we sometimes do the opposite with problems, short-comings, and struggles: we maximize our own and minimize the other person's. Others seem more clever, more attractive, more popular, more relaxed, more athletic, more whatever, than we are, and so therefore (it seems) they lead charmed lives. Likewise, other people, we surmise, face no real problems in their lives. Or if they do face problems, we think, their problems are not as bad as ours.

But no one leads a charmed life. Everyone's life is a full measure of graces and blessings—as well as struggles and challenges. "Every house has its problems," as my mother would say when we would drive through wealthy neighborhoods and envy the lives of the rich. And if we consistently compare our own complicated reality with the supposed perfection of another's life, is it any wonder that we wish we were other than who we are?

Compare and despair, as a Jesuit friend likes to say.

How do you move toward becoming who you are? Here are a few important steps, with some Ignatian highlights, for this lifelong journey of discovery.

BECOMING YOURSELF

First, *remember that God loves you*. As David liked to say, paraphrasing the psalms, "God takes delight in you!" Or as the theologian James Alison suggests, God *likes* you. If you doubt this, a quick examen of the things for which you're grateful may help you see the way that God has blessed you, and loves you. Reading the first few verses of Psalm 139—"You knit me together in my mother's womb"—often helps as well.

Second, realize that God loves you *as an individual,* not simply in the abstract. God cares about you personally, much as a close friend would. Remember how God speaks to you in personal, intimate ways, in your daily life and in prayer, which only you can appreciate. This is a sign of God's *personal* love for you.

Third, accept your desires, skills, and talents as things *given to you by God* for your happiness and for others. These are gifts from the Creator.

Fourth, *avoid the temptation to compare* yourself to others and denigrate or undervalue yourself. Remember: compare and despair.

Fifth, *move away* from actions that are sinful or that keep you from being compassionate, loving, and free. And *move toward* actions that make you more compassionate, loving, and free. Think of the meditation on the Two Standards from the Exercises to help you with this.

Sixth, trust that *God will help you* because God desires for you to become who you are meant to be. And pray for God's help.

Seventh, recognize that the process of becoming the person you are meant to be is a *long process* and can take time.

It WILL TAKE SOME time before you are able to integrate your insights fully, and longer before they translate into action, and still longer before you find that you have changed inside and outside.

Remember the story of Ignatius if you doubt this.

Five years after I entered the Jesuits, I returned to Campion Center, in Weston, Massachusetts, where I had made my very first retreat. My director that year was a light-hearted Jesuit named Harry, who had lived with us as a spiritual father in the novitiate. It was almost impossible to be sad around him: he was consistently joyful and funny. When one of the three original members in our novitiate class decided to leave, leaving only two behind, he instantly coined a motto for our little class, taken from a Greek phrase: *Ou polla, alla pollou*. Not many, but much.

During that summertime retreat, I lamented to Harry that I didn't seem to be changing quickly enough. I knew the kind of person I wanted to be: free, open, relaxed, loose, compassionate, patient, mature, generous. But my imperfections held me back. How would God change me? When would I change? Why wasn't it happening *faster?*

The Slow Work of God

Patience is an important companion on the path to discovering your own vocation, to becoming the person you would like to become, and, in fact, to any change. Pierre Teilhard de Chardin, the Jesuit paleontologist, who knew about the slow working of time, wrote this in a letter to a friend, on patience:

Above all, trust in the slow work of God.

We are quite naturally impatient in everything to reach the end without delay.

We should like to skip the intermediate stages.

We are impatient of being on the way to something unknown, something new.

And yet it is the law of all progress that it is made by passing through some stages of instability—and that it may take a very long time.

And so I think it is with you; your ideas mature gradually—let them grow, let them shape themselves, without undue haste. Don't try to force them on, as though you could be today what time (that is to say, grace and circumstances acting on your own good will) will make of you tomorrow.

Only God could say what this new spirit gradually forming within you will be.

Give our Lord the benefit of believing that his hand is leading you, and accept the anxiety of feeling yourself in suspense and incomplete.

Harry smiled and looked out the window to the grounds of the retreat house. "You see that tree over there?" he said.

I glanced at a large maple tree on a knoll, which I passed frequently as I wandered through the woods. "It's green now, but in a few months it will become a beautiful red." Then he paused.

"And no one will see it change," he said.

The Salt Doll

Ultimately we find our identity and our vocation in God. Our desires come from God and lead to God.

To wrap up our discussion about vocation, let's end with one of my favorite stories from Anthony de Mello, which beautifully illustrates this concept. It's called "The Salt Doll," and is about, well, a doll made of salt.

A salt doll journeyed for thousands of miles over land, until it finally came to the sea.

It was fascinated by this strange moving mass, quite unlike anything it had ever seen before.

"Who are you?" said the salt doll to the sea.

The sea smilingly replied, "Come in and see."

So the doll waded in. The farther it walked into the sea the more it dissolved, until there was only very little of it left. Before that last bit dissolved, the doll exclaimed in wonder, "Now I know what I am!"

CHAPTER FOURTEEN

The Contemplative in Action

Our Way of Proceeding

ONE OF MY FAVORITE moments in film is from a foreign movie, first released in 2006, called *Paris, Je T'Aime,* a series of twenty vignettes by a group of international directors. Each story takes place in Paris. One depicts a love affair; another a meeting between a father and daughter; another a violent and bloody murder. In one vignette, Alexander Payne, the director of the film *Sideways,* offers the story of Carol, a mail carrier from Denver, who has saved her money for a dream vacation to Paris. She's even taken French language lessons for the past two years in preparation for her big trip.

Carol, played by Margo Martindale, seems a good soul, a middle-aged woman who lives with her two dogs, and who has traveled to Paris alone. Though she describes herself as happy and speaks about her friends, an element of loneliness suffuses her wanderings. Her tale, which takes the form of an oral report to her French class back home, is told in a voiceover. Carol's thoughts are conveyed in very simple words—since those are the only ones she knows in French.

Toward the end of a long day of sightseeing and sampling local restaurants, Carol wanders into a sunlit park and sits on a wooden bench. During the morning, she was surprised to find herself so pensive—about her work, her friends, her two dogs, her lost love, and her mother, who has recently died from cancer. As she sits silently, Carol sees signs of life all around her: couples talking animatedly, children in a playground, a woman resting on the green grass. A breeze gently stirs her brown hair. Then something extraordinary happens.

In her halting French, translated for the viewer in the English subtitles, Carol says this:

> Sitting there, alone in a foreign country, far from my job and everyone I know, a feeling came over me.
>
> It was like remembering something I'd never known before or had always been waiting for, but I didn't know what. Maybe it was something I had forgotten or something I've been missing all my life.
>
> All I can say is that I felt, at the same time, joy and sadness. But not too much sadness.
>
> Because I felt alive.
>
> Yes, alive.

As she says this, a look of peace washes over her tired features.

I'm not sure if the filmmaker intended to portray a spiritual epiphany (though Alexander Payne went to a Jesuit high school). And I'm not sure if Carol, who is the star of, after all, a five-minute movie, was intended to be a spiritual person. But in simple words, she not only expresses what we spoke about in an earlier chapter as an "uncommon longing," but opens a window onto one of the goals of the way of Ignatius: to be alive.

Yes, Alive

In these pages we've traveled together along the way of Ignatius. Now you have a right to ask: Where does that way lead? What's our destination?

In our first chapter, we talked about how five hypothetical Jesuits would define the way of Ignatius. Four answers were suggested: being a contemplative in action; finding God in all things; looking at the world in an incarnational way; and seeking freedom and detachment. These are all goals for the traveler along the way of Ignatius.

The first goal is illustrated by the fictional Carol, who feels, perhaps for the first time in her life, alive. She notices. She is aware. As she sits on that Parisian park bench, she discovers a connection. Significantly, the next words in her voiceover are: "That was the moment I fell in love with Paris. And I felt Paris fall in love with me." Awareness moves her to love.

In real life, Carol would have a choice to make—beyond simply deciding whether to change her hotel reservations and stay a few more days in France. Or even beyond deciding that Paris is now her favorite city. She can accept her experiences as just "feelings," or she can wonder if they might have another source.

The *contemplative in action,* according to St. Ignatius Loyola, not only contemplates the active world and sees wonderful things, but also sees in those wonderful things signs of God's presence and activity. The contemplative in action is deeply aware of God's presence even in the midst of a busy life. It is a stance of awareness. Awareness of God.

That leads us to a second goal: *finding God in all things.* By now you've seen how everything can be a way to experience God. In the past chapters, we've talked about encountering God in prayer, worship, family, love, music, nature, decision making, working, living simply, friendship, even during times of suffering. In all things. And in all people. And we've talked about an easy way to jump-start that awareness, to help you find God in everything: the examen. The contemplative in action seeks God and seeks to find God in action.

That means that he or she sees the world in an *incarnational way,* a third definition. God dwells in real things, real places, and real people. Not just "up there" but "all around." (Though I'm not denying that God is also "up there" in heaven, wherever or however that is.) For Christians, Jesus is the incarnation of God, but you don't have to be Christian to have an incarnational worldview. The more you travel along the way of Ignatius, the more you see the incarnational God.

And the more you travel along the Ignatian way, the more you will want to go further. The more you experience God, the more you will want to experience God more. The more you know God, the more you will want to know God more.

To do this, you need to maintain a measure of *detachment and freedom,* a fourth goal. You desire freedom from anything that prevents you from following along the way. You want to free yourself from any excess baggage. You want, as Ignatius said, to be free of "disordered attachments." And you have to be careful not to start down paths that will lead you away from God. As Ignatius would say, you have to "discern."

So tying it all together, you could say this: *Contemplatives in action* seek to *find God in all things* by looking at the world in an *incarnational* way, and, in their quest, they realize their desire for *freedom and detachment,* which helps them move even closer to God. That's probably a fair summary of Ignatian spirituality.

That's been my experience, too.

In the past few chapters, I've offered some personal examples of God's activity in my life, not because my life is more important than anyone else's, or more spiritual, or even normative. Rather, it's to show you that *anyone* can experience God if he or she moves along the path of Ignatius.

When I entered the Jesuit novitiate at twenty-seven, I had little experience of prayer. I couldn't imagine that I would ever have a "personal relationship" with God. I couldn't imagine that I would be free of some of the unhealthy patterns that had been with me since childhood. I couldn't imagine walking along a new path. I couldn't imagine a new path *at all*. I couldn't imagine, in a word, change.

But God had already imagined it.

The path of Ignatius has invited me to continual growth, freedom, and movement toward becoming more aware, more loving, more authentic, and, "yes, alive," to quote Carol. I've tried to show how this happened in ways that are personal, because that's where God is usually most alive, in our most intimate selves, *intimior intimo meo*, nearer to me than I am to myself. If we allow it to happen, God can work that way in all of our lives, which is why I include some real-life stories from the Jesuit saints, Jesuits I've known (some of whom seemed like saints), and many other friends and companions, both men and women, whom I've met along the way of Ignatius.

But those qualities—growth, freedom, movement, love, authenticity, even feeling alive—are not the final goals. The goal of the Ignatian way is not a quality, but something else.

The Road Is Our Home

The goal is God.

I've tried to write this book in a welcoming way so that as many readers as possible will be able to use it—from the doubtful seeker to the devout believer. Ignatian spirituality is a resource for a wide variety of people, not just Jesuits, not just Catholics, and not just Christians. Just as there are insights from Zen Buddhism that are useful to me as a Christian, so there are practices and techniques from Ignatian spirituality that can help the Zen Buddhist. And the person who is Jewish or Muslim, too. Anyone can use these practices to better his or her life.

But to understand fully the end of the journey, you have to understand the destination. For Ignatian spirituality is meaningless without God. The end is not a place. It's God.

Remember the analogy I used about the Spiritual Exercises at the beginning of the book? The Exercises are not meant to be read, they're meant to be experienced. It is similar to an instruction book about dancing. It wouldn't do you much good if you just read the book; you have to *dance* before you can understand it.

Well, there's a partner in that dance: God. It's a cheesy image, I know. (At this point you might be imagining yourself dancing with an old man with a long white beard—or if you weren't, maybe you are now!) But it's a reminder that the goal of the path is a relationship with God, who wants to be in relationship with you. Who wants to dance with you.

For me, Ignatian spirituality has been the primary way through which I've met God in my life. It's been my path to God. And to Jesus Christ. Ignatius's practices and insights have enriched my appreciation for my religious tradition, for Scripture, for community, for prayer, for . . . almost everything. The way of Ignatius has helped to lead me into relationship with God, something I would have thought impossible at age twenty-seven.

But no one, in this lifetime, reaches the end of the journey. After our deaths, I believe, we shall meet God "face to face," as St. Paul says. But on this earth we will always be pilgrims along the way.

That's why the image of the path has been the dominant image that I've used for Ignatian spirituality. That's also why I like what Jerónimo Nadal, one of Ignatius's early companions, said: "The road is our home." He meant that Jesuits were always traveling, always en route to some new mission, always open to move.

But Nadal's comment carries another meaning, too. It means that we are always on the road to God, and the more we come to understand the destination, the more we feel at home on that road.

God is the goal. So is our offering of ourselves to God. That's part of the friendship. In any real friendship, there is, as Ignatius says, an exchange of gifts. "Each shares with the other." God offers himself (or herself) to us, and we offer ourselves to God. So that's why I would like to end this book with a challenging prayer, taken from—what else?—the Spiritual Exercises. It's about giving something to God.

Yourself.

TAKE, LORD, RECEIVE

Throughout these past chapters, we've mentioned the four weeks of the Spiritual Exercises. As we moved along, I introduced you to selected aspects about each week as they related to the topics we were discussing. The First Week invites you to look at gratitude for God's gifts in your life, and then your own sinfulness. You're led to a grateful awareness of yourself as a loved sinner. In the Second Week, you imagine yourself accompanying Jesus of Nazareth in his earthly ministry of preaching and healing. The Third Week takes you, imaginatively, into the story of Jesus' passion and death, which gives you new perspectives on suffering.

But there's one more week we haven't yet talked about: the Fourth Week, which focuses on the Resurrection.

By the end of the Spiritual Exercises, most retreatants are delighted to be able to meditate on the joyful stories of the Resurrection: Jesus appearing to Mary Magdalene and the disciples, Jesus forgiving Peter for his betrayal, and Jesus feeding his disciples by the Sea of Galilee. And in a burst of pious enthusiasm Ignatius even *added* something to the New Testament: a scene of Jesus meeting his mother after the Resurrection. "Although this is not stated in Scripture," he writes, "still it is considered as understood by the statement that he appeared to many others."

At the close of the Fourth Week Ignatius invites us into a wonderful contemplation, which is often rushed through by people anxious to wrap up their retreats. (People on retreats are human too!) It's called the Contemplation to Attain Divine Love.

Said differently, it's a contemplation designed to help us understand God's love for us. To help us do so, Ignatius offers us one thought exercise and then a variety of typically rich metaphors.

First, he suggests, remember "with deep affection how much God our Lord has done for me" and "how much he has given me of what he possesses." This is similar to the type of gratitude included in the examination of conscience.

Second, says Ignatius, think about the way that God "dwells" in all his creatures. In the elements, God gives them existence. In the plants, life. In the animals, sensation. In human beings, intelligence. And in yourself, in whom God dwells, "giving me existence, life, sensation, and intelligence; and even further, making me his temple, since I am created as a likeness and image of the Divine Majesty." How does God "dwell" in you?

Third, consider how God labors in all of creation. That's always been a powerful image for me. God labors on our behalf and on behalf of all creatures, "giving them their existence, conserving them," helping them to grow and be themselves.

Finally, think of how all these gifts—and others, like justice, goodness, piety, and mercy—descend from God "as the rays come down from the sun, or the rains from their source." God is at work, with you, and for you.

All these images are beautiful invitations to think about and experience God's love for you.

But there's more. Within that final contemplation is one of the most famous, and perhaps most difficult, of all Ignatian prayers. It's often called the *Suscipe,* taken from the first word of the Latin prayer. Coming at the end of the Exercises, the *Suscipe* prayer is an offering to God. After the four weeks of the Exercises, after meditating on God's wholehearted love for you, people are often moved to respond wholeheartedly. Like many of the Ignatian ideals— including indifference, detachment, humility—this prayer is a goal.

> *Take, Lord, and receive all my liberty,*
> *my memory, my understanding, and all my will—*
> *all that I have and possess.*
> *You, Lord, have given all that to me.*
> *I now give it back to you, O Lord.*
> *All of it is yours.*

Dispose of it according to your will.
Give me love of yourself along with grace,
for that is enough for me.

Like I said, a tall order. It is a prayer of total surrender. I offer you everything, God. All I need is your love and grace. This is all I need to be "yes, alive."

Why am I ending this book with such a "hard" prayer? To remind you that the spiritual life is a constant journey. For me, I don't think I've ever been able to say that prayer and mean it completely. That is, I still want to hold on to all those things. And I'm not sure that I can say yet that all I need is God's love and grace. I'm still too human for that. But as Ignatius said, it's enough to have the desire for the desire. It's enough to want that freedom. God will take care of the rest.

So together you and I are still on the way to being contemplatives in action, to finding God in all things, to seeing God incarnate in the world, and to seeking freedom and detachment.

The way of Ignatius has been traveled by millions of people searching for God in their daily lives. And for that way—easy at times, difficult at others, but always moving us closer to God—we can thank our friend, St. Ignatius Loyola.

Acknowledgments

The examen starts with gratitude. This book ends with it. So let me recall some of the people for whom I am grateful.

First, I would like to thank my spiritual directors over the past twenty years, who have taught me more about Ignatian spirituality than could ever be contained in one book—especially those Jesuits who have accompanied me for extended periods, sometimes years at a time, during my training: David Donovan, Ken Hughes, J. J. Bresnahan, Jack Replogle, Dick Anderson, George Drury, Ozy Gonsalves, George Anderson, Jeff Chojnacki, and Damian O'Connell. Also, to those men and women who have directed my annual retreats and deepened my appreciation for God's activity in my life, heartfelt thanks: Ron Mercier, Joe McHugh, Jim Gillon, Phil Shano, Harry Cain, Jim Bowler, Bill Devine, Jim Keegan, Paul Harman, Dick Stanley, John Kierdejus, Paul Fitterer, Pat Lee (Jesuits all) as well as Gerry Calhoun and Maddy Tiberii, S.S.J. Thanks also to Bill Creed, S.J., and Martha Buser, O.S.U., who led me through a summer-long training program on the Spiritual Exercises at the Jesuit Spiritual Center in Milford, Ohio, and to Maureen Steeley, S.U., and Eleanora Murphy, S.U., for their spiritual direction practicum at the Linwood Spiritual Center in Rhinebeck, New York.

Second, thanks to a group of exceedingly wise, generous, and patient men and women who read this book in its early stages and offered their wisdom, insights—and corrections! Some are experts in Ignatian spirituality, others in Jesuit history, others in Scripture, theology, or psychology. Some were asked to read the manuscript with a particular audience in mind. All of them spent a great deal of time poring over what I had written in very rough form. And all of them helped make this book more accurate and more accessible.

Acknowledgments

So abundant thanks to the following Jesuits: Bill Barry, John O'Malley, John Padberg, David Fleming, John Donohue, Charles Shelton, Dan Harrington, Drew Christiansen, Richard Leonard, as well as to Margaret Silf, Maureen Conroy, R.S.M., Ron Hansen, Robert Ellsberg, and Matt Weiner—and to my mother, Eleanor Martin, and my sister, Carolyn Buscarino. Also thanks to the following Jesuits who helped with specific portions of the book: Jim Siwicki, Joseph Koterski, Peter Schineller, Antonio Delfau, and Bill Campbell.

Third, thanks to my dear brothers in the Society of Jesus, to whom this book is dedicated—*fratribus carissimis in Societate Jesu*—for accompanying me along the way of Ignatius. For more than twenty years they have offered me their love, friendship, encouragement, and prayers, as well as their insights on Ignatian spirituality and their example as faithful priests and brothers. Special thanks to the members of my faith-sharing groups over the years, and also to George Williams, Steve Katsouros, Bob Reiser, Chris Derby, Dave Godleski, Ross Pribyl, Kevin White, Matt Cassidy, Bob Gilroy, David McCallum, Tim Howe, Myles Sheehan, Jack McClain, Bill Campbell, Tom Reese, Brian Frain, George Witt, and Kevin O'Brien.

Fourth, there were some generous souls who helped me type this manuscript when my carpal tunnel syndrome was acting up, including Veronica Szczygiel, P. J. Williams, Kaitlyn Rechenberg, Regina Nigro, and Jim Keane, S.J.

Fifth, thanks to Heidi Hill, possibly the world's best fact checker, who saved me from numerous factual errors (which included misquoting something from one of my own books).

Sixth, thanks to my literary agent, Donald Cutler, for helping to shepherd this book to completion, and to Roger Freet at Harper-Collins for his initial and continued enthusiasm for the project and his superb edits and suggestions, which greatly helped to tighten and focus the book. Also great thanks to Carolyn Holland and Mary Ann Jeffreys whose careful editing improved the book greatly and saved me from some real howlers.

Finally, thanks to—who else?—St. Ignatius Loyola. And, of course, God, with whom all things are possible.

For Further Exploration

Rather than include a lengthy bibliography of the books used in writing this one, I thought it would be more helpful to recommend some favorite books for specific areas. This list is also by way of thanks to these authors, whose superb works have helped me to follow the way of Ignatius.

The Life of St. Ignatius Loyola

The starting point for any study of Ignatian spirituality is the *Autobiography,* a relatively short book of which there are multiple editions and translations. My favorite is by Parmananda R. Divarkar, S.J., called *A Pilgrim's Testament.* For a more straightforward account of his life try *St. Ignatius Loyola, the Pilgrim Years: 1491–1538,* by James Brodrick, S.J.; *Ignatius of Loyola* by Candido de Dalmases, S.J.; Mary Purcell's *The First Jesuit;* and Philip Caraman's *Ignatius Loyola.* John W. O'Malley, S.J.'s *The First Jesuits* recounts the life of Ignatius and his early companions as part of his larger story of the Society's first years.

The Letters of St. Ignatius Loyola, edited and translated by William J. Young, S.J., is a compact compendium of the saint's letters to Jesuits and other friends. So is the slightly more scholarly *Ignatius of Loyola: Letters and Instructions,* edited by John Padberg, S.J., Martin Palmer, S.J., and John L. McCarthy, S.J. Also, Joseph Munitiz and Philip Endean have edited a book called *Saint Ignatius Loyola: Personal Writings* that incorporates into a single volume the text of the *Spiritual Exercises,* many letters, and hard-to-find excerpts from the saint's journals.

THE SPIRITUAL EXERCISES

Reading *The Spiritual Exercises* is not like doing them, but it is an essential resource nonetheless for the pilgrim along Ignatius's way. Two of the best translations are *The Spiritual Exercises of St. Ignatius: A Translation and Commentary,* by George E. Ganss, S.J., which provides an analysis of some key words and concepts, and *Draw Me into Your Friendship,* by David Fleming, S.J. Fleming offers two side-by-side translations—one hewing completely to the original text, the other more contemporary and free-form. Other excellent books on the Exercises (helpful for directors and retreatants alike) include *Letting God Come Close* and *Finding God in All Things,* both by William A. Barry, S.J.; *Seek God Everywhere,* by Anthony de Mello, S.J.; *Spiritual Freedom,* by John English, S.J.; *Stretched for Greater Glory,* by George Aschenbrenner, S.J.; *The Spiritual Exercises of Ignatius Loyola, with Commentary,* by Joseph A. Tetlow, S.J.; and *Like the Lightning,* by David Fleming, S.J.

If you're interested in a line-by-line analysis of the Exercises, perhaps the best book is Michael Ivens's *Understanding the Spiritual Exercises.* This is the most detailed of the books on the Exercises included here, and it can be used profitably by the newcomer and the expert, not to mention spiritual directors. For a woman's perspective on the Exercises, try *The Spiritual Exercises Reclaimed,* by Kathryn Dyckman, Mary Garvin, and Elizabeth Liebert. Finally, Paul Mariani, a layman, husband, father, and poet, wrote a memoir of his time making the Spiritual Exercises at Eastern Point Retreat House in Gloucester called *Thirty Days.*

IGNATIAN SPIRITUALITY AND PRAYER

Margaret Silf's *Inner Compass* is a lovely invitation to Ignatian spiritual practices for the beginner. William Barry has written several terrific books that explicitly and implicitly use Ignatian spiritual themes. My favorites are *God's Passionate Desire, Seek My Face,* and *A Friendship Like No Other.* George Traub, S.J., has collected articles on a wide variety of topics in *An Ignatian Spirituality Reader.* A wonderfully concise book is David Fleming's *What Is Ignatian Spirituality?* A more detailed and intensive approach to Ignatian spirituality is *Eyes to See, Ears to Hear,* by David Lonsdale, which has especially good chapters on discernment and Ignatian contemplation.

For exploring prayer in general, an excellent starting point is William Barry's *God and You: Prayer as a Personal Relationship.* Also *Armchair Mystic,* by Mark Thibodeaux, S.J., is a user-friendly introduction to prayer in general with an Ignatian flavor. Thibodeaux's *God, I Have Issues* looks at prayer during different emotional states. *The Discerning Heart,* by Maureen Conroy, R.S.M., talks about both prayer and the practice of spiritual direction.

Good books on the practice of discernment and decision making in the Ignatian tradition include *Making Choices in Christ* by Joseph A. Tetlow, S.J., *Wise Choices,* by Margaret Silf, and *The Discernment of Spirits,* by Timothy Gallagher, O.M.V.

JESUIT SPIRITUALITY

When I use "Jesuit spirituality," I'm referring to aspects of the spiritual life distinctive to Jesuit life. The *Constitutions of the Society of Jesus* are, of course, an important foundation, though, except in some parts, they make for dry reading for all but Jesuits. A superb summary of the *Constitutions* and a reflection on its overarching spirituality is *Together for Mission,* by Andre de Jaer, S.J.

The granddaddy of books on Jesuit spirituality is *The Jesuits: Their Spiritual Doctrines and Practice,* by Joseph de Guibert, S.J., first published in 1964, which, while absolutely fascinating in places, is heavy going in others. Perhaps the best short book on Jesuit spirituality is by William Barry, S.J., and Robert Doherty, S.J.: *Contemplatives in Action,* which describes the variety of "tensions" (between activity and prayer, to take one example) inherent in Jesuit life, community, and governance. Chris Lowney's *Heroic Leadership* applies Jesuit practices to corporations, and William A. Byron, S.J.'s *Jesuit Saturdays* is designed for laypeople working in Jesuit institutions, introducing them to our "way of proceeding." Finally, F. E. Peters's memoir *Ours* is a window into the life of American Jesuits in the middle part of the twentieth century.

The History of the Society of Jesus

The gold standard of studies on the history of the early Jesuits, which also includes a précis of the life of Ignatius, is John O'Malley's *The First Jesuits*. It combines the author's superb skills as a historian with his elegant prose. (A good companion is *Year by Year with the Early Jesuits*, a firsthand account by Juan de Polanco, S.J., who entered the Society in 1541.) William Bangert's *A History of the Society of Jesus* is a comprehensive (though somewhat dry) look at the Society's entire history, from the early days until the early 1980s. James Brodrick, S.J., wrote both *The Origin of the Jesuits* and *The Progress of the Jesuits*. Other lively retellings of the almost five-hundred-year history of the Society of Jesus include *God's Soldiers*, which focuses on the early centuries, by Jonathan Wright, and *Jesuits: A Multibiography*, by Jean Lacouture, which does a superb job highlighting the stories of some notable Jesuit priests and brothers. Also Thomas Worcester, S.J., edited a fine series of essays collected in *The Cambridge Companion to the Jesuits*.

Focusing on particular aspects of Jesuit history are two books I would like to recommend. First, Liam Brockey's *Journey to the East*, a scholarly and fascinating look at the Jesuit mission to China from 1579 to 1724 (including the story of Matteo Ricci). And for those interested in the artistic heritage of the Jesuits (particularly the distinctive heritage of "Jesuit architecture" as well as how Jesuits used arts in the "missions"), see *Jesuits and the Arts: 1540–1773*, a gorgeously illustrated book edited by John O'Malley and Gauvin Bailey. It includes marvelous photos of the Jesuit "reductions" in South America and illustrations of stage sets that exemplify the history of "Jesuit theater."

Jesuit Saints and Other Lives

Start with Joseph Tylenda, S.J.'s *Jesuit Saints and Martyrs*, which packs into a few hundred pages the stories of the members of the Society of

Jesus who have been canonized, beatified, or are otherwise on their way to sainthood.

The list of books of Jesuit saints, blesseds, and holy men have (literally) filled libraries. Some of my favorites, in no particular order, are: *The Quiet Companion* (about Blessed Peter Favre, S.J.), by Mary Purcell; *Saint Francis Xavier*, by James Brodrick, S.J.; *Jean de Brébeuf* (about one of the North American martyrs), by Joseph P. Donnelly, S.J.; *With God in Russia* and *He Leadeth Me*, autobiographical works by Walter Ciszek, S.J.; *Conquistador Without Sword* (about Roque Gonzalez, S.J., one of the workers in the "reductions") by C. J. McNaspy, S.J.; *Spirit of Fire* (about Pierre Teilhard de Chardin S.J.), by Ursula King; *A Testimonial to Grace*, a memoir by Avery Cardinal Dulles S.J.; *Gerard Manley Hopkins,* by Paul Mariani; *Edmund Campion* by Evelyn Waugh; *With Bound Hands* (about Albert Delp, S.J., killed by the Nazis), by Mary Frances Coady; and *One Jesuit's Spiritual Journey*, a series of interviews with Pedro Arrupe. And I'll add one hard-to-find book: a one-volume work by Georg Schurhammer, S.J., (summarizing his colossal four-volume one) called *Francis Xavier: The Apostle of India and Japan.*

NOVELS, POEMS, FILMS, WEB SITES, AND OTHER RESOURCES

Almost anything by Anthony de Mello, S.J., is worthwhile; my favorite collection is *The Song of the Bird*, which includes several of the parable-like stories told in this book. *Hearts on Fire,* edited by Michael Harter, S.J., is a short compendium of Jesuit prayers penned since the time of Ignatius. Ron Hansen's novel on Gerard Manley Hopkins, *Exiles*, makes a natural companion to Paul Mariani's scholarly biography of the poet. Speaking of Hopkins, read his poems "God's Grandeur," "The Windhover," and "In Honor of St. Alphonsus Rodríguez," as a way of getting to know this great Jesuit artist.

Mary Doria Russell's *The Sparrow* is a popular science-fiction novel that imagines Jesuits in the near future exploring another planet. The films *The Mission* and *Blackrobe* provide good ways of beginning to understand the Jesuit missionary tradition: the first one is based on the South American "reductions"; the second, more loosely, on the lives of the North American martyrs, specifically St. Isaac Jogues.

The Web site jesuit.org, run by the U.S. Jesuits, offers a wealth of resources on Jesuit and Ignatian topics, and sacredspace.ie, run by the Irish Jesuits, provides daily prayer meditations in the Ignatian tradition.

Two Theological Topics

There are two specific theological topics touched upon briefly in this book, which, if treated fully, would have taken up several hundred more pages—at least: the existence of God and the "problem of suffering." One useful overview on the "proofs" or "arguments" for the existence of God can be found in the magisterial *A History of Philosophy*, by Frederick Copleston, S.J., which covers the major theological arguments for God, including, most notably, those of St. Anselm and St. Thomas Aquinas. A more focused and user-friendly look at that specific question is contained in *The One and the Many*, by W. Norris Clarke, S.J. The "problem of suffering," and how it is approached in the Old and New Testaments, is lucidly presented in *Why Do We Suffer?* by Daniel J. Harrington, S.J. *Created for Joy*, by Sidney Callahan, provides a broad overview of Christian theologies on suffering.

More by the Author

In Good Company tells the story of my move from the corporate world to the Jesuit novitiate. *This Our Exile* recounts two years working with refugees in East Africa as a Jesuit scholastic. *Becoming Who You Are* speaks about vocation and how desire plays a role in becoming our "true selves." *A Jesuit Off-Broadway* tells of six months working with a theater company and includes a brief history of "Jesuit theater." And *My Life with the Saints* focuses on holy men and women who have been influential and inspiring to me, including three Jesuits: St. Aloysius Gonzaga, Pedro Arrupe, and—who else?—St. Ignatius Loyola.

Index

Abandonment to Divine Providence (de Caussade), 285

Addictive behaviors, 65–66

Agnostics/atheists, 34–36, 54; author Martin and, 37–38; desire for God and, 63–64; the Examen as "prayer of awareness" for, 101; Ignatian spirituality and, 28; "secular saint," 35; story of the atheist caught in the flood, 35–36; suffering, question of, 38, 39, 54; totalitarianism and, 45

Allen, Woody, 228

America, 278, 280, 286, 288, 348

Amos: 3:3, 116

Anger, 123–24

Aquinas, St. Thomas, 44, 162, 163, 180

Aristotle, 140

Armchair Mystic (Thibodeaux), 113

Arrupe, Pedro, S.J., 51, 195, 198, 211–12, 218–19, 274, 300, 364

Aschenbrenner, George, S.J., 87–88, 207, 208

Asselin, David, S.J., 131

Auden, W. H., 73–74

Augustine, St., 9, 56, 64, 166, 173

Autobiography (Ignatius Loyola), 12, 14, 23, 52–53

Awake My Soul (Cunneen), 144

Awe, 71

Baltimore Catechism, 134–35

Bangert, William, S.J., 249, 366, 370–71

Barnes, Julian, 67, 83

Barry, William A., S.J., 32, 115, 122, 137, 142, 167, 244, 246, 260, 268, 272, 343

Bartimaeus, 57–58, 340

Beauty, 74

Benedict, St., 3

Benedictines, 3, 21, 24

Berchmans, John, St., 233–34

Bergan, Jacqueline Syrup, 170, 344

Berrigan, Daniel, S.J., 26

Bible: prayer based on (*lectio divina*), 155–62; scripture as path to God, 117–18. *See also specific books*

Birth: A Guide for Prayer (Bergan and Schwan), 170, 344

Bishop, Jim, 302

Bobadilla, Nicolás, S.J., 241

Borgia, St. Francis, 191

Brackley, Dean, S.J., 183, 203

Brideshead Revisited (Waugh), 74

Broët, Paschase, S.J., 241

Buddhism, 10, 163–64, 165–66

Burghardt, Walter, S.J., 8, 86, 114, 377

Burrows, Ruth, 69, 70

Call of the King, 293–94

Campion, St. Edmund, 25, 107

Campion Renewal Center, Weston, Massachusetts, 106–10, 178, 387

Career, 341, 342. *See also* Work; Vocation

Carmelites, 3, 15

Castro, Fidel, 4

Catherine of Siena, St., 45

Catherine the Great of Russia, 18

Celibacy. *See* Chastity

Centering prayer (Third Method), 162–67

Change, 134–39, 142, 170, 261; acting as a leaven agent of change, 355, 360–61; Ignatius Loyola on, 310–11; patience and, 387–88

Chariots of Fire (film), 351

Charism (founding spirit), 3, 21

Chastity, 174–75, 176, 213–30; celibacy vs., 216–17; difficulty of, 226; first Jesuits and, 213–14; freedom and detachment and, 220–21, 270, 279; lessons from, 215; love and, 217–30; lust and, 222; married priests, 216–17; popular thinking, 215; religious chastity, 217, 220–27
Cistercians, 3, 15
Ciszek, Walter, S.J., 25, 30, 31, 280–82, 284, 285, 289, 294, 297, 304, 354, 375
Clarity (insight), 75, 130
Clarke, Thomas E., S.J., 165
Claver, St. Peter, 244–46, 361, 372–73
Clement XIV, Pope, 18
Cloister Walk, The (Norris), 175
Cloud of Unknowing, The, 162, 167
Code of Canon Law, 135
Codure, Jean, S.J., 241
Colloquy, 167–68, 298
Compassion, 31, 94, 129, 159, 227, 228, 234, 254, 258, 273, 289, 298, 339, 360, 368, 386
Competition, 260–61
Conroy, Maureen, R.S.M., 262
Conscience, 166; "account of conscience," 268; Ignatius on, 202; Peter Favre and, 238; sting of "with remorse," 327. *See also* Examen
Consolmagno, Guy, S.J., 137
Constitutions, The, 16, 21–23, 240; analogous to "rule" of a religious order, 21; on chastity, 213; dismissal from the order, 272–73; length of, 135; love, value of in Jesuit training, 368–69; moderation counseled in, 310; need for health and bodily strength, 187–88, 310, 358; on obedience, 266; on poverty, 186; restrictions on ambitions, 190–91, 260; suggestions about living in, 22–23; superior general, qualities of, 368–69
Consumerism, 181–86, 362–63; Brackley's twelve steps and, 183–85; ladder model of society and, 184
Contemplation, Ignatian, 145–55; author Martin's contemplation of the storm at sea, 152–55; author Martin's Los Angeles retreat, 298–304; "compose the place," 145–50; pay attention to God's voice, 151–52; "sacred events" and, 151
Contemplation to Attain Divine Love, 395–96
Contemplatives in action, 7–8, 15, 350, 389–97; finding time for God and you, 350; summary of Ignatian spirituality and, 392
Contemplatives in Action: The Jesuit Way (Barry and Doherty), 268, 272
"Corporal works of mercy," 196
Corridan, John, S.J., 26
Cozzens, Donald, 216
CrazyBusy (Hallowell), 358–59
Creed, Bill, S.J., 76
Cunneen, Sally, 144
Curry, Rick, S.J., 266–67, 379–80

Daily Office, 111, 169
Daley, Brian, S.J., 208
Damascene, St. John, 113
Davis, Thurston, S.J., 280–81
Day, Dorothy, 44, 96, 170
Day Christ Died, The (Bishop), 302
Dead Man Walking (Prejean), 117
Death: fear of, 67; openness to God, 79–80
De Brébeuf, St. Jean, 25
De Caussade, Jean-Pierre, S.J., 95, 284, 285
Decision making, 1, 27, 305–38; advice in *The Constitutions,* 22; author Martin's bad decision, 330–32; "best self" clarification, 324–25; changing paths, 310–11; choosing between desires, 225; commitment and, 311; confirmation as "rightness of our choice," 320–21, 347; deathbed clarification, 324, 346; detachment and, 9–10; discernment, 48, 62, 305, 326–37; drawbacks of good decisions, 337–38; emotions and, 322; experience and, 337; feeling downcast after, 311–12; First Method, six steps, 319–20, 322–23; First Time (clear and unmistakable choice), 313–15; God's help in, 305, 308; between "goods," 311; Ignatian

spirituality and, 9–10; Ignatius gets a haircut and, 307–12; Ignatius's practical techniques, 306–38; indifference and, 306–7, 311, 319, 322, 323, 365; Last Judgment clarification, 324, 346; meditation and, 316–20; no changes during time of desolation, 330–32; "pointer of a balance" image, 307; "pushes" and "pulls," 329; "reflection-action-reflection," 322, 365; Second Method (imagination), 317–18, 323–25, 346; Second Time (less clear), 315–18; spiritual consolation and desolation as central to, 308–9, 316, 320; Third Time (no obvious choice), 318–25; the "three times," 313–25; three ways the "enemy" works, 332–36; of vocation, 343–47; what is "of God" and what is "not of God," 326–29. *See also* Career; Discernment

De Guibert, Joseph, S.J., 2–3

De Jaer, André, S.J., 22, 188

Delp, Alfred, S.J., 290, 374

De Mello, Anthony, S.J., 40, 81, 89, 91, 136, 177–78, 384, 388; parable of "The Little Fish," 102; parable of "The Diamond," 177–78

De Polanco, Juan, S.J., 191, 196

De Sales, St. Francis, 258

Descartes, René, 135

Desire, 57–85; analogy of stream, 344–45; arising in prayer, 133; author Martin and, 59–62, 71–72, 75; clarity and, 75; common longings, 66–69; as communication from God, 61, 67, 75; competing, choosing between, 225; distinguishing between deep and shallow, 343; dreams of the heart, 344, 369–71; exaltation or happiness and, 72–74, 75; experiences of the desire for God, 63–80; feelings of incompletion and, 64–66; finding your vocation and, 339–88; to follow God, 76–77; for friendship, 265; the God who seeks and, 80–81; for holiness, 77–78; holy, 59, 61, 133; Jesus and Bartimaeus and, 57–58; Margaret Silf on, 60, 63;

material wants, 58; "Outside-In" or "Inside-Out" approach, 63; praying for what you desire, 343; sexual, 58, 125–26; uncommon longings, 69–72; vocation and, 342–47; vulnerability and, 78–80

Detachment, 9–10, 121, 391, 392; from "drive to acquire," 183; friendship and relationships, 243–46, 253; indifference and decision making, 306–7, 365; love and, 223; second degree of humility and, 207; of St. Ignatius Loyola, 18; in work environment, 360

Dineson, Isak, 75

Discerning Heart, The (Conroy), 262

Discernment, 48, 62, 305–38; individual, 268, 269; joke about, 317; Lonsdale on, 309, 316; obedience and, 272; "of spirits," 189, 278, 326–29, 332–37; rules for, 326–37; spiritual consolation and desolation as central to, 308–9; "the drop of water," 327–29; your desires and God's desires for you, 279, 308, 316, 320, 338. *See also* Decision making

Discernment of Spirits, The (Gallagher), 189, 326

Disordered affections, 9, 180; defined, 10

Dissatisfaction or incompletion, 64–66

Doherty, Robert, S.J., 268, 272

Donovan, David, S.J., 5–7, 383; on falling in love, 224; God meets you where you are, 81, 143–45; God of Surprises, 49; God's love for you, 385; God's use of Ignatius's pride, 12; on humility, 258; on *lectio divina*, 155; mother of, and praying the Rosary, 170; on prayer, 96, 114, 115, 140, 146, 151, 181, 328; "shoulding all over yourself," 329; "you can't put part of your life in a box," 6–7, 27, 301, 334, 351

Dostoevsky, Fyodor, 230

"Downward Mobility" (Brackley), 183, 203

Draw Me into Your Friendship
(Fleming), 207

Drinan, Robert, S.J., 273–74

Dulles, Avery Cardinal, S.J., 86–87, 234

Duty of Delight, The (Day), 96, 170

Dyckman, Katherine, 58

Easterbrook, Gregg, 182

Education: early work in, 24;
famous people educated by Jesuits,
4, 17, 390; Jesuit colleges and
schools, 4

Egan, Harvey, S.J., 162, 163

Elijah, 133

Emotions: arising in prayer, 132, 152,
168, 301–2; clarity and, 75; decision
making and, 322; exaltation or happiness, 72–74, 75; fear, nearness of
God and, 68–69; feelings about
God, 110; gift of tears, 302; hearing God's voice in prayer and, 130;
incompletion and dissatisfaction,
64–69; intense, as communication
with God, 53–56, 67; as spiritual
experience, 67–68

English, John J., S.J., 151, 336

Ethics, 359–62

Examen, 87–97, 343; for agnostics
and atheists, 101; awareness of
God in the present and, 356; for
busy people, 349–50; closing
prayer, 95; Dorothy Day on, 96; to
examine your life, 100; final step,
asking for grace of God's help, 95;
first step, gratitude, 88–89; in five
steps, 97; fourth step, forgiveness,
95; grace and, 96–97; gratitude
and, 264, 385; to help you find God
in everything, 391; preparation for,
88; second step, "know my sins,"
89–91; seeing God in retrospect,
97–100; as spiritual lifesaver,
349–50; St. Francis Xavier on, 90;
third step, a review of your day,
91–95; using, variations for individuals, 95–97

Exiles (Hansen), 376

Exodus: **4:11–12**, 118; **20:21**, 162;
33:19–20, 98; **34:5**, 162

Eyes to See, Ears to Hear (Lonsdale),
309, 345

Failure, 374–77

Faith: analogy of garden, 32; not just
a question of you and God, 46–47;
one pitfall of, 32; Path of Belief and,
30–32; Path of Return and, 36–39

"Faith sharing," 254–58

Favre, Peter, S.J., 82, 89, 214, 236, 237,
238–39, 240, 245, 306, 355; as the
"Second Jesuit," 239

Fear: of change, 136; of death, 67; *mysterium tremendum et fascinans,* 69; of
nearness to God, 68–69; resistance
during prayer and, 161–62

Fermor, Patrick Leigh, 345

Finding Grace at the Center
(Pennington, Keating, and Clarke),
165, 166

Fink, Peter, S.J., 95

First Jesuits, The (O'Malley), 20, 24,
186, 213, 239, 250, 270

Flaubert, Gustave, 83, 100

Flaubert's Parrot (Barnes), 67, 83

Fleming, David, S.J., 88, 146, 207, 209,
263, 296, 297, 309, 316, 318, 369

Following Christ in a Consumer Society
(Kavanaugh), 182

Forgiveness, 229–30, 259, 312

Franciscans, 3, 15, 24

Francis of Assisi, St., 3, 17, 44, 45, 186,
196, 217

Freedom, 121, 391, 392; admitting your
own powerlessness and, 259; chastity and, 220–21, 270; friendship
and, 243–46, 261; indifference and,
306; love and, 223, 229; obedience
and, 270; simple life and, 203; spiritual poverty and, 211; voluntary poverty and, 270. *See also* Detachment

Freeing Celibacy (Cozzens), 216

Free will, 127

"Friendship in Jesuit Life" (Shelton),
241, 243

Friendship Like No Other, A (Barry),
32, 137

Friendship and relationships, 27, 230,
231–65; barriers to healthy, 246–48;

being honest, 122–26; changing and, 134–39; chaste love and, 230; communication and, 252; communication with God and, 243, 254, 331; danger of exclusivity, 262; "faith sharing," 254–58; forgiveness and, 259; freedom and, 243–46; with God, 115–42; gratitude and, 263–65; healthy, elements of, 259–63; humility and, 258–59; impairing relationships, 248; Jesuits and, 231–34; with Jesus, 108–10; learning, 116–21; listening and, 126–29; maintaining difficult, 248–50; married couples and, 247; openness of heart and, 236; Presupposition, 234–36, 249, 256; silence and, 139; spending time, 116; suffering and poverty, analogy of, 208; union of hearts and minds, 251–54
Fülöp-Miller, René, 367

Gallagher, Timothy, O.M.V., 189, 326
Ganss, George E., S.J., 306–7
Garvin, Mary, 58
Genovesi, Vincent J., S.J., 216
Gilead (Robinson), 77–78
God, 173; as Almighty Artisan, 383; anger at, 123–24; asking God for help, 103–5, 124; awe and, 71; beauty as passage to, 74; as beyond comprehension (unknowable), 162, 163; clarity as communication from, 75, 130; communication through imagination, 146–50; communication with, 12, 49, 53–56, 67, 83–85, 110, 114, 120, 128–29, 130–34, 145–73, 243, 331 (*see also* Prayer); conscience as voice of God, 166; constancy of, 142; decision making and, 306–7, 316–17, 320, 338 (*see also* Discernment); desire as communication from, 61, 316; desire for, recognizing, 63–80; easier to see in retrospect, 97–100; the examen and finding God, 87–97; experienced in the natural world, 163; faith community and, 49; feminine imagery

of, 137–38; finding around you, 351–55; finding by noticing, 86–87; finding and letting God find you, 86–102; finding in all things, 5–7, 27, 50–51, 99–100, 116, 281, 304, 350, 391–92; friendship as communication from, 243, 254; friendship with, 115–42; goal of following, 295; as goal of Ignatian spirituality, 393–97; God of Surprises, 49–50, 61, 138, 153; God the Far-Away One, 43, 49; the God who seeks, 80–81; gratitude, peace, joy, and, 56; as the Great Problem Solver, 37, 38, 39, 103, 137; hearing God's voice, 127–28, 130–34, 317, 356; Holy Spirit, discernment, and decision making, 309; human connection to, 79–80; as incomprehensible, 9, 286; inner emptiness as the "God-shaped hole," 65–66; intentional time with, 116; knowing, 9; learning about, 116–21; listening for, 126–29; lives of holy men and women and, 120; *magis* and, 369–71; nearness of, 392–93; obedience to, 267, 271, 279–85, 304; paths to God, 28; "pocket-size God," 41; the poor and brokenhearted and, 199–201; relationship with, 81–85, 110, 113, 115–42, 253, 276, 392–94; reliance on, in the working world, 378; Scripture and, 117–18; search for, and simple things, 68; signs of presence and activity, 391; silence and, 139–41; six paths to seeking, 29–44, 138; suffering and, 38, 39, 54, 285–92, 391; as transcendent and incarnational, 8–9; Two Standards meditation and, 188–90; where to look for, 82; willingness to trust in God's providence, 364; will of, 207, 279–85. *See also* God's love
God, I Have Issues (Thibodeaux), 126
God and You: Prayer as a Personal Relationship (Barry), 115
God of Surprises (Hughes), 136
God's love, 128, 142; chastity and, 222; Contemplation to Attain Divine

God's love *(continued)*
Love, 395–96; experiencing, 1, 20;
God meets you where you are,
81–85, 378–81, 384; "loved sinner,"
76; parable of the Prodigal son, 91;
as personal, 385
God's Mechanics (Consolmagno), 137
*God's Soldiers: Adventure, Politics,
Intrigue, and Power—A History of the
Jesuits* (Wright), 4
Gonzaga, St. Aloysius (Luigi), 159,
197, 214
Gonzalez, Roque, S.J., 370
Goupil, René, 296–97
Grace, 54, 62, 82, 86, 88, 89, 91, 95,
96–97, 113, 164, 186, 241, 282, 288,
301, 307, 384, 385, 397
Gratitude, 20, 55, 66, 70, 76, 88–89,
124, 395; friendship and relation-
ships and, 263–65; Ignatius Loyola
on occasions for, 88–89; self-
acceptance and, 385
Greeley, Andrew, 32–34
Guidelines for Mystical Prayer
(Burrows), 69
Guilt, 89–90, 91, 202, 229

Habits of the Heart (Bellah), 47
"Hail Mary," 143–44, 169
Hansen, Ron, 49–50
Harrington, Daniel J., S.J., 117–18,
156, 286
Harry Potter series (Rowling), 189
Haughey, John, S.J., 373
Healthy life, 357–58
Hebrews: **4:15,** 292
Hecker, Isaac, 48
Heroic Leadership (Lowney), 341, 364
Heschel, Abraham Joshua, 44, 71, 286
History of the Society of Jesus, A
(Bangert), 249, 366, 370–71
Hitchcock, Alfred, 4
Honesty: chastity and, 223; in feelings,
318; in friendships and relation-
ships, 215, 216, 254, 260; Ignatius
and, 251; in prayer, 122–26; in the
work world, 360
Hopkins, Gerard Manley, S.J., 73,
124–25, 269, 325, 376–77, 381–82

How Can I Find God? (Martin, ed.),
97–98, 117
Hughes, Gerard W., S.J., 49, 136
Humility: friendship and relationships
and, 258–59; Jesuit joke, 208; poverty of the spirit as, 206–7; religion
and, 48; sin and, 90; three degrees
of, 207–8, 295, 361
Humor, 121, 210, 263

Identity: acceptance of self, 378–81;
becoming oneself, 385–88; compare
and despair/individuality, 381–85;
finding true self, 378–88; poem,
381–82
Ignatian spirituality, 51; as available
to everyone, 1–2, 28, 44, 392; being
spiritual and religious, 44–50;
career or vocation and, 339–88;
charism (founding spirit), 3–4;
chastity and, 174, 175, 176, 213–30;
choosing the more difficult path
and, 295; communication with God
and, 110; compassion and, 298;
contemplatives in action, 7–8, 15,
350, 389–97; decision making and,
305–38; desire and, 57–85; discernment and, 305–38; "discernment
of spirits," 189, 332–36; experts in,
25; finding God in all things, 5–7,
27, 50–51, 99–100, 116, 281, 304,
350, 351, 390, 391; four simple ways
of understanding, 5–11; freedom
and detachment and, 1, 9–10,
391; friendship and relationships,
231–65; God as goal of, 393–97;
gratitude and, 263–65; helping
souls, 263, 361; Ignatian contemplation, 145–55; as an incarnational
spirituality, 8–9, 390–92; "living
rules," 25, 194; on love, friendship,
and human relationships, 234–65;
meditation on life of Christ,
292–93; obedience and, 174, 175, 176,
266–85, 297, 304; poverty and, 174,
175, 176, 177–212; prayer traditions,
143–73 *(see also* Prayer); questions
proper to, 7; "reflection-action-
reflection," 322, 365; resources for

understanding, 19–25; riches to honors to pride and, 188–92, 294, 361; simple life, 7, 22, 136, 174–212, 238, 279; six paths to seeking God, 29–44; *The Spiritual Exercises* and, 21 (*see also Spiritual Exercises, The*); a spirituality of work, 347–63; on suffering, 285–98; summary of, 392; Two Standards and, 188–90, 207, 294–95; the way of Ignatius, 25–28; ways the "enemy" or "worst self" works in our lives, 332–36; what a spirituality is, 2

Impairing relationships, 248

Indifference. *See* Detachment

Ingenuity, 365–68

Inner Compass: An Invitation to Ignatian Spirituality (Silf), 63, 95, 100

In Pursuit of Love (Genovesi), 216

Islam, 81, 138

Ivens, Michael, S.J., 309, 320, 330

James, William, 18

Jay, Claude, S.J., 241

Jeremiah: **29:11**, 138

Jesuit Order/Jesuits. *See* Society of Jesus

Jesuit Refugee Service, 195–96, 198, 277, 303

Jesuits, The: Their Spiritual Doctrine and Practice (de Guibert), 2–3

Jesuit Saints and Martyrs (Tylenda), 100

Jesus of Nazareth: "blessed are the poor in spirit," 209–11; blind beggar and, 57–58, 340; coming to people, 85; as craftsman or carpenter, 372; desire for holiness and, 77; Fourth Week of the Spiritual Exercises and, 395–96; as friend, 108–10; imitation of, 176, 197, 207–8, 295; love of, 81–82; meditation on life of Christ, 20, 292–93, 295–98, 299–304; ministry to the poor, 203; obedience and, 267; parable of the Prodigal Son, 91; parables of, 119–20; points of entry into the life of, 300; on the poor, 196; preaching in the synagogue, 156–60; promise of "hundredfold" return, 233; as reli-gious man, 45; the "rich young man" and, 179–80, 186; rules to disciples, 135; Second Week of the Exercises and, 147; Sermon on the Mount, 205; on sinfulness and the Good Samaritan, 89–90; speaking to on the cross (colloquy), 168; story of the storm at sea, 147; suffering of, 294, 295–98; Third Week of the Spiritual Exercises and, 295–98; unmarried state of, 224; "vowed life" and emulation of, 176; weep-ing, 300; as the Word made flesh (incarnation), 8, 119; words after the Resurrection, 223

Job, Book of: **10:1**, 123

Jogues, St. Isaac, 25, 271, 296–97

John, Gospel of: **9:2**, 287; **14:9**, 163

John III, King of Portugal, 249, 250

John of the Cross, St., 66

John Paul II, Pope, 274, 362

Johnson, Elizabeth, C.S.J., 137

Joseph, St., 373

Journaling, 170

Joyce, James, 4

Juana, regent of Spain, 214

Julius III, Pope, 22

Kane, Jim, S.J., 106

Kavanaugh, John, S.J., 182

Keating, Thomas, O.C.S.O., 165

Keenan, James F., S.J., 89–90, 258

Kennedy, John F., 280

King, Martin Luther, Jr., 44, 45

1 Kings: **19:12**, 133, 356

2 Kings: **5:1-19**, 67–68

Knowing oneself, 339–40. *See also* Identity; Vocation

Kolodiejchuk, Brian, M.C., 139

Kolvenbach, Peter-Hans, S.J., 98

La Colombière, St. Claude, S.J., 165, 378

Laínez, Diego, S.J., 17, 240–41

Langford, Jeremy, 349

Last Days of Judas Iscariot, The, 39–40

Lectio divina, 155–62; action, 159–60; alternate method, 160–62; finding time for, 350; four-step process,

Lectio divina (continued)
156–60; meaning of, 155; medita-
tion, 157–58; prayer, 158–59; reading,
156–57
Lee, Peggy, 64
Leonard, Richard, S.J., 137, 142,
290–92
Lewis, C. S., 70, 190
Liebert, Elizabeth, 58
Listening: compassionate, 227–28;
"faith sharing" and, 254–58; for
God's voice, 126–29, 356; Ignatius
Loyola on, 257; obedience as, 267–71
"Living rules," 25, 194
Loneliness, 130–31, 133–34, 226, 301–2
Lonsdale, David, 309, 316, 320, 345, 351
Lord, Daniel, S.J., 210
Lord of the Rings (Tolkein), 189
Love: chastity and, 216, 217–23,
227–30, 270; commitment and,
224; six chaste acts of love, 227–30;
freedom and detachment and, 223,
229; humility and "three ways of
loving," 207; Ignatius's dictum on,
197, 220, 227, 229; Jesuits in love,
224; leadership and, 364, 368–69;
learning to, 27; owning, 223; Pedro
Arrupe on, 218–19; praying for
loved ones, 230; value of in Jesuit
training, 368–69. *See also* God's
love
Lowney, Chris, 341, 347, 364, 369
Loyola, St. Ignatius: asceticism and,
178, 187–88; *Autobiography*, 12, 23;
battle as key metaphor for, 189;
being spiritual and religious, 50;
character, 217; companions of, 8,
15, 22; composition of place, the
Nativity scene, 149; on conscience,
202; *Constitutions*, 16, 21–23, 135, 240;
contemplating the night sky, 17;
contemplative attitude throughout
day and, 350; death of, 16; decision making and haircut, 307–12;
on decision-making of superiors,
272–73; on deeds as manifestation
of love, 197; on desire, 63; dictum
on love, 197, 220, 227, 229; the discerning mule and, 325; divesting of

possessions, 186–87; the examen
and, 87–97; feast day of, 271; finding
God in nature, 171, 172; founding
of Society of Jesus, 15–16; Francis
Xavier and, 241–43, 260; on friendship, 254; friends of, 237–43, 244,
248–50; "gift of tears," 302; God as
the Almighty Artisan, 383; God as
the center of his life, 28; identity
of, 1; on indifference, 319; inexplicable feelings during prayer and,
132; ingenuity and leadership, 365;
initial conversion, 51, 52–53, 77, 186,
225, 317; Inquisition and, 15, 54; on
judging intentions not actions, 235;
on *lectio divina*, 155, 161; letters of,
23–24, 237, 239, 242–43, 249, 369; life
of, 11–19, 52–53, 237–43; on listening,
257; *loquela* (speech) from God, 127;
in Manresa, 187; as mystic, 13–14, 18,
70, 309; ordination of, 16; on "over-
loading," 357; path of moderation
taken by, 310; perception of, 17–18;
poverty and, 176, 186, 195, 201;
prayer and, 145–46; quote on going
forward by different roads, 145, 384;
reliance on God and, 378; Rubens's
painting, 17; Simon Rodrigues and,
248–50; simple life and, 238; sin
of ingratitude and, 264; *Spiritual
Exercises* and, 9, 14, 19–21, 51, 62,
75, 81; Two Standards meditation
and, 188–90; "union of hearts and
minds," 251; women and, 214; writing, prayer, and guidance for, 22
Luke: **1:26–28**, 131; **1:30**, 68; **2:10**, 69;
2:52, 372; **4:16–30**, 156–60; **5:10**, 69;
8:22–25, 147; **9:58**, 176; **10:29–37**,
119; **15:3–10**, 80–81; **15:11–32**, 91;
18:21, 179; **22:42**, 176

Machiavelli, Niccolò, 368
Macmurray, John, 39
Magis, 369–71
Maimonides, 44
Main, John, 165
Making Choices in Christ (Tetlow),
150, 312
Mariette in Ecstasy (Hansen), 49–50

Mark, Gospel of: **1:29–31**, 216; **3:32**, 176; 4, 119; **10:22**, 179–80; **10:46–52**, 57–58; **12:41–44**, 201

Marriage, 61, 176, 214, 216–17, 221, 224, 225, 226, 227, 229, 230, 231, 247, 253, 258, 261, 275–76, 279, 283, 307, 333, 337–38, 340, 342, 349, 377

Martin, James, S.J.: at *America* magazine, 278, 288, 348; bad decision made by, 330–32; celibacy and, 130, 222–23; colloquy and, 168; confusion about God, 42–43; contemplation of the storm at sea, 152–55; David Donovan as spiritual director, 6 (*see also* Donovan, David); death of friend and Path of Return to God, 37–38; decision to enter Jesuits, 314–15, 342, 345; decision to stay or leave the Jesuits, 276–79, 305; desire for priesthood and, 59–62; directed retreat of, 106–10; divesting of possessions, 179, 204; entering the novitiate, 178–80; falling in love and, 224–25, 276; father's illness and death, 78–79, 204, 283–84, 285; friendship and, 244, 251–54; at General Electric, 43, 181, 269–70, 314, 343, 347–48, 368; God as the Great Problem Solver and, 37; Ignatian spirituality and growth, 392–93; incompletion and dissatisfaction, feelings of, 43; intense joy, experience of, 66; as Jesuit novice in Boston, 6, 110–14, 392; job at packaging plant, 352–53; loneliness and, 130–31, 133–34, 205–6, 301–4; Loyola University, Chicago, ministry, and examen, 92–94; mother and, lesson of Presupposition, 236; in Nairobi, Kenya, 83–85, 195–201, 205–6, 209–11, 219, 276–77, 303, 331–32; nature prayer and, 171–72; obedience to decision to delay theological studies, 276–79; Off-Broadway play and, 39–40, 101, 222–23; ordination of, 75; personality test results and, 383; prayer and, 103–14, 115, 129; relationship with God, 81; seeing God in suffering, 287–89; return to Campion Center, 387–88; self-acceptance and, 383–84; Spiritual Exercises and, 293, 298–304; temptations that come to, 335; uncommon longings, 71–72; writing career, 278

Maslow, Abraham, 56

Mass, 169; daily, 112

Matrix, The (film), 337

Matthew, Gospel of: **13:33**, 355; **25:40**, 196

Maxwell, William, 131

Mead, Margaret, 361

Memories: during prayer, 130–32

Merton, Thomas, 34, 43, 106, 165, 166, 293, 314, 342

Messiaen, Olivier, 173

Metz, Johannes Baptist, 206–7

Meyer, Dick, 363

"Ministry of presence," 228

Mission, The (film), 370

Mitford, Nancy, 46

Monastic orders, 8, 15; "vowed life," 175–76, 186

Moonstruck (film), 226

Morality, 207

Moses, 118, 140, 162

Mother Teresa: Come Be My Light (Kolodiejchuk), 139

Murray, John Courtney, S.J., 190, 274–75

Mysticism: Auden's experience, 73–74; definition, 69; everyday, 69; Ignatius Loyola as mystic, 13–14, 18, 70; uncommon longings and, 69–72

Nadal, Jerónimo, S.J., 8, 18, 311, 350, 351, 394

National Shrine of the North American Martyrs, Auriesville, New York, 297

National Theatre Workshop of the Handicapped, 379

New Dictionary of Catholic Spirituality, The (Downey, ed.), 162

New Yorker cartoon, 259, 354

Niebuhr, Reinhold, 44

19th Annotation Retreat or the Spiritual Exercises in Daily Life, 19–20

Nixon, Richard M., 274
No One Sees God: The Dark Night of Atheists and Believers (Novak), 45
Norris, Kathleen, 175, 266
North American College, 6
Norton Simon Museum, California, 17
Nothing to Be Frightened Of (Barnes), 67
Nouwen, Henri, 65, 183
Novak, Michael, 45

Obedience, 174, 175, 176, 266–84; acceptance and, 268; accepting the unacceptable, 304; apostolic, 269; benefits, 270–71; in corporate world, 269; in everyday life, 283–84; everyday life of a Jesuit, 271–73; freedom and, 270; Jesuit joke, 268; as listening, 267–71; Pedro Arrupe and, 300; religious superior and, 266–68, 271–73; as surrendering to God's will, 267, 271, 279–85, 304; surrendering to the future, 283–85, 297, 304; two stories about, 273–79; Walter Ciszek and, 280–82
O'Keefe, Vincent, S.J., 219
O'Malley, John W., S.J., 20, 24, 186, 187, 196, 213, 239, 247, 270
One Jesuit's Spiritual Journey (Arrupe), 211–12
On the Waterfront (film), 26
Otto, Rudolf, 69
"Our Father" (Lord's Prayer), 169–70
Our Town (Wilder), 101–2
Out of Africa (Dineson), 75, 303

Padberg, John W., S.J., 9, 264
Papacy: Jesuit's fourth vow and, 270; obedience to, 274
Paris, Je T'Aime (film), 389–90
Patience, 386–87
Paul, St., 166, 297, 394; Damascus experience, 313, 315
Paul III, Pope, 16, 22, 196
Paulists, 48
Paul VI, Pope, 275
Payne, Alexander, 389–90
"Peak experiences," 56
Pennington, M. Basil, O.C.S.O., 165, 166

1 Peter: 5:8, 335
Peter, St., 216
"Pied Beauty" (Hopkins), 73
Polish, Daniel, 286
Poverty, 177–212; as cause of "great delight," 178; in the *Constitutions*, 186; contemporary Jesuit life and, 193–95; dehumanizing involuntary, 197; in East Africa, 195–201, 205, 209–11; Pedro Arrupe and, 211–12; getting to know the poor, 204–5; as imitation of Christ, 176, 178; Jesus on the poor, 196; learning about, 198; relationship with God and, 199–201; remembering the poor, 362–63; "rich young man" of the Gospels, 179–80; simple life and, 177–212; of the spirit, 205–11, 289; voluntary, 174, 195, 197, 270; vows of, 175–76. *See also* Simple life
Poverty of the Spirit (Metz), 206–7
Power and Secret of the Jesuits, The (Fülöp-Miller), 367
Prayer: anger in, 123–24; answer to "Why doesn't God answer my prayer?," 98–99; "apophatic," 162, 163; author Martin and, 103–14, 115, 129; being honest, 122–26; Burghardt's definition, 8, 86, 114; celebration of Mass, 169; centering prayer (Third Method), 162–67; changing through, 136–39; colloquy, 167–68; communal, 169; Contemplation to Attain Divine Love, 395–96; contemplative, 112–13; Daily Office, 111, 169; David Donovan on the Rosary, 143–45; decision making and, 316–17, 319–20; deepening, 27; definitions, 113–14; desire arising during, 133; directed retreat, 106–10; emotions arising during, 132, 152, 168, 301–2; the examen, 87–97, 391; finding time for God and you, 348–51; four weeks of The Spiritual Exercises and, 20–21; on the gifts God has given you, 76; Ignatian contemplation, 145–55; Ignatian traditions, 143–73; imagining yourself speaking

with God, and God's reply, 128–29; as intentional time with God, 116; Jesuits as contemplatives in action, 7–8; journaling, 170; "katapatic," 162, 163; *lectio divina,* 155–62; listening and hearing God, 126–29; for loved ones, 230; meditation on life of Christ, 20, 292–93, 295–98, 299–304; memories arising during, 130–32, 133–34; music, 173; nature prayer, 170–72; no "right" way, 96, 143–45; for our desires, 62; petitionary prayer, 103–5, 113, 124, 126–27, 199–200; physical feelings arising during, 132–33; prayer from Teilhard de Chardin, 164; praying the Rosary, 143–45, 169; Quaker "gathered silence," 40; reflecting on daily life, 133; repetition, 153; resistance during, 161–62; rote prayers, 104, 106, 169; sadness in, 125; sexual desire and, 125–26; silence and, 139–41; on sinfulness, 76; *Suscipe,* 396–97; as transformative, 303–4; ways of hearing God's voice in, 130–34; what it is, 110–14; for what you desire, 343; work as, 173

Preaching to the Converted (Leonard), 142

Prejean, Sister Helen, C.S.J., 117

Presupposition, 234–36, 249, 256

Pride, 180, 210

Professions of Faith (Langford and Martin, eds.), 349

Progress Paradox, The (Easterbrook), 182

Psalms: **23**, 132, 160–62; **34:18**, 201; **42:7**, 77, 356; **64**, 105; **139**, 385; **139:1**, 122; as basis for prayer, 111

Quaker "gathered silence," 40

Rahner, Karl, S.J., 49, 69, 113, 119, 338, 374

Rebecca (film), 327

Rejadell, Teresa, 358

Relationships. *See* Friendship and relationships

Religion: change and relationship with, 138; humility and, 48; image of God and, 137; negatives and positives,

44–50; Path of Independence, 32–34; "real" vs. "illusory," 39; rule-based, 135; search for perfection in as futile, 34; social dimension of human nature and, 49; spiritual but not religious (SBNR), 44–50; "spiritual home," 40, 41; spirituality and, 28, 50

Religious of Jesus and Mary, 283

Ribadaneira, Pedro, 171

Ricci, Matteo, 26, 365–66

Robinson, Marilynne, 77

Rodrigues, Simon, 241, 248–50

Rodríguez, St. Alphonsus, 99–100, 244–46, 372

Roman Catholic Church, 26, 48, 51, 361, 364; celibacy and clergy, 216–17, 221; *Code of Canon Law,* 135; communal prayer and, 169; First Communion, 245; founding of Jesuits and, 15–16; Jesuits in clerical office and, 46, 191; Mass, 111, 169; sexual-abuse crisis, 33, 215, 221; suppression and restoration of Jesuits, 18, 19

Rosary, 143–45, 169

Roser, Isabel, 214

Rubens, Peter Paul, 17

Rule of St. Benedict, 21

Rumi, 44

Sacrament of the Present Moment, The (de Caussade), 95, 285

Sadness, 125

Saints and Sanctity (Burghardt), 377

Salmerón, Alfonso, S.J., 241

"Salt Doll, The," 388

Salvadoran Jesuits, martyrdom of, 25

Satan, 188–90, 278, 294; masquerading as a good spirit, 336–37; three ways the "enemy" works, 332–36; what is "of God" and what is "not of God," 326–29. *See also* Two Standards

Saying no, 357–58

Schurhammer, Georg, S.J., 240

Schwan, Marie, C.S.J., 170, 344

Screwtape Letters, The (Lewis), 190

Second Vatican Council, 272; "Declaration on Religious Freedom," 275; "universal call to holiness," 341

Self-awareness and self-acceptance, 339–40, 364, 365, 378–88

Self-care, 187–88, 310, 357–58

Selfless Way of Christ, The (Nouwen), 65

Seven Storey Mountain, The (Merton), 34, 43, 314, 342

Sex and sexuality, 58, 125–26, 174–75; abuse scandals, 215, 221; celibacy and, 130; chastity and, 216, 220–21, 227–30; purity and, 214. *See also* Chastity

Shakers, 173

Shelton, Charles M., S.J., 226–27, 241, 243, 246, 248, 252, 253, 259, 260, 261

She Who Is (Johnson), 137

Silence, 139–41

"Silencing," 275

Silf, Margaret, 60, 63, 95, 100, 140, 167, 343, 346

"Simple Heart, A" (Flaubert), 83, 100

Simple life, 7, 22, 27, 136, 174–212, 238, 279; closeness with God and, 195–201; consumerist culture, demands of, 181–86; contemporary Jesuit life and, 193–95; de Mello's parable "The Diamond," 177–78; distinguishing between needs and wants, 204; downward mobility, 201–3; freedom of, 203, 270, 279; humility and, 207–8; as imitation of Christ, 176; moderate asceticism, healthy poverty, 188; possessions and, 181, 202, 204; poverty and, 177–212; riches to honors to pride and, 188–92, 294, 361; the "rich young man" and, 179–80, 186, 202; three steps to achieving, 203–5

Sin: contemplating one's sinfulness, 20, 76, 89–91; guilt, conscience, and, 88, 89, 90; Jesus and, 81; "loved sinner," 76, 81, 91; meeting God and, 85; religion and, 45, 47; sins of omission, 90

Sisters of St. Joseph, 127

Six Paths (to God), 29–44; Path of Belief, 30–32, 138; Path of Confusion, 42–43; Path of Disbelief, 34–36; Path of Exploration, 39–42, 138; Path of Independence, 32–34;

Path of Return, 36–39, 138

Sketches of God (Vallés), 139

Sobrino, Jon, S.J., 363

Society of Jesus (Jesuits): accomplishments, 4, 16; account of conscience, 268; anecdote, *Suntne angeli?*, 232–33; chastity and, 224–26; in China, 365–66; community life of, 232–34, 247, 270; *Constitutions*, 16, 21–23, 135; desire, importance of, 62–63; director of novices, 368; discernment and, 268–69, 272; dismissal from, 273; early Jesuits, 15, 17; education as mission, 4, 17, 24, 365–66, 390; everyday life of a Jesuit and obedience, 271–73; "explicit articulation" of charitable works, 196–97; "faith sharing," 254–58; first American cardinal, 86; first Jesuits, 240–41; flexibility of, 366–67; founder, St. Ignatius Loyola, 1; founding of, 1, 15–16; "fourth vow" of, 270; friendship and, 231–34; future of, 364; goal of, 16; ingenuity and, 365–68; Italian Jesuit saying on opinions, 5; jokes, 208, 268, 317, 363–64; kindness in governance, 368; as loving and supportive place, 369; Lowney's four pillars of Jesuit leadership secrets, 364; martyrdom of Jesuit saints, 296; mission of, 196; obedience and, 266–85; "particular friendships" and, 262; *personalia* (monthly stipend), 194; plague victims of Perugia and, 197; in Portugal, 249; as practical, 2, 4–5, 22; pride and, 4, 16; promise not to "ambition" for high office, 48; restoration of (1814), 19; saints of, 24–25, 120; *S.J.*, meaning of, 24; superior in, 266–68, 271–73, 276–79, 305; suppressed by Clement XIV (1773), 18; theatrical productions, 367–68, 379; Thirty-Day Retreat or Long Retreat, 19; training of Jesuit priest, 153; "way of proceeding," 364; work and, 348; work aptitudes and God's desire, 269, 271; working with the poor, 195–201; worldview, 188–90, 294;

yearly list of assignments (*status*),
271. *See also* Ignatian spirituality
Solitude, 355–59
So Long, See You Tomorrow (Maxwell),
131–32
Song of Songs, 126
Song of the Bird, The (de Mello), 102
Sophia (Wisdom), 138
Soul: good and evil spirits and, 328–29;
saving of, 50
Spellman, Francis Cardinal, 275
Spiritual but not religious (SBNR),
44–50
Spiritual Exercises, The, 14, 19–21, 50,
51, 395–97; author Martin and,
298–304; Call of the King, 293–94;
centering prayer (Third Method),
162–67; clarity and, 75; colloquy,
167–68, 298; Contemplation to
Attain Divine Love, 395–96; contemplative or imaginative prayer in,
145–55; date of writing, 9; decision-
making and spiritual consolation
or desolation, 308–9; discernment/
decision making practices in,
305–38; examen, 87–97; experiencing, not reading, 20–21, 393; First
Method, 155; First Week, 20, 168,
299, 395; Fourth Week, 20, 264,
395; four weeks of, 20; gratitude
references, 264; imagining yourself
speaking with God, and God's reply,
128–29; "laboring" with God in,
373; *lectio divina* (Second Method),
155–62; on love, friendship, and
human relationships, 252, 253; 19th
Annotation Retreat or the Spiritual
Exercises in Daily Life, 19–20;
Peter Favre and, 238–39; praying for
our desires, 62, 343; Presupposition,
234–36, 249, 256; Principle and
Foundation, 293; "Riches to honors
to pride," 188–92; Second Week,
20, 76, 147, 293, 294, 299; *Suscipe,*
396–97; Third Week, 20, 295–98;
299–304; Thirty-Day Retreat
or Long Retreat, 19, 299; Three
Degrees of Humility, 207–8; the
"three times" of decision making,
313–25; Two Standards, 188–90, 207,
294–95, 386
Spiritual Exercises Reclaimed, The
(Dyckman, Garvin, and Liebert),
58, 129, 214, 313
Spiritual Freedom (English), 151, 336
Spirituality, a: bridge analogy, 3;
charism (founding spirit), 3, 21;
"family tradition," 3; types of
Christian spiritualities, 2, 3; what it
is, 2; of work, 347–63
Spiritual poverty, 205–11, 289; as path
to freedom, 211; relying on God not
oneself and, 209; saying no and, 358
Stretched for Greater Glory
(Aschenbrenner), 207
Studies in the Spirituality of Jesuits, 241
Suffering ("mystery of evil"), 27, 292,
391; acceptance, obedience and,
282–83, 296; belief in God and, 54;
choosing the more difficult path
and, 295; Christian life and, 294;
explanations in Scripture, 286–87;
finding a personal perspective
on, 290; finding God in the midst
of, 39, 285–92; Job and, 286, 289;
meditation on life of Christ and,
20, 292–304; as only one question
to ask about God, 38; "reality of the
situation" and, 283, 284, 285, 289,
300; some Ignatian perspectives,
292–98; vulnerability and God,
78–80; working world and, 376
Surprised by Joy (Lewis), 70
Suscipe prayer, 396–97

Talking About God (Polish), 286
Tang, Dominic, S.J., 26
Teilhard de Chardin, Pierre, S.J., 26,
120, 164, 386–87
Temptation: author Martin and, 335;
three ways the "enemy" works,
332–36
Teresa of Ávila, St., 44, 45, 114
Teresa of Calcutta, Mother, 45, 196,
217, 293; "dark night" of, 139; hearing
God's voice, 127
Testimonial to Grace, A (Dulles), 86
Tetlow, Joseph A., S.J., 150, 312

Theater, 367
Thérèse of Lisieux, St., 17, 49–50
Thibodeaux, Mark, S.J., 113, 126
Thirty-Day Retreat or Long
  Retreat, 19
"Thou Art Indeed Just, Lord"
  (Hopkins), 124–25
Three Degrees of Humility, 207–8
Time: for contemplation, 351; the
  examen for busy people, 349–50;
  finding time for God and you, 348–51
Time to Keep Silence, A (Fermor), 345
"To Be More Like Christ" (Daley), 208
Together for Mission (de Jaer), 188
Tolkien, J. R. R., 189
True Church and the Poor, The
  (Sobrino), 363
Two Standards, 188–90, 207, 294–95, 386
Tylenda, Joseph, S.J., 100

U2, 64
Uelmen, Amelia, 349
Understanding the Spiritual Exercises
  (Ivens), 309

Vallés, Carlos, S.J., 139
Vidal, Gore, 185
Vocation, 339–88; being called to, 341;
  confirmation as "rightness of our
  choice," 347; desire and, 342–47;
  dream job, 344; finding meaningful
  work, 27; having it revealed, 343–47;
  how to bring your best self to work,
  363–78; identity or true self, 378–88;
  individuality and, 381–85; overwork
  danger, 350; patience and, 386–87;
  "The Salt Doll," 388; a spirituality
  of work, 347–63
Voltaire, 4

Waugh, Evelyn, 46, 74
Way of Ignatius. *See* Ignatian spiri-
  tuality
"Way of proceeding," 1–28, 241, 250,
  362, 364, 389
Weston Jesuit School of
  Theology, 283
What Is Ignatian Spirituality?
  (Fleming), 263, 297

Whitman, Walt, 41
"Why Become or Remain a Jesuit?"
  (Rahner), 374
Why Do We Suffer? (Harrington), 286
Why We Hate Us (Meyer), 363
Wilder, Thornton, 101–2
Wisdom of Solomon, 138
Wise Choices (Silf), 343, 346
With God in Russia (Ciszek), 30, 31, 281
Women: desires, naming, 58; feminine
  imagery of God, 137–38
Woodstock College, Maryland, 275
Work, 341, 342; acceptance of failure,
  374–76; acting as a leaven agent of
  change, 355, 360–61; best practices,
  372–78; as "cocreator" with God,
  373; dignity of work, 372–74; doing
  better, greater, 369; finding God
  around you at, 351–55; finding time
  for God and you, 348–51; finding
  time for solitude, 355–59; heroism and leadership, 364, 369; how
  to bring your best self to work,
  363–78; Ignatius Loyola on "over-
  loading," 357; ingenuity and leadership, 364, 365–68; Jesuit way of
  proceeding and best practices, 364;
  love and leadership, 364, 368–69;
  Lowney's four pillars of Jesuit leadership secrets, 364; *magis* in, 369–
  71; overbusyness, 358–59; parable
  of the stone-carver, 373; reliance on
  God, 378; remembering the poor,
  362–63; "riches to honors to pride"
  danger, 362; self-awareness and
  leadership, 364, 365; a spirituality
  of work, 347–63; suffering and, 376;
  working ethically, 359–62. *See also*
  Vocation
Work, 341. *See also* Vocation
Workaholism, 209
Working world. *See* Job
Wright, Jonathan, 4
Wright, Vinita Hampton, 129

Xavier, St. Francis (Francisco Javier),
  15, 237, 239, 240, 241–43, 244, 260,
  271, 365; on the Examen, 90; failure
  and, 377; relic of, 379–80